Accessibility and the Bus System: Transforming the World

Second edition

ice | Institution of Civil Engineers
publishing

Accessibility and the Bus System: Transforming the World

Second edition

Nick Tyler

Published by ICE Publishing, One Great George Street, Westminster, London SW1P 3AA

Full details of ICE Publishing sales representatives and distributors can be found at: www.icevirtuallibrary.com/info/printbooksales

Other titles by ICE Publishing:
Practical Road Safety Auditing, Third Edition.
M. Belcher, S. Proctor and P. Cook. ISBN 978-0-7277-6016-6
Transportation Engineering (ICE Textbook series).
J. Wright. ISBN 978-0-7277-5973-3
Highways, Fifth edition.
C. O'Flaherty with D. Hughes. ISBN 978-0-7277-5993-1
ICE Manual of Highway Design and Management.
I. Walsh (ed.). ISBN 978-0-7277-4111-0

www.icevirtuallibrary.com

A catalogue record for this book is available from the British Library.

ISBN 978-0-7277-5980-1

© Thomas Telford Limited 2016

ICE Publishing is a division of Thomas Telford Ltd, a wholly-owned subsidiary of the Institution of Civil Engineers (ICE).

Commissioning Editor: Amber Thomas
Development Editor: Maria Inês Pinheiro
Production Editor: Abigail Neale
Market Development Executive: Elizabeth Hobson

Typeset by Academic + Technical, Bristol
Index created by Nigel D'Auvergne
Printed and bound by TJ International Ltd, Padstow

FSC
www.fsc.org
MIX
Paper from
responsible sources
FSC® C013056

Contents

About
the author

Nick Tyler CBE, MSc, PhD, ARCM, FICE, FREng,
FRSA is the Chadwick Professor of Civil Engineering at
University College London, where he teaches and
researches the ways in which people interact with their
immediate environments. He set up the Accessibility
Research Group within the Centre for Transport Studies,
with a team of researchers investigating many aspects of
accessibility and public transport, including the Pamela
pedestrian environment laboratory, which is being used
to develop models for accessible pedestrian
infrastructure.

Nick is also the Director of the UCL CRUCIBLE
Centre, which is a centre for interdisciplinary research on
lifelong health and wellbeing, and a Co-Director of UCL
as urban design research studio.

He is a Fellow of the Institution of Civil Engineers and a
Fellow of the Royal Society of Arts. He was appointed a
CBE in the New Year's Honours 2011 for services to
technology and elected Fellow of the Royal Academy of
Engineering in 2014.

Preface

Transforming the world is a big task, so one should not embark on it alone. The intention of this book is to be a companion, to start a conversation about what people need from their cities and bus systems that provide the means to reachtheir desired activities, and how we can stimulate and make the changes that will indeed transform the world. The idea is that the conversation should take unexpected turns, start from unusual places and lead to new ways of thinking, not only about the bus system, but about the world. However, what have buses to do with transforming the world? Buses and the bus system are often disregarded, unseen or ignored, but they enable people to reach – or miss – their life-changing events. A city cannot function without some sort of publicly accessible transport system and the default way of providing this is the bus system.

Crucial, yet ignored, buses form part of the essence of the city. The French impressionist composer Claude Debussy said about the nuances of music: 'La musique est le silence entre les notes' ('the music is the silence between the notes'), that without the almost imperceptible silences between the notes, the notes would just be meaningless sounds. The same is true of a city: a city is people and its essence is the unobserved link between their activities – without those links the activities are just meaningless points in a calendar, buildings are just buildings, not the 'loci of foci' made by people coming together to create something better, and the people just live their lives without the benefit of being in a society. These links are created in an ever-changing world of interactions between people and their immediate environment: the way these combine into that essence of the city is provided by the bus system.

Yet people often do not see it this way. They see buses as negative, polluting, obstructions, messy, dirty, inefficient … Why do they not see the bus system for the positive contribution to their lives that it is? My case is that the reason for this misperception is the way the bus system is conceived and designed. It is conceived as a way of doing the minimum, making money, creating employment by moving people, and is designed to do this at the lowest possible cost. The aims of the system are often not designed to improve society or the quality of life but simply to carry as many people as possible (and to do the same the next day). My hope is that this book will, in the manner of a companion, help to focus the mind on the positives, what the bus system could do if we were to think more of it, give it higher aims, and treat it with the respect, value and investment it deserves. The bus system should be one of the glories of a city – let's make it so!

The ubiquity and variety of buses and bus systems around the world means that they can be a real force for change. Instead of thinking of them as expensive but necessary problems that need to be tolerated, we can think of them as forces for good, with the capability of improving quality of life and wellbeing in society through the way they are designed and operated. My intention in writing this book is to show ways of thinking about the bus system that help to change perceptions and to make it possible for the bus system to transform the world and to make it a better place for everyone. Alternatively, for those people who wish to transform a city in terms of the way in which people relate, both to each other and to the city itself, the book should capture their minds and show them things that they could do – if only they could just stop thinking about the bus system in the same old way.

Just as a companion can be quite a challenging person, this book is structured in a number of different ways. The thought processes behind the bus system (what it is trying to do, how it relates to a city and, more importantly, its people) come at the beginning – the 'why'. Then I move on to what a bus system might need to be to meet these aims – the 'what'. Then I consider some approaches to achieve this, including the science (knowledge and thinking behind the processes) – the 'how'. However, it is important to recognise that sometimes the reason for things being done in an inappropriate way is not the design or the thinking per se, but the way people make the decisions that need to be made. So the decision-making process also comes under scrutiny.

The book does not contain all of the answers; just like a companion, it is there to ask the questions and lead you towards creating the answers yourself, through explanations, illustrations, analogies and examples, because transforming the world starts with transforming ourselves.

Acknowledgments

The ideas expressed in this book are mine, but they can only arise because of the inspiration that I receive from the people with whom I have the pleasure to work, think and create. It is hard – and wrong – to single out anyone in particular. It is the result of a genuine mixing of open minds and sharing of different expertise. I am really fortunate to have such people around to keep me in line, inspire and encourage me to look at things in an open, innovative and 'no baggage' kind of way.

Nevertheless, I would like to acknowledge some people who have been particularly inspirational in different ways in the course of writing this book: Sara Adhitya, David Ashmore, Simon Buxton, Martha Caiafa, Tsu-Jui Cheng, Anna Clark, Brian Collins, Emily Digges la Touche, Taku Fujiyama, Catherine Holloway, Peter Jones, Xenia Karekla, Makoto Okada, Adriana Ortegon, Liliana Ortega, Nikos Papadosifos, David Price, Claudia Ramírez, Kristy Revell, Ian Scott, Paulo Silva, Roselle Thoreau, Pam Turpin, Tianyu Wang, Nigel Wilson and Jo Wolff – any one of whom could have written parts of the book. I take the blame for mixing their ideas and putting them together, possibly in ways they had not envisaged, and presenting the resulting blend in the book as a whole. Each one of these people (and many more) has helped by chipping and polishing the rough pebble of an idea towards making it a multifaceted diamond. I hope the resulting book does all their insights and help the justice they deserve. I am indebted to Janette Yacoub, who helped me put my ramblings into some order so that the manuscript would be intelligible to the publisher. Of course, I have a huge debt of gratitude to my wife, Katrina, and Quincy, who together kept me in one piece during the whole process.

Introduction

The bus is one of the most common artefacts of city life, almost unseen because of its ubiquity in cities all over the world. It is impossible to know exactly how many there are in the world, but most cities of any size have several thousand. Yet, as a system, the bus system is barely understood – by the passengers who use them, the public in general, the industry or its regulators. This book seeks to change this situation so that people can use the bus system to improve their quality of life so that they can live, work and play in cities around the world.

The key concept here – and the rationale for the title of his book – is that the bus system does not exist for those people who are not able to access it, so it is essential that we make the bus system accessible. What we mean by 'accessibility', its importance and the influence it has on quality of life is discussed in Part 1 of the book. The first edition of this book sought to show the outcomes of research that help to improve the accessibility of the bus system. Many of those concepts still stand and research in the intervening 10 years or so has refined and improved on these and introduced more. This technical side of the process is set out in Part 2. Some examples of bus systems around the world are analysed in Part 3 to show what has been done in bus systems to change the travel opportunities in cities around the world. Part 4 brings these three strands together to develop a strategy for using the bus system as an integral part of improving people's lives in cities around the world.

A word about engineering ...

The word 'engineering' is used a lot in this book. However, I have a particular way of looking at 'engineering' and it is important to understand this in order to understand the core message of the book. 'Engineering' comes from a Latin word '*ingeniare*' meaning 'to contrive or to devise'. It is not too difficult to see that other modern English words stem from the same root – such as 'ingenious' or 'ingenuity'. It is reasonable to say that, to the modern English ear, the word 'engineer' suggests the person who makes an engine work (in US English, it is the person who drives a train) and that the more ephemeral implication of being ingenious – devising ways of making things happen – is a little lost.

Vitruvius wrote the first books about buildings, in which he set out three principles: buildings should be simple, useful and beautiful. This is an excellent ambition for engineers. The first person of record to hold the title of 'Engineer' was Leonardo da Vinci, arguably one of the world's most ingenious people. He was clearly in line with Vitruvius (he even drew the 'Vitruvian Man', which shows that how to achieve the Vitruvian ideal it is necessary to encompass both the technical and sociopolitical worlds). When you read the words 'engineer' and 'engineering' in this book, you should interpret them in the da Vinci way – visionary, curious, innovative, unafraid to challenge received knowledge, unabashed at trying new things, looking at the world in a new way in order to reach a new outcome for a new world – and with his illustration of the Vitruvian ideal in mind. This does not only apply to hardware (such as engines) but to whole systems, ideas, concepts, society ... to think that the humble bus can transform the world ...

Part 1

Philosophy – Why?

Accessibility and the Bus System: Transforming the World
ISBN 978-0-7277-5980-1

ICE Publishing: All rights reserved
http://dx.doi.org/10.1680/aabs2ed.59801.003

publishing

Chapter 1
Buses and the city

1.1.   Why?

Why are buses so important? 'A man who, beyond the age of 26, finds himself travelling on a bus can count himself a failure' is a quote often ascribed to Margaret Thatcher, but with no verifiable source. Perhaps it owes its life as an apocryphal axiom to the thought that it sums up a very common view of the bus system and its users – one often held by people who do not use buses rather than those who do. That it is no more true than any other simplistic generalisation of a group of the travelling public, does not limit its compelling premise – or the more insidious logic that flows from it, that as a consequence it is not worth making the bus system effective, just to make it as cheap as possible and to minimise as far as possible its burden on the rest of society.

How wrong that is!

Let us look at an example of a bus system in a major city. Between 28 April and 4 May 2013 buses in London carried some 49.5 million trips, more than the total number of trips in the rest of England (TfL, 2013) and every day there were some 6.5 million trips by bus in London. Buses provide about a quarter of all trips in London and without this contribution the city would grind to a halt. In some parts of London the situation is already difficult, as can be seen by anyone visiting Oxford Street, with its long queues of buses, very low speeds and high levels of pollution. However, the trend in London is also positive, as shown in Figure 1.1, where the rise in bus use can be seen in comparison with the smaller rise in metro ('underground') use. Buses are therefore a key component of travel in London, even where there are other alternatives. One of the reasons for this is the density of the network – the 500 million bus kilometres and 76.2 million metro train kilometres operated in 2011/2012 represent around 40 billion passenger kilometre spaces on the buses and 783.8 billion passenger kilometre spaces on the trains, carrying a total of 7.714 billion bus passenger kilometres and approaching 10 billion underground passenger kilometres. The access points are also rather more common – 19 500 bus stops compared to 270 underground stations – so the bus system is more likely than the Underground to be near to journey origins and destinations, as can be seen when comparing geographical maps of the bus and metro networks.

So buses are important.

However, to discover why all this movement is undertaken we need to take a few steps back and to look at how a city works.

3

Figure 1.1 Passenger travel volumes in Greater London: daily average number of journey stages (millions), Bus, rail and walk, 1993–2012 (TfL, 2013)

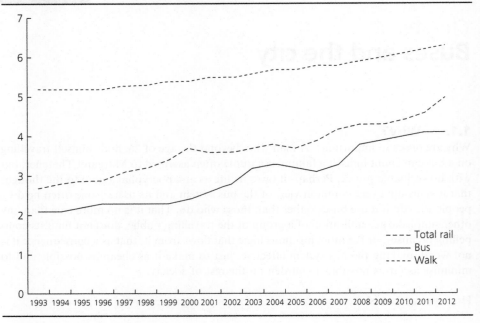

Since cities first emerged in ancient Sumeria some 7400 years ago, they have been about the agglomeration of activities. Initially organised for the provision of shelter, water, food and security for nomadic tribes, they eventually became more stabilised and established themselves as centres of employment, trade and, in some cases at least, government and/or religion, although the majority of people lived in rural areas rather than in cities. So it remained across diverse cultures and geographies until the Industrial Revolution in northern Europe, when the conversion of natural energy to power meant that industry could be centralised and based in a single place. This transformed cities from relatively small and singular places to large metropolises based around one or two dominant industries. This increased the number and size of cities over a very short period of time and led to our current perception of cities as providers of employment, centres of financial and political power, where the ensuing economic activity makes them attractive to people seeking to improve their lot in life. Now, we have over half the world's population living in cities, with some countries (e.g. the UK) having over 80% of their population living in urban areas. The growth in size of these cities has increased the dispersion of activities within their boundaries and thus the need for movement is generated. Cities are no longer predominantly pedestrian in nature – as they were until little over a century ago – and they have become dominated by vehicular, particularly motorised, movement. It should, however, be realised that this change has happened only over the last 200 or so years, at a rapidly increasing rate over the last century and really quickly in the last 50 years. *Traffic in Towns*, Colin Buchanan's seminal work (Buchanan, 1963) on transport planning, was really about how to accommodate urban traffic in a civilised way. Jane Jacobs (1961) looked at how the planning of cities – often driven by the need to accommodate vehicular, particularly private car, traffic – was failing society, but she was seen as rather a maverick at the time. It is only recently that the dominance of the car as the main driver of needs in city planning has been questioned to any great extent, and then mainly in Europe – this has still to spread to any great extent across the Atlantic or into Africa, the Middle East or Asia, for example. Charles Montgomery's book, *The Happy City* (Montgomery, 2013), which argues for a more people-centred approach to city planning and operation, has appeal for planners, but has yet to catch the ear of politicians. This illustrates the constraints under which a surface transport system must operate, but also the opportunities for a reappraisal of the functionality we could develop for such systems in the twenty-first century. Key to that reappraisal is the relationship between the bus system and the people who could use it.

An issue that is also important in the coming years is that of energy use and emissions resulting from the use of fossil fuels. Particular emissions issues concern CO_2, NO_x and sulphur, but the general use of energy and the ability to deal with peak load are also problems that require innovative solutions. A particular health concern is the proliferation of 'black carbon', a major emission from fossil fuel combustion, especially diesel, largely in the form of particulates. Walton *et al.* (2015) show that in London in 2010 3537 deaths were attributable to $PM_{2.5}$, the permitted maximum size of particulates in vehicle emissions, and 5897 deaths were attributable to NO_2 (this is the first study to examine the specific effects of NO_2). To put this in context, there were 126 deaths in London in the same year due to road traffic accidents (TfL, 2011). $PM_{2.5}$ and NO_2 are characteristic emissions of diesel engines. Buses, trucks and cars with conventional internal combustion engines (usually these are diesel, even in hybrid vehicles) are a major target for reducing this problem. Two approaches for dealing with these issues are the general reduction in motorised travel and the spreading of peak demand in order to reduce the need for high energy-density fuels. Both of these suggest that there is a benefit to be gained from a shift from private motorised transport modes to public transport and non-motorised modes. The more pressing need is to devise transport systems in such a way that the need and desire for private motorised transport is reduced so that current non-users of private cars remain that way while being able to achieve their own needs. This heightens the need to understand how public transport could fit the needs of people in the twenty-first century at a level that is rather greater than has hitherto been the case.

There are three basic areas of interest in making such a change: the sense of social justice that can be delivered by a public transport system; the achievement of a sense of wellbeing that could be achieved from a public transport system; and the sense of the functionality of a city that could be served by a public transport system. Drawing these together in a way that shows how the bus system can contribute to the concept of an ideal city puts the subject of this book into the wider context.

1.2. Social justice

A society is a social community living in close proximity on the basis that as a group they face a better chance of survival than by acting individually. However, by coming together, people juxtapose their different lifestyles, needs and desires. This can be seen clearly in

5

areas of high population density where many people give up their individual preferences for the sake of living close to their neighbours. However, this is not only a feature of high-density neighbourhoods – some people in rural communities also give up individual preferences in order to live in small communities. For example, for many people the anonymity of city centre living is preferable to the common knowledge of one's affairs, which can easily be the experience in village communities in remote rural areas.

Recent literature, well summarised by Montgomery (2013), has suggested that we should re-examine the concept of such 'choices'. Not everyone can choose where to live and many choices are determined by reasons other than simply the location: reasons such as work, access to schools or other activities, or the financial burden are also often cited as reasons for choosing a place in which to live. The move to the suburbs in the USA and elsewhere has dictated not only the location of residence away from work but also the need to commute. This has been possible because of improvements to transport – in the late nineteenth century such an option was raised by the development of the railways; in the twentieth century it was driven by the availability of private cars. In the former case, this tended to join existing residential locations to major cities, in the latter, it has brought about the expansion of cities and the development of new dwelling locations, often on the outside of existing settlements or occasionally in new ones. The length of time taken for the commute has begun to dominate the working day. Although in the UK there is a seeming constant daily travel time of around 1 hour (Metz, 2008), in the USA this is often in excess of 4 hours per day.

Such travel times, especially when combined with extended working times, has had a major impact on the real availability of activities for people to do beyond their work or travel commitments. Montgomery cites Sandow (2011) to suggest that this is in part to blame for increasing divorce rates in Sweden, where she notes that those having a commute of more than 45 minutes were 40% more likely to divorce. One of the issues that marks out living in societies is that people, who as individuals choose to take on an activity, often desire – or need – others to participate in order for the activity to be feasible. A football team or an orchestra could not happen without the coming together of a number of like-minded individuals. The spreading of suburbs into 'exurbs' makes such community activities a lot harder to happen. It also has impacts on other societal needs, such as the availability of health or education services or cultural activities that serve to retain the cultural diversity that helps to maintain the heritage of society for future generations. As with many similar issues, this is an aspect of societal life that impacts most severely on people on lower incomes, older people and those who find it most difficult to move around.

There is a functional difference between activities undertaken individually and those that depend on joint or social activity. There is also a difference in terms of where the activity can take place. Individuals could review their stamp collections in isolation at home, but in order for them to trade with like-minded people they must find some place to congregate. Even in these days of electronic trading by way of the internet there seems to be a need for face-to-face contact between like-minded individuals. In other, more obviously gregarious activities such as football, participation can only be undertaken in places where people can gather.

Some social activities provide pleasure (e.g. sport) and others enable the economy to turn (e.g. employment or trade). Yet others are concerned with the wellbeing of members of society (e.g. healthcare, social services or education) or of society itself (e.g. the democratic process). These are examples of 'societal activities' and constitute a major part of living in society. If someone is denied access to one of these activities they are being denied full membership of society.

There are many ways in which societal activities can be denied to people – either deliberately or unintentionally – because of unsuitable access arrangements, for example:

1   Locating an activity very far away might make it available only to those with access to a car.
2   If the only access to an activity is a flight of stairs it prevents a wheelchair user from participating in the activity.
3   Lack of thinking about third-party needs such as family and friends visiting someone in hospital. Patients might have been able to reach the hospital (e.g. in an ambulance), but their families have the opportunity to provide family support denied to them because the hospital is too far away and/or difficult to reach on public transport.

Whatever the reason for denial, preventing a person from gaining access means preventing him or her from participating in the activity. Failure to provide adequate access means that some people will be denied opportunities for leisure, employment, trading, healthcare, education – even for taking part in the electoral process. Accessibility is not just about being 'nice' to people with difficulties, it is about ensuring that the benefits and responsibilities of living in society are truly available to, and are shared between, all its members. Understanding this becomes more important if the outcome of a decision is likely to result in an unequal distribution of benefits – whether these are of income, accessibility or other societal concerns such as education or health. So it is useful to have a look at the distribution of benefits in more detail. It is more common to consider distribution of benefits when considering income, so I shall start by considering this and then showing how accessibility is distributed unequally within society.

1.2.1   Trade-offs

Most societies contain rich and poor people. In many cases, a lot of society's activities are directed towards ensuring that the poorest members of society are not left in what is considered to be a state of unacceptable poverty. The resources used to achieve this are redistributed from people in better economic circumstances, often through taxation. It is not the purpose of this book to discuss the rights and wrongs of taxation or of any particular taxation policy. Nevertheless, there are some issues that arise when thinking about taxation that will help to understand accessible bus systems.

The first issue is the concept of thresholds defined by society over which it considers that people should not pass. For example, society could declare a level of poverty that it considers unacceptable. This can be defined in several ways – one is the level of income below which the state decides to contribute towards household income through some statutory payment (another is the level of income at which income tax becomes payable). However, some people may require more resources than others in order to survive and thus the level of payments needs to be adjusted according to individual circumstances.

Another way of describing this process is that some people may be eligible for payments from the state (granted in the name of society) while others may not. Who should be in receipt of such payments or the associated adjustments to their income? The answer to this question is defined by a set of eligibility criteria that are determined by society (by means of intervention by the state or some other body). The general point here is that there is a default level of income that is determined by society (through its willingness to support levels of contribution through taxation) and which can take into account the particular circumstances of different individuals. There may be much debate about what that default level of income actually is, but the principle holds in any case, even where the threshold is set for reasons of affordability rather than pure social justice.

Although described here in terms of the concept of state provision of income support, the principle applies in many other ways. For example, permission (formal or informal) to beg in some societies is determined on the basis of class, caste, gender, race or other social determinant. This denies access to income just as surely as ineligibility in relation to legally determined criteria for official state support in other societies – perhaps the major difference being that the determinants identified here are relatively unchangeable, whereas it might be at least possible in principle to change one's circumstances to meet an income-based criterion.

Other aspects of communal living are also subject to thresholds. The education system in those societies that have one, for example, attempts to ensure that every member of society has some basic skills (e.g. reading, writing and numeracy). We can consider these levels as society's consideration of the basic level of education that its members should have. Society devotes resources towards establishing and maintaining such education standards. The health system is another example where society takes a view about the basic level of health of a member of society and this is set as a default. In the UK this is enshrined in the level and type of healthcare available under the National Health Service (NHS). Some treatments are not deemed to be necessary to ensure that every member of society is able to live above a certain threshold, but others are. Some treatments are considered differently in different circumstances. Elective cosmetic surgery might be considered to be beyond the scope of treatment within society's norms in one case, yet if required as the result of injuries sustained in a road accident could be deemed to be within society's scope. Such principles are not without controversy – for example, the arguments around the introduction of widened availability of 'free' healthcare in the USA as proposed by Barack Obama has caused deep divisions in political circles.

The basic principle is that there are activities for which society declares an interest in the level of provision and expresses this in a form that sets a minimum acceptable standard of access that should be provided to what might be considered a human life. Because accessibility is the definition of access to other activities, it should be considered in a similar way.

Many approaches to accessibility work on a similar basis: people in wheelchairs may have their access to a bus restricted unless they can use a chair up to a certain size. We can debate what is a reasonable maximum size for a wheelchair – and we could change our views about this over time (e.g. as technology changes). However, in the end, society decides on a reasonable size to use when trying to make buses accessible and, in some cases (for example, the UK), expresses this decision in the form of legislation that must be followed until a change is deemed to be desirable. However, the practice is more complicated. In 2014, the Court of Appeal ruled in *Paulley* v. *FirstGroup PLC* (8 December 2014) that the law does not give a right of access for a disabled person over and above the rights of other people; instead the law presumes that people will not be selfish in refusing to move to make a wheelchair space available to a wheelchair user.

Why are these defaults important? The principles by which decisions are made in the examples just given are examples of society taking a decision about a base acceptable level (e.g. of income, education or health) and allocating its resources in a way that attempts to establish and maintain the quality of society above that level. It says nothing about the quality of society below this threshold. Different societies have different views about what should be the default value – the UK is different from the USA, Sweden or France in its choices just as surely as, at a more local level, two counties in England or two boroughs in London might make different choices about how society will function in their area. In each of the aspects I have discussed so far (and of course there are many more), there is a concept of unequal distribution. Some people are better off than others – whether we are looking at income, health, education or accessibility – and it is up to society to define a base acceptable level below which nobody should fall in each case.

We can consider the 'quality' of some aspect of society (e.g. income) in two ways:

1 we can measure the default or fundamental level below which it is deemed unacceptable to allow members to fall ('base acceptable level')
2 we can count the number of people at various levels above and below the base acceptable level (e.g. at different levels of income).

We can consider these as, respectively, the 'level' and the 'distribution' of whatever aspect of society we are considering. In either case, this means establishing some method for measuring the levels attained by members of society. In the case of income this is reasonably easy, and even in the case of health or education this can be done in an understandable way. It is much harder – and no less essential – to measure accessibility in a similar way.

We need to look at both the level and the distribution of 'quality' in order to gain a complete picture of the effects of a given policy and to avoid perverse results. For example, if a policy were based only on income distribution it would be based on proportions of the population in different income percentiles, and would take no account of the levels involved, thus leaving no consideration of what the threshold of acceptability would be. The result of such a policy would be that some people could be in absolute poverty yet this could still appear to be acceptable to the policy-makers because there is no definition of the 'base acceptable level' of income. Similarly, some people could be unable to reach any activity because of the poor accessibility on offer, yet the overall consideration of the accessibility level could still be described as acceptable (this is the practical outcome of the *Paulley* v. *FirstGroup PLC* case). This means that it is important to be careful about the way we use and cite statistics. Simple measures such as 'mean', 'average', 'standard deviation' are too simplistic for these purposes. It is important to find ways of describing the distribution in much more detail.

A useful compromise between the simplicity of describing a distribution in broad terms and highly complex attempts to describe what is actually going on, is the use of terms such as 'median' and 'percentiles'. These capture how much of the distribution lies below the measure. This is important when considering policy about accessibility because it is so important to understand the implications for people who are otherwise unconsidered. So the acceptability or otherwise of a policy where 90% of the population can access the bus system depends entirely on what is done for the other 10% and it is all too often the case that such minorities lose out in the desire to satisfy the needs of the majority.

However, analysis of only the level means that we would consider only the actual level (e.g. of income). We could choose to examine a high level (e.g. the maximum) or the average or even the lowest level of income. Under this sort of regime, the average – or some percentile – income could be maintained at an acceptable level, but could leave some people destitute, simply because there are enough people with enough affluence to offset the effects on the statistics of the number of people on unacceptably low incomes. Considering only the highest level of income takes no account of how many people are living below the base acceptable level. This would also permit highly unequal income distributions to be perceived as acceptable in a society while there are in fact people living within that society in abject poverty. Many emerging economies face this problem and it is not unknown in countries such as the UK or USA.

The issue covered in this book is that of accessibility rather than income: a society can be highly mobile which lends credibility to planning and engineering solutions that assume a given desirable level of mobility and accessibility, yet leave tranches of society unable to reach activities that are important for social inclusion, indeed survival in some cases. Many societies around the world, including those considered to be in higher income categories, face this issue. Transport for London (TfL), for example, has tried to deal with this issue. TfL's *Accessible Bus Stop Guidance* (2014) states that bus stops should be spaced every 400 m (closer in town centres or residential areas may be desirable). This is an impressive goal in terms of accessibility, yet even this provision means that some people would have to travel over 500 m in order to reach their nearest bus stop – a distance too far for many people, so TfL also aims to ensure that there is a bus stop within 10 minutes of everyone in London and has gone to great lengths to ensure that all buses are accessible (within the current UK legal definition). (See Chapter 3 for an explanation of these distances.)

We therefore need to find a policy appraisal method that takes level as well as distribution into account. John Rawls, a political philosopher, proposed a particularly interesting approach to this problem in his book *A Theory of Justice* (1971). Rawls considered the distribution of economic benefits to groups of members of society. I shall continue to use these as the topic for this discussion, as they are relatively easy to understand. I shall argue that the same principles apply to the consideration of accessibility.

1.2.2   Social Justice and fairness

Acknowledging the ubiquity and usefulness of utility theory in establishing the distribution of benefits following a given policy decision, Rawls set out to consider how to incorporate the analysis of the level of benefits into policy appraisal. Rawls framed his thoughts in the context of social justice. He felt that the weak consideration of the distribution of benefits usually incorporated in utility-based decision assessments meant that some people could be intolerably worse off as a result of a decision, even though the analysis of benefits showed a net gain to society as a whole. The key word here is 'intolerably': very few policy decisions result in everyone being better off, but Rawls maintained that society, to be just and fair, should ensure that nobody should fall below the minimum acceptable level and that the people who were the worst off before the decision should at least be in no worse a position afterwards. The key issue for Rawls was the difference between the net expectations obtained by the least well-off compared with those obtained by the better off. Rawls expressed this as:

... the higher expectations of those better situated are just if and only if they
work as part of a scheme which improves the expectations of the least
advantaged members of society. (Rawls, 1971, p. 75)

Rawls called this the *difference principle* and explained it by comparing two groups following a policy decision.

Figure 1.2 shows the contribution to the expectations of the less well-off group (X2) as a result of the increased expectations of the better off group (X1) following a decision. If X2's expectations increase exactly in line with X1's, both groups benefit in equal measure and the curve would be equidistant from the axes as shown in Figure 1.2 by the line OA.

Rawls considers the situation where the expectations of X2 as an effect of the increased expectations of X1 are represented by the curve OP in Figure 1.3. In this case, the difference principle is perfectly satisfied only where OP is at its maximum. This is where the expectations of benefits from the decision are maximised. Subsequent increases in the expectations of X1 are only achieved as those to X2 are reduced. This suggests that the quality – amount – of justice and fairness in the society thus depicted depends on the state of the least well-off group in that society. This means that a socially just system must search for the solution at which the expectations of the least well-off group are maximised. Seeking to improve the benefits to the other group beyond this point will always be at the expense of the less well-off and thus to the quality of social justice and fairness in society as a whole. The maximum point on the curve OP in Figure 1.3 represents a compromise. X1 could accrue more benefits (although X2 could not), but would do so only if society were to accept the unfairness of the resulting position for X2. This compromise is not

Figure 1.2 Equal expectations of benefits to better off (X1) and worse off (X2) groups following a decision

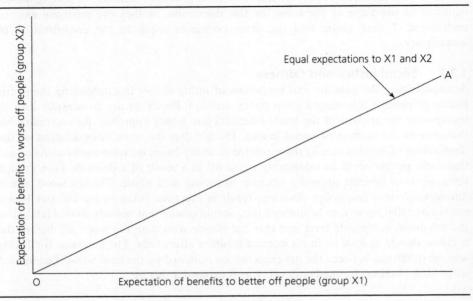

Figure 1.3 Unequal expectations of benefits to better off (X1) and worse off (X2) groups following a decision

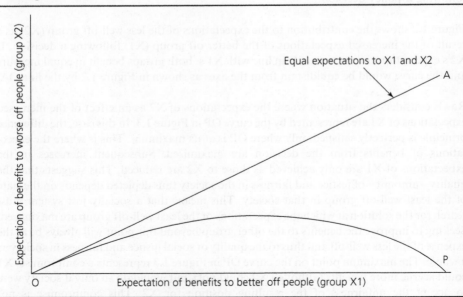

necessarily ideal for any group, but it does seek to ensure that the worst off in society do not become even more worse off after a given decision has been made.

Rawls was trying to establish how social justice could be brought into the decision process regarding the movement of wealth. There is an equivalent concern in relation to other aspects of society, for example decisions about the provision of healthcare or education. Replacing the idea of poverty with that of healthcare shows how social justice could affect policy decisions about a non-quantitative issue. Consider a decision to locate a certain level of healthcare intervention in a centralised facility. As the concentration of specialisms increases, so the benefits to patients must surely increase: patients will be able to reach all the necessary experts in a single place – possibly during the same visit. This presupposes that patients can reach this facility. Those patients with access to their own transport would receive increasing benefits as more treatments become available at the centralised facility and a single journey suffices for a lot of treatments. Those with no such access also receive some benefits if they can reduce the amount of travel by arranging several treatments on the same visit. Even if the journey is longer and more complex than the simple local journeys it replaces, it is still just one journey instead of many.

However, after a certain point patients begin to lose, because the greater concentration means that local facilities, to which they would have access for many treatments, close, thus forcing patients to make longer and more complex journeys to the larger centralised facility. So concentration of health facilities has a point beyond which it cannot go without causing an overall loss in social justice and fairness, because of the impact it has on the transport system. The people who had least access in the first place (because they had no access to their own transport) are even worse off because they are unable to reach any facility at all. I shall discuss below how this approach affects the view of accessibility and the use of the transport system.

Rawls' approach can also be used to assess accessibility provision. If accessibility (to the hospital specifically or more in general) is delivered to one group in particular, the benefits to other groups can start to diminish if they are not also kept under direct consideration. We can take the Rawls diagram in Figure 1.3 and, for example, make Group X1 car drivers and Group X2 public transport users. Increasing accessibility for car drivers will improve public transport accessibility up to a point, but this is soon overcome by disadvantages to the public transport users as buses are excluded from greater and greater areas of the network and subjected to congestion. Or, X1 could be one group of people with specific needs – for example, wheelchair users – and X2 could be another group – for example, ambulant elderly people. The ramps that are so useful for wheelchair users are actually very difficult for many ambulant elderly people because of the strain they apply to their ankles, knees and hips. So an increase in ramps would start to exclude the ambulant people and cause them disbenefit.

Another solution, for example raising the roadway at crossings (where possible) so that level crossing is provided for both groups, would change the tipping point in the distribution – and yield better benefits to both groups at the same time. Figure 1.4 refers to a case where

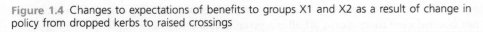

Figure 1.4 Changes to expectations of benefits to groups X1 and X2 as a result of change in policy from dropped kerbs to raised crossings

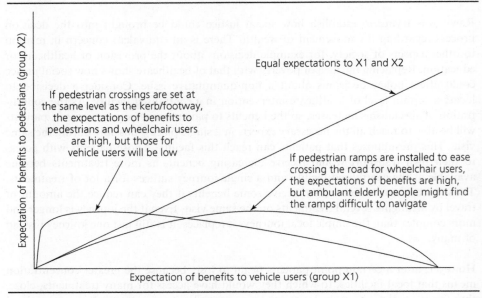

a pedestrian crossing could be made either by installing dropped kerbs to assist wheelchair users (but risking increasing difficulties for ambulant elderly people), or by raising the road level to that of the footway. The latter case would inconvenience vehicle users by placing a vertical obstacle in the roadway. As shown in Figure 1.4, the expectations of benefits to vehicle users are reduced by the presence of the crossing, even with dropped kerbs, as compared with having no crossing at all. Expectation of benefits increase to wheelchair users from having the crossing with dropped kerbs, but ambulant elderly people would find this difficult. The relevant curve looks similar to OP in Figure 1.3.

If, however, the road level were made the same as the footway level, no ramp would be required, so the wheelchair users and ambulant elderly people would both have high expectations. Vehicle users would have low expectations of benefit because the ramp being imposed on them creates a disadvantage. This situation can be seen in the other curve in Figure 1.4, where the expectation of benefits to group X2 are high and those to X1 are low. This approach might be adopted where there is a desire to raise the priority of pedestrians and reduce the speed of traffic.

Social justice is much more than simply choosing the correct trade-offs. It is about ensuring that everyone has at least some fundamentally acceptable amount of health, wealth, education, accessibility and wellbeing before determining how the overall benefits should be distributed. Rawls' model shows that simply improving things for one sector of society can only be justified to the point at which another group begins to become worse off. In the end we have to learn to deal with compromises where perhaps nobody feels that they have received as many benefits as they deserve, but where the delivery of social justice is maximised. To make compromises of this sort work in practice we have to be reassured that the improvement in social justice will be delivered, that it is worth having and that the corresponding 'losses' of benefits are justified. One way of providing reassurance that future actions will be delivered is to enter into a contract. In the case considered in this book the contract is between individual members of society and the controllers of its transport system – a sort of 'transport contract'. The first edition of this book advocated a 'transport contract' for this function. I have since broadened this to a 'mobility contract' for two reasons. First, the transport system should not be seen in isolation of the rest of the societal offer and it is important that the whole concept of how people are able to reach and use their desired activities is included. Second, 'transport' carries a sense of movement (sometimes restricted to motorised movement) whereas part of the way in which society may choose to implement its policies could be to increase accessibility while limiting (motorised) movement. The mobility system is the set of planning, design and transport systems in the area of concern, including the provision of activities and their locations and the means whereby people can reach and use them.

1.2.3   A mobility contract

The first thing to say about this concept of a mobility contract is that it is not about the specific duties placed on mobility system designers, operators or planners. We are dealing with the wider issues from which such duties might result: what society needs from its mobility system and what the mobility system requires from society. In this sense it is similar in concept to the Social Contract of Jean-Jacques Rousseau in which the 'contract' was between a sovereign and the citizens (Rousseau, 1762). In the case of a mobility contract, it is a contract between society and its citizens in relation to the availability and accessibility of the activities people require in order to attempt to attain their aspirations.

So far, I have identified that people living in society undertake a variety of activities, many of which are located some distance from their homes so that at least some people will have to travel to undertake them. I have also established that a failure on the part of society to ensure that such access is possible for everyone results in some people being excluded from some activities, with a consequent reduction in social justice and fairness. The next step is to determine the points at which social justice is maximised – the maximum point in Figure 1.3 – for various aspects of society's needs from the mobility system. To consider this further, I shall consider two simple examples: (a) concerning access to a health centre and (b) the arrangement of bus stops along a corridor.

1.2.3.1   Access to a health centre

Suppose that society has determined that an equitable and socially just level of access to a health centre is that everyone should be able to reach it comfortably from their home within 30 minutes. Some people will require more resources than others in order to meet this standard. For example, some people may live within 30 minutes' walk at their comfortable walking speed. Others may need to walk more slowly than this and therefore would require some form of conveyance to the health centre in order to meet the criterion. Their alternative would be to move home, but requiring this would be unlikely to meet social-justice criteria. As a result, a social duty is placed on society to ensure that:

1   the provision for walking to the health centre is such that the journey could be completed comfortably, securely and safely
2   suitable transport provision is made for those members of society for whom the criterion would otherwise be unachievable.

The requirement for good-quality, safe pedestrian infrastructure is a matter of social responsibility on the part of society. The same also applies to the provision of transport for those who cannot take advantage of that infrastructure. Our mobility contract has to define the minimum requirements for planning, design, operations and information provision so that socially just access is available to everyone. This could be set out in terms of network design (e.g. a bus stop within 10 minutes' walk from a journey origin), but it should not specify how this would be achieved. These minimum requirements are derived from knowledge obtained from people about what they need from the public transport system in order to use it. As we shall see throughout this book, such needs can be expressed – and met – in the form of design criteria for infrastructure, operations, vehicles and the supply of information. As with any contract, evaluation criteria must be set out so that achievements can be checked against the requirements.

1.2.3.2   Bus stops along a corridor

Perhaps Lima is an example of one of the freest of free markets in bus operation. Despite great efforts by the municipal government during recent years, there is still a high level of informal bus provision, meaning that most of the 30 000 or so buses operating in the city are subject to only minor regulatory control – routes are more or less defined, but where the buses stop is in fact up to a negotiation between the passenger and driver. Consequently, the most common request is for the driver to stop 'by the corner'. This is not surprising, as 'corners' represent an increase in possible directions or connections with other buses. However, one result of this behaviour is that although it is superficially convenient for the passenger leaving or wishing to board the bus, it is a cause of much congestion, increased travel time and general inconvenience to everyone else. I would argue that one of the worst results of this behaviour is the impatient and cavalier way in which drivers in the city treat each other – and, importantly, pedestrians, leading to a state where just attempting to move around the city is a major stress-inducing experience which restricts access to activities just as surely as any physical barrier and thus can degrade the quality of society as a whole.

Figure 1.5(a) illustrates this case in a simple form. Assuming that the major flow is travelling from left to right of the diagram and traffic is driving on the left, the solid circles show the bus stops by each corner – approximately every 100 metres – for buses heading in the direction of the major flow. The empty circles show the case for the opposite direction. The solid/empty squares show some other services which cross this major corridor on main routes.

A common solution to this problem is to reduce the number of bus stops and to place these at major intersections, usually (although not always) upstream of the junction

Figure 1.5 Three possible arrangements for bus stops in a corridor. The direction of major flow is from left to right

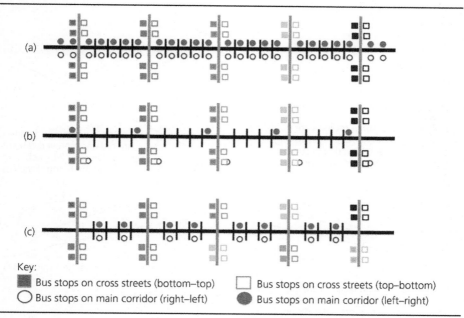

Key:

■ Bus stops on cross streets (bottom–top)   □ Bus stops on cross streets (top–bottom)
○ Bus stops on main corridor (right–left)   ● Bus stops on main corridor (left–right)

so that buses can take advantage of red traffic signals to reduce the need to stop separately at the traffic signal and the bus stop. This situation is shown in Figure 1.5(b). This would serve the passengers well if they are travelling along the corridor as it could reduce delays caused by frequent stopping. It would also, however, reduce the benefits to those passengers who need to leave the corridor – their access to the areas on either side of the corridor is much reduced. This is therefore a case where the economic model for locating bus stops makes sense (the delay reductions on the major flow outweigh the imposition of additional delay to the other flows) but where the disadvantage to the people needing to use the minor flow directions is not taken into account. This shows a situation to the right of the optimum point in Figure 1.3, where the expectation of benefits to the major flow passengers (Group X1) can be delivered only if the expectation of benefits to the minor flow passengers (Group X2) are reduced.

Figure 1.5(c) shows a different approach to this problem. This is an attempt to bring the decision closer to the optimum position shown in Figure 1.3. In this case, a reorganisation of the bus services in the minor flow directions has been designed so that they no longer only cross the major corridor at the major intersections, but join the corridor briefly so that they can share a bus stop designed to facilitate interchange between the major and minor flow services and thus permit better access to the minor flow directions while reducing the number of stops along the major flow. The major flow now has more stops than shown in Figure 1.5(b), but these are better distributed and, if properly designed could render shorter dwell times and thus provide a better journey time for the major flow passengers as well as better connectivity for the minor flow passengers. This

17

Figure 1.6 The expectations of benefits arising from the cases shown in Figure 1.5

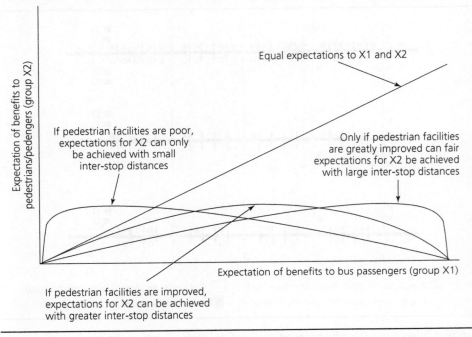

is an example where design is paramount to the delivery of a socially just mobility system.

Obviously the details of such a design will be determined by the particular circumstances in any given situation, but the principle being used to check the sufficiency of the bus stop arrangement is that of Rawls' difference principle. Figure 1.6 shows this situation from the perspective of Rawls' difference principle (this is discussed in more detail in Chapter 3).

The Rawls-type approach means that these points are not determined on the basis of a trade-off but are set by the point at which the expectation available to the most disadvantaged groups in society is maximised. Richard Sennett (2013) describes a state of 'civility', which he sees as a combination of the human capabilities of competition and collaboration. These range from a pure form of collaboration – altruism – where a person gives up his or her life for the sake of the community (Joan of Arc being an example), to pure competition, in which the 'winner takes all' in a dog-eat-dog situation. Between these two extremes lie three grades of collaboration-competition combination: 'win-win' in which a deal is made so that everyone wins, 'differentiating exchange', in which people exchange ideas, can change their minds as a result and then come to a reasoned compromise and 'zero-sum', in which the deal is struck where one person gains and the other loses but the overall total benefit is the same. For Sennett, 'civility' lies in this mid-range, with a distinct preference for the greatest civility being achieved with differentiating exchange. The Rawls difference principle is, in a way, a form of codifying the differentiating exchange between two groups, realising that the groups are highly unlikely to be equally disposed prior to the decision. Thus, social justice ensures that the relationship between them might change but not in a way that the worse off group loses even more, and is a controlling condition on the differentiating exchange.

The sort of informed discussion that is involved in differentiating exchange is one of the drivers for public participation in decision-making. It is not, however, the easiest path to tread in terms of action. The combination of competition and collaboration, of which differentiating exchange is a version, needs work. Humans have survived through a combination of collaboration and competition, but the evolutionary concept of 'survival of the fittest' is a powerful driver, which tends to veer in the direction of competition rather than collaboration, thus favouring actions between win-win and winner-takes-all. Civility, when combined with social justice, embraces the idea of competition in a collaborative context and thus a civilised society should aim to base its decisions on the combination of differentiating exchange and the difference principle to ensure that decisions are taken in a spirit of information, discussion, mutual respect, innovation and socially-just compromise. However, because this is a civilised, rather than a natural, state, it is likely to be necessary to frame this approach to decision-making in some form of agreement.

So, the mobility contract between society and its members comes into play. The intriguing thing here is that of course 'society' is made up of the people who are its members. The relationship is not one-sided though. On the one side, people can determine what they require from the public transport system; on the other, society can determine what is required of the people. Meeting particular demands might place obligations on the public budgets, thus requiring changes to the amounts, sources and ways in which public money is spent. The concept of a contract has another effect: the statement that there are minimum requirements means that the system has to be designed to meet them. Failure to do so would mean that the contract would have been broken. The contract acts as some protection for people who would be disabled by the failure to design a system that provides the ability to reach and use facilities that are available to others. The socially just minimum requirements – the minimum acceptable level – are, by definition, those that can meet the needs of the most disadvantaged groups in society. However, this does not mean that everyone has to have access to, for example, a low-price, door-to-door transport service. It acknowledges that some people will require such a service and that this should be provided for them so that their requirements can be met. There are many reasons why people may need special transport services in order to function more completely in society. These include the presence of some circumstances that make it difficult to use conventional transport services. However, it should be noted that the more accessible the conventional services are the more inclusive they will be and, thus, fewer people will require the specialised services. Therefore, usually the overall cost of providing equitably accessible transport to society will be lower.

Of course, the minimum requirements have to be defined. The temptation is to define standards in terms of inputs (e.g. measurements of size or distances). However, these become very inflexible and can become outdated very quickly. Also, it is very easy for a standard that has been set as a minimum to become the norm in practice, thus tending to reduce the possibility for improvements over time. This also tends to reduce the basic standard very quickly to that of the worst acceptable level. A further problem with standards defined in this way is that they stifle inventive thought about meeting the requirements. It is all too easy for standards to become the last refuge of the incompetent, and we need much higher skills in the course of designing a socially acceptable public transport system than simply working towards meeting an existing standard. This route leads to torpor and rigid inability to adapt to changing circumstances.

Another way of looking at standards is on the basis of outputs, usually expressed as levels of performance. Performance-based requirements determine what should be achievable. For example, rather than define the minimum dimensions for a wheelchair space, a performance-based requirement would require that a wheelchair user can reach, enter and leave the wheelchair space comfortably and with dignity in a forward direction. A performance requirement needs to be devised with users. It is necessary to find out what users need from the performance, then extract from this the elements that are both repeatable and testable as measures of performance. These might be described in terms of time (e.g. to enter the wheelchair space within 1 minute of entering the bus, in a forward motion with a minimum of reversing, in a dignified manner and at a safe speed). This would only be to provide guidance to the technicians overseeing the test. It is not a target for 'real' users in a 'real' situation. The test should be designed so that it can be repeated with the same results at different testing stations and when carried out by different people. Performance-based requirements are harder for manufacturers to work with than dimension-based criteria, but if determined properly they are much better for users. They also allow manufacturers and designers to be creative about how they are achieved. On the whole, a performance-based criterion means more pre-production practical testing and user involvement, but once a design has been produced that satisfies the performance test its dimensions then become the production design and the manufacturer can construct the product accordingly, safe in the knowledge that the performance test will be satisfied.

The 'mobility contract' is therefore a mechanism for ensuring that differentiating exchange is the means by which society and its members determine how the bus system meets the needs of its users and acknowledges intrinsically that these are likely to change over time. Thus, a solution devised and acceptable in 2015 may well be inappropriate in 2017. This is because of changes in demographics, improvements in longevity, introduction of innovative technologies and acknowledgement that if the solution works well it is likely to attract more users. This itself could yield another set of problems – for example, is one wheelchair space in a bus sufficient? For example, a very good question to ask in London is whether the bus system is actually saturated. Testing solutions against the 'mobility contract' maintains the force for improvement in performance on the basis of ensuring that social justice has been satisfied – a measure of satisfaction that is constantly changing, becoming ever more challenging, but always geared to the improvement of society and the betterment of mankind.

It is this last condition that drives the answer to the question about what buses are for: the overall vision is not to have a bus system but to have a fair, equitable society that improves the wellbeing of its members. The bus system is one of the ways to help achieve that – it is neither the only one, nor is it working in isolation of the rest of the city and its constituent systems. The city needs a sensible approach to the environment in which it operates, one which needs to enable people to reach the activities that enable them to achieve their aspirations. This can be achieved by a variety of means, including determining where the activities are as well as the means to travel between them. It is that determination that requires the combination of Sennett's civility and Rawls' social justice in order to achieve an equitable and fair outcome for all. A city needs to ensure that it has enough buses operating in a city to provide a service in which activities are reachable by everyone in a civilised manner. This book seeks to stimulate thinking about how that might be achieved.

1.3.   Wellbeing and aspirations

Of course, people do not usually choose to travel for the sake of it – they have some other purpose for making a journey. In conventional transport models, these purposes are often represented as work, leisure or education. However, it seems that people are making much more specific decisions and, if we want to make the world better for future generations, we need to think in a rather different way. This is what I call the 'outcomes-based' approach and starts from a premise that decisions are made on the basis of attempting to reach desired outcomes. At the highest level it is possible to conceive that people are seeking to improve their wellbeing – however they define this for their own purposes.

The first step on the way to improving wellbeing is to aspire to achieve some goal. For example, a person could aspire to obtain a university degree or vocational training, to improve his or her self-image, earn (more) money, enjoy an arts or sporting event. These aspirations are the precursor to taking on some activity – going to school, university or training college, buying certain products, finding a job or visiting a museum, theatre or sports arena. Indeed, it is the activity that joins the aspiration to the achievement of wellbeing. Activities are therefore a critical point in the transformation of an idea – an aspiration – to a reality and, as such, form the crucial element of the achievement of wellbeing. Denial of access to activities is therefore a denial of the realisation of achieving an improved state of wellbeing. In any city, it is highly unlikely that these activities would all be in the same place so it is therefore necessary for some system to be in place to provide equitable access to, from and between them. That system is the transport system, including all its various components, such as pedestrian facilities, and public and private transport systems. If this system is not accessible to all members of society, we are denying access to the possibility of improving wellbeing to at least some people.

For the past 100 years or so, the thinking has been that the key to better accessibility is to increase movement, signified by improvements in networks to increase journey speed and reduce journey time, in particular by encouraging the use of the private car, which was seen as the liberator of people from the limitations of their locality. However, speed increases are only really available to people who are well-off enough to make use of technology – the rest have to make do with walking, for which changes in speed over time are inevitably small.

By transferring the means of movement from feet to motors, the whole concept of accessibility changes. Distance becomes less of a constraint as speed increases allow the distance covered in a given time to increase. People can live further away from their work, the sources of their daily needs, education, healthcare systems, sports or cultural activities, seemingly without penalty. However, this is an illusion. There are indeed penalties – the consumption of finite energy resources, the emission of noxious substances into the air, the social disconnect between people who are separated from each other by distance (or merely by being individuals in separate cars) all take a toll on the cohesion that might otherwise be achieved by society.

However, if we were to shift the objective from one of increasing movement to that of increasing accessibility, the outcome would be much more equitable: ensuring access to the activities which render the aspirations realisable and to make this available to all. This suggests that thought needs to be given to the location of activities and the equitable means of access between them – based on walking, cycling and public transport rather than by private motorised modes. The drive for speed over the years has meant that a lot of activities have moved in response and considerable effort is required in many cases to bring daily activities within reach of people without recourse to private motorised transport. However, such a shift is now essential as the need to reduce energy use and greenhouse gas emissions means that there is a need to reduce the amount of motorised transport altogether: this will not happen unless there is a reconsideration of the location of activities, especially those that imply a need for daily access. This is why we need to think in terms of a mobility, rather than a transport, system.

As noted in Section 1.2.3, the decisions about locations of activities can be made using a combination of Rawls' difference principle and Sennett's civility. For this, effort needs to be expended on obtaining information about aspirations, desired outcomes and the requisite activities from the local population so that meaningful discussion (differentiating exchange) can occur. To start with, the aim should be to bring as many of the desired activities as possible within walking distance of the population. This suggests clusters of activities within a reasonable walking distance. These clusters can then be linked by public transport so that the activities required to meet aspirations can be reached easily by all the population without the need for using private motorised transport. We can also determine whether the network needs to remain the same all day. There is a tendency to design public transport networks on the basis of the morning/afternoon peak hour demand, but this could be completely irrelevant for meeting the needs of those people whose aspirations need to be met at other times. Thus we can see how wellbeing and aspiration objectives can give rise to the dynamic design of the bus network and the service operation.

It is desirable to rethink the objectives of transport engineers, planners, architects and urban designers – away from easing movement and towards increasing accessibility. So how would a city be if the goal of increasing wellbeing were set as its objective?

Jan Gehl set out a model of a city that is directed towards the 'human dimension', which he sees as a necessary new way of looking at planning (Gehl, 2010). His model is to look at four key goals: a city should be lively, safe, sustainable and healthy. In each of these four dimensions, he shows the importance of walking as the key component. This is an important shift from previous planning tenets in that it places people, rather than the accommodation of traffic, the design of buildings or urban space, very firmly at the pinnacle of the city's objective. I looked at the same desirable goal and started to describe it in a slightly different way, in order to emphasise the improvement of wellbeing as the overall vision. I now explain the resulting model in a little more detail.

1.4.   The five-cities model

With the improvement of wellbeing in mind, I started to reconsider the purpose of a city – why do we have them? Perhaps in trying to improve the means of making a city work, we have somehow lost the view of the overall vision, the fundamental purpose of creating a location where people live. I see a city as people, rather than buildings or infrastructure, so placing people at the centre of the model I could then start to figure out how a city could act to improve their wellbeing.

In trying to understand that fundamental purpose, I looked at a number of cities around the world and asked what is necessary for them to become civilised. In order for a city to reach its goal of improving the quality of life and wellbeing for its population it would need to place people at the centre of its processes and to see this goal as the overarching vision for the entire city. One of the problems I detected was that cities tended to see themselves as a collection of systems – transport, housing, health, education, sanitation and so on – each of which with its own set of goals, but neither individually nor collectively having a clear link to the city's high level reason for existence: the improvement in wellbeing and quality of life of its population. It was clear that this link had to be made, not through each of the systems in isolation, but in all of them together, each and all working with a clear and common purpose. Therefore, it would be helpful to have a set of principles that rose above the individual systems and provided guidance to each of them, both individually and collectively, to help them achieve, together, the improvement of quality of life and wellbeing that was being sought. This set of principles became what I now call the 'five cities model'.

The basis for the five cities model is a city that seems to have made an extremely successful transformation from one of a place with immense social problems to one of a high level of social achievement in a couple of decades. To see what facilitated such a change, I will now describe that transition.

The city of Medellín in Colombia (this is described in more detail in Chapter 8) was famous all over the world as the capital of the illegal drugs industry, with immensely challenging results:

> ... in 1990 [Pablo Escobar] killed 500 policemen in Medellín, ... he killed four presidential candidates. He killed General Ramírez, the director against [narco] traffic; he killed the attorney general of the nation; and, with a car bomb he killed 157 people in Bogotá ... (General Rosso José Serrano Cadena, Director General of the Colombian National Police, quoted in Boon *et al.*, 2010: p. 62)

The city set out to change this and, after just 20 years, has transformed itself into one of the most civilised cities in the world, where its transport system is seen as a social integrator rather than just a means of transport.

> The word 'innovation' perhaps best describes Medellín: the second most populous and one of the most vibrant cities in Colombia. Some of the following examples attest the creative wealth of the city: Linear parks, quality playschools, the 'Talleres del Sueño' ('workshops for dreams'), a creative community programme to strengthen identity and to develop a sense of place, the 'Explora' Park an innovative idea of social inclusion and scientific development and the 'Medellín a Home for Life' a comprehensive perspective of long-term urban development that puts people first. (UN Habitat, 2014)

The transformation is an object lesson in what can be achieved if we shift the vision from one of simply trying to make a city work cohesively to provide, for example, a transport system to one of trying to achieve an improved state of wellbeing.

In looking at Medellín – and other cities – I started to work with my team on how to shift from just the 'vision', to how this could be implemented, and realised that it would be helpful to break down the concepts a bit to make them easier to achieve. We ended up with the concept that a city needed to be seen in terms of five different principles, each of which would apply to the whole city and its population, and which we called the 'five cities'. These cities are described as follows, with explanatory examples based on the city of Medellín, using its metro system as an example of how a working system can be seen through the lens of each principle (Tyler, 2013):

> **A courteous city**: a city in which mutual respect is prioritised through design which encourages behaviour which emphasises the social, rather than individual, priority. *The Medellín metro is principally a social integrator, with a role in education and social spheres as an example of good social behaviour – known as 'Metroculture'. It is easy to use, is accessible, is integrated with other innovative public transport systems such as the Metrocables, buses, the Metroplus Bus Rapid Transit system, the public escalators, public bicycle system, monorail, tram and car sharing scheme, conveys social messages and facilitates good social practice in community health, culture, crime reduction etc.*

> **An active and inclusive city**: a city needs many activities in order to thrive. These include economic activities, social, educational, health, leisure and so on. These have to be distributed around the city and there is a need for every activity to be available and accessible to the entire population to avoid exclusion and social isolation. *The Medellín metro is accessible, and includes connections to the poorer hard-to-reach parts of the city so that economic, social and educational activities are truly available to all. The city believes that one of its strongest drivers is the civilising effect of reading and thus uses every opportunity to encourage reading – provision of libraries of course, but also providing book dispensers at each station in the metro system so that people can borrow books to read on the train.*

A city of public space: a city's public space needs to be available, attractive, aesthetic and accessible to all users of the city and they need to feel safe and secure to enable people to feel able to continue their desired activities. The people need to feel that they own their public space and enjoy being in it – and share the responsibility for keeping it safe, secure and accessible to all. *The Medellín Metro has opened up public parks, libraries, ecological areas to the whole city. Public escalators have been designed to encourage ownership by the citizens, especially the young people, of the public space. Local school students are engaged to look after the public escalators and to help people use them.*

A healthy city: a city should actively enhance improvement in the health of its occupants through good design, the use of appropriate materials, clean technologies, minimising the use of energy and associated harmful emissions so that the population achieves a higher quality of life, physical and mental health and an increased healthy life expectancy. *The Medellín metro provides zero-emission mobility, provides access to health centres and public health education.*

An evolving city: a city needs to open opportunities for future generations to meet the needs and desires they will encounter (and which are currently unknown), by ensuring the design is adaptive and able to change, whilst delivering a sense of 'stable change' to the population over time. An acceptance of the fact that what works today might not work tomorrow (and vice versa) drives this approach to design. *The Medellín metro, by employing university students to drive the trains, is showing them at first hand how important the metro is in delivering the social cohesion desired in the city; these students will become the future engineers, planners, architects, doctors, business and political leaders and will carry this ethos into their future decisions.*

There is still plenty to do in Medellín – the congestion and pollution in the city centre are dreadful, but the mission of improving the quality of life for everyone is embedded in the city and these will be tackled in the same spirit.

The five cities are shown figuratively in Figure 1.7 and the whole city bring these together in the way that it engages space, time and rhythm. The point about the five cities model is that the ingenuity required to meet these challenges must be centred on people and their needs and is the means by which civilisation happens. Rather than think about the design of a bridge or the provision of a road, it thinks first about why the bridge or road is needed in the first place – the principal question being 'how does the function that the new resource would perform respond to the needs of the people?'. Answering this question first determines (1) whether a given solution is needed at all, (2) what the functionality required of the solution should be, and (3) – and only when the first two issues have been resolved satisfactorily – the consideration of how the solution could be designed to provide that functionality to meet the needs of the people. In the case of the five cities model, of course there is also the question of ensuring that the five cities' needs are also met – the solution needs to fit and be tested against these needs as well.

The principles mean that the city needs to look at itself as five different cities, each of which defines certain requirements across the entire city which, in combination, need

Figure 1.7 The five-cities model

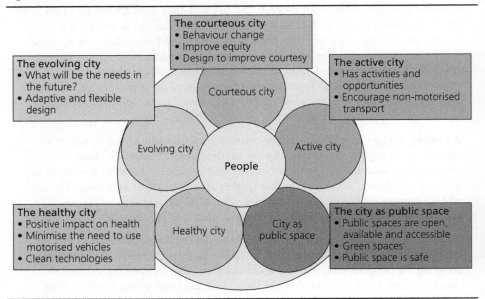

The courteous city
- Behaviour change
- Improve equity
- Design to improve courtesy

The evolving city
- What will be the needs in the future?
- Adaptive and flexible design

The active city
- Has activities and opportunities
- Encourage non-motorised transport

The healthy city
- Positive impact on health
- Minimise the need to use motorised vehicles
- Clean technologies

The city as public space
- Public spaces are open, available and accessible
- Green spaces
- Public space is safe

to be fulfilled in order to satisfy the people's needs. They are not aligned at all with any particular city sector, but each and every sector can align itself with all of the principles. Housing designed to enable easier social interactions and 'differentiating exchange' will lead towards a more courteous city. The planning of the city then has to ensure that employment and other activities are accessible, making use of a public environment of which people are proud and over which they have a sense of ownership and responsibility. Ensuring that the air people breathe and the water they drink are as pure and health-giving as possible will contribute to the city as a healthy place. The ability of the housing to adapt and change for upcoming needs is an important element for the continuing survivability of the city. Each of the normal city sectors could tell a similar story. They interact with each other in driving towards these goals, but with this view the overarching vision – improving quality of life and wellbeing – sets the agenda throughout for the differentiating exchange.

1.5.   Value engineering

The five cities model stimulates thought about the function of each aspect of a city. Basing the approach on function means that we need to think about how we could engineer – that is, be ingenious about – functionality. This means we need a robust way to evaluate functionality in engineering terms. In the 1950s Larry Miles developed an application of engineering principles, known as 'value engineering', in order to obtain a better approach to production engineering (Miles, 1989). It proves to be quite constructive to think about the meaning of function and functionality in terms of engineering for value in the context of how a city could act as the bridge between a person and their aspirations on the one hand and the improvement of social wellbeing on the other.

Value engineering has recently become a rather tainted term. It has come to be interpreted by some as how 'value' can be distorted to infer an outcome that is somehow more acceptable to its proponents. This is not the sense in which the term was invented. In the context of this book, I take it to mean the way in which the true value of a project is derived from the totality of the project and its components. This raises the question of what is meant by 'true value'.

The five cities are essentially directing attention to the achievement of qualities that lead towards improving a sense of wellbeing in the people. How do we know if this is being achieved? The answer is to consider wellbeing as one of the functions of the activities that the person would undertake. Then we can use techniques from value engineering to enable us to consider how to evaluate the functions. For this we need to be particular about what we mean by the word 'function' and its property, 'functionality'.

In semantic terms, a function consists of a noun and a verb. An example of a noun could be a coffee cup. To make a coffee cup function, we need to add a verb, such as 'to hold'. The primary function of a coffee cup is 'to hold coffee'. This leads to certain requirements in the design and manufacture (the engineering) of the cup: it needs to be heat resistant, hold a sufficient quantity of liquid, retain the heat of the coffee without transmitting this to the hand holding it, and so on. The cup could have a secondary function – for example, it could be edible. This has other requirements for the engineering of the cup, which must not break the primary function. There can be many secondary functions – to look beautiful, to maintain heat for longer and so on. When we add up the primary and various secondary functions, we arrive at a sense of the functionality of the cup. We can then compare this functionality with the cost to establish its value. Value engineering in the Larry Miles sense is therefore the establishment of functionality and comparing this to the cost.

However, let's think about functionality in another way. Functionality suggests something about the extent to which the functions actually work: does the function satisfy the need? I see resources other than money used in the creation of the function. Therefore, functionality can be seen to be satisfaction compared with a more general use of resources (i.e. not just financial cost). So, what is meant by 'satisfaction'? If someone aspires to do something, then the extent to which they manage to achieve it is a mark of the extent to which they have satisfied their aim. So satisfaction can be considered to be the measurement of achievement compared with the originating aspiration. Perhaps satisfaction is achievement compared with the aspiration involved in trying to change wellbeing. I can now consider value to be achievement, compared with aspiration, given the required use of resources, and can represent this shift in a series of relationships, starting with Larry Miles' original equation:

$$\text{Functionality} = \sum_{i=1}^{n} \text{function} \tag{1}$$

$$\text{Value} = \frac{\text{Functionality}}{\text{Cost}} \tag{2}$$

To be acceptable, functionality should signify the satisfactory result of the various functions so I can widen the concept of 'cost' to include resources in general, including financial, human, environmental and so on. So:

$$\text{Value} = \frac{\text{Satisfaction}}{\text{Use of Resources}} \tag{3}$$

However, the definition of satisfaction for these purposes is actually the extent to which the activities manage to achieve the aspirations which are driving the initial wish to improve the state of wellbeing. This is important in the planning, design and operation of a city because in order for a person to achieve an improvement in their quality of life and wellbeing, they must first aspire to change something, with some activity leading from that aspiration towards the achievement of wellbeing. So:

$$\text{Satisfaction} = \frac{\text{Achievement}}{\text{Aspiration}} \tag{4}$$

Rearranging the value equation then gives a relationship between value, achievement, aspirations and the use of resources, to give an 'enhanced' view of value:

$$\text{Value} = \frac{\text{Achievement}}{\text{Aspiration} \times \text{Use of Resources}} \tag{5}$$

This sequence suggests a rethinking of engineering, planning and design, from the 'hard' 'nuts and bolts' product-based view (which drove the original concept of value engineering) of functions in equations (1) and (2), towards a softer view, which requires in addition the understanding of the psychology, anthropology and culture that jointly define the context for the generation of those aspirations and the sense of wellbeing as exemplified in equations (3), (4) and (5). The sequence shows the shift in emphasis from function to aspiration and achievement – while maintaining the core competence required as a *sine qua non* of engineering. This is highly important when we are trying to establish a way of securing a robust way of improving wellbeing in a city and it changes the whole concept of engineering into what I like to call 'civilised engineering' – a blend of hard engineering, design, architecture, planning, psychology, anthropology, art – in which person-centred design forms a major component. I shall discuss functionality further in Chapter 2.

However, there is a hidden assumption that needs to be exposed – that the resources needed to convert aspirations into achievement are openly available to everyone. The word 'resources' includes money of course but also individual capability. Neither money nor individual capabilities are naturally distributed in an even or fair way unless some process is put in place to ensure that the most disadvantaged in society are somehow able to turn their aspirations to achievement – or even to be able to have the aspirations in the first place. At one level this is the domain of the social justice approach described in Section 1.2, and one important implication from the Rawls approach is that it is essential, in order to attain a socially just society, that attention is paid, as part of the defining criteria, to the expectations of the worst off. Rawls dealt with economics so he was discussing economic wellbeing. However, I am also talking about people who challenge the *status quo* in other ways. The use of the word 'accessibility' in the title of this book is a deliberate choice to include the idea that an activity has to be accessible in every way – financially, but also physically, cognitively, sensorially, socially – without prejudice. Society will never be just if some people are excluded because some characteristic precludes them from being able to access their pathway from aspiration to wellbeing. So the ideal city needs to be accessible.

Two issues concern me at this stage. First, the relative accessibility of people in general and, second, the relative accessibility of people with different capabilities. If accessibility is equally available to all, the expectation of benefits – being able to reach activities – would be equal to people with greater or lesser capabilities. If accessibility is provided on the basis of the availability of a car, for example, the accessibility of society to those without a car will decline. In the second case, we can consider accessibility afforded to one group of people where this implies a lack of accessibility for another group. An example could be the need for a wheelchair user to have smooth height changes in the footway whereas a blind person may need the information available from, for example, a kerb to tell them where the roadway starts. As accessibility is provided increasingly for one group, so the opportunities available to the other group decline. This situation needs to be remedied in some way or other – the provision of tactile paving at pedestrian crossings is one such attempt. The problem is that (1) wheelchair users find the tactile paving uncomfortable, (2) visually-impaired people dislike the slope and (3) ambulant elderly people find the combination of a slope and the tactile surface reduces their contact with the ground, thus providing a difficult sloping surface which, especially in wet conditions, can become very slippery and the cause of slips and falls. To see our way around this problem, we need to consider accessibility and capabilities.

1.6.   Accessibility issues
1.6.1   Disability
For a long time the concept of disability was dominated by the medical profession. Disability was seen as a problem of a person arising from some form of medical condition or traumatic event that resulted in the loss, or reduction in use, of some physical, sensory or cognitive function. The problem rested with the person concerned and the medical profession attempted to relieve or remove the offending condition. Failure to remove the problem resulted in a person being unable to carry out some function (i.e. he or she had a disability). The easiest way to treat a person with a disability was to put him or her in some form of hospital unit at which medical facilities could be provided and, for this reason, many disabled people were kept in institutions, away from any involvement in society.

The medical view of disability ignored many of the social dimensions of the issue, especially where these were not under the direct control of the person concerned. This gave a very narrow view of disability, in which all the problems were seen as 'belonging' to the individual, who therefore had to adapt (or be adapted) to 'fit in' with the rest of society as best they could.

During the latter part of the twentieth century, it became increasingly apparent that the medical model of disability was unable to reflect the needs of disabled people. It was difficult to understand how society could function legitimately while excluding many of its members simply on the basis of a disability. The concept began to emerge that disability was a problem of society rather than the individual. In this view, a person does not have a disability which prevents them from doing something; rather, they might be disabled by society's inability to design a facility in such a way as to permit them to use it. This view has been termed the *social model of disability*.

People can be excluded from an activity by all sorts of barriers, whether these are physical, sensory, cognitive, social, psychological or economic. The social model places the emphasis on society to resolve the problem: society has the disability, which then disables the person. The consequences of the social model are that much more attention must be paid to the design of all facilities so that people are not excluded from them.

The medical model tends to depersonalise disability in the sense that it views a person simply as a collection of conditions. The social model positions the disability firmly within society, thus removing the problem from the person. It is interesting that in both cases the person at the centre of the issue is actually ignored in favour of either the medical condition or the environmental state. Neither is a particularly good way of looking at the problem if we are trying to improve wellbeing in society.

Instead, why not look at the issue from a different perspective? Why is something inaccessible? Basically, because it requires the person wishing to do it to be able to perform in some way in which they cannot. This 'performance' could be to pay enough money, or it could be to be able to walk a long way or to be able to climb a stairway, hear an announcement, or read a sign. Accessibility is about the relationship between this requirement – what I call the 'required capability' – and the ability of the person to be able to fulfil the requirement – the 'provided capability' – and this brings us to the third model for considering accessibility: the capability model. Elvezia Cepolina and I started thinking about Capabilities in this way while we were developing a pedestrian simulation model (Cepolina and Tyler, 2004) and I went on to develop it as a more explicit model (Tyler, 2006). It is now a much more generic approach to how a person could reach and use an activity in order to strive to realise their aspirations and improve their wellbeing.

The three models – medical, social and capability – are shown in diagrammatic form in Figures 1.8, 1.9 and 1.10 respectively for comparison. Figure 1.8 shows how the diagnosis of the inability to walk leads to the prescription of a remedy – a wheelchair – that would enable the problem of not walking to be resolved. Figure 1.9 shows that the problem being presented is that a person cannot climb a kerb, so the societal response needs to be to lower the kerb to a height at which it would be possible for the person to cross the barrier. Figure 1.10 shows that the understanding that the kerb provides a set of required capabilities (e.g. the need to be able to climb a given height) needs to be compared with the provided capabilities (the person's ability to climb a given height) so that it can be determined whether the relationship between the required and provided capabilities needs to be resolved and, if so, whether this is done by reducing the

Figure 1.8 A simple representation of the medical model of disability

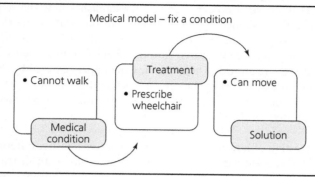

required capabilities (e.g. changing the kerb or providing a hand rail) or by increasing the provided capabilities (providing some form of mobility assistance). Accessibility is thus the outcome of a satisfactory relationship between required and provided capabilities.

Figure 1.9 A simple representation of the social model of disability

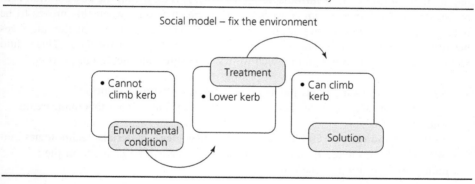

Figure 1.10 A simple representation of the capabilities model

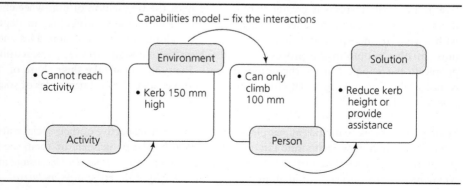

The capability model places the person at the centre of the process in question, places their objective as the desired outcome and then establishes how the requirements can be met by capabilities provided by the individual in one way or another. The model shows also that the requirements could be reduced by altering the environment and the provided capabilities might be increased through medical inputs – but at the end of the day what matters is the relationship between the capabilities required by the activity in its environment and those provided by the person. Social justice mandates that this relationship is such that the outcome should ensure that the provided capabilities are at least as great as those required by the system.

This raises the question of how we can ensure that the social justice criteria are being met for everyone. As discussed earlier in this chapter, the bus is an instrument of social justice, but it might prove impossible to provide a bus that everyone can use, and we therefore have to consider how society can meet its social justice obligations in such circumstances. Inevitably, this brings forward the issue of who is excluded from the bus. The broad intention is to provide a bus that is accessible to everyone. The reality is that there will still be some people who will have to use other means of transport to reach their chosen activities because it is currently physically impossible to design a bus to accommodate them. In order to ensure that society can meet their particular needs, their requirements must be taken into the design process. It is clear that the best solution is to make sure that the bus system is accessible to them. It is only when this proves to be impossible that we should look at alternatives. For this we must look at the interfaces between their needs and the facilities that can be designed to cater for them. This would seem to advocate an approach in which we try to ensure that the design process:

1 accommodates as many people as possible in a mainstream solution
2 determines how to provide the service for those excluded from this mainstream solution
3 works continuously to find and incorporate new ideas, materials, technologies and methods into on going designs so that more people can be included in the mainstream solution in the future.

There is, however, a personal element to the detail of the problem, because barriers have different impacts on different people. The range of capabilities among wheelchair users is vast and in some respects is greater than that amongst the population of non-wheelchair users. This means that designers need to understand individuals' difficulties in depth, with a view to incorporating their needs in the development of a solution. Designers must involve people in the process of establishing their design criteria. This requires people to participate fully in the design process. Everyone must take their share of the responsibility for making society function in accordance with the best principles of social justice and fairness.

Society should seek to include all people in all its activities, irrespective of their social status, intellectual capability, economic circumstances, health, age or gender, or their social, psychological, physical, sensory or cognitive abilities. I refer to this as *social inclusion*, and where an activity succeeds in including people in this way, I describe it as *inclusive*.

1.6.2   Accessibility, movement and mobility

In order to simplify the discussion in the first edition of this book, I used particular definitions of the words accessibility, mobility, and movement. Now I have moved on a bit and have revised those definitions a little and added a fourth: connectivity.

1   *Mobility* is the overall status describing the ease of movement from place to place, and thus represents the ease with which a person can reach an activity. This consists of four elements: location, movement, accessibility and connectivity. The mobility system is the spatiotemporal network joining the distributed activities together – you can think of it as a map in space and time which shows what is accessible to whom and when.

2   *Movement* is the act of moving (i.e. the physical displacement required in order to reach the activity). Sometimes the movement required to reach a facility is minimal, but in many cases there is a need to use some form of conveyance (e.g. a vehicle) to enable this displacement to occur. If it is not possible to reach and use this vehicle, the movement is impossible and the activity cannot be reached. Movement is facilitated by speed, which reduces the time for displacement for the person who is moving, but often at the cost of increasing journey time for other users of the mobility system.

3   *Accessibility* is the ability to approach, reach and enter a desired activity. If an activity is not accessible to some members of society, in effect it does not exist for them. The systems that facilitate movement also need to be accessible to all, thus it is crucial that basic forms of movement – walking, cycling, public transport – are accessible in order that the activities are accessible to everyone, wherever they are within the city.

4   *Connectivity* is the extent to which the network as a whole delivers the opportunity to join places together in a way that is independent of particular modes of transport (e.g. a car). A large part of the design of a public transport system, and its network in particular, is to provide connectivity, hence the importance of interchanges, such as bus stops and intermodal interchanges, which are the initial points of accessible connection in the encounter with the public transport system. This set of connections is what I call the connectivity system. It is a debate in my mind at the moment as to whether connectivity embraces mobility (in other words, the mobility system joins the connections together to form a connectivity system) or if the mobility system embraces connectivity (in other words, the mobility system requires connections in order to function). Whichever way around, the two systems are intertwined and the way in which they work together generates the sense of availability of activities within the city. Rather like the double helix of DNA, they provide the scaffold on which accessibility is built and the interactions between them form the opportunities for generating new ideas about how equitable accessibility can be achieved.

To make a positive difference towards achieving the vision, it is necessary to maximise accessibility, maximise connectivity, and minimise movement to maximise the mobility in the city.

Transport has a leading role in making sure that activities are accessible and available to all. The ability to use a facility is dependent on its accessibility and part of that accessibility is governed by the transport system. The bus system is fundamental to this societal driver because it is the default public transport system. It can collect people near to their journey origin and deliver them to their journey destination and thus alleviate problems of long walking distances. It can integrate with other transport systems – the pedestrian network obviously, but also metro, train, bicycle, taxi and others in order to give a city-wide opportunity for people to find the activities they need in order to improve their wellbeing.

London's 19 500 bus stops and 800 bus services provide a much more connected and reachable system than is possible with 'just' the metro system in the city, with its 270 stations and 13 lines, even though this is one of the most comprehensive in the world. The bus system is also much more evenly distributed around the city. Looking at the London Underground network in the geographical context of London as a whole, actually it provides a quite partial coverage of the city, influenced by the potential markets perceived by the private developers who initiated it in the latter years of the nineteenth century. This rail system is supplemented by the overground railway network of the London suburbs, which provides a lot of commuting capacity and covers many of the gaps left by the underground network. Many of these lines were also developed in the latter years of the nineteenth century as the national railway network expanded. By contrast to both of these networks, the bus network in London covers much more of the city than either of the railway networks. It connects with both of them to provide a good level of connectivity to the public transport system as a whole, but the bus network provides something that neither railway network does to any great extent, namely the ability to move around the city without being so dominated by the city centre. This provides a very important level of connectivity to those living in one suburb but needing to reach activities in another. Emphasising these orbital connections reduces the pressure on activities in the centre, and thus on the radial routes.

What would be the result if the bus system were to be designed on the basis of connectivity? For example, a major consideration in the thinking that underlies many transport decisions has been related to facilitating movement between one place and another – seeking time savings, reductions in delay and so on. Making it easier to travel further and faster implies that measures to increase speed would be helpful and the need to locate activities close together could be reduced. However, such movement-based objectives could have unfortunate effects – for example, travel time could be decreased by increasing the distance between bus stops and thus increasing the commercial speed of the buses. However, this would make the bus stops less accessible to people experiencing difficulties in walking to the bus stop and would thus reduce the social justice being generated by the system.

Accessibility to the bus system is the ease with which people can reach and use it. We could, for example, improve accessibility by moving the bus stops closer together, thus reducing the distance it is necessary to walk to the bus stop. However, this would tend to reduce the commercial speed of the buses and thus work against the movement-enhancing objective discussed earlier.

A failure to meet movement-based objectives will act as a disincentive to travel. However, failure to meet accessibility-enhancing objectives would prevent, rather than just reduce, travel and thus would result in the exclusion of some people from society. Indeed, enhancing movement for some might actively reduce accessibility for others (if, for example, movement for cars is prioritised over movement for pedestrians). So, if we want a socially just society, we need to change our view about the objectives of a transport system, from those of increasing speed and movement to that of accessibility enhancement: maximise mobility, connectivity and accessibility and minimise movement.

Referring back to the earlier discussion on Rawls and the bus system, I can begin to see how the design of the transport system could be affected by considerations of accessibility maximisation. The point I am seeking is where the maximum acceptable movement-enhancing objectives coincide with the maximum acceptable accessibility-enhancing ones. As noted above, it has tended to be more common in the past to think in terms of increasing the rate and amount of movement and, as a result, accessibility-enhancing objectives have often lost out. As inaccessibility prevents – rather than discourages – travel, it is better to meet accessibility objectives before tackling movement-enhancing ones. After all, a person cannot benefit from easier movement if they cannot reach the means of transport that provides it. A decision to make society more accessible for everyone means that, even if there are some disadvantages in terms of movement, society will be a more inclusive, more just and fairer place. It would seem that a socially just sense of mobility must place accessibility above movement when prioritising decisions about transport. Design objectives should therefore reflect this order.

1.6.3   The accessible journey chain

Accessibility objectives need to be applied throughout the journey in order to eliminate all barriers. A public transport journey is a set of linked elements, each of which has to be accessible for the whole journey to be achievable. Frye (1996) calls this the 'accessible journey chain'. We can illustrate this concept with the example of a journey involving travel on a bus. This stresses the importance of the accessibility of every link in the transport chain:

1   The bus stop will not provide access to the bus if the walk to reach it from the origin is not accessible.
2   It will not be possible to enter the bus if either the bus stop or the bus is not designed for accessible boarding.
3   The bus cannot be used at all if it is not designed to accommodate the needs of users.
4   The walk to the destination cannot be achieved if it is impossible to alight from the bus because the bus and bus stop are not designed to provide an acceptable interface for alighting passengers.
5   The destination cannot be reached if the walk from the last bus stop to the destination is impossible.
6   None of the above will be possible at all if the potential passenger cannot find out that the service exists and how to use it by means of an accessible information system.

Figure 1.11 The accessible journey chain

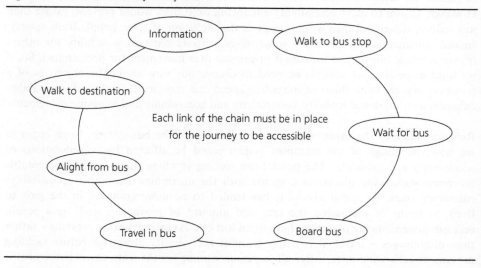

The final link is that every element in the chain feeds into the information used when undertaking the next journey, and thus the chain forms a connected whole. Figure 1.11 presents the accessible journey chain and shows that the journey is not possible if any element of the chain is not accessible.

A potential passenger needs to be certain that the entire journey is accessible before they can have any confidence in setting out on the trip. Some people require more certainty than others about more of the journey in order to have this confidence. This is because they are more sensitive to barriers than others and are thus susceptible to very small changes in the details of a journey. Whereas some people could easily adapt to a barrier (e.g. by changing route), others would not be able to do so without a lot of difficulty. In such cases they have to establish that the entire chain is accessible to them, including any possible diversions, before they can contemplate setting out on a journey. This can only be done if the information system is able to provide sufficient information to give this level of confidence. The inability of an information system to provide this exacerbates the difficulties encountered during the actual journey to such an extent that it could prevent journeys from being made even if they were actually quite accessible. Putting accessibility into practice depends on correct and adequate performance in detail of all aspects of the journey chain at all times. It is for this reason that the design details throughout the transport system are so important.

1.6.4 Accessibility gap

What happens if the chain is broken? By and large in the UK, buses are now low-floor and accessible in accordance with the Public Service Vehicles Accessibility Regulations 2000 (PSVA, 2000a, 2000b), but, although there has been some progress, especially in London and some other major conurbations, there has been little achievement in relation to the accessibility of bus stops. I mentioned earlier the example of bus stops

Figure 1.12 The accessibility gap between conventional bus and specialised transport services

CB	Accessibility gap	Specialised transport

CB, conventional bus

being set too far apart for some people to reach them. What is the resolution to this problem? To think through the answer to this question, it is helpful to imagine a conventional bus network (large, high-floor buses, infrequent, reasonable route coverage on main routes but poor elsewhere, poor information provision, no special bus stops). For a person who cannot use this bus system – maybe because the bus stops are too far apart – there is no alternative except to rely on a taxi or possibly, in certain circumstances, transport provided on behalf of some statutory authority. For brevity in this discussion, at this point I shall call these *specialised transport services*. There is a difficulty here: people who are just unable to use the conventional bus system, but who for some reason are not eligible for the specialised transport services, will be unable to make a journey using the transport system. They fall into what we call the 'accessibility gap' which arises between the mainstream public transport services and provision for people for whom these are not sufficient. One reaction to this is for people to use a car for their journeys: another is not to travel at all. Even where specialised transport services are being used, society acknowledges that there will inevitably be people using these where they could use conventional transport if only it were more accessible. The accessibility gap – between the most accessible available conventional bus system and the specialised transport services – is illustrated in Figure 1.12. In this case, the use of the conventional bus services is illustrated by the area to the left of the diagram. Specialised transport services are indicated by the area to the right and the accessibility gap is represented by the area in the middle.

Because of the renewal of the bus fleet towards more accessible vehicles, more people are able to use the new bus system. Some of these 'new' passengers come from the accessibility gap and some would have been using the specialised services. This is illustrated in Figure 1.13, where the gap as shown in Figure 1.12 has been reduced due to the introduction of the new buses. The reduction in the accessibility gap is shown in two parts: the increase in the area on the left represents the new opportunities for people who are currently in the accessibility gap and cannot travel. The area on the right represents the people who, prior to the change, had to use specialised transport services but who, following the change, can use the improved bus service. Figure 1.14 shows how the gap

Figure 1.13 The accessibility gap between low-floor bus and specialised transport services

CB	Accessibility gap		Specialised transport	
+ LFB			+ LFB	Specialised transport

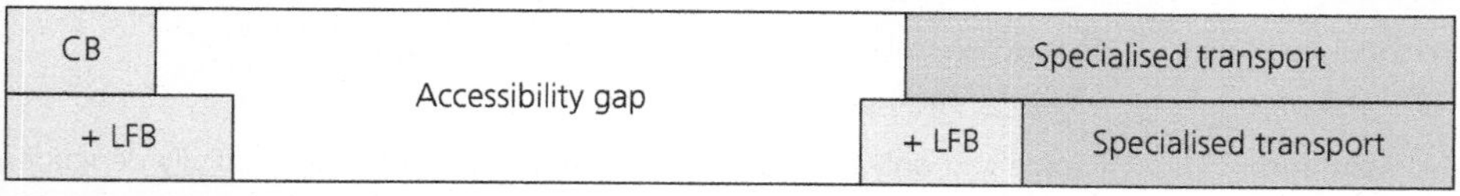

CB, conventional bus
LFB, low-floor bus

Figure 1.14 The accessibility gap between bus (with low-floor buses, accessible network and accessible information) and specialised transport services

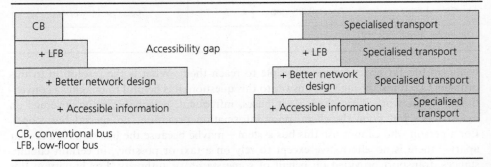

CB, conventional bus
LFB, low-floor bus

could be reduced further by improving the design of the network to bring buses closer to the people and by providing accessible information about the services.

1.6.5 Dependence and independence

For some people, the possibility of using the public transport system means that they can have some control over their choices in life. Most specialised transport services are scarce and must be booked in advance. Therefore, a spontaneous journey – whether for pleasure or necessity – might not be possible if it relies on the availability of a specialised transport service. The opportunity to act spontaneously is a sign of independence and control over one's life, so it is interesting to consider how accessibility and independence interact. To do this, I have divided the concept of independence into five categories, as shown in Table 1.1.

Table 1.1 Independence categories

Category	Assistance required to make a journey	Dependence on others
No assistance	People can travel alone without the need for any technical or personal assistance	Independent
Technical assistance	People can travel alone if they have the aid of some form of technical assistance (e.g. hearing aid, assistance or guide dog, wheelchair)	
Personal assistance (localised)	People can travel alone if they have some personal help at specific points in the journey (e.g. to board a train)	
Personal assistance (continual)	People can only travel if they are accompanied by someone throughout the journey	
Full assistance	People can only make a journey if some form of specialised assistance is available throughout the journey	Fully dependent

These five categories suggest differences in the need for assistance, ranging from complete dependence at one extreme to independence at the other. The accessibility gap is one reason why people need assistance to make a journey, and thus reducing the accessibility gap is one way to increase independence. For example, a wheelchair user who is unable to use a conventional bus cannot complete a bus journey. If low-floor buses were introduced (together with the associated infrastructure improvements) they would be able to use the buses (as long as they could reach the bus stop). In this case, they would have increased their independence even though they would remain in the 'technical assistance' category.

Some people could change category as a result of a change in the required capabilities – such as an improvement in public transport. For example, people might need a wheelchair because the distance to the bus stop is too far for them to walk. An improved network design that brings the bus closer to their house could enable them to make the journey without the assistance of a wheelchair. This would help them change from the 'technical assistance' category to the 'no assistance' category and thus increase their independence – the required capabilities have been reduced and their provided capabilities are now sufficient. In this way, improved design of the bus system makes a fundamental difference to the choices available and the degree of independence that can be achieved and also changes the need for some provided capabilities.

Comparing the accessibility gap with the independence categories shows how changes in accessibility can affect independence. The improvements shown in Figures 1.12–1.15 reduce the accessibility gap, but it is not removed entirely and it is reduced at each end rather than in the middle. The importance of these reservations, especially the latter, can be seen by comparing the accessibility gap with the independence categories. Figure 1.15 suggests that accessibility is most difficult to deliver to people who require momentary, yet vital, assistance. Although people in this category depend on such assistance for only a short time in the journey, the assistance is crucial and its absence will render the

Figure 1.15 Accessibility and independence

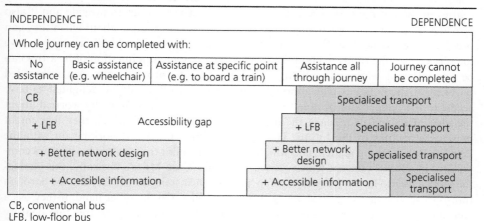

CB, conventional bus
LFB, low-floor bus

journey impossible. It is also extremely difficult to organise such localised assistance so that it can be guaranteed to be present at the right time and in the right place. A traveller cannot start their journey unless they are certain that this assistance will be at the right place at the right time. Unreliability in this respect negates whatever system has been put in place to provide assistance. The same problem arises with the reliability of technical assistance – non-functioning bus ramps have the same effect. This would move the passenger from the 'technical assistance' to the 'personal assistance (localised)' category if someone was needed to help him or her onto the bus, with the consequent loss of independence. Such failures reduce the extent to which a person can feel able to travel – and make the choice about travelling – independently.

Figure 1.15 also shows that people in other categories can gain independence in the ways described above as a result of improvements in accessibility to the bus system. Accessibility helps to deliver independence, but only if it can be relied on. It is therefore better to design accessibility into a system in such a way that it relies as little as possible on personal or technical assistance at particular points along the journey.

Independence can be challenged unwittingly in some circumstances. For example, consider the case where a person offers his or her non-car-owning neighbour a lift to the supermarket. Kind and generous though the offer may be, it can put the recipient of the offer in a position where he or she feels overly dependent. The person is unable to refuse because he or she needs to go to the supermarket and has no other way of going, but this reinforces the person's dependence, not on the lift, but on the kindness and generosity of the neighbour. The result is a reduction in the amount the person travels because the lift-taker tries to reduce inconvenience to the lift-giver (and with it the sense of dependence engendered by the acceptance of the lift). I have found examples of just such a reaction in a number of our research projects. This is not to say that people should not offer others a lift, just that such an act can have unintended consequences.

Simm Gill and I are working with the London Borough of Camden to capitalise on this relationship. Camden provides specialised transport services to take people to day centres in the borough. However, this is a very expensive service to provide and it also provides quite severe restrictions on the service users, for example about when they can travel. As the payment for the transport services is being 'personalised' (a policy to give the service user the funds to choose how they travel), there is a question of how this can be administered while still fulfilling the legal duty to provide care. An unintended problem of the policy is that although some service users would be delighted to have access to the budget and be able to use it as they wish, others are really worried about the idea of having to manage the money and make decisions which they fear might present difficulties in the future. The solution Simm and I are working on with the London Borough of Camden, and which is due for its pilot trials as this book nears completion, involves a concept which gained the name 'Care Miles'. Basically, this enables the service user to have a points system to 'pay' for their transport. If they use the borough transport service they can do so using their Care Miles. On the other hand, if they use a conventional bus, they would be able to use their Freedom Pass (the free fare delivery system for public transport in London and is administered by Transport for London), and accumulate Care Miles which can then be used for other trips, which would not normally be funded through the borough systems. This would mean that they could use their Care Miles to make a trip to a supermarket, rather than just to Day Centres. The point of the Care Miles system is that it provides some link between the specialised and conventional transport systems so that for people who fall in the gap between them can have a better transport service to enable them to reach the activities they desire.

1.7. Buses and their contribution

The discussion so far has raised some issues about accessibility, independence, the burden of responsibility within society and the concept of social justice and fairness.

1.7.1 Public transport

A public transport system is one that is available to the general public to use. For the purposes of this book, there is no concern about who owns it, operates it or who controls it – just on what it is that the system should deliver. The key concern is its availability to the public, and this presents considerable constraints and responsibilities to the designers of a public transport system to ensure that it is accessible and connected. Public transport is the fundamental – default – transport system: the system which everyone should be able to use without the need for private resources such as a car and that should be designed into the city systems in tandem with the complementary pedestrian network.

The prime requirement of public transport design is to ensure that the accessible journey chain is maintained so that the activities are reachable and the vision can be attained. Capacity or speed (the conventional main objectives) only make sense if passengers can actually reach and use the system, so they must be secondary to accessibility as an objective. Systems must be designed so that they provide accessibility throughout the chain even where different owners and operators are responsible for different parts of the chain. Although the various owners and operators – and their technologies – might be different from each other, this should be transparent to the user, who, after all, is simply trying to make a journey to reach their desired activity. A principal outcome from this is that someone needs to 'own' the network. The societal needs of the network to provide access to the activities means that this is unlikely to be in the province of a commercial entity. These are unlikely to have the breadth of concern to encompass the needs of the city, even if a single company were to operate all the buses in a city, its interests would still be in generating its profit rather than providing a consistently accessible service to the city's population. This means that peripheral areas and less popular routes would be less likely to survive, even though, for the people who live there, they might be vital. Society needs to own the network so that the overall city vision can be maintained. This is the case in London, where the services are provided by private companies but the network and service specification is set by TfL in the name of the Mayor.

One of the difficulties for designers of accessible transport systems is that over the last century or so the main influence on transport design has been the private car. This has spawned design objectives and techniques geared to ease the use of cars and, in addition, has raised expectations of the ease of movement for the private individual. Accessibility is based on the need to improve wellbeing and to ensure this in a way that is consistent with the principles of social justice and thus may conflict with design objectives directed towards the enhancement of movement. One of the first impacts of basing transport design on accessibility objectives is that the public transport system would be truly available to everyone in society, whatever their accessibility needs. This does not prevent other people from using their private resources to obtain access to a private car, but it places the requirement on society to design first for the default system, which is available to everyone, and then to design for other forms of movement. If we insist that this default system is accessible to everyone we place constraints not only on its design – of network, infrastructure, vehicles, operating systems and information provision – but also on what we include in this 'public transport system'. However, I see these constraints as challenges and opportunities for innovative design and implementation.

Trains and buses are usually considered to be public transport, but what about taxis, specialised services, ambulances, footways and other pedestrian infrastructure or public bicycles? In the sense of our definition of a transport system that the public can use, each of these examples is public transport. The accessible journey chain includes phases such as the walk to and from the bus stop and the provision of information. As each of these must be accessible in order for the chain to be complete, they must be included in the public transport system. The search for a just and fair society in which people can reach and use the activities they wish must begin by ensuring that the whole public transport system is fully accessible. Nobody should be excluded from society because they are unable to travel on society's default transport system.

1.7.2 The bus system

I have chosen in this book to concentrate on the type of public transport offered by buses. Although not every form of road-based public transport might be considered to involve buses, I have used the bus system as the main focus for research, and therefore this is the main source of examples for the discussion. Even where there is a railway system, it is likely that it will be necessary to use a bus (or some other form of road-based public transport) in order to reach the railway station. Therefore the bus system – in its broadest interpretation – is the default public transport system: if the bus system is not accessible, the rest of the public transport system is not accessible.

I include in the bus system: the network of fixed- and variable-route scheduled bus services; bookable taxi and bus services; on-demand taxi services; specialised transport services provided for reasons of health, social services or education; and, because of its importance in the accessible journey chain, the pedestrian network.

I chose the bus system as the focus because:

1   it incorporates every aspect of the accessible journey chain
2   it involves the design of vehicles and infrastructure and the interface between them
3   it highlights the conflicts and opportunities between the public and private sectors
4   it is far more common than any other public transport mode

5 its operational characteristics enable us to think in more practical terms about implementation

6 it is (at least in principle) easier to introduce innovations than in other more constrained systems

7 I can test ideas about all of the above more easily (this would be much more difficult if I considered only, for example, a rail-based system).

I have the opportunity to think anew about the bus system, not so much as a part of the transport chain but as the golden braid that links aspirations to wellbeing. This places a quite different set of objectives and tests to ingenuity, including what is considered to be the value of the bus system. Measuring the success of a bus system in delivering achievement on aspirations will be rather different from simply reducing its cost to the taxpayer and accordingly we need to change society's mentality. To achieve this, I need to raise the vision of what I expect the bus system to do and then to work out how to use our ingenuity to make that vision happen.

The 26-year-old person with whom I started this chapter may well have another three-quarters of a century – 3–4 times his or her present lifespan – yet to live, throughout which he or she will have the opportunity to improve his or her wellbeing. That journey he or she is making on the bus, far from being a caricature of his or her failure, is enabling them to achieve that lifetime of improving wellbeing. If we can enable buses to do this for everyone, everywhere, all the time, he or she really will transform the world.

1.8.   Conclusions

Before thinking about how to design a bus system, it is essential to have a clear vision of the ultimate purpose of the system. This requires thinking about what a future society aspires to. I have suggested in this chapter that this vision is for an improved quality of life and wellbeing and the rest of the book is dedicated to how the bus system can contribute to that end through its interactions with people and cities.

A utopian society, where everybody has instant access to everything, does not exist, but every reduction from this ideal results in someone being excluded from something. So, to increase social inclusion we need to consider how to identify and deal with these exclusions. Some exclusions are the result of a lack of accessibility to the bus system, and these are the subject of this book. Transport is the means by which society coheres, people meet each other and manage to carry out their daily lives. The transport system is the means by which concepts such as freedom of choice and independent living are made real. The provision of more access to all sorts of activities must therefore be available to everyone, and for this reason we must ensure that there is a transport system which really is inclusive. The design of this transport system has to be directed towards eliminating barriers to access (or reducing their impact if they cannot be removed). Not all transport systems can be made completely inclusive: some people will inevitably be excluded from even the most accessible system. However, by including concepts such as justice, fairness, inclusion and accessibility in the creation of the design objectives, it is possible to make decisions about the transport system, where the inevitably suboptimal choices can be made on the basis of maximising social justice rather than on achieving some other, less socially coherent, objectives.

The socially just and fair approach to transport policy places public transport at the top of the agenda for transport investment and improvement but only if it provides the connectivity and accessibility that society needs. This is because it is the practical statement about the levels of mobility and connectivity all members of society require in order to be able to live in a free and independent society. The main aim should be to maximise social justice by making decisions on the basis of assuring the level of provision for the people experiencing the greatest difficulty in using the public transport system that enables them to be involved in whatever activity they choose.

The design of the public transport system is important because it is the default transport system for everyone in society; the bus system, in its widest sense, is the default public transport system. I aim to encourage design of bus systems that is directed towards the achievement of a fully accessible journey chain for every journey. Where this cannot be achieved in full, suboptimal solutions are required and the key to choosing these solutions rests with maintaining and enhancing social inclusion. The attainment of other transport-related objectives (e.g. time savings) can only be sought after the overall aim for social inclusion has been satisfied.

However, the design of the bus system is not the end objective: it is one part of the means of arriving at a state of improved wellbeing and we need to keep in mind that the higher level vision for society is to achieve that improvement. Buses have their part to play in this – and their contribution to every part of the five cities model is an essential part of the delivery of an equitable access to the activities that people need to undertake in order to achieve their aspirations. Changing the focus from the provision of movement to the provision of accessibility changes the focus of what we expect the bus system to do and that in turn causes us to think about the functionality of the bus system and how we measure its performance. It is that functionality that enables us to assess the true value of the bus system in the context of its contribution to society. This book is basically about how to achieve this vision.

REFERENCES

Boon K, Huq A, Lovelace DS (2010) Terrorism: Commentary on Security Documents, Vol. 105. Oxford University Press, p. 2.

Buchanan C (1963) *Traffic in Towns*. Her Majesty's Stationery Office, London.

Cepolina EM and Tyler N (2004) Microscopic simulation of pedestrians in accessibility evaluation. *Transportation Planning and Technology* **27(3)**: 145–180.

Frye A (1996) Bus travel – a vital link in the chain of accessible transport. *Proceedings of Bus and Coach '96, Birmingham, UK*. John Wiley & Sons, Hoboken, NJ, USA.

Gehl J (2010) *Cities for People*. Island Press, Washington, DC, USA.

Jacobs J (1961) *The Death and Life of American Cities*. Random House, New York, USA.

Metz D (2008) The Myth of Travel time Saving. *Transport reviews* **28(3)**: 321–336.

Miles LD (1989) *Techniques of Value Analysis and Engineering*. Lawrence D Miles Foundation, Madison, WI, USA.

Montgomery C (2013) *Happy City: Transforming our lives through urban design*. Penguin, London, p. 54.

PSVA (Public Service Vehicles Accessibility) (2000a) Public Service Vehicles Accessibility Regulations 2000, http://www.legislation.gov.uk/uksi/2000/1970/contents/made (accessed 15/10/2015).

PSVA (2000b) Public Service Vehicles Accessibility (Amendment) Regulations 2000. http://www.legislation.gov.uk/uksi/2000/3318/made (accessed 15/10/2015).

Sandow E (2011) *On the Road: Social aspects of commuting long distances to work*, PhD thesis, Department of Social and Economic Geography, Umeå University, Sweden.

Sennett R (2013) *Together*. Penguin, London.

Rawls J (1971) *A Social Theory of Justice*, Oxford University Press, Oxford, UK.

Rousseau J-J (1762) *The Social Contract* (trans. Cranston M). Penguin, London, UK (1975 edition).

TfL (Transport for London) (2011) *Casualties in Greater London During 2010*. TfL, London, UK. See https://tfl.gov.uk/cdn/static/cms/documents/casualties-greater-london-2010.pdf (accessed 15/10/2015).

TfL (2013) Travel in London report 6. TfL, London.

TfL (2014) See http://www.tfl.gov.uk/cdn/static/cms/documents/accessibile-bus-stop-design-guidance.pdf p. 10 (accessed 31 December 2014).

Tyler N (2006) Capabilities and radicalism: Engineering accessibility in the 21st century. *Transportation Planning and Technology* **29(5)**: 331–358.

Tyler N (2013) A vision for cities – the five cities model. ARGNote **1(5)**. See http://www.cege.ucl.ac.uk/arg/Pages/ARGnote.aspx (accessed 5 May 2014).

UN Habitat (2014) Urban Equity in Development Cities for Life. Concept Paper for the World Urban Forum 7, 1–5 April, p. 8. World. See https://www.medellin.gov.co/irj/go/km/docs/wpccontent/Sites/Subportal%20del%20Ciudadano/Nuestro%20Gobierno/Secciones/Plantillas%20Gen%C3%A9ricas/Im%C3%A1genes/2013/WUF7/Concept%20paper%20WUF7.pdf (accessed 14 August 2015).

Walton H, Dajnak D, Beevers S, Williams M, Watkiss P and Hunt A (2015) *Understanding the Health Impacts of Pollution in London*. Report for Transport for London and the Greater London Authority. King's College London, London, UK.

Accessibility and the Bus System: Transforming the World
ISBN 978-0-7277-5980-1

ICE Publishing: All rights reserved
http://dx.doi.org/10.1680/aabs2ed.59801.047

Chapter 2
Functionality of a bus system

2.1. Functionality

In Chapter 1 I mentioned the concept of evaluating the bus system on the basis of its functionality and its performance in relation to achievement of aspirations in the context of the use of resources. This chapter looks at what I mean by 'functionality', how this is determined, what sorts of functionality I might be looking for and how that translates into a specification for functionality for a bus system against which I can evaluate existing systems and potential designs.

As discussed in Chapter 1, functionality is a set of functions evaluated on the basis of their ability to deliver achievement of aspirations given the wise use of resources. Therefore, there is a confluence of the achievements required in order to meet our vision and those that can be provided by the various systems that could contribute to that achievement. It should be obvious that the bus system cannot enable an improvement in wellbeing all on its own. However, the bus system is a facilitator. It enables other things to happen which can improve wellbeing. So the first of our functionality requirements is that the bus system needs to be able to act as the facilitator as well as being a generator of improved wellbeing in its own right.

Acting as a facilitator means that there has to be a recognition of the interconnectedness between the bus system and other elements of the city system. To improve the value it is necessary to understand that connectivity, and know how to meld the bus system into the other elements – this means that there is potentially a need for changes to the bus system and to the other elements as well. In 'systems-speak', this is integration. The marker we are looking for here is that of an improvement in value – achievement of aspirations – not necessarily just a smarter bus system or a better appointed city. Let's start by thinking about the function of a bus system.

At first sight, the function of a bus system is to carry people from one point to another using the road network and vehicles which can carry more than one person and multiple trips – in other words, the same vehicle could be providing a part of a journey for many people undertaking many different trips. Why would that be a good thing to do? Surely, this would actually satisfy very few people – because of its agglomerative characteristic of bringing lots of trips together, it will be very unlikely to meet the needs of every one of the trips, even if it could satisfy any at all. The end result is a system with vehicles that have many people in them but no overall satisfaction of needs.

47

Even in a city, such as London, with a hugely comprehensive bus system, average occupancy of the bus system is of the order of 20% (for comparison, the average occupancy of the London Underground metro is around 10%), so it seems like a very expensive way of providing at best only partial delivery of the function of carrying people from one point to another. The net outcome from this view of the function of public transport is that public transport – especially the bus system – is a costly and inefficient activity, where the only beneficiaries are the passengers and everyone else suffers. In this world view, the main objective of the system owners would need to be to reduce the negative impacts – cost, pollution, energy use and so on – and to try to ensure that provision is as small as possible while being sufficient to enable some revenue to be generated which could cover these costs and if possible make a profit. That view is what drives the bus environment in the UK outside London and in many cities in the world. It means that a relatively small proportion of the network where the demand is perceived is overprovided and overloaded for a small part of the day and other parts of the city are under served, if served at all, for a large part of the day. Looking at public transport networks in this way delivers these perverse outcomes. It is necessary to change the paradigm to something that is more likely to deliver on the improvement of quality of life and wellbeing for the city and its population.

Change the perspective of functionality and things change. Remember that the achievement of wellbeing from aspirations depends on having equitable access to the activities that make those aspirations real. This means realising that people's aspirations, not some performance characteristic of a transport system, are the real driver for what we are trying to achieve.

Suppose the primary function of the bus system was defined as being to provide an equitable link between the activities that help to materialise people's aspirations to achieve an improved state of wellbeing. What is equitable and even what serves as a suitable (let alone equitable) link is in the determination of the people. In this view, the value of the bus system would increase if more activities were linked to each other and if those links were truly available to everybody. This suggests that the operational network should be defined by access – how near to the activities does the network reach? – and how we choose to locate the activities – how near to the network can we place our activities? – but this is not only a spatial question: the issue is also about when the access is available. Which activities are included in this scheme is absolutely a matter for the people – not planners and not politicians – to decide.

So the concept of defining a network becomes one of finding people's needs and then defining a space-time continuum in which the physical manifestation of the bus services, routes, schedules and access points is defined by requirements of the people's needs and time. On the one hand, the bus network is therefore defined by the pedestrian network and its available routes – the buses serve to deliver and collect pedestrians/passengers at strategically useful points in space and time within the pedestrian network. On the other hand, the pedestrian network complements the bus network by providing the access between the buses and the various activities chosen by the people. This symbiosis between the bus and pedestrian networks is crucial to enhancing connectivity and thus meeting that overall objective of improving wellbeing by achieving aspirations through activities.

So, for example, if a person was able to walk at a speed of 1 metre per second, and it was decided that equitable access meant that they should be able to reach an access point to the bus system (or reach an activity from the bus system) in less than 15 minutes, this would imply a walking distance of around 900 m. Actually, 15 minutes of sustained walking at 1 m/sec would be unachievable for many older people or people with young children so it could be more equitable to have this access available at a distance defined by a walking speed of, say, 0.5 m/sec, which implies an access distance of 450 m. The point here is that this is defining the density of the network, not on the basis of some economic consideration of demand and supply but on the basis of equity and feasible access distances based on the capabilities of a person to walk. Put another way, this is defining the functionality of the access network: to deliver a person to their chosen activity and determining requirements for that network on the basis of equity – and this is determined in terms of their capabilities.

Actually, the London bus network is indeed defined on the basis of such policy statements: 'An ideal spacing for bus stops is approximately 400 m, although a closer spacing in town centres and residential areas may be necessary to meet passenger requirements' (TfL, 2006), with commensurate measures of performance, such as: 'More than 94 per cent of Londoners live within 400 metres of one of the 19 000 bus stops' (TfL, 2014). In fact, a spacing between bus stops of 400 m implies a walking distance from a journey origin to the bus stop of more than 500 m so these two statements conflict. At 1 m/s, 500 m would take 500 seconds – over 8 minutes. Nevertheless, by defining the access distance, the spacing of bus stops on the street is determined by passenger needs rather than operator convenience. The actual walking distance is increasingly being brought into use.

Transport for London is introducing a new version of accessibility calculations, based on public transport accessibility levels (PTALs – these are discussed in Section 3.1.2) but using access distances calculated using GIS rather than straight-line distances) (Webpetals, 2014). Of course, the siting of most bus stops in London was done long before such measures were considered but the current rationalisation is one of delivery of a service standard. The risk in terms of the generation of demand is taken by TfL: its contracts with the operators require them to deliver a bus service of a given frequency and capacity to those bus stops. Thus, the network design in terms of routes, access points and service frequencies is defined by TfL on the basis of delivery by the combination of TfL and its contractors, of the functionality of equitable access to the bus system for the population of London, not on the basis of calculations of demand between points. Route and schedule improvements are based on improving this performance – or, in the terms I raised in Chapter 1, on improving the value obtained by improving achievement over aspiration by the wise use of resources.

I will go one step further. People are not cars, which need to be constrained to operate at managed speeds and directions in order to maintain safety and capacity. People can walk at different speeds, they can travel in different directions and they can stop. This variety enables some pedestrians to proceed along the footway, others to turn into shops or other activities and others to meet for social encounters. This is all part of the social fabric and serves to improve the wellbeing of people in society. It all becomes possible once people are no longer boxed into their cars, when none of these activities can happen. In other words, being a pedestrian is a social function. So part of the function of the bus system is to deliver people to this social activity. Those metres between the access point of the bus system and the entrance to the various activities then become part of that achievement of aspiration. They are not simply part of the transport capacity of the city: they are part of that delivery of wellbeing and we should think about how to make them more attractive. So, why a speed of 1 or 0.5 m/sec?

I would like to change the way in which we think of walking speed, from the utilitarian approach of covering the greatest distance on foot in the shortest time, to a more sensorial based one in which the way in which a person responds to the environment drives the speed at which they walk. What makes the network comfortable to traverse at one speed or another? Maybe a desirable speed should be defined, not by the time it takes to walk along a given section of the network but by the availability of sensory stimuli along the way. We could design our pedestrian networks on the basis of encounters with sensory stimuli and people can adjust their speed in order to enjoy, rather than tolerate, their walk. The speed at which people walk is then an output of, rather than an input to, the design process.

Making the walking part of the journey attractive – for example, by presenting foci of interest, feeding the senses through haptic, visual, olfactory and aural stimuli and suffi-cient space to allow people to move or not as they wish and presenting these as people move around the pedestrian network is part of delivering a rhythm to the pedestrian act which makes walking as pleasant as people wish it to be. Sara Adhitya (2013) suggests that thinking of an urban area as rhythmic – how such stimuli are presented over time – also helps to constitute a way of thinking about what happens where in the city. If the pedestrian network were as active as this, then another function of the bus system would be to deliver people to the pedestrian network so that they can enjoy its gifts. I will discuss this is in more detail in Chapter 4.

If the primary function of the bus system is to provide an equitable link between activi-ties, what then is the primary function of a bus? Conventionally, this is often seen as the ability to carry people. This leads to the idea that we should try to carry as many people as possible with the minimum of resources. The major component of resources used in operating bus is the driver. Therefore, there is a sense that a large vehicle with one driver is a good way of providing this function. Unfortunately, it is not quite as simple as that!

In the overriding function of providing equitable links, the bus provides the moving part and other elements of the bus system provide other parts – access from the local area to the bus at the bus stop and access to the local area from the bus at the bus stop, for example. The movement of the vehicle is interrupted by the need to stop at bus stops in order to provide that access and so it is necessary to think about the functionality of the bus, not only in terms of its movement, but also in terms of its accessibility. As with any network system, the bottleneck of the system lies at the interface between two (or more) elements of the system, such as junctions in streets, valves in pipelines – and bus stops in bus systems. How a bus manages this interface is crucial to its ability to contribute to the functionality of the bus system.

So, before the bus becomes the moving part of the system, it must first be the portal – or at least part of the portal – to the movement. So, as a bus cannot carry people unless it has first enabled them to board the vehicle it is necessary to think about how the access to the vehicle can be made equitable. The availability of doors and smooth access into and out of the vehicle is therefore a crucial aspect of the design of the vehicle. Maximising the availability of seats, in particular to older people, is another important requirement, as is the availability of circulation space within the vehicle. If people cannot move easily around the vehicle, the time spent at bus stops will become extended and the whole journey becomes uncomfortable and unpleasant. In part, these are issues for design of the vehicle, but they are also factors of interest in the design of the operation – a higher frequency service will deliver more doors and seats, reduce pressure on the circulation space in the vehicles and reduce overcrowding at bus stops. I discuss these issues in more detail in Chapters 5 and 6.

Once passengers are on the bus they need to have a comfortable experience. If it is not a pleasant experience, people will, at the first available opportunity, cease to use the bus system and it is not in society's interests to encourage such a shift. This means having a sufficient number of seats to enable those who need to sit while travelling to do so. It also means that it is necessary to have enough space inside the vehicle to allow circulation around the vehicle for those who are wishing to alight. Failure to do this slows the bus down at the bus stops. In Chapter 6 I will discuss what this means in terms of bus design but it is also a function of bus service planning – a higher service frequency means that fewer people will try to board each bus, thus allowing for a more civilised environment inside each vehicle as well as better performance at the bus stops. This suggests the need for a policy about how many people a bus should carry. Most bus designs come with a maximum occupancy constraint. However, this does not mean that this is the occupancy at which buses should be operated (this is considered further in Chapter 6). Enabling buses to provide other facilities – for example, the opportunity to read, access the internet and so on – increases their attractiveness and their role as a facilitator in society. Maybe it could be possible to have an app that enables passengers to listen to music or poetry with an affinity to the bus route, linked to the location of the bus so that it can also indicate the next bus stop (or just the one desired by the listener). Some drivers in London make free newspapers available to passengers – maybe this could be extended to include a book library as is the case in the metro system in Medellín. After all, if it is possible to have a multisensorial walking environment which is enjoyable and attractive, why should it be difficult to take the same approach to the design of the bus?

The bus system delivers people to, and receives people from, the pedestrian network, so how the service is organised affects the number of people in the pedestrian network at any one time and the routes they take. Infrequent bus stops deliver large clumps of people at specific points in the network and these need to be accommodated within the pedestrian facilities. Smaller spacing between bus stops means fewer people being inserted into the pedestrian space at a time. A denser bus network would have a similar effect. The detail of how any of this can be achieved will be covered in Chapters 4, 5 and 6: here I am only concerned with the point that a primary element of the functionality of the bus is its ability to receive and deliver passengers from and to the pedestrian network and that the equity issue in the primary functionality of the bus system means that this access has to be equitable. That both travelling on the bus and walking in the pedestrian environment should be pleasant experiences is part of the functionality of the bus system.

The points at which people transfer between the bus system and the pedestrian network are, in the main, bus stops. So what functionalities do I expect from a bus stop? First of all, the transfer process is complicated – many things have to happen to effect the change from being a pedestrian to being a passenger and vice versa. Imagine.

First, the pedestrians moving along the footway need to be able to locate the correct bus stop. Then they need to stop at the bus stop and wait for the bus. Often, the arrangements they have made for walking along the footway will be different from those they need to employ while they wait at the bus stop. For example, the arrangement of the bags they are carrying will be different as the people stop moving. They also need to prepare to move the bags into the bus, which might require a different arrangement from the one used along the footway (for example, perhaps all the bags need to be held in one hand to allow the manoeuvre into the more confined space inside the vehicle). They may need to be able to sit down while waiting. Also, it might be necessary to locate the means of payment for the bus journey. It is also necessary to ensure that the passengers are aware of the arrival of the correct bus and to position themselves appropriately in order to board – and of course to be able to board the bus when it arrives.

Passengers arriving at the bus stop on a bus need space to step into from the vehicle. Then it is necessary for them to be able to rearrange their bags in order to proceed along the footway. They may also need information about the locality – the activities available around the bus stop and other bus stops nearby.

In order to ensure that the interface between the vehicle and the bus stop provides a smooth transition for the passengers/pedestrians, it is important that the bus stop is designed in order to make it as easy as possible for the bus driver to stop the bus smoothly and consistently at the right place so that people can be assured that they can board and alight easily and safely. This means ensuring that there is sufficient capacity for those buses that need to use the bus stop at the same time – they must be able to arrive, stop and leave without interference from other buses or other traffic.

The bus stop needs to provide all these functions.

Table 2.1 shows some examples of how the requirements for functionality might impact on the bus system. As can be seen in Table 2.1, the remedies are not beyond the capabilities of the bus system – indeed the right-hand column is a starting point for defining what the bus system should be aiming to deliver in terms of functionality. However, they do challenge the way in which we might think about designing the system, including how we measure its success.

If you are designing the bus system for people and with a view to achieving aspirations so that people can reach the activities they wish to undertake, then you need to make sure

Table 2.1 Example functionalities and their implications for the bus system

Functionality requirement	Means of delivering the functionality	Implications for the bus system
A wide choice of different activities to meet aspirations	Many different activities dispersed around the city	Dense network designed on the basis of location and timing of activities and setting access points at suitable locations to provide equitable access to all activities
Daily needs met within walking distance	Polycentric city with many local centres defined by walking distance	Needs to link polycentres – orbital as well as radial links
Provision of main commuting capacity	High-capacity corridors fed by well-designed feeder services so that access is easy	Need for high-capacity operation means well-designed bus stops, vehicles, integrated fare systems, etc. People should be inspired by the commute to want to use the bus system for other journeys
Provision of access to relevant locations in the off-peak	Peak demand does not necessarily correspond to the needs of off-peak travellers so route and service flexibility should be included in the system design	Good information systems, open operational arrangements to enable the bus fleet to perform many different functions at different times of day
Improve quality of health	Reduce noxious emissions, noise, stress levels	Look at new technologies, electric or hybrid buses and operating practices and information systems
Improve cultural aspects of society	Make reading more prevalent	Make books more widely available to people through bus stops and other public transport outlets
Enable the city to evolve	Ensure that systems are adaptive and respond to changing needs	Be prepared to be flexible – services can change according to changes in need; recyclable infrastructure
Equitable access to activities	Attractive pedestrian networks which are accessible to all; affordable accessible bus system	Location of access points to ensure that the remainder of the journey is attractive; management of fares so that the system is affordable to everyone
Pleasant travelling environment	Interesting surroundings, attractive rhythm of stimuli, sufficient capacity to avoid overcrowding, smooth transition from/to the bus/pedestrian networks	Design of bus services and vehicles to be a seamless whole, at one with the pedestrian environment; sufficient space and time to allow different movements to happen; easy to walk; bus stops can be a great and inspiring element of the public realm

that the bus system itself is able to deliver higher order outcomes. If the walk to the bus stop is uncomfortable and frightening, however attractive the activity at the end of the journey might be, the ability to reach the activity is compromised and therefore the achievement of aspirations to be gained from performing the activity will be reduced. Therefore, it is incumbent on the bus system to ensure that it is able to deliver on aspirations for a pleasant experience. Table 2.2 gives some suggestions for how aspirations and

Table 2.2 Some suggested aspirations, types of achievement and indications of satisfaction for the bus system

Aspiration	Achievement	Satisfaction
My walk to the bus stop is enjoyable	Pleasant sensory stimuli Opportunity for social encounters Not too far to walk Feels safe	The environment is designed to be interesting, with rhythmic interactions with sensory stimuli Bus stops are located a suitable distance from activities Bus network brings the buses reasonably close to the activities Good lighting, visibility, acoustic environment Pedestrians prioritised over traffic The bus stop is made into a great place to be – maybe a destination in its own right
My wait for the bus is comfortable	A good environment for waiting High-frequency bus service Reliable bus service so waiting times are predictable Information about bus arrivals Information about downstream performance, alternative routes, etc.	Provision of shelter from weather Seating, lighting Sufficient space for the expected number of waiting passengers and their baggage Real-time information about the bus system performance, maps, available destinations, etc. Bus service frequency sufficient to keep waiting times to an acceptable level Bus service is reliable
It is easy for me to board the bus	Easy access to the bus Buses stop consistently at the same place It is clear which bus to board How boarding works is simple to understand Crowding around the doorway is eliminated	Bus stop and bus are designed to provide a smooth step-free access The bus stop is designed to make it easy for the drivers to use well Signage for different bus lines is clear Information is available about which doors to use, how payment is arranged, etc. Bus service frequency is sufficient to reduce the numbers boarding each bus

Table 2.2 Continued

Aspiration	Achievement	Satisfaction
I enjoy the journey on the bus	Comfortable seats Good air quality Good heating/cooling system Large windows Good circulation space Good handrails Smooth driver operation Good information about where the bus is, where it is going, connections, etc. Reliable service so that the journey time is predictable	Enough seats available and accessible for older people to use Air circulation, heating and cooling are adequate for the number of people on the bus in the prevailing weather conditions There is sufficient space for people to move around the vehicle when required and there are sufficient handrails to provide adequate support Drivers trained and driving systems designed to make bus operation smooth and safe with no jerks Real-time information system about present location and forthcoming bus stops Circulation space on the vehicle is sufficient to enable people to remain seated until the bus stops and still feel they have the time to reach the door to alight
It is easy for me to alight from the bus	Knowing when it is necessary to prepare to alight Easy access to the bus stop platform Buses stop consistently at the same place How alighting works is simple to understand Crowding around the doorway is eliminated Space and information is available at the bus stop to allow passengers to prepare for walking on the footway	Information on the bus about forthcoming bus stops Good design of bus and bus stop to facilitate alighting The bus stop is designed to make it easy for the drivers to use well Information is available on the bus about which doors to use, etc. Information is available at the bus stop about the local area, activities, local bus stops, etc. Bus service frequency is sufficient to reduce the numbers alighting from each bus
My walk from the bus stop to the activity is enjoyable	Pleasant sensory stimuli Opportunity for social encounters Not too far to walk Feels safe	The environment is designed to be interesting, with rhythmic interactions with sensory stimuli Bus stops are located a suitable distance apart Bus network brings the buses reasonably close to the activities Good lighting, visibility, acoustic environment Pedestrians prioritised over traffic

achievement might be related to satisfaction and, through equation (4) (see Section 1.5 in Chapter 1), its contribution to the value that could be delivered by the bus system, with a view to ensuring that the use of the bus system is a pleasant and civilised experience throughout the journey.

Table 2.2 shows that the requirements for a well-designed bus system would include outcomes such as 'pleasant walks to and from the bus stop', 'pleasant waiting experiences', 'good boarding and alighting experiences' and 'pleasant journeys on the bus'. The key point here is that I am defining the functionality of the bus system – and therefore what I require it to do – on the basis of needs and desires outside the bus system itself. These are not to make just the bus system better (although undoubtedly they would achieve that) – they are to make society better. These are not costly add-ons to a basic system – they are core requirements for a civilised bus system. All the operational requirements stem from this core.

2.2. Vision

The functionality discussed thus far in this chapter has highlighted the feasibility of using the bus system to help achieve the societal vision of improving wellbeing. Determining the functionality of the bus system can therefore only happen if the bus system designer has a clear view of the vision which the bus system is going to help to achieve – the improvement in wellbeing to which people aspire. Given the diverse nature of a population, it is easy to realise that there will be several different ways of turning even a relatively common aspiration into a reality in terms of improvement in wellbeing. One of the benefits of living in a city is that it becomes possible to provide many different activities for people to try. How to achieve equitable access to all these activities is a crucial issue, which has implications for the way society designs and operate our cities. To illustrate how direct this influence can be, let us examine two ways of providing access to activities: a car-based system and a bus-based system.

In a car-based society, the best way of making all these activities available in a city would be to have clusters of activities in a number of different places. This is because at this level distance is not really an issue and the person can have a great choice of versions of their chosen activity once they have arrived at this particular selection: park the car and you have many opportunities all within easy reach. So this mega-activity place would need to have easy car parking. In this way you could have a maximum choice of gyms, cinemas, schools or whatever available to you as soon as you have parked your car. If you want to go to a restaurant afterwards you could drive to another locale where there are many restaurants to choose from. Maybe, the competition from similar activities in close proximity would reduce prices, which might also be a benefit.

In a society facilitated by public transport, the same vision could be met but the result would be different. It would be better to have more mixed activities close to each other so that, having arrived in the high street there are many different opportunities to choose. Parking is not a problem because it is not necessary and the question is how to fit as great a diversity of activities as possible in the area near to the bus system's access points.

In terms of equitable access, the car-based arrangement would work very well – but only for those with access to a car. The distances between different activities would be large – probably beyond walking distance – and so a person without a car would only have available the selection of similar activities in the place they managed to reach by public transport. The public transport-based option, however, would allow for greater choice for more people and thus reflects the diversity of society and its choices. Wellbeing would be more broadly scattered among the population and there would be many different ways of improving it.

So, what is the vision for the bus system? To provide a seamless accessible integration between people and the activities they choose in a way that, of itself, improves wellbeing. How does this fit with the overarching vision for the ideal city as expounded in Chapter 1?

Figure 2.1 is a simple representation of how the five cities model described in Chapter 1 might be supported by the bus system. That crucially important element of the courteous city will be propelled forwards by a bus system which is operated in a way that allows people to use it without feeling desperate that the bus that is here is the last bus on the planet. That could mean a high-frequency service operating in a dense network with lots of access points over the entire day, so that nobody feels that, come what may, they must fight off everyone else to board the bus. Recognising that it is serving people's needs for a variety of activities means that this dense service has to be operated when the activities

Figure 2.1 Some implications for the bus system if we wish it to deliver social cohesion to the overarching vision of an ideal city

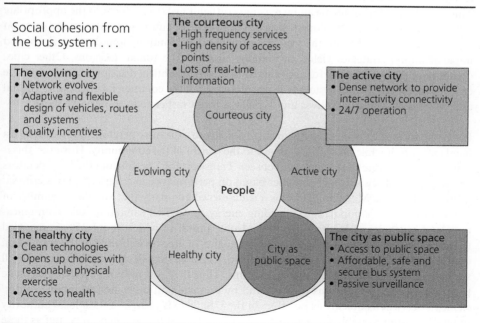

Social cohesion from the bus system . . .

The evolving city
• Network evolves
• Adaptive and flexible design of vehicles, routes and systems
• Quality incentives

The courteous city
• High frequency services
• High density of access points
• Lots of real-time information

The active city
• Dense network to provide inter-activity connectivity
• 24/7 operation

The healthy city
• Clean technologies
• Opens up choices with reasonable physical exercise
• Access to health

The city as public space
• Access to public space
• Affordable, safe and secure bus system
• Passive surveillance

Courteous city

Evolving city   Active city

People

Healthy city   City as public space

are taking place – so it is quite possible that 24-hour operation 7 days per week might be required. The use of the bus system to ensure that public space is indeed usable by the public and the use of clean technologies to ensure that noxious emissions from vehicles are minimised also go towards improving the quality of society in an equitable way. Walton *et al.* (2015) would seem to suggest, for example, that diesel-based operation should be removed as a priority. The need to make the system adaptive so that future generations also have the service they will need means keeping in constant communication with the public so that options are kept open for the future without ceding to planning blight as a result of indecision. The examples I have given here are just that – there are many other ways in which the bus system should be designed to meet the principles of the five cities model!

2.3. Strategy

If all we needed were a vision, it would be easy! However, it is also necessary to think hard about how the vision can be made real. In a city such as London, where the transport system is in the control of a far-sighted process that keeps it innovative while the politicians are acting as stewards for the city's long-term future, the processes are in place to be able to make the sort of decisions that are required to follow this approach. It is also feasible to think that in cities where there is a strong mandated mayor there will also be a strength in maintaining such an approach. However, these are not as settled as the London case – Bogotá is a case in point, where after a succession of three mayors with keen societal views and implementation plans for the city, including the Transmilenio bus system, the outcome has been allowed to subside without the required maintenance and investment to keep it operating properly and the system has fallen into some disrepute – because the political will has shifted from the bus system to other priorities. This gives the technical teams an increasingly difficult task to perform to the appropriate current societal levels – let alone trying to improve it for future generations. Reliance on a political power without the constraining hand of binding long-term visions and implementation strategies yields an inability to make the tough decisions. Other cities do not have the opportunity for even this form of single political decision-making. In these cases the nature of the bus system falls into the world of the commercial operators – formal and informal – whose objectives are to make a profit rather than to improve society.

Profit and societal wellbeing are not mutually exclusive – the bus operators in London turn a handsome profit while providing a service to the benefit of the community. However, this is because of the nature of the contract between Transport for London and the bus operators and its system of rewards and penalties based on performance in relation to TfL's criteria. Empresas Públicas Medellín (EPM) is a state-owned company that supplies a number of services to the city's population, including energy, water and sanitation, telecommunications and much more. It also turns a handsome profit, of which about 35% is returned to the city. It has a firm vision to improve the quality of life and wellbeing of the population of the city. Where there is no such guiding hand, it is more than likely that the operators will see individual services as their income streams. Thus they will respond by trying to make those services as profitable as possible and by removing all other non-profitable routes/elements/services as quickly as possible. In the UK there is provision for a local authority to tender for unprofitable services to be provided at a cost to the community, but as these are subject to the availability of finance and do not have the compensatory contribution from the more profitable services, they are fragile at best. Thus the contribution of the bus system to the overall vision of a city is lost.

So, to put the vision in place it is necessary to have a strategy to ensure that the operators, designers and planners of bus systems are working to the overarching objective of improving quality of life and wellbeing. The strategy requires a legal and/or contractual framework that places this as the highest requirement of the bus system and allows performance criteria to be set accordingly. In the city context, it is crucial that this strategy always meets the vision, even though the implementational details might change from time to time for political and other reasons. The way to achieve this is to have a firm decision-making process that acts to ensure that all appropriate considerations are taken into account when making decisions, including the active involvement of the people, and to ensure that the decisions are based on an explicit definition of the desired outcomes that should be obtained as a result of the decision having been made. I call this the outcomes-based decision model and I will introduce this now.

2.3.1   Outcomes-based decision model

As the name implies this decision model is based on the predefinition of the outcomes that are desired as a result of the decision. There are four components to the model:

1   the desired outcome
2   the 'success factors' that will act positively in order to reach the desired outcome
3   the 'limitations' that will act negatively against achievement of the desired outcome
4   the 'actions' that are necessary to amplify the success factors and eliminate
    (or mitigate if elimination is not possible) the limitations.

There are three important points to make about the outcomes-based decision model. First, the whole decision is framed by the situation one wishes to see after the decision has been implemented in full. This requires thought and, in most cases, a great deal of consultation and discussion with the people who might be affected by the decision. In the end, the outcome has to be accepted by everyone, even if some might have had a preference for another outcome. This tends to raise the game – in order to obtain such agreement the level of the outcome has to be raised to one that can obtain broad agreement. I stated in Section 2.1 that in the present case I am setting the 'vision' (a particular type of desired outcome) as being the equitable improvement of wellbeing and it is hard to find someone who would not agree with that level of vision – although one can imagine several disagreements about how this vision might be reached.

It really is worth striving for agreement at this high level. It is this agreement that enables long-term strategies to be adopted and thus to secure long-term consistency in decisions. This is particularly vital in the political arena, especially where political influence changes strongly and frequently, so that society is not confounded by sharp changes in direction as the political wind shifts. The 20-year London strategies, which are revised on a 4-year public consultation cycle, give a good compromise between long-term consistency and political preference. The revisions allow for considerations about how the longer-term strategy could be delivered while the overall direction is maintained, whatever political party or leaning is in power at any one time. Contrast this with the sharp changes in practice that occur as a new mayor takes over a city who changes not only the policies but also the people charged with running the city. Transport is a major – but not by any means the only – loser in such environments because of the long-term nature of its investments in comparison with the usual political cycle. The real losers are the people who live in, work in or visit the city.

Second, most decision-makers are fairly clear – if rather optimistic – about the success factors. Many decisions are made on the basis of an assumption that the success factors will be successful and that the success factors and the actions are somehow the same. The outcomes-based decision model encourages a more realistic appraisal of exactly what is actually going to support achievement of the desired outcomes.

The optimism bias is tempered in the model by the equal consideration of the limitations – those elements, actions, policies and so on that will act against achievement of the desired outcome. Some limitations will be applicable to specific success factors. Others will be identifiable as obstacles in their own right. However, having a clear assessment of both the positives and negatives helps to ensure that the decision-maker considers all aspects that are pertinent to the desired outcome. In the case of both success factors and limitations, it is essential to be aware that these will not fall neatly within the confines of a single area of knowledge. At some sub-level they might be something to do with a single intellectual line of knowledge, but they can be characterised in general as being multifunctional and multi-factorial systems – most being 'systems of systems'. What might be referred to at this stage in the process as a single success factor is in fact a complex system of many dimensions. Thus, the decision process inherently includes decisions associated with wicked and complex problems and the decision-maker will have to deal explicitly with that complexity.

Third, the result of the analysis of success factors and limitations gives a set of actions which will amplify the success factors and limit the limitations. It is these actions that will be the most obvious results of the decision-making process – at least until the desired outcome has been achieved. It is crucial that the actions are not 'just' implementing the success factors (this is where so many decisions go wrong) but that they also explicitly deal with the limitations. There may be compromises in order to achieve sufficient success given immovable limitations, but as the process is only complete when the desired outcome has been achieved, such compromises must not reduce attainment of the desired outcomes.

It is important to realise that success factors cannot achieve success on their own, but they might help the achievement of success (this is why they are factors and not indicators), whereas limitations not only hinder, but can also prevent the achievement of success.

Figure 2.2 shows the outcomes-based decision model in a simplified diagrammatic form. However, actually there is a more complex process to be considered. Figure 2.3 shows in more detail how the model works. Clearly shown in Figure 2.3 are the desired outcomes, success factors, limitations and actions as given in Figure 2.2 and described above, but in addition there is closer consideration of the parts of the process that occur between

Figure 2.2 Basic outcomes-based decision model

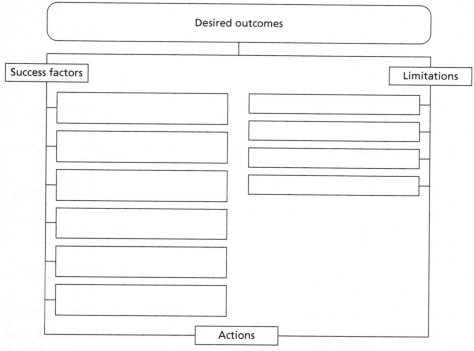

these headline elements, and the cyclic nature of the process. I would like to make some comments about the process as a whole.

First of all, the decision is based around people. It is the people affected by the decision who have the greatest right to a say in what the desired outcome should be. This requires careful consideration about who might be affected by the decision and it is probably safest to consider, at the highest decision level at least, everyone. Simply asking the people is not enough though. We need to understand the meaning behind their wishes. This requires considerable processing. For example, to most people living in a city the bus system is a matter of having a bus where they want it when they want it, but they are less clear about the wider implications of having a bus system, such as its impacts on congestion, pollution, energy consumption or social cohesion. To extract desired outcomes from statements from the public requires skilled interpretation to ensure that the underlying meaning for the bus system is understood. This may need to be played back to, and discussed with, the public a number of times in order to establish the correct outcome. Starting at the highest level is helpful in achieving this because in general people are not experts in the bus system, but they are expert about their own aspirations. The skill is to interpret these aspirations in a form that leads to a desired outcome. It is this process that has led to the point, raised in Chapter 1 and repeated earlier in the present chapter, that people are seeking to improve their wellbeing by aspiring to achieve

Figure 2.3 Extended outcomes-based decision model showing interactions with people

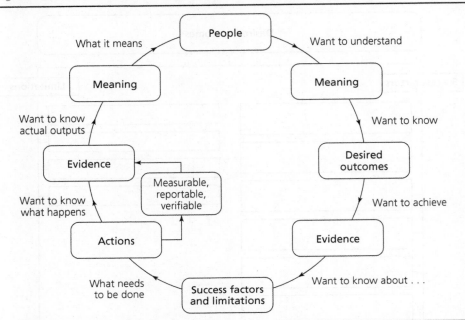

something in their life, which usually means undertaking some activity. It is the availability and accessibility of that activity that is the core requirement for the achievement of their wellbeing and this is where the bus system enters the process. Planners and designers of bus systems must therefore become able to make that connection between aspirations, activities and the accessibility afforded by the bus system.

Having determined the desired outcome the next requirement is to determine what would be the evidence required to know whether or not (or the extent to which) the desired outcome has been achieved. It is this evidence that determines what the success factors and limitations will be, so a realistic appraisal of how we would know achievement when it occurs (and also how we know when failure is imminent) is absolutely essential to the development of a sound decision.

As mentioned above, the actions are the way in which we implement the success factors and mitigate the limitations. It is crucial that the actions lead to evidence which shows how progress is being made on the desired outcome. Therefore, the actions should be designed to be measurable, reportable and verifiable so that they can be understood. This terminology emanates from the United Nations Clean Development Mechanism, where it was necessary to be able to prove how much carbon had been mitigated so that it could be traded on some realistic basis. However, it also serves as a good framework for defining actions in other contexts so that the resulting evidence is believed and understood by all appropriate parties to the decision. Simply having the evidence is not sufficient. The evidence needs to be understood, especially by the public affected by the decision.

There is a tendency to supply data as evidence: clearly, data are necessary in order to provide evidence, but they only become useful when interpretation has been applied in a robust and rigorous way so that the meaning which the data are describing is understood by all the people who are involved in the decision. This means converting scientific data and results into meaningful statements that explain what the data mean. Take the example of noise, where there are distinct measures of noise level, which are routinely not understood by people outside the acoustics field. I have heard public inquiries spend days discussing different experts' versions of data about noise, using a variety of measures, but the meaning of any of it is completely unclear to anyone else (or maybe even to the experts). The meaning is about what the noise would actually be like and whether the noise levels would be intolerable, uncomfortable or acceptable, not whether they are one value of dBA or another. It would have been a whole lot simpler for everyone if the inquiries had been able to hear the different noises that were being discussed so that people could understand what was being talked about. This needs to be played back to the people so that they can assess whether they believe the actions have led to the desired outcome. As Figure 2.3 shows, this is a cyclic affair – as the people understand the meaning of the evidence so they may wish to update the desired outcome, and the process continues. This is, in effect, the revision process to which all societal decisions should be subjected.

Most decisions, especially in the public sphere, are more complex than this simple model, so the model can be nested in order to deal with more complex situations. Figure 2.4 shows how the actions determined at one stage of the process become the desired outcomes for the subsequent stage. Figure 2.5 shows how the cycle shown in Figure 2.3 is actually simply a particular 2D view of the process. In reality, the process is a helix – the process proceeds around the cycle and then, when the meaning of the evidence produced by the actions has been understood, the process moves to another level before repeating. Thus, although the process at each level is the same, the decision-makers are never in the same position – they always have the additional information available to them, both from the previous cycle and from their new vantage point in the process, when attempting to make a new decision. This is how the more complex decisions are made and how more detailed aspects of a decision become determined from a higher towards a lower level. Eventually, those high-level desired outcomes – for example, the improvement of wellbeing – become, after many cycles, a lower-level outcome, such as the colour of a bus.

The strategy is therefore to implement this succession of decisions in a way that develops our pathway to improved wellbeing. As can be seen from the outcomes-based decision model, there will be many actions required and these actions can be construed as a sort of programme of projects, where each project is related in some way to an action which delivers a desired outcome. The outcome of each project/action is the evidence that enables us to reappraise the strategy and ensure that it is still moving towards the desired outcome, as expressed in the vision.

The vision and strategy come together in a four-step process an illustrated in Figure 2.6. First the vision is set at a high level, as discussed earlier in this chapter. The vision gives rise to the need to set fundamental principles and objectives for the strategy. I have illustrated this in Figure 2.6 as the five cities model from Section 1.6. These should be described in as much

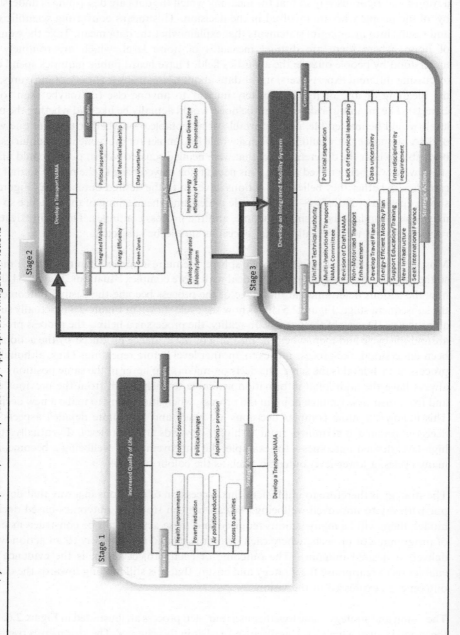

Figure 2.4 Nested outcomes-based decision model: the actions from one stage become the desired outcome for the next: the case of developing a NAMA document for Peru (Tyler and Ramírez, 2012). NAMA, Nationally Appropriate Mitigation Actions

Figure 2.5 Detailed view of the nested outcomes-based decision model. L, limitations; SF, success factors

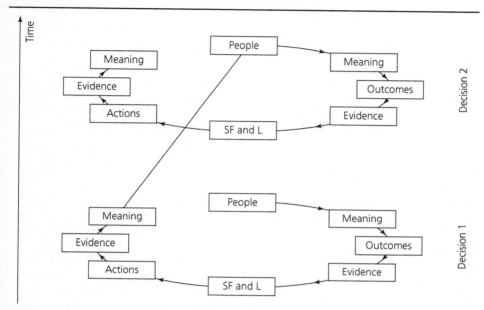

detail as possible so that every aspect of city existence is covered across all of them. The salience of these principles needs to be tested with the people so that they are all-inclusive, understood and accepted by the people as a whole. This activates the outcomes-based decision model so that the cycle of meaning, outcomes, evidence success factors/limitations and actions is engaged throughout the development of the strategy so that implementation embraces the people as well as the team responsible for developing the strategy.

I consider a strategy to be a sequence of executive decisions, directed towards achievement of the aims and objectives (declared in this example) through the five cities and leading towards attainment of the overall vision. Each decision follows the outcomes-based decision model as described in Figure 2.3. This sequence is described as follows.

1 Define the plans, projects and any necessary changes in regulation (or even law if necessary).
2 Determine the financial, investment and political support for the process and initiate this to include as much of the political spectrum as possible.
3 Start the implementation of the programme of projects and actions.

Comments about the detail of each step of the strategy in relation to the contribution of the bus system to the improvement of wellbeing follow.

2.3.1.1 Adoption of the five cities model

The model of the five cities describes different types of needs that are required in a city, and the functions that a city should have in order to make it easier for its citizens

Figure 2.6 The strategy process. L, limitations; SF, success factors

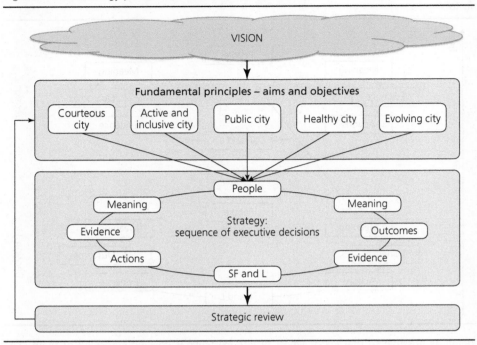

to achieve wellbeing. The model provides a framework for creating a long-term vision. The strategy by which this vision is put in place focuses on the fundamental principle within the vision that urban development focuses on people, and therefore their wellbeing. Cities are by their nature crowds of people, activities and a diversity of opportunities that facilitate achieving the general 'wellbeing'. However, a crowd is actually a mass of individual people, who respond to both large and tiny stimuli in the environment and to the associated responses of other people. This is why crowds are such complex beasts. It is important to ensure that the activities are accessible and affordable to everyone, to ensure equity, reduction of poverty and violence, and so on. It is also vital to ensure that the means available to access the activities are planned and designed so as to minimise the negative impacts on health (respiratory diseases, accidents and stress) and the environment (emissions, energy use and scarce resources), in order to ensure the general wellbeing of current and future generations. Therefore adopting the basic principles of the five cities model may be used to frame and guide the scope of the general wellbeing and sustainable economic development in all cities.

2.3.1.2 Adoption of the accessibility, connectivity, mobility, movement and transport concepts as a set of requirements to meet

The strategy is based on people and therefore it is important to understand why people move and how to facilitate this shift. Everyone seeks their wellbeing and this is conceptualised through aspirations. To achieve these aspirations and perceptions of welfare, people need to undertake a variety of activities (study, work, shopping, sports, access to health centres, etc.) that allow them to approach this wellbeing. These are activities that encourage movement and this is an essential concept that the transport sector needs to recognise: people move to gain access to the activities they desire and not just to be 'transported'.

So, the displacement creates the need to move and the 'transport' system is simply a tool to sort some of the necessary movements for people to achieve mobility. Therefore, it is essential to consider accessibility to the activities as the primary goal for people, mobility as the distribution of activities and their access routes, connectivity as the link to the transport system, and the transport system as the movement management tool required to access the activities. This consideration is necessary because it places the emphasis for the transport system on delivery and not on what it looks like or how it works. Similarly, it is also crucial to understand that it is useless to have a transport system unless it has easy access for everyone regardless of their mental, physical and financial capacity, journey times are reasonable and it generates zero or acceptably low and benign emissions. Therefore, to contribute successfully to achieving the vision, the key for the transport system is that it should maximise accessibility and minimise movement, and in doing so reduce transport energy consumption and greenhouse gases emissions.

For this it is necessary to modify the thinking about transport needs by adopting an accessibility and connectivity maximisation approach, which also minimises energy use, thus reducing emissions. An important element of this approach is to make mobility more local. That is, reducing the need to travel or facilitating activities so that they could be reached through the use of non-motorised transport and then prioritising the use of public transport for those journeys that could not be achieved using non-motorised modes would change the objective of 'maximising capacity' to 'maximising accessibility and connectivity' and at the same time would have the benefit of reducing energy use and emissions production.

2.3.1.3 Development of plans based on the analysis of where they are in relation to the 'systems functionality' approach

The analysis of the functionality and cost of a system consists of the development of a structured process that sets the value of the relationship between the 'function' (satisfaction of needs (goals)) and the resources used to meet them. The steps included in this process are: planning, procurement of information, analysis, creativity, evaluation and reporting. Value engineering, described briefly in Chapter 1, is a specific technique to make this type of analysis in a rigorous way.

Central to value engineering is the determination of the functionality ('value') of the system elements. Therefore, to design the urban transport system it is essential to determine the necessary functions of each one of the system's elements. For example, a bus stop may have a variety of functions: access to buses, access from buses to the local area, a point of information near the transport system, a place to rest, a place to display the system logo, a positive element of the urban realm and so on. The way these functions are prioritised, determines the design of the bus stop and its contribution to the overall system's functionality. The focus on each element's function means that the implementation would be directed to the functionality of the system – the general understanding of isolated functions is not enough – you also need to have a clear view of the joint functions and how they – individually and in combination – are related to the high-level vision.

The consideration of macro factors in the different spheres is a process which should involve all the citizens and this is an initial process in which everyone expresses their views. Similarly, to obtain a successful plan for implementation it is necessary that the public understands what can be done – and what cannot (and why). This analysis is expected to identify a set of clear actions in specific areas of intervention. Also, it is recommended to set timeframes and processes to measure, report and verify.

2.3.1.4 Definition of plans, policies and regulations to facilitate the implementation of the strategy

In order to achieve the vision, projects and programmes should be defined, including actions to achieve the strategy objectives. These actions must be translated into plans, policies and regulations to facilitate the implementation of the strategy and thereby facilitate the decision-making processes. These plans should be developed with the aim of providing the decision-makers with the required autonomy and freedom to adjust policies to meet the requirements for the particular needs in each case. Sometimes it might be necessary to remove, change or add regulatory requirements in order to facilitate 'doing the right thing'. This should be done with great caution, but if it is necessary the change should be made and embraced.

2.3.1.5 Financial and institutional support for the implementation of plans that meet the strategy requirements starts

Typically, the design of transport networks aims to create the necessary capacity to meet peak demand. This encourages large investments in high capacity infrastructure (but is often unsuccessful because it is not understood well enough how capacity operates in transport systems, especially near to the limits). In the model presented here, this strategy aims to prioritise investments that will not only help to reduce energy use and carbon emissions, but would be aligned with the vision and the five cities model. Funding of projects, institutional capacity, clear definition of actors and their functions, and the consensus among stakeholders have been presented repeatedly as critical elements for the development of programmes and projects. Given these elements, scarce resource scenarios in which different sectors compete for funding, or political scenarios characterised by the multiplicity of institutions and overlapping of functions, further increase the difficulty of the project development. However, to make the proposals viable in the context of the principles of this strategy, it is possible to identify funding and institutional mechanisms that contribute to the project's sustainability while promoting the achievement of the basic objectives of the transport strategy. So the approach should encourage the selection of a variety of funding and institutional mechanisms to structure both institutional and financial strategies in line with the capabilities and needs of each city. This means, for example, the design of financing and institutional plans that combine both private and public sectors, in such a way that there is a clear understanding of responsibilities taken by each party in the future – in terms of the share of investment income, risks and responsibilities in the event of difficulties taken on by each party.

The analysis of the funding and institutionalism for the implementation of the strategy may focus on developing regulatory mechanisms, or institutional viability required to obtaining certain funding levels or institutional capacity required. Nevertheless, funding and institutionalism are not the only tools needed to implement the strategy, and therefore it is necessary to design it in detail so that it is politically feasible and allows successful programmes and projects to develop which transcend the political cycle. It is, then, important to consider that the main determinant for the design of funding and institutional systems is related to policy decisions that influence the selection of one funding model over another. Against this, it is crucial to ensure that the decisions that are taken are focused on achieving the vision and not necessarily to fit the currently favoured political model.

2.3.1.6 Execution of the plans and actions starts

Once extensive planning processes have been carried out, it is important to start the process of execution and implementation of the elements defined at the beginning, ideally, by the process of reform and institutional strengthening to allow the identification of actors that will have the technical capacity and could be in charge of leading the development of the whole strategy. The start of this execution process refers to the start of different elements and steps required to carry the plans from the *paper* to *reality*. This process may be related to legal or economic processes (i.e. definition of contracts, tendering process, etc.), design processes, engineering processes and/or technical (e.g. infrastructure construction, operational changes, etc.) or consultation processes and stakeholder engagement, among others.

2.3.1.7 Initiate the establishment of monitoring, reporting and verification system to evaluate the strategy's performance

It is necessary to evaluate the performance of the designed system in terms of its scope to meet the required objectives. This has to start at the very first point in the process – when ideas are first discussed with the local community. Otherwise subsequent measurements will have no basis for comparison. The problem is that the objectives defined in the light of the basic principles are generally not directly measurable on comparable terms. For example, because interest income cannot be easily compared with the benefits of the courteous city, it is necessary to use multi-criteria analysis tools to make the required assessments. It is also necessary to include measurement systems at the beginning of the design of the city systems, to ensure that the monitoring is sufficient for the analysis and evaluation.

With multicriteria analysis methods, it is necessary to assess each of the elements using the same criterion. Whereas some are indicated in quantitative terms (e.g. speed, time, money), others are more qualitative (e.g. comfort). The value engineering approach described in Chapter 1 provides one possible route towards finding this measure.

In Chapter 1, the concept of value was considered to be:

$$\text{Value} = \frac{\text{Achievement}}{\text{Aspiration} \times \text{Use of resources}}$$

The concept of value could be ascribed to any of the functions of the bus system and thus could be used as a common measure for the evaluation of the outcomes. In some cases, either or both the aspiration and the achievement might be expressed in quantitative terms (e.g. a specific level of noise) or in qualitative terms (e.g. acceptability of a noise level). However they are determined, as long as each one is determined objectively and consistently, we can have a measure of value that relates the extent that the aspiration has been achieved and that takes into account the extent to which resources have been used in order to achieve that outcome. In quantitative terms this could be a percentage (e.g. achieved noise levels are 10% more than the aspiration). In qualitative terms, this could be expressed in the acceptability of the achieved noise levels (e.g. 'almost acceptable'). This could be expressed as a qualitative reading on a number line – e.g. as a point on a scale between 0 and 100, where 100 is complete achievement of the aspiration. This would give a percentage in which 'almost acceptable' could be expressed as, say, 85% of the aspiration (it would be better to calculate using ranges to represent qualitative descriptors, but for simplicity here I will just use single numbers). To estimate the value taking into account all the criteria, it is then simply a case of combining the assessments of the different criteria. The easiest and simplest way to do this is to use a 'radar' graph, where each axis represents one criterion, the score for each criterion is entered and the points then joined. The value is then the area of the region encompassed by joining all the points together. The outcome with the greatest area has the greatest value. This process can be seen in Figures 2.7, 2.8 and 2.9.

Figure 2.7 Evaluations of three different transport actions intended to improve various aspects of health

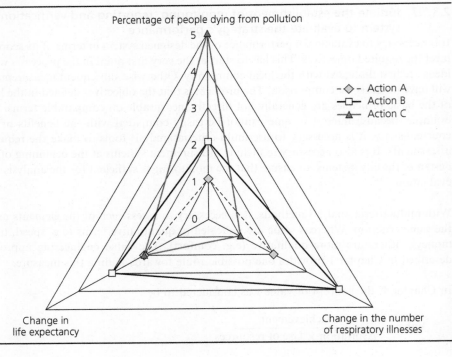

Figure 2.8 Comparison of the transport actions in Figure 2.7 in terms of a range of criteria, including health

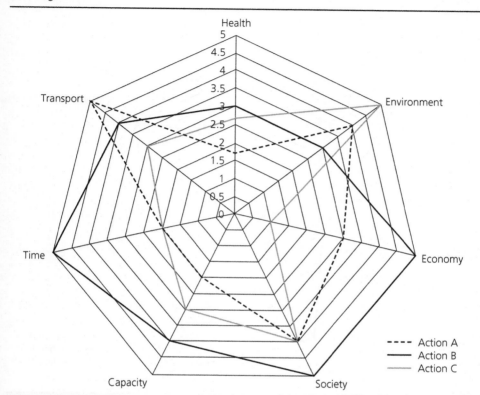

Figure 2.7 shows the output obtained from an assessment of each of three hypothetical transport actions when assessed against a set of three health-related criteria. The three criteria are probably assessable on a quantitative basis, but they might not be (e.g. one of them might have been 'level of discomfort'). The scores are plotted on a radar graph so that each criterion is represented by one axis. The score obtained for each action against each criterion is plotted and the points for each action are then joined.

In this case, the view was taken to use the average scores for each action across the three criteria and transferred to a radar plot in which six other criteria are considered as well. This is shown in Figure 2.8, in which the overall plots for each of the actions can be seen. in this case, the action with the greatest area (i.e. with the highest overall average scores) is Action B. However, if the view had been to take the maximum scores in each case, the result would have been as shown in Figure 2.9. The result would have been to choose Action C in this case as opposed to Action B in the previous example.

Of course, in reality, it is probably necessary to weight the criteria differently to account for relative differences in importance – this would alter the score plotted on the radar

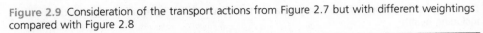

Figure 2.9 Consideration of the transport actions from Figure 2.7 but with different weightings compared with Figure 2.8

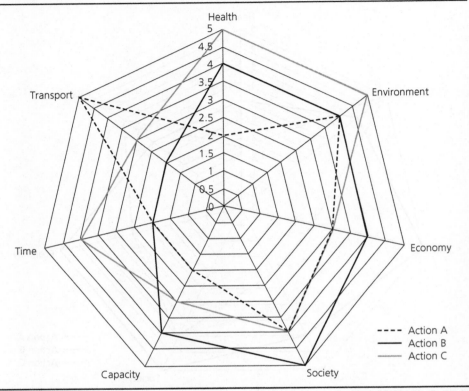

graph, but not the method. Another approach, which seeks to avoid this problem, is to evaluate the outputs of the individual assessments for each criterion and then appraise these according to a qualitative scale, say from 'highly unacceptable' to 'highly acceptable' and combine them as before in the radar plot. The difficulty with this is that it is necessary to adopt a consistent way of evaluating what the various categories on the qualitative scale actually mean. I have seen this done using a panel of stakeholders, or a panel of technical experts. It could be done using a technical panel and a panel drawn from the general public, meeting separately and then combining the two results. This tends to produce outcomes such as 'technically successful, but with outcomes which are unsatisfactory for the public'. At least it is clear where the problems lie with such an approach. I am researching a method for generating a consistent qualitative evaluation of different quantitative and qualitative outputs that could be used for this purpose.

Moreover, it is essential to create mechanisms that facilitate measuring, reporting and verifying (MRV) the integration of urban and transport planning, including feedback required to make adjustments at the level of specific actions. Similarly, these mechanisms should measure the improvement of accessibility and equality so that it is clearly visible whether it has improved or not. The key is that the results have to be consistent.

2.3.1.8 Initiate the review of the strategy after 5 years

It is essential to define a timeframe to evaluate the strategy after implementation so as to identify the aspects that are working, what needs to be changed and what adjustments must be made in order to continue to achieve the vision. Therefore, it is important to include a date to evaluate this strategy in order to ensure its success and make the necessary changes to maintain progress towards the vision. It is important that the strategy review is technical, and not political – political reviews are made within the democratic process – and that it is made through the value engineering model, including especially an analysis of macro and micro functions. I recommend a period of 5 years to review the strategy, so that it provides the opportunity to evaluate substantive progress. This period of 5 years should have covered the periods of implementation, transition, and initial monitoring to facilitate reviewing whether it would be necessary to change something to ensure the successful path towards the vision. TfL revises its strategies every 4 years. This period is used because that is the time it takes to develop, consolidate and include all the public participation outcomes in the process. This seems to be a reason the time for review of the Strategy.

2.4. Conclusions

In this chapter I have set out the underlying thinking about the functionality of the bus system: what society should expect the bus system to be able to do in order to contribute to the improvement of wellbeing. The first issue is to realise that the bus system is the means to attain this outcome but it is not the end objective in itself: the measure of success lies in the extent to which it makes activities available and accessible to the population so that everyone can have an equitable opportunity to transform their aspirations into achievement as part of their pathway to an improved state of wellbeing. Satisfaction, when measured in this way, means that achievement is more likely if the bus network is accessible, connective, spatially dense, operates with a high operating frequency and has plenty of accessible access points. The watchword is accessibility and connectivity rather than movement.

Consequently, I defined some examples of functionalities for the bus system and the functions that might be required in order to provide the overall functionality. The details of how these might be achieved will be discussed in later chapters.

Exactly what the design of a bus system should be is dependent on local needs. In order to have a consistent way of determining these and thence how they can be met requires a coherent decision-making process. I have described the outcomes-based decision model and shown how this can be used to maintain outcomes as the key decision driver. This functions if and only if it considers those factors which will support achievement as well as those that will act as limitations to achievement, resulting in a clear set of appropriate actions that, when nested, form the desired outcome for the next stage in the process. Collectively this will give an approach to achieving the higher-level desired outcome. Figure 2.10 shows the first stage of the outcomes-based decision model applied to the overall ambition for a city – to create an ongoing improvement in societal wellbeing – and how the achievements of the five principles will help to create the successful achievement of this vision. It also indicates just a few of the limitations (for illustrative purposes,

Figure 2.10 A summary of the outcomes-based decision model in relation to the top level of the decision process in relation to the achievement of an improvement in societal wellbeing

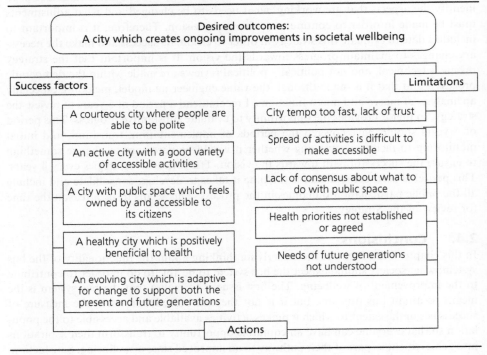

only one per city) that might prevent such an achievement, and thus which must be tackled in order to ensure success. The actions that follow from this part of the process form the matter of the rest of this book.

These decisions are a major element of the strategy for implementing the vision. This needs to be formulated around principles that aim towards achievement of the vision and must include the process of review of the strategy so that although it is possible to work towards an accepted vision based around some form of belief system that this is the right direction, the best way to proceed can be redefined according to changing circumstances. I have suggested that it might be necessary to use multicriteria analysis to evaluate system performance against the huge variety of criteria, especially when these are not all measured in the same way. Overall, in this way it is possible to have stability without fossilisation: a consistent, adaptive stability which improves wellbeing and leaves options for future generations. How to achieve this is considered in the next four chapters.

REFERENCES

Adhitya S (2013) *Sonifying Urban Rhythms: Towards the spatio-temporal composition of the urban environment.* See http://rice.iuav.it/400/ (accessed 15/10/2015).

TfL (Transport for London) (2006) *Accessible Bus Stop Design Guidance*, p. 10. See http://www.tfl.gov.uk/corporate/modesoftransport/1548.aspx (accessed 4 January 2014).

TfL (2014) *Roads Task Force Technical Note 7. What Are the Trends and Patterns of Bus and Coach Traffic in London*? TfL, London, UK.

Tyler N and Ramírez C (2012) *Developing Low Carbon Transport Policies in Peru With Capacity-Building for their Implementation: Draft Transport NAMA* See http://www.ucl.ac.uk/arg/international/latinamerica/peru.

Walton A, Dajnak D, Beevers S, Williams M, Watkiss P and Hunt A (2015) Understanding the Health Impacts of Pollution in London. Report for Transport for London and the Greater London Authority. King's College London, London, UK.

Webpetals (2014) See http://www.webptals.org.uk (accessed 31 December 2014).

Accessibility and the Bus System: Transforming the World
ISBN 978-0-7277-5980-1

ICE Publishing: All rights reserved
http://dx.doi.org/10.1680/aabs2ed.59801.077

Chapter 3
The bus system and the city

3.1.   Passenger needs

As discussed in Chapter 2, the functionality of the bus system includes the process of reaching the system in the first place. This is because the access points – bus stops – are defining points of the interface between the buses and the rest of the city. How the bus system relates to the rest of the city is therefore defined by the bus stops. The bus services simply link the bus stops together on one side of the interface and the pedestrian network links them together on the other. Ultimately, the fundamental requirement comes from the locations of the activities around the city. The bus stops form the fulcrum of the whole system – the balancing points of the city which enable it to deliver these activities to the population. As a result, ensuring that these interfaces are equitable – in terms of where they are, when and how they work – is crucial if the city is to deliver a socially just and fair society which is able to improve its wellbeing and that of its individual members in space and over time. So we need to think about how a person can use the whole system: how they can reach the buses, and the barriers that must be overcome in doing so, so that we can start to define how the buses can make the activities genuinely available to everyone. This is the precursor to specifying the bus service, including its network, routes, access points and schedules.

The first point to bear in mind is the status of the person within the bus system. A person is at one and the same time both a person and: (i) a pedestrian, or (ii) a passenger – or (iii) a person in transition between being a pedestrian and a passenger, or vice versa – a sort of 'pedenger' (a state in which they are simultaneously exhibiting the properties of both and yet the idiosyncrasies of each). The way a person carries their goods (and how much they carry), the clothes they wear, the route (both walking and using the bus) they take are all defined by the passenger, 'pedenger' and pedestrian singularities in combination. We need to understand this 'triality' in order to understand how to define the bus service.

Table 3.1 gives some simple examples of how people might change their priorities as they consider themselves first as pedestrians, then as passengers and finally as 'pedengers'. Of course, whether people are, at any given moment of time, passengers, pedestrians or pedengers, they are always a person – these distinctions are second-order characteristics of people in given circumstances at a given time. The key is that in order to use the bus system people have to take on all three sets of characteristics – the bus stop being the place at which the 'phase transitions' between them take place. It is possible to see some dichotomies – for example, what clothes to wear could mean having to carry other clothes on the journey. To be perfectly attired to use the bus system, one might want

77

Table 3.1 Trialities: sets of characteristics for a person when they are also a pedestrian, passenger or 'pedenger'

Person	Pedestrian	Passenger	'Pedenger'
Smart shoes for the office	Comfortable walking shoes	Shoes that can withstand crowded situations	Comfortable walking shoes, maybe carrying smart shoes in a bag
Smart clothes for a meeting	Suitable for the prevailing weather conditions	Suitable for being inside a vehicle	Light/cool/warm/waterproof outer garments, telescopic umbrella
Amount of shopping	Weight limited by needing to carry in two hands	Best if only one bag, to leave one hand free	Some shopping could be carried in a backpack; easy to rearrange shopping bags for one- or two-handed carrying
Shortest, easiest route	Walking route with fewest road crossings, least crowds	Walking route according to both ends of the bus journey	Choice of bus stop, bus route, interchanges, etc. affects and is affected by the choice of walking route at each end of the journey, total journey time, etc. needs a bus stop with more space to change role, seats, shelter, etc.
Most interesting route	Walking route with most interesting stimuli	Opportunity to do 'other' things during the journey (read, email, meet people …)	Choose route with greatest opportunity for multitasking even if it involves more walking, greater journey time. Needs to be convenient to complete other tasks before moving to the other state
Cheapest route	Be prepared to walk more in order to save money	Shortest or tactically cheapest bus journey affects choice of bus stop(s)	Choose route with lowest fare; minimise the number of changes
Most reliable journey	Be prepared to walk more as walking speed is the most consistent	Some services are more reliable than others	Experience of reliability affects choice of route; easiest to know when bus is coming, its destination, etc.

to change clothes in order to use the bus (e.g. when it is cold and raining), but this is usually difficult to achieve conveniently at a bus stop, so some sort of compromise has to be made. The carriage of shopping – or business equipment – is another area where what might be tolerable or convenient as a pedestrian could be quite difficult to manage as a passenger, particularly if the bus is crowded. The pedenger state is where the change is made to accommodate the different circumstances for people when inside a bus as opposed to being in the pedestrian environment.

But what difference does this triality make to the design of the bus system? Well, for example, the need to provide sufficient options for a choice of route suggests a dense network with many access points; the need to be able to travel with more than one bag could mean thinking about fare collection methods; the potential level of crowding in the bus and bus stop could affect the operational frequency; the desire to make the journey interesting could imply designing the pedestrian route to be engaging and ensure good wi-fi availability at bus stops and on the bus.

3.1.1 Activities

A person is always undertaking an activity, even if that activity is 'being at home'. So the word 'activity' includes the fact of being at home as well as being at some other place. The desired activities in the city can be more numerous than the size of the population and it is likely that many will be duplicated, either because of the need to have them within a reachable distance of members of the population or because there are nuances of style that make people prefer one example to another. That element of choice is important in the process of improving wellbeing.

In an ideal world, everything would be reachable within an easy walking distance. However, this is simply not feasible in most city environments so we need to make choices. The growth of supermarkets over the last few decades has reduced the prevalence of small local shops based near to local residential areas and shifted the goods these used to supply to larger out of town sites. These are inevitably difficult for public transport systems to reach and even where there is a good public transport service the encouragement to buy large amounts of goods makes the carrying of the shopping difficult if this has to be done by hand. Supermarkets are primarily designed around the car rather than the person, but they can also provide a wide range of choices. The same applies to multiplex cinemas, sports arenas, large general hospitals and so on. If they are difficult to reach by public transport, they are certainly difficult to reach by walking. The decline of shops in the town centres as a result of shifting the shopping to the out-of-town site means that the commercial activity in the town centre reduces and the attractiveness drops, making even those shops that are not in direct competition with the supermarket suffer a fall in income.

Planning decisions can have long-lasting effects. Houston, Texas, is considering encouraging development out of town for large supermarkets and other attractors specifically as a way of reducing city centre congestion. Given that the sprawling nature of the city means that it is generally necessary to drive a car to do anything in the city, this might be an inevitable outcome from decisions taken several decades ago – an example of what happens when decisions ignore the requirements of the evolving city. Changing the city towards a more person-oriented development strategy would be very difficult. This does not mean that this should not be done, just that the political and social upheaval will be considerable as people have come to expect driving as the normal way of obtaining mobility.

Activities should be structured according to a base level at which they should be reached without recourse to motorised transport, a secondary level where they can be reached using the bus system, and a third level where longer distance public transport (e.g. metro) would be the preferred means of transport. Only when these have proved to be impossible should cars be seen as the main mode of access. The situation in Houston suggests that there is a lot of work to be done around the underlying access structure before any hard proposals for solutions would be anywhere near ready for consideration.

Of course, shopping is not the only activity! However, the principle still applies that we should consider what activities constitute potential improvements to wellbeing and the extent to which this means that they should be sufficiently close to people that they do not require motorised transport at all. Items such as staple food which is available on a daily basis, newspapers, or opportunities for social interaction could all be activities that fall into the category of being within walking distance. In some communities this might include religious observance or availability of space (and sometimes equipment) for exercise, or a park. Jaime Lerner's 'urban acupuncture' seeks to facilitate activity in person-scale interventions which can be implemented quickly and which respond to the people's needs and desires – sometimes to act and sometimes to sit back and relax (Lerner, 2014). Each of these interventions is an activity in space and time. Setha Low's study of the Plaza de la Cultura in Costa Rica (Low, 2000) shows how a community can use a simple public space for a variety of uses, how these can evolve over time and how the design of the space can help or hinder such activities.

The next level is the type of activity that is good to have near but which might not always be feasible to locate within walking distance. This is where I begin to look at the bus system as a service that brings people from one group of walkable activities to another. This concept can then be extended over greater distances. More linear systems, such as Bus Rapid Transport (BRT) and Metro, come into play eventually in this schema, but only become sensible when the distances and level of aggregation desirable for their operation match the needs of the people. Without well-designed feeder systems, they are not very accessible. The underlying principle is to try to maintain activities close enough to people to minimise the amount of motorised movement necessary in order to reach them. The city thus becomes a series of 'people centres' in each of which is a set of walkable activities and, in combination, there is a whole range of activities which can help to improve wellbeing.

In most cases, changing a city from a car-based/supermarket-focused environment to a walkable one will require retrofit. It might be the case that incentives would be required to encourage trades and activity providers to set up initially. However, it does seem clear that a concerted effort to discover from the community what sort of activities could be suitable for which scale of operation (walk, small bus, large bus, BRT, metro) is a very good place to start. This can lead, in turn, to the concept of doing small things that people can enjoy – both in the creating and the using – and that encourage an important sense of interaction, ownership and responsibility which creates a true and deep social culture. Adhitya and Tyler (2014) show how the use of 'little things' can really help to transfer the way in which city infrastructure is viewed and used – and the importance of transforming elements within the urban realm such as bus stops or benches, in improving the wellbeing of the community.

3.1.2 Accessible networks for users

It is necessary to think about how people can gain access to the network in order to start the journey to reach their chosen activity. First, how people and their activities are distributed around an area affects the ways in which people travel to reach the bus. So the question is how to define a bus network so that accessibility to the bus system might be set as part of a policy based on access to activities.

Having determined the activities that need to be served by bus services, the next stage is to think about the access network required in order to reach them. The first issue is that of direct pedestrian access to the activities. The second is how the bus stops, which are required to enable access to the bus services, are located within the access network. In fact the two issues are the same – the difference is only that in the former case there is direct access from the access network to the activity and in the latter there is direct access from the access network to the bus services, which usually works better if a bus stop is provided. The design of bus stops and the pedestrian infrastructure will be discussed in Chapters 4 and 5: in this chapter, the discussion is about the way in which the access network works in relation to its delivery of people to either a bus stop or an activity. As I am talking about the bus system in this book, I will discuss this issue in relation to bus stops – but the main issues also pertain to the interface with the activities.

Although the bus stop is the gateway to the bus, it is not much use if an intending passenger cannot reach it. A first consideration about this is the distance that a passenger has to walk in order to reach a bus stop. The location of bus stops within the street network defines how far we expect people to have to walk in order to reach their chosen activities as well as the bus system. This is one of the first issues to address when designing an accessible bus system. I mentioned some initial thoughts about this in Chapter 2. I am now going to look at it in a little more detail.

Normally, bus stop location is thought about after a bus route has been determined, but this makes no sense if the bus stops are considered on the basis of their relationship to activities. In fact, bus stops are the hinges of the city – on one side are the buses that carry people to other parts of the city and on the other is the pedestrian network that brings people to and from the city's activities. Bus stops are usually thought of as a part of the bus system – which they are – but actually they are also part of the urban realm. Arguably, they could be seen as being more closely associated with the urban realm than with the bus system – they are present in the urban realm as a permanent fixture, whereas their role in the bus system is mainly associated with the arrival and departure of buses –

but they are really the connection between the two, hence the image of a hinge. Although this might seem a little prosaic, it is important. The bus stop is the source of what is often thought of as the penalty of bus operations – it is where buses have to stop and collect passengers and therefore it imposes a cost on the operation; passengers would be there anyway, whatever the actual nature of the bus stop. In this view, there is no need to spend resources – this would only increase the capital and possibly the operational cost. However, this view is quite wrong. If bus stops are the portals of the bus system, then it is certainly worth investing in them. They need to be operationally efficient and they are the main static physical representation of the bus system – they convey the fact that the bus system exists, and the image of what that system is like to both users and non-users of the bus system. If they seem to be cheap, shoddy and unwelcoming, this is how the bus system will seem. Interestingly, this is not a view taken by the metro systems of the world, where stations are often seen as the shop window of the system – look at the Paris, London or Moscow metro systems for examples.

There are relatively few metro stations in a city – London has less than 300 metro stations, but its 19 500 bus stops are a great opportunity to make a strong city-wide statement about the public transport system and the dynamism that the city is offering. Therefore, bus stops need to be seen in the context of the pedestrian network on which the bus network is superimposed in order to obtain the best balance between the bus and the pedestrian elements of the journey.

As discussed briefly in Chapter 2, most conventional approaches to the location of bus stops at this scale consider only the distance between bus stops along a route and try to balance the time delay to passengers on the bus caused by stopping at the bus stop and that imposed on passengers waiting to board the bus when it arrives at the bus stop. We need to explore the distance and time required of a passenger to reach a bus stop from their chosen activity (the *access distance*) and vice versa.

However, in all considerations of bus stop location it is important to consider the social justice implications of the system. Invoking Rawls' difference principle (see Chapter 1) gives a different perspective from the economics-based one usually advocated. Figure 3.1 shows how the equitable outcome of different bus systems changes as bus stop distances increase. Expectations of benefits to a bus and its passengers (Group X1) increase as inter-stop distances increase. If these were to be transferred equally to pedestrians approaching (and pedengers occupying) the stop (Group X2), the expectations of benefits to Group X2 from increasing inter-stop distances and thus increasing the expectation of benefits for Group X1, would follow the straight line as shown in Figure 3.1. Poor pedestrian and bus stop infrastructure will mean that the maximum expectation of benefits for Group X2 could only be achieved at very short inter-stop distances, thus penalising Group X1 and, after the maximum point, increasing the inter-stop distance would result in decreasing expectations of benefits to this group.

If the pedestrian infrastructure and bus stop facilities were improved, this would improve the expectations of benefits in the sense that the maximum expectation of benefits could be achieved at greater inter-stop distances, but this is limited – even the best

Figure 3.1 Expectations of benefits to passengers in a bus and pedestrians/pedengers in relation to bus stop distance

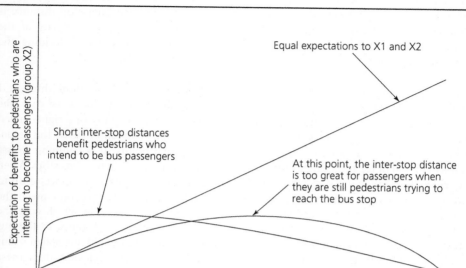

infrastructure will not compensate for the disadvantage of having to walk further and wait longer for a bus and the social justice of the system fails. This situation is indicated in Figure 3.1 by the location of the maximum value of expectations of benefits to the right of the equality line and the decrease in expectations as inter-stop distance increases beyond that point. Only if the walk to the bus stop could be eradicated – for example by the provision of an accessible feeder service – would it be possible to increase the stop distance beyond this point and maintain social justice.

This approach suggests that the inter-stop distance policy should be determined by the social justice implications and that Rawls' concept that the worse off should not become more worse off as a result of the decision comes to the fore. The interesting point in this example is that people in Group X2 turn into people in Group X1 once they board the bus, which is why it is important to make sure that there is an equity between the two groups. This is not based on their value of time or factors differentiating between the value of time of people on the bus compared with people walking towards or waiting for the bus, but on their sense of fairness and the way in which the infrastructure and operational systems combine to provide an equitable access to the bus system.

Fairness would suggest that the pedestrians and pedengers (Group X2) have the tougher deal – they put up with the weather, the footway quality (or lack of it), the complications of crossing the network to reach the bus stop, crowding in the bus stop (as fewer stops means more pedengers in each one), whereas the passengers (Group X1) have to deal with a potentially longer journey time in the bus as a result of having more bus stops. This suggests that, where footways are bad, the access network is complex and the number of passengers is high, the maximum point would move to the left, and to the right if they were respectively excellent, simple and low, or the need to walk were reduced as a result of a well-designed accessible feeder service. Thus the inter-stop distance is conditioned by the quality of the infrastructure, topography, and complexity of the access network and these should always be taken into account when deciding the inter-stop distance, rather than some conceptual notion of economic value.

To start with, and to make the explanation of network density easier to think through, I will assume that the road and footway network is a grid pattern. In the worst case, the straight-line distance between two points in this case is the hypotenuse of a right-angled triangle. The other two sides of the triangle are then the representation of the actual route to be followed along the footways between the two points. It is common to use a norm of 400 m for the straight-line distance from a journey origin to a bus stop. When considered in this way, a 400 m straight-line distance means a walking distance of up to 566 m to reach a bus stop if it were located at the point where the access route meets the bus route. It may not be possible to put a bus stop at this point, in which case the walking distance would be even greater. If the straight-line access distance to the bus stop is 400 m, the worst situation for the inter-stop spacing would be 566 m. This would provide rather less than 2 stops/km. What is even more relevant than these theoretical distances though is the actual distance it is necessary to walk in order to reach the bus stop.

Several years ago, some students of mine tested walking distances in Bloomsbury in London, which has a street network that is nearer to a grid pattern than many in London. They examined a number of bus stops and identified a selection of random locations at a straight-line distance of 400 m from these bus stops. They then measured the shortest distance along the footway network from each selected location to the associated bus stop and calculated the overall mean access distance to reach a bus stop where the straight-line distance was 400 m. We found that the mean access distance was 528 m (Tadesse and Islam, 1996). This was more or less expected – the higher figure mentioned earlier would be the worst case (i.e. when the right-angled triangle was isosceles).

They then repeated the exercise assuming that there was an additional constraint: the access route used in the exercise had to be accessible to a person in a wheelchair. This meant that only routes that had footways of sufficient width for a wheelchair and with access ramps (or level access) for crossing roads could be included (there was an assumption that the wheelchair user knew that these routes existed and which route to take so that turning back and attempting a second route was not included in the analysis). This constraint had a dramatic effect: the mean travelling distance between the selected points and the associated bus stops rose from 528 to 930 m. Similar effects can be found if other accessibility constraints are applied. For example, blind people may need to adapt their walking route in order to cross roads in locations where they can hear traffic more easily or can take advantage of accessible pedestrian crossings. Similarly, deaf people may need to find crossings where they can see traffic more easily, or people worried about their personal security might wish to alter a route to avoid a threatening street environment.

Table 3.2 Percentage of people with a mobility impairment able, with assistance, to move at least the stated distance without a rest (Barham *et al.*, 1994)

Group	Distance: m				
	18	68	137	180	360
Wheelchair users	100%	95%	95%	40%	15%
Visually impaired	100%	100%	95%	50%	25%
Walking aid users	90%	75%	60%	20%	5%
Ambulatory, no walking aid	95%	85%	75%	30%	20%

In these circumstances, it is necessary to consider how far people can actually travel before the distance becomes a problem which is sufficient to cause them to abandon or avoid the journey altogether. Research carried out at Leeds University showed that these distances are actually quite short. Table 3.2 shows a summary of the distances achieved by people walking along a measured path and observed during that walk. It can be seen from the table that only 15% of wheelchair users and only 5% of people with a walking aid could manage a distance of 360 m without stopping for a rest. The distances mentioned above therefore exclude many people from using the bus system, simply because of the distance required in order to reach it.

The effects on people of the location of points of access to the bus system can be examined by bringing together the two notions of bus stop distance and the distances people are able to walk. This involves comparing two views of the same object: what is a bus stop to a bus driver is an access point to the passenger. Assuming the grid network as before, if a maximum walking distance of 360 m were to be adopted, the straight-line distance to an access point would be 254 m and the distance between the bus stops would be 360 m (about 3 stops/km). Table 3.2 shows that this would still exclude some 95% of people using sticks as a mobility aid from using the bus system. This could make the bus system accessible to another 15% of elderly people with a walking aid by reducing the walking distance to the access points from 360 m to 180 m. This would give a straight-line distance of 127 m and a distance between the bus stops of 254 m, yielding about 4 stops/km, but even so it would still exclude some 80% of elderly people with a walking aid from the bus system.

However, as discussed in Chapter 2, I prefer to think about walking distance in a different way, which leads to a different view of how we should be considering the distribution of bus stops. This is based on the walking speed of older people, for example taking a walking speed, say, 0.5 m/sec (slightly less than 2 km/hour) and providing resting points at 50 m intervals along the way, a 10-minute walking time would mean a walking distance of 300 m and those who find it difficult to walk continuously for this distance could rest in one or more of the available resting locations along the way. The provision of resting points is therefore a fundamental aspect of ensuring that the access distance is accessible. A resting point could be a seat or it could be a shelter or it could be just somewhere comfortable to lean. It could include a water supply or telephone or the provision of community information – really it could be as simple or as complex as desired: the key point is that it invites people to use it as a place to ease their difficulty of walking along the footway to the bus stop or activity. Good provision and design means that using such a facility is a pleasure and is not at all something only for those people who cannot walk as far as they would wish. Of course, resting in this way during the walk to the bus stop means that the access time increases. For those in such situations, however, this is not the greatest of their concerns – as long as the overall distance is not too far. On this basis, TfL's norm of a walking distance of 400 m would be feasible if, but only if, suitable resting points are provided.

The theoretical examples above based on a simple grid network are much simpler than would be the case for most real networks. Kunaka (1996) examined the nature of the footway network bringing people to a bus stop and how this related to the 'main route' where the bus stop was located. In the environment considered by Kunaka (Harare, Zimbabwe), the passengers selected the access points and the vehicles stopped where the passengers had accumulated. This was therefore a case where the convenience of passengers' access determined the location of the bus stops. One of the results of Kunaka's work is that, under these circumstances, the design of the access network has a strong impact on the location of a bus stop. A minor change in bus stop location could have a profound effect on the walking distance in one case, yet a much larger change elsewhere could make hardly any difference because the access network provided a different level of access to the main route served by the buses. Knowledge of the access network must include a detailed knowledge of how people use it and the impacts of different barriers. It is therefore necessary to examine the access network to establish actual access routes in some detail before deciding on bus stop locations.

It is unlikely that the required level of knowledge about the access network will be obtainable from just looking at maps. The study in Bloomsbury, mentioned previously, showed that the access route differs for people who are disabled by different barriers. It is necessary to evaluate all these access routes for people who are affected by different barriers when determining the accessibility of a pedestrian network. These assessments need to be undertaken on site – they can rarely be made from maps because of the multi-dimensional nature of the detail concerned (e.g. available footway width, sightlines, echo effects from buildings or bridges, they 'feel' of a place). Catherine Holloway and Steve Hailes at UCL (University College London) are working on an app-based device which links sensor data from a wheelchair (for example) to inform the person occupying the chair and others who might be wishing to use the same route of the topographical, surface and other relevant characteristics of the route.

Considering the walk to the bus stop as an enjoyable and social part of the journey should be a major target for the designers of bus networks. They should make the walking journey 'interesting' by ensuring that it has a number of stimuli to draw the interest – consciously or not – of the pedestrian as they walk along. This could be by way of works of art such as images (2D) or sculpture (3D), dynamically-changing performance or interactive art (4D), trees or other natural environmental features, or it could be done more subtly by affecting the rhythmic sense of the journey – changes to the building line, or making use of other senses, such as hearing or smell, and altering the frequency or regularity of encounter with stimuli and so on. This could be incorporated into the provision of resting points, which could then become the foci of social interactions.

I always like to bear in mind that the whole point of accessible public transport is to make places and activities accessible to people in order to help improve their wellbeing. It is worth spending a lot of effort to consider how accessibility will be dealt with when planning the location of places and activities. Poor consideration of accessibility at this stage may render a new development inaccessible to people who rely on public transport, or it could make public transport extremely difficult to provide in an accessible manner. The accessibility of the pedestrian access network is therefore the starting point for planning and developing bus stops, bus services and bus routes and should be based on the location of the desired activities. This should be worked out before considering other issues such as operating costs, traffic impacts, infrastructure design or environmental effects. The quality of the pedestrian network directly affects the way in which the bus system can operate – Figure 1.6 in Chapter 1 suggests that the better the quality of pedestrian access and bus stop facilities, the greater can be the inter-stop distance in order to achieve an equitable system. However, increases in inter-stop distance can only be considered if the fundamentals of need for access can be enjoyed by the whole population and this tends to shift the maximum amount of expectation of benefits to the bus passengers to the left of the graph. The graph in Figure 1.6 is actually quite simplified – it assumes that the maximum expectation of benefits in the three cases are equal. I think it is quite likely that this might not be the case in reality and that the three distributions could each have a different maximum value of expectations of benefits.

Transport for London (TfL) and some other larger city transport planners (e.g. Manchester) use an interesting measure to help it evaluate the provision of public transport in relation to a proposed development. This takes into account the distance from public transport access points to a given location. This is combined with the service frequency to provide an estimate of the *public transport accessibility level* (PTAL) (TfL, 2014). At the time of writing, TfL is updating the system in order to use actual walking distances; Manchester only uses straight-line distances. The model only includes quantifiable measures, such as time and distance, and does not incorporate issues such as perception or degrees of mobility impairment. As PTALs only consider walking distances and public transport service frequencies, they do not take any other form of barrier into account. As a result, they do not measure 'accessibility' in the sense that it is used in this book. I consider the PTAL approach as a useful means of including the 'availability' of public transport rather than its 'accessibility', given the current use of the latter term.

PTALs are calculated on the basis of the measured walking distance from a proposed development to the various public transport access points within a maximum distance (15 minutes for rail and 10 minutes for bus (LBHF, 1994). There has been a move to represent this in terms of distance (960 m for rail and 640 m for bus). If a straight-line distance is used, a factor is applied to account for the difference between the straight-line and the actual walking distance. The factor normally used provides an estimate of walking distance that is broadly in line with the results from our Bloomsbury work noted above. Walking speed is assumed to be 4.8 km/h (1.33 m/sec), which is a lot faster than the speeds that would be appropriate when discussing older people. Access time is then calculated by adding the walking time from the 'doorstep' of the location of interest to the boarding points and the scheduled waiting time (adjusted by an assumed reliability factor). The *equivalent doorstep frequency* (EDF) for each boarding point is taken as the reciprocal of the access time. The EDFs are then summed over all boarding points, with the smallest access times multiplied by 30 and the others by 15, to give an *accessibility index* (AI). Ranges of AIs are then used to divide the borough into zones, currently ranging from 1 with the lowest accessibility level (AI between 0 and 5) to 6 for the highest level (AI greater than 25). The zone value is then used to determine aspects of a development (e.g. the amount of office space to be permitted).

PTAL analysis is an attempt to ensure that public transport availability is included in planning decisions which might otherwise only consider access by private car.

However, there are difficulties with PTALs. PTALs only consider what services are intended to function in the proposal. They do not distinguish between the usefulness of what might be on offer. So, for example, it would rate a service better with six buses an hour terminating one stop after the one nearest to the starting point than one with five buses an hour which operates into the city centre. It is also very limited by its parameters. So, for example, a station in London could be rated as a 6 (very high accessibility) within 960 m, but if the location of interest is 961 metres away, it drops to a level 2 (very poor accessibility). Also, no account is taken of differences in accessibility obtained by people with different walking speeds. A speed of 4.8 km/h may be an average value, but it is quite a high average – reasonable estimates for walking speed tend to suggest a rather lower speed (4.3 km/h) (TRB, 2000). However, even these estimates do not take into account the slower walking speeds obtained in practice by elderly and disabled people (we have measured examples as low as 0.25 m/s (0.9 km/h)). Speeds are generally reduced further by design features such as crossfalls, road crossings, and/or the need to rest during the journey.

A study of crossing speeds at mid-block pedestrian crossings in Australia (Akcelik and Associates, 2001) showed that the 15th percentile for walking speeds by people with a walking difficulty in this environment was 1.0 m/s (3.6 km/h). However, this is an environment where people feel under pressure to walk faster and the distance is relatively short.

Another gap is that there is no allowance made for people to choose routes other than the shortest in terms of physical distance because they are more accessible. PTALs are used when making decisions about planning consents. As PTALs do not explicitly include such routes in the analysis, disabled and elderly people can all too easily be effectively excluded from consideration in some planning decisions unless there is a conscious effort to ensure that they are included. Failure in this respect could, for example, exclude disabled people from working in a new office development even though the development itself complies with current accessibility regulations and is fully accessible. This could also apply to new facilities such as healthcare or day centres, which, although accessible in themselves, may only be reachable in practice by specialised transport or private car because suitably accessible access routes from local public transport are not assured. This is not only an issue for urban areas. The nature of the bus network and the location of bus stops is also a key issue for rural areas. Indeed, in some cases the problem is much worse in rural areas. The sparse road network and lack of roadside footways mean that people are often required to walk along the road in order to reach a formal bus stop. This is neither attractive nor safe. Nevertheless, the use of PTALs does ensure that public transport is taken into consideration in planning decisions and this might be its greatest value.

Both the bus network and the access network need to be adapted in order to accommodate the accessibility needs of the population. The result of this approach is that it is necessary to fix the bus stop locations on the basis of the accessibility of the pedestrian network (including such factors as the availability of resting points, the number and ease of pedestrian crossings etc.) before worrying about the design of the bus services that will join them together. Figures 1.6 and 3.1, with their consideration of the quality of the pedestrian network and its implications, should be kept strongly in mind when making decisions about the location of bus stops.

3.1.3 Accessibility requirements of bus stops

A number of issues should be considered with respect to the bus network in both urban and rural areas:

1 Formal bus stops are needed so that they can:
   (a) indicate where the bus service will be found
   (b) indicate to the bus driver where the passengers might be waiting
   (c) provide an accessible place to board and alight from the buses
   (d) provide appropriate waiting facilities and shelter
   (e) act as a source of information about the bus service
   (f) act as a source of information about the local area.
2 Bus stops must be located so that access distances are appropriate. This may mean ensuring that buses go into local residential areas or villages rather than pass them by on the main road.
3 Bus services combine smoothly with the local pedestrian network and together these must serve the local community, making it easier for people to move around and reach their desired activities within their local area, as well as making it easier to travel further afield when necessary. This means including resting points, ensuring that pedestrian crossings are adequate and easy to use. A lack of such facilities means that bus stops will need to be closer together.
4 There must be accessible interchanges between the local services and longer distance services (bus and rail) to provide access to activities that are not available locally.
5 The service routes and frequencies must be appropriate to provide satisfactory access to the requisite amount of activity when and where this takes place. This must take into account the maximum desirable access time, waiting time and journey time, and the satisfactory level of occupancy of the infrastructure and vehicles. This could affect frequency, the size of the vehicles and the density of the route network. The application of Rawls' thinking to accessibility discussed in

Chapter 1 makes it clear that there is a minimum level of accessibility that society must provide, and this will indicate requirements in terms of the demand to be met which might be quite different from those obtained from the conventional calculations. This leads to perceiving the bus system as a service, which includes the pedestrian environment, rather than as a set of bus routes and vehicles.

I can now summarise the steps that need to be taken in recognition of the needs of bus users – including potential users – to be included when considering the design of an accessible bus network.

1   Set out the accessibility requirements for reaching and using the bus stops, based on the location of local activities. Without this, all the other measures will be wasted. This involves ensuring that the pedestrian network is accessible, and that the bus network ensures that access distances are appropriate and the time taken to reach a bus stop is reasonable.
2   Determine the maximum waiting time. This indicates the service frequency, which determines the number of buses needed to operate the service and thus the number of buses that each bus stop has to accommodate.
3   Calculate the minimum capacity of the bus stop for passengers (and, therefore, the associated facilities) and the size of the buses on the basis of the overall spatio-temporal passenger demand.
4   Ensure that the system is user-friendly, comfortable and convenient to use. This is a primary element of a city's ability to connect its activities for the benefit of all the population and there is no reason why it should be shoddy or unpleasant.
5   Work out the provision of the accessible information that will guide people to and from the bus system.
6   Finally, once all these have been completed, the whole system can be put in place.

In summary, the essential ingredients of an accessible bus system, against which any proposal should be measured, include:

1   Provision of an accessible pedestrian network, including:
    (a) the removal of sensory, cognitive and physical barriers, or the reduction to an acceptable level of their impact on users
    (b) the provision of sufficient accessibility enhancements (e.g. use of appropriate materials, dropped kerbs, increased footway widths, safe and secure resting points with seating, information and signage)
    (c) the design and construction of the pedestrian network so that its quality is such that using it is an enjoyable experience.
2   The definition of appropriate access times and distances between journey origins/ destinations and bus stops, and thus the location of bus stops.
3   The definition of accessible service schedules, including consideration of the effects on accessibility of frequency, route and interchange (e.g. access times, waiting times and journey times).
4   The definition of appropriate capacities, such as pedestrian network capacity, bus stop capacity (for passengers and buses) and bus size.

5   The provision of appropriate passenger facilities at bus stops, such as seating, shelter and information, taking the full range of users' capabilities into account.
6   The provision of adequate accessibility features on and in vehicles, and training for staff in their use.
7   The provision of updated training in disability awareness for all staff associated with the bus service.
8   The provision of accessible information throughout both the access network and the bus network, including access to information at journey origins.
9   Ensuring that the system is comfortable and enjoyable to use.
10 The implementation of the accessible bus system.

3.1.4   Spatial accessibility

Some accessibility issues are defined in terms of space; I have already mentioned some aspects of distance. The principles underlying the notion of this 'spatial accessibility' to the bus system are that the distance between a bus stop and a journey origin or destination where the activities happen should be achievable by the population. Analytical models currently used to analyse the distance between bus stops do take passenger access times into consideration, but the 'conversion' of space into time is performed by using speed, which means that the speed that is chosen is highly important. All those models accept the premise that all passengers have the same value of time, concept of walking and waiting times and ability to walk at a given speed. I believe that it is not reasonable to hold such a view. A speed that is too high will exclude from consideration in the design all those who walk more slowly.

I will now discuss the effects of considering the possibility that different pedestrians might have different needs with respect to the distance between their journey origins/ destinations and the bus stops. Basically, this means considering how to ensure that people are not excluded from the bus system because their journey origin or destination lies too far away from the existing (or proposed) bus network.

Every activity must be accessible to everyone, yet physically this cannot be the case. One of the ways of resolving this conundrum is to have a bus system where the accessibility is provided by means of the combination of vehicles (to resolve major distances) and access points (to provide accessible access to these vehicles). It is therefore essential to ensure that every activity has at least one reachable bus stop within an accessible distance. Bus stops have to be located around the network in such a way as to provide reasonable access to the bus system and the bus network must be thought of primarily as a network of access points – bus stops. The measurement of the adequacy of a physical bus network is the extent to which people are able to reach its bus stops from their activities. If the access distance to a bus stop becomes too large or too difficult, some people will be unable to reach it and this inability will exclude them from the activities they would otherwise be able to reach by using the bus system. The pedestrian network and its infrastructure is thus an integral part of the service being provided by the bus system.

So far, I have talked about exclusion in terms of distance, but the 'distances' used to define it are usually described in terms of time. This brings me back to the speed/access issue. It seems more sensitive to describe access to the bus system in terms of time rather than distance. I like to think of a bus stop as having an 'inclusion zone' within which people are able to reach the bus stop, and an 'exclusion zone' where the bus stop is basically inaccessible. The inclusion zone would become smaller (and the exclusion zone larger) as the access speed decreases. A single stop could have several inclusion zones to allow for people with different maximum access distances as a result of their different access speeds. I like thinking about it in time rather than distance because it makes it possible to have a consistent policy (e.g. 'everyone should be within 10 minutes of a bus stop'), yet allows it to be interpreted flexibly to take account of the needs of different people and the different environments they encounter on the way to the bus stop. This also encourages the identification of access problems so that remedial measures can be identified and implemented. Access time includes waiting time, so the expected waiting time should also be taken into account. Waiting time can be perceived very differently if different provision is made. Waiting in the wind and rain will feel much worse than wait-ing in a comfortable environment, so the value of waiting could be quite different and the use of a simple measure related only to the time spent waiting is not suitable for assessing waiting time. I will discuss how this access time can be estimated in Section 3.1.6).

The further away a journey origin is from a bus stop, the more likely it is that some form of personal or technical assistance, for example, a walking aid or resting points) might be necessary in order for a journey-maker to be included within the inclusion zone. The more accessible the access network, the more inclusive the bus system will be. I noted in Chapter 1 how important independence is to the development of a high quality society and the crucial role played by accessible public transport – especially bus systems – in the encouragement of independence. The design of an inclusive access network is central to the development of an inclusive bus system and thus to the encouragement of this independence.

An accessible access distance is defined precisely for a person under the particular circumstances that arise for them in the location of interest. This is the actual access distance which they can achieve comfortably within the access time considered to be inclusive. The access distance can therefore be radically changed by the addition (or removal) of infrastructure (e.g. a footbridge or accessible crossing). Catherine Holloway carried out some experiments to discover how much work (force required to move over a given distance) is required to proceed along a typical footway (these are described in more detail in Chapter 4). One important outcome is the extent to which the level of work required increases as 'standard' design features (e.g. a crossfall (the gradient aligned across the footway, usually for drainage)) or the use of a walking aid such as a crutch, are emphasised. The use of geographical information systems (GISs) for this purpose could help to show the effects on access distance as a result of the introduction or removal of such infrastructure or the removal of certain barriers. This could then define who is being excluded from the bus system by the combination of bus stop locations and the access network using a measurable quantity based on the work required to cover the access distance in the local circumstances.

People who are unable to reach a bus stop for any reason are located in its exclusion zone. This can be remedied in principle by the addition of another bus stop, not necessarily on the same road or bus route as the (exclusive) original stop. Plotting these access points on a map will yield a mass of dots and inclusion zones spread over the area. The process of network design is then one of defining the access points (bus stops) needed in order to make as much of the overall area as possible lie within inclusion zones. The next step is to design the ways in which these points could be joined together to form a set of services.

There are many ways in which a set of points can be joined to form a bus route. In the simplest case, it is a question of joining them together and then working out how feasible the resulting service would be. The set of bus stops selected in order to maximise the amount of an area that can be considered to be within inclusion zones can then be compared with the operating cost of the bus services that are required to call at the stops under the desired operating regime (e.g. whether buses can overtake each other or not).

The consideration of inclusion zones for bus stops means that I am defining areas around a bus stop that exclude certain people from using the bus. This is set against the operational idea of a bus service which has constraints on the number of times it is sensible to stop a bus on its journey. One solution to such exclusion is to have more bus services spread around the area and thus to have more opportunities to have bus stops without imposing too many stops on each route. This increases the amount of an area that falls within inclusion zones. Bus services combine to form networks and it is these networks that can help to reduce the exclusion from the bus system, but only if the resulting network is easy to understand, interchange is easy and there is no fare penalty for changing buses.

Defining a network on the basis of bus stops and thinking in terms of access distance means bringing buses nearer to journey origins and destinations. This is not good for longer routes as the increased number of bus stops would increase the journey time and thus the number of vehicles required to operate the route. One way of solving this problem is to bring a number of the local services together as a 'micronetwork' – a small network that covers a local area – and to connect this to one or more 'main routes' in a 'mesonetwork' which can connect the micronetworks to each other and to other access points in the city (see Figure 3.2). This sort of network has main routes which provide the high capacity point-to-point bus services and smaller routes which feed into the main routes from outlying areas. The concept is quite common, but it is important to think about it in more depth. A network designed on the basis of feeder services will have a number of small services serving a main interchange point. Usually, the feeder services will start some distance away from the interchange, call at a few intermediate points and end at the interchange. This is analogous to the sort of arrangement envisaged for an integrated inter-modal system where the main mode is a railway, but in this case it is an 'intra-modal' integration between different types of bus service.

3.1.5   Micronetworks

Whatever the design of a micronetwork, its viability is important. These services bring people from parts of the network that are more difficult to reach by conventional bus services (maybe because of distance, road type or traffic restrictions) to join activities to the main bus services at a convenient point. If there is a reasonable demand for the

Figure 3.2 Micronetworks joining into a mesonetwork to connect local areas with others and a more major destination

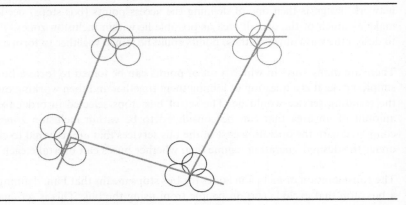

main service, the feeders may well bring additional passengers who simply cannot reach the main service at its current location. The design of a bus network that is integrated in this way allows the main services to follow more direct routes, thus reducing their journey time and costs. However, it is important to realise that the level of demand for a service is not the only reason for having it: providing access to the local high street or other public transport services may outweigh the simple profit and loss analysis of any route.

The trouble with thinking in terms of 'feeder services' is that this implies that their main cause for existence is to 'feed into' the main service, thus making them some sort of subsidiary derivative, which depends on the main service for survival. Remember that the objective is to make activities accessible. Actually, it is the micronetworks that deliver the activities and they are essential in order to make these reachable from other parts of the city because in the majority of cases the main services are incapable of coming close to the desired activities. I think of the micronetwork as the essential element of the service as it makes the activities accessible and what are otherwise thought of as the 'main services' as additional services which serve to widen the accessibility of the activities. So it is a mistake to view feeder services merely as tributaries to the main network: we must also think they interact with the area in which they are situated.

A well-designed micronetwork also provides a service in its own right which enables people to travel within a local area or out of one local area into another, whether or not this is for the purpose of changing bus. The small high street may only be surviving by serving those people who have no access to transport to take them to the larger super-market in the second area. Small shops often also find it very difficult to offer the same breadth of goods at the same quality and price as their larger supermarket counterparts, which are reachable by private car. People without access to transport – including those on restricted incomes – are therefore often condemned to buying more expensive, poorer quality goods with less choice than their better-off neighbours. The provision of accessible intra-community bus services is, therefore, one way of enhancing choice and inclusion and extending economic benefits to local areas. It should also encourage the local community to be cohesive, paying attention to how people in the community inter-act with each other in both social and economic terms. The provision of a transport system can threaten this cohesion as well as facilitate it, and it is important to design the service to ensure that the encouragement of social cohesion outweighs any potential economic disadvantage that might be perceived. As I shall show, a well-designed bus service can encourage people to shop locally: access to a car is much more of a threat to the local community than access to a bus service.

I devised a bus service that encouraged people to come to the local high street rather than go to the more distant supermarket. This approach consisted of a network design that consisted of joining the access points in such a way that buses were led towards the local shopping street. Making it easier to shop at the local high street helps to sustain the local economy and provides opportunities for local social cohesion. This is not to say that it should be impossible to reach the supermarket. A more distant supermarket could be reached via an accessible, well-designed interchange; that is, it is still possible, but slightly less convenient than going to the local shops.

One way of approaching this would be to locate the interchange between the micro-network services and the main services in the local high street. Bus services (possibly using small accessible buses) could provide a frequent service from the hinterland towards the local high street, where they would provide an interchange that enabled people to transfer easily to another service which would take them to other parts of the hinterland or further afield. However, a local area exists as a community in which activities happen. A bus system is the default means of transport which society should design in order to ensure that all these activities are accessible to everyone. A bus network which is conceived just as a main service and its feeder services is in danger of ignoring this issue. Simply designing a bus network to provide access to itself is a waste, especially if this means that it is easy to leave a local area to carry out activities elsewhere. We should think about the way in which the bus network could help the local economy to survive a little better.

A bus service aimed to help a local high street needs to provide a service from neighbour-ing areas (whether these are local villages in a rural area or residential areas in a town) to the high street and back again. Inevitably, the high street will attract a number of bus services, thus affording the possibility of interchange between them. Some of these bus services may connect with other communities, thus providing the possibility of travelling further afield in order to visit amenities that are not available in the immediate locality. The high street would become the focus of these services but it is important that they do not swamp the high street 'eco-system'. This suggests that a small interchange facility, designed to ensure accessible transfer between vehicles, should be included. This need not be a major structure – in most cases it would be a set of well-designed accessible bus stops. It would need to be planned and designed to ensure that the buses did not cause congestion in the high street.

However, remembering that the aim is to support the high street, the concept of inter-change alters a little. Instead of trying to accommodate the interchange between two services as quickly as possible, we could try to insert enough time to allow some activity to take place in the high street during the interchange period. Thus, a passenger could arrive on one service and make some purchases, enjoy a coffee, visit the post office, or whatever, before boarding the second service that would take them onwards. The concept is not novel – airports thrive on forcing passengers to loiter in the proximity of retail and catering facilities while waiting for transport services. The difference is that 'bus stations' are not normally the sort of place one would expect to do this – they are often located too far away from the high street, or are too complicated with too many badly integrated services to make such a scenario attractive. They are also often designed to accommodate the bus operations rather than the passengers – and they rarely attempt to integrate with the local community.

So, I see a great opportunity for a bus network to work as a set of micronetworks, in which accessible bus services operate at reasonable frequencies, work together to form an overall network for the area, make it easy to have choices about and make journeys between local centres, and connect with longer distance services. The micronetworks are each defined on the basis of access points as described above. Each micronetwork provides transport for the inclusion zones – in combination they should be able to reduce the number of excluded people so that they can be accommodated by other means. The micronetwork then acts as a feeder service to longer distance services, providing access to other areas by means of a simple and accessible interchange.

Why have I come to this view about the bus system? In the first edition of this book we discussed two projects which involve micronetworks: the Hackney and the Cumbria Plusbuses. Although I will not provide a detailed description in this edition, I will discuss some features of these projects that help to explain the progression of my thinking.

When setting up the Hackney Plusbus, I wanted to incorporate the views of potential users in the route design. Working with Hackney Community Transport, a social enterprise, we tried to find out where people wanted to go, but instead we found that they were unable to tell us. This was because their transport had been so inadequate for so long that they had simply closed down their world to the activities that they could reach on foot or via a specialised transport service organised by someone else. To establish the Plusbus route required by the local community in Hackney, we had to plot the access points as best as we could and then join them together, taking into account operational requirements and other factors such as traffic management (Lynas, 1998). We then put this route into operation and revisited the users a few months later. It was clear that the Plusbus had awakened their interest in activities outside their hitherto normal regime and other destinations had become desirable. We then adjusted the route to include as many of these as possible.

The Cumbria case was a little different. Before the start of the Cumbria Plusbus operation, journeys were undertaken by car or not at all (with the occasional exception of journeys made on foot or bicycle, some over quite long distances). For a non-car-owner or driver in Cumbria, the need to travel meant an infrequent trip to one of the larger towns (about 50–60 kilometres away), made with the help of a car-owning neighbour or family member.

Before they could make such a journey they had to ask for a lift or the lift-giver had to know somehow that such a need had arisen: independent travel was not possible.

Once an accessible bus service was introduced, the attractions of local activities were made available to people. Independent travel became a possibility and quite suddenly – and seemingly on a reasonably long-term basis – people opted to use the new bus to reach local shops independently rather than to visit the supermarket further away as part of a pre-arranged trip. In both the Hackney and Cumbria cases, the demand for transport within the local area was not apparent due to the ways in which the residents dealt with the lack of accessible transport and the provision of an accessible service opened up opportunities that had been unavailable.

Why is this? A number of issues seem to be important in answering this question:

1 People could make their own decisions about when and where they went out.
2 The difficulty of travelling was eased so that people could choose how to undertake an activity rather than how to make a particular journey (e.g. to shop locally rather than far away).
3 Some trips (e.g. to a hospital out-patient appointment) could be undertaken without the need to wait around for the 'official' vehicle, even though this would have provided a door-to-door service.
4 Apart from the occasional trip on the bus 'just to get out of the house', journeys generally have a non-transport purpose. However, what makes people choose a service that is not door-to-door, is scheduled and is restrictive in terms of destination and departure time, rather than the apparently more comfortable and convenient alternatives? It seems it is the freedom to make that choice and the social interactions that arise. In both Hackney and Cumbria people of all ages make trips for social reasons: shopping or even visits to a health centre become a social event in addition to their prime purpose. In some cases the availability of company on the bus acts as a means to reduce isolation. So one of the Functions (see Chapter 2) of the bus service is to provide social cohesion through the availability of social contact. Transport can therefore be seen as playing an active role in the local economic and social life of a community, rather than as simply being a bus service. I conclude from this that one of the effects of a community-centred micronetwork is to facilitate social cohesion – helping people to function within their community rather than merely helping them to travel to the locations further afield.
5 The Hackney Plusbus has opened up opportunities outside the local area: it has provided interchange with accessible mainstream buses which enable users to reach the centre of London (some 10 km away), a journey which might have been unachievable on an independent basis for many years. The Cumbria Plusbus enabled people to travel between villages in the area, thus making visits to friends and family – and even some work trips – easier.

The difference between the Hackney and Cumbria cases is that, before the change, in Hackney the journeys were either not made at all or were made on specialised transport before the arrival of the Plusbus, whereas in Cumbria journeys were generally being made to distant locations by car. In Hackney, the specialised transport journeys transferred to the Plusbus but the destinations did not really change. There were also many new trips to the local facilities. In Cumbria, the longer car journeys were exchanged for shorter bus journeys to the local market town. Often several short bus journeys each week replaced one car trip to a distant town for ostensibly the same purpose (Brown and Tyler, 2001) but actually so that additional opportunities arose to meet people and engage in social contact. In both cases, the new transport service has provided some independence, resulting from the ability to choose, which is so important in the quality of life of the community. In short, they contributed to an improvement in local wellbeing.

3.1.6 Time and frequency

I have discussed the issues surrounding the access to a bus stop and how that affected my thinking about network and bus stop density. Now I can explore the way in which time is affected by the service density and how this affects accessibility. This has an impact in two ways: the effect on departure time choice and the impact of service frequency on waiting time. I shall consider waiting time first.

There is a fairly common consensus that a 10 minute wait is about the maximum that is tolerable for many people – for some this would be an absolute maximum as a result of pain resulting from standing or sitting. This brings the need to ensure that this limit is not exceeded. There is a common line of thought that suggests that the average waiting time in a high-frequency service is half the headway. This is based on the idea that people arrive at the bus stop in a random manner and thus although someone would just miss the bus as it leaves, others would arrive randomly until someone else just manages to catch the following bus. As a result, the average waiting time is half the interval between the buses. Thus to achieve an average 10 minute wait, it would be necessary to have a reliable service with a 20 minute headway. However, I am not talking about an average wait – I have said that the maximum wait should be no more than 10 minutes. This means that it is necessary to run the service with a 10 minute headway so that nobody waits for more than 10 minutes or that a lower frequency service operates so reliably that a passenger can know when to arrive at the bus stop so that their maximum wait would be less than 10 minutes.

A 10 minute headway would deliver a maximum wait of 10 minutes only if the service were to operate perfectly reliably – that is, every bus arrives exactly 10 minutes after the previous one. This is actually very hard to achieve as a result of differences in operating conditions over time – one bus might have to wait at one more traffic signal than the previous one or perhaps pick up a few more passengers at a previous stop. Either of these would cause a bus to run slightly late in comparison to both the one in front and the one behind. The converse would apply if the bus were to run slightly faster than the schedule and thus appear early at a downstream bus stop.

The maximum wait requirement could be achieved by having a high-frequency service or by having a service that is so reliable that it is unnecessary to wait for longer than 10 minutes. Shorter routes, being easier to operate reliably, are therefore useful in this respect.

This is another reason for using a micronetwork to provide access to local services (including other bus services). The ability to operate reliably is also an important way in which to reduce the need to run a high-frequency service.

However, there is another element to think about when considering time, especially waiting time, and this is that although the network 'owner' and bus operator might be thinking about service frequency, headway reliability and journey time, the passenger is actually thinking in terms, not of actual waiting time, but their perception of time spent waiting. People routinely overestimate the time they spend waiting for anything and buses are no exception. This overestimation can be of the order of 1.5 to 2 times the actual time spent waiting. So that maximum 10 minute wait I have been talking about might be perceived to be between 15 and 20 minutes, which is well above that maximum 10 minute threshold. As a result, the threshold is actually perceived time, not actual time. So really, the 10 minute maximum should be somewhere between 5 and 7.5 minutes in terms of actual time. These perceptual errors refer to time spent in the present but when they consider time in the past or future a wholly different approach is adopted.

There is a tendency for people to distort their perception of time when thinking of the past or future, according to their propensity to think about events in the past or future. If we ignore the transcendental perception of time, there are five common perceptual states adopted by people. Zimbaldo and Boyd (2008) suggest that people who are highly positive about the past tend to remember large amounts of detail about past events and to think these are nearer to the present than they actually are, wishing that these pleasurable circumstances could be repeated – and being certain that they could be, whatever their current time constraints. People who think negatively about the past tend to amplify their past difficulties and seek to avoid them in the present and future, often thinking that they are unable to affect whether or not they reoccur, whether or not the time would be available for this to happen. People who are obsessed with the present tend to want to do everything 'now' whatever the time constraints. People anxious about the future tend to want to avoid future events and people who are positive about the future want to plan their lives into the future to maximise the opportunity for doing all those things that they could possibly want. These perceptions mean that the concept of time is extremely elastic – most people will have a mixture of these perceptions – and across the population there is a variety of time perceptions which have to be understood.

Hammond (2013) discusses a common experiment where people are asked about high profile events in the past. There is a really common tendency for people to make quite large errors when trying to do this. Typically, if the event happened more than a couple of years before the tendency will be to shorten the time period so that the perception is that it happened much closer to the present than was actually the case. Errors can be of the order of several years, even decades, and always in the same, shortening, direction. Why is this important for our wellbeing-improving bus system?

Hammond's discussion suggests that previous experience of waiting for a bus can be stretched into a very long perceived time, so that the very thought of repeating the experience is that of a complete and frustrating waste of time. Or it could be that whatever

Figure 3.3 Sensing Time 1: Waiting time is often overestimated when compared with the actual time that has elapsed while waiting

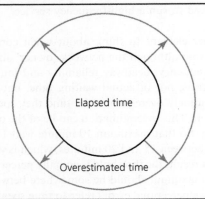

happens the waiting time will be longer than desired (or expected or hoped). Or that however short the waiting time might turn out to be, it will frustrate the ability to carry out some preferred 'proper' task. Waiting time therefore inevitably turns into a negatively-perceived time which is longer than can be tolerated and generally something one should not do.

Figure 3.3 represents the normal view of waiting time, where the perceived duration is more – often much more – than the actual elapsed time spent waiting. This is the background for estimating the value of time spent waiting as 2–3 times that for travelling in a vehicle. However, this assumes that waiting time is not useful and that the whole of the waiting time is equally undesirable. The time spent changing from a pedestrian to a pedenger is, for example, useful – when there is not enough time for this and the person arrives at the stop at the same time as their bus for example, the lack of time for this change presents difficulties. Figure 3.3 shows real elapsed time as a circle which is extended to reach the perceived time shown as a larger circle.

The effect of real-time bus information can be seen in Figure 3.4, where the evidence of there being a bus and a continuously updated estimate of how long it will actually be before it arrives at the stop acts as a constant revision of the passage of actual time and thus reduces the overestimation of waiting time so that the perception of time is (nearly) the same as actual clock time. It can also allow for decisions to be made about the use of time – so that, for example, the simultaneous arrival of a bus and person could be offset by information about a subsequent bus arrival, which could allow the pedestrian to change more comfortably into a pedenger and take the next bus. Placing the decision into the hands of the person is a strong way of enabling them to feel that they can manage their own journey. Figure 3.4 shows the perceived time being compressed to the size of the elapsed time.

Real-time bus information does nothing about the perception of waiting time itself which has been generated either by the (probably) incorrect perception of past

Figure 3.4 Sensing time 2: Real-time bus information helps to reduce the overestimation of waiting time so that it becomes closer to actual elapsed time

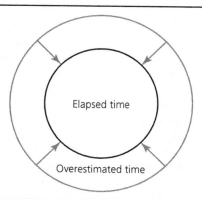

experience or from anecdotal knowledge of others' past experiences, projected onto the present, thus distorting the situation. There is therefore a strong case for making the waiting experience enjoyable, in order to allay these negative experiences. The aim is to try to change the perception of time to one which is less than the actual passage of time. Instead of thinking that waiting time is twice as long as it actually is, the passenger would feel that time has flown by while they were waiting for the bus and their frustration/surprise is actually that the bus has arrived sooner than they expected and their pleasurable experience has been curtailed! Some of the work my team and I are working on at the moment, with TfL, is to see how we can improve the bus stop experience so that the perception of elapsed time is less than the actual time (see Figure 3.5). The presence of real-time information allows the person to decide how to use their time at the bus stop – enjoy the facilities and take the next bus, or catch the first bus to arrive. Once again this is enabling them to make their own decisions about the use of their time.

Figure 3.5 Sensing time 3: Better facilities at bus stops could help to reduce the perception of waiting time so that it becomes less than the actual elapsed time

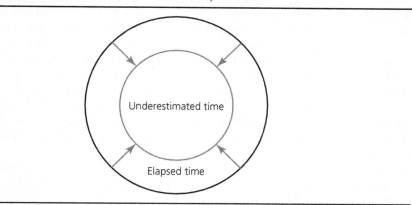

I will say more about how this might be achieved in Chapter 4, where I consider the design of bus stop environments.

Reliability is of course the most effective way of making perceived time equal to actual time. Reducing unreliability is very difficult, especially in mixed traffic conditions. The average waiting time provides a description of the service but without an associated indicator of the service reliability (e.g. a comparison between actual and scheduled waiting times) the average waiting time is fairly meaningless. TfL uses a measure called excess waiting time (EWT) to determine the reliability of the bus service. This is the calculation of waiting time above the average (calculated as being half the headway for high-frequency services) that is experienced. This incorporates both the unreliability of the buses in service and that caused by a failure to run one or more scheduled buses. In accessibility terms, the important issue is the maximum rather than the average waiting time. We need to base the service frequency on the longest time that people can wait, rather than the average that might be delivered, and to ensure that this is not exceeded.

Frequency is thus an important part of accessibility. Rethinking it as a part of the service rather than just as a means to provide capacity brings opportunities for providing more accessible bus systems. The conventional view about the design of service capacity is to think in terms of calculating how many buses of a given size are required to provide sufficient capacity for the number of passengers to be carried past the maximum load point. Thus this line of thinking would suggest that if you need to carry 1000 passengers per hour past the maximum load point and your buses can accommodate 100 passengers each, you would require ten buses per hour. There are three reasons why this is a bad way to think about service frequency.

First, the carriage of passengers is not the limiting factor for a bus service: this is the time spent stationary at bus stops, which is largely determined by the time taken by the passengers moving between the bus and the infrastructure at each bus stop. This is strongly affected by the number of passengers off and on the vehicle of course, but also by the number, location and design of the entrances of the bus and the bus stop. Second, it is affected by the amount of space inside the bus that is available for passengers to circulate as they start to prepare to leave the bus or after they have entered. Third, it is affected by the ability of the bus to enter and leave the bus stop when it requires and not to be delayed by other buses or traffic. I will discuss in Chapter 5 how the vehicle and the bus stop infrastructure can be designed to minimise these effects, but a clear aspect of the service design that can affect this issue is the service frequency. It is useful to think of the frequency of doors, rather than the frequency of vehicles. The number of vehicles arriving within a time period determines the number of passengers who will be boarding, alighting and travelling in each vehicle, but it is the number of doors that determines how long these processes will take. It is quite likely that the service frequency should be higher than that suggested by simply looking at the carrying capacity of the vehicles.

For accessibility purposes, we need to shift the perception of frequency towards that of the user rather than the operator or planner. The key issues are then based on how a user could use the bus service:

1 how long a user must wait for a bus
2 how long before it is possible for the user to make a return journey
3 the freedom of choice of departure time.

Although a maximum waiting time of 10 minutes implies a maximum headway of 10 minutes, this is not necessarily required in order to meet the maximum waiting time requirement. Where a service is relatively low frequency, an acceptable maximum waiting time can be arranged if the service is able to deliver a reasonable level of reliability. Thus the Hackney Plusbus operates at 30 minute intervals, but waiting time is rarely as much as 10 minutes because of the reliability of the service and thus the predictability of its arrival time at a stop. The same applied to the Cumbria Plusbus, which operated with a 3-hour headway.

Making a return journey is important for most trips. The ease of arranging this depends on the frequency of the service in the same way as the freedom to choose the departure time. However, there is a difference between the outward and return journey in terms of being able to know about the available services before departure. This is particularly important if the journey involves transfer between a micronetwork and a main service. It is all too easy to think about this connection in one direction but to forget it in the other. Some rural services may not even provide a return service, and in almost every case it would be necessary to know the times of the last available connections of the day for the return journey.

Connectivity requires the connections in both directions to be easily understood. In the case of the return journey it is determined by the last connection required in the journey. This, in turn, determines the previous one, and so on.

3.2. Bus needs

In Chapter 1 I argued that bus stops are the principal points of access to the transport system, so it is important to understand how they might affect accessibility. Some aspects of this are of course concerned with the actual design, construction and operation of the bus stops, and these issues will be discussed in Chapters 4 and 5. I discussed earlier in this chapter the effects of bus stop location for passengers. That discussion did not take into account the needs of buses in relation to the location of stopping points. It is also important to determine how the accessibility effects of the relationship between the location of bus stops and the access network will affect the bus operation. It is important to know what costs and difficulties the design of an accessible access network imposes on the bus system before it is possible to work out how to ensure that such a system could be implemented and made viable.

Most models used to optimise distances between bus stops are derived from the approach used for railway stations, where the issue is to find the distance at which operating costs and overall access costs are equal. In these models, no account is taken of the distance of a journey origin or destination away from the route: the access path from the journey origin to the station is only considered in terms of travel parallel to the route. Inter-stop distances have traditionally been treated in terms of economics, but this approach barely touches on the accessibility issue. I am going to look at the bus stop network and use some simple models to indicate the effects of different locations of bus stops. This is not to suggest that these models, or any others based on similar principles, are the best means for locating bus stops: I am just using them to illustrate the effects of different bus stop densities on bus operations, passenger access and so on. In reality, bus stops are located according to the practicality of placing them near to suitable origin and destination points (network effects of bus routes are discussed in Chapter 4). Simple economic models are not useful for determining where a bus stop should be located, but they can help to show how operations might appear if different policies about location were to be adopted.

The density of bus stops is the number of bus stops per unit area, not per unit of distance along the route. As far as a single bus route is concerned, this is derived from the number of bus stops in a given route distance, and this is where I start the discussion. To consider this in more detail along the route I will look at some simple models of bus operations. Before doing so, it would be useful to clarify the difference between what I shall call 'stops' and 'stoppings'. I will use the word *stop* to refer to a formal or permanently generally recognised official place where buses stop. A *stopping* is the act of the bus coming to a halt, which might be due to congestion, or it could be in order to pick up passengers at a formal or informal stop. A bus may or may not stop at a bus stop or, in some cases, it could stop more than once at a bus stop or it could stop where there is no bus stop, and thus the number of stoppings along a route could be different from the number of stops.

3.2.1 Speed
In terms of accessibility, speed is not, of itself, of much importance. The issue of importance is duration in time, which is of course affected by speed, but it is crucial to separate the two issues because many factors affect the journey time which are nothing to do with how fast the vehicle is travelling. In the urban environment it is relatively unusual for there to be significant periods at which a vehicle can travel at a constant speed – it is routinely affected by the need to decelerate and stop for junctions, other traffic, pedestrians, other vehicles and – in the case of the bus system – bus stops. To understand how this can affect the accessibility of the bus system, it is necessary to consider the concept of speed in more detail. To do this, I will describe briefly what we mean by speed:

1 *Design speed* is the speed for which the infrastructure is designed.
2 *Maximum speed* is the highest permitted speed.
3 *Operating speed* is the speed at which the vehicles are able to travel.
4 *Running speed* is the highest cruise speed obtained under the relevant infrastructure and traffic conditions.
5 *Average speed* is the mean speed over a distance while the bus is in motion (e.g. between two bus stops) and includes consideration of acceleration and deceleration.
6 *Commercial speed* is derived from the time for which the bus is in business, namely the average speed calculated from the time of departure from the first stop on its route to the time of arrival at the last stop. It includes consideration of delay resulting from bus stops and general congestion.

7   *Journey speed* includes the entire journey from origin to destination, including all the stops and time spent walking to, from and within the bus system.

Comparing these speeds can give a very rough impression of where an operational problem might lie:

1   The difference between design speed and maximum speed indicates the extent to which it is believed that the design is safe. A large difference here would indicate that, for some reason or other, the design is not perceived to be as safe in practice as it was designed to be.
2   The difference between maximum speed and operating speed indicates the extent to which the vehicles are capable of achieving the maximum speed (or of over-achieving it).
3   Comparing the running speed with the operating speed shows the extent to which the infrastructure or traffic conditions might reduce the cruise speed for the vehicles of interest. This might indicate that it is necessary to look at traffic management, bus priorities and other such measures.
4   The difference between running speed and average speed gives an indication of the loss in performance resulting from aspects of the bus operation, such as its ability to accelerate and the distance between stoppings. The more stoppings there are, the more it will reduce the average speed compared to the running speed.
5   The difference between average speed and commercial speed indicates the effects of bus stops (congestion will have been included in the consideration of both running speed and average speed). This shows the effects of the delay at bus stops caused both by passengers boarding and alighting and by congestion between buses within the bus stop area.
6   The difference between commercial speed and journey speed is the consideration of the operator's view as opposed to the passenger's view. It shows where there are insufficiencies in the service provision, either in the network (causing walking distances to be longer) or in the service frequency (causing waiting times to be longer).

Table 3.3 summarises the different speed types and indicates a possible place to start analysing the system, given large differences between these speeds. For example, if the difference in speed lies between the design speed and the maximum speed, it is pointless looking at the bus stop design: this will not affect the maximum speed between bus stops. However, if the difference is between average and commercial speed, then it is likely that the problem lies in the design of the bus stops.

The relationships between the maximum, running, average and commercial speed for a hypothetical road with a length of 5 km as a function of the stop density are shown in Figure 3.6. For this graph, the maximum permitted speed (V_{run}) is 40 km/h, the running speed (V_{max}) is 18 km/h, and the average (V_{av}) and commercial (V_c) speeds, respectively. The graph indicates the effect of stopping a bus and thus shows at what point attention should be paid to the quantity of bus stoppings. This illustrates why I distinguish between stops and stoppings – the accessibility of a bus system is, as I have discussed

Table 3.3 Different ways of looking at speed and what this can indicate

	Description	A large difference between the speed defined in this and that in the previous row indicates:	Look at first:
Design	Speed for which infrastructure was designed		
Maximum	Highest permitted speed	(a) Inadequacy of design (b) Cautious speed limits	(a) Design of infrastructure (b) Speed limits
Operating	What the vehicles can achieve	Extent to which vehicles can achieve maximum speed	Adequacy of vehicles for this operation
Running	Normal cruise speed attained	Extent to which vehicles are affected by congestion	Congestion measures and bus priorities
Average	Mean speed while in motion	Extent to which vehicles are affected by the number of stoppings	(a) Route and service design (b) Power/weight ratio of vehicles
Commercial	Mean speed including stopped time	Extent to which vehicles are affected by the duration of stoppings	(a) Number of bus stops (b) Bus stop design
Journey	Mean speed from origin to destination including access and waiting times	Extent to which the bus network density and/or service frequency is able to provide good access within tolerable distance and time from the journey origin to the bus service and from the bus service to the destination. This also includes the time spent in interchanges	(a) The service network in relation to the pedestrian network and the location of activities (b) The service frequency in relation to appropriate maximum waiting times

above, heavily concerned with the distance it is necessary to walk to reach a bus and the time this takes. This is inevitably connected to the number of bus stops along the bus route, but it is also heavily influenced by both the actual service network and reliable service frequency. At first sight, an improvement in accessibility would therefore seem to provide a devastating effect on the commercial speed of the bus service. The resulting journey times would not be attractive to other passengers and attention must be paid to

Figure 3.6 Comparison of the maximum, running, average and commercial speeds

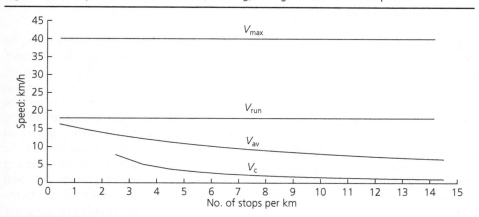

resolving this issue in order to ensure that the bus system is both accessible and attractive. The issue becomes one of being astute with the design of the network and services so that stoppings are distributed in a way that reduces the impact on users of particular services, while retaining good accessibility to the system as a whole. This is discussed in more depth in Chapter 4.

The inference is that, depending on the nature of the problem in a given street, attention should be spent on either the reduction of traffic impacts on bus operation, or on the effects of poorly designed bus stops, or on the design of the service network, or on the delivery of reliable service frequencies. Analysing the different types of speed, as described at the beginning of this section is a very simple way to know where to start trying to resolve the problem. It is therefore useful when collecting speed data to include an assessment of the reasons for the stoppings, as this will help to direct attention to the cause of the problem of bus delay in each situation.

The average speed also changes with respect to the distance between the stoppings on a particular route. For example, the commercial speed given by the model proposed by Gibson *et al.* (1989) as defined for the London example above would be of the order of 14 km/h if the distance between bus stops were 250 m. With a stop distance of 500 m, the commercial speed would be higher (a little under 16 km/h). A 10 km journey would take (under the same congestion conditions) 43 minutes and 38 minutes, respectively, and one might think that reducing the inter-stop distance in this way would not be so bad for the bus operation, given the improvement in accessibility this would offer. However, as we shall see below, the reduced inter-stop distance will have an important impact on the cost of operation (the additional time taken to operate the route with 250 m spacing would result in the need for one extra bus and crew to keep a 10 minute headway). The impact on bus operations of making the network accessible is, therefore, potentially considerable. We need to ensure that increased costs that arise from a more accessible service are compensated through better operational conditions and reduced impacts of bus stops. However, it is little use having a bus service that is not accessible to the people who need to use it.

The example in the previous paragraph is also interesting in terms of the journey speed. As pointed out, the increase in commercial speed obtained by doubling the inter-stop distance is a little less than 2 km/h and the associated time saving is around 5 minutes. If we consider as an example that the access distance for the case of the 250 m stop spacing was set at 400 m from a particular origin, access to the stop if the spacing were 500 m would be 525 m. The access time in the 250 m case would be 400 sec (assuming a walking speed of 1 m/s) and in the latter case it would be 525 sec. This would give journey speeds of 10.7 km/h and 10.81 km/h respectively. The difference lies in what is required of the passenger in terms of using the service. The increase in access time as a result of increasing by 250 m the walking distance necessary to reach the bus system would be an additional 125 seconds at each end of the bus journey, which would add a further 4.5 minutes to the passenger's journey time. This is why the increase in journey speed is smaller than that for commercial speed when the longer inter-stop distance is used – but it is still an increase! However, this means the passenger having to walk a total of over 1 km in order to reach and leave the bus: how reasonable an expectation is that? Thus the saving made by the bus operator is simply taken up by the additional time and effort the passenger has to spend walking to and from the bus. These issues are discussed in detail in Chapter 4.

3.2.2   Access costs and accessibility

The previous section has portrayed one view of the impacts of the number of stoppings on a bus operation, taking into consideration the impacts on accessibility arising from changing the distance between bus stops. We should note that the models just discussed do not include passengers except in the most simplistic way as an element of the dwell time of the buses at the bus stops. I can now discuss what happens if I include passengers in the consideration of the optimum distance between bus stops by examining some bus stop location models.

Most bus stop location models are derived in some way from railway station location models. This is quite understandable: inter-station distances are important on railway systems, given the capital cost involved and the impacts on operations. It seems only natural to consider buses as small trains and to use the same model. After all, they are both based on fixed routes and schedules. However, these models only consider vehicle operations – there is no direct reference to passengers, except in the simplistic treatment of dwell time. I can start to introduce passengers to the bus stop density models by including a simple evaluation of time associated with arriving at a bus stop located at a given distance from its neighbours.

Figure 3.7 shows the curve that results from normal result of inter-stop distance analysis: the optimum distance increases at a decreasing rate as the vehicle flow increases relative to the passenger density. This is because the model assumes that when one vehicle stops all the others will have to stop behind it. Thus, as the frequency increases, the effect on the overall delay to the bus system increases. This delay should be caused as infrequently as possible, and therefore the distance between bus stoppings should be increased. One

Figure 3.7 The optimum distance between bus stops, assuming no overtaking

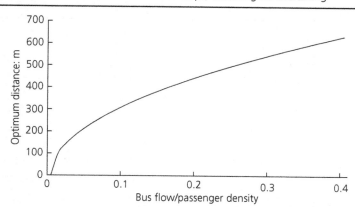

way of achieving this is to allow overtaking at bus stops, thus removing the effect of one bus upon another at bus stops. When the outcomes of this approach are plotted, it is possible to see what would happen to the optimum inter-stop distance. Figure 3.8 shows that this gives a surprisingly short inter-stop distance compared with the one that would be calculated with the same parameter values used to generate Figure 3.7. This suggests a rethink about how bus networks are designed and evaluated.

I have discussed above the need to consider an exclusion penalty in the consideration of bus stop location. The exclusion penalty should apply to everyone who:

1   is within the inclusion zone, but whose access speed is different from the average
2   is outside the inclusion zone.

The Rawlsian approach suggested in Chapter 1 would say that nobody should be in an exclusion zone, so system designers should not begin to calculate distances between bus stops until they have satisfied this condition. Nevertheless, it is interesting to see what would happen to the optimum stop distance if excluded people were taken into account. First, I consider all the people within the inclusion zone who cannot reach the bus stop and those who can reach the bus stop albeit at a slower walking speed than the average used in the calculations. Then I count all the people outside the inclusion zone who might have been associated with this bus stop. If I assume that the exclusion penalty is paid simply by hiring a local taxi to carry the person to the bus stop, then I can begin to see the effects.

What Figure 3.9 shows is that when the effects of exclusion are included the access costs are so high that they completely dominate the consideration of inter-stop distances. In fact, the situation is much worse than this: the real 'cost' to people who are excluded from the system because they cannot manage the access distance from their home to the bus stop is that they cannot go out at all. As I discussed in Chapter 1, I do not accept that a society should be designed in such a way that some people are excluded. Also, as noted

Figure 3.8 The optimum distance between bus stops, comparing overtaking and no-overtaking operations

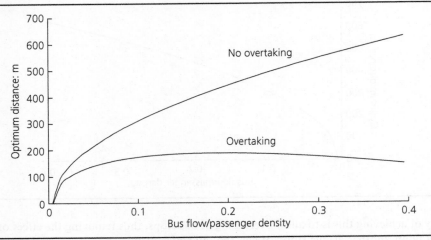

in Chapter 2, such exclusion imposes costs on society in the performance of its other duties (e.g. the provision of healthcare, social care or education).

I therefore need to resolve the issue of how to enable buses to operate feasibly within a system conceived to be accessible to the people who need to use it. For this reason, and if buses are to transform the world, it is necessary to consider again how the bus system operates but, from now, including the point of view of some other characteristics. The key is the evaluation of functionality – what the bus system is being required to do for society – as discussed in Chapter 2. This means looking again at the science of how the bus system works. I shall do this in Chapters 4, 5 and 6.

Figure 3.9 Access costs, differentiating between inclusion and exclusion, compared with the costs of stopping buses as a function of inter-stop distances

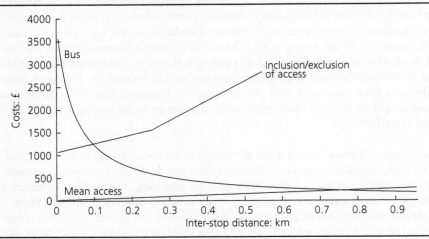

3.3.   Conclusions

In this chapter, I have examined the functionality of the bus system and how it might be able to achieve the requirements imposed by society. I have looked at how this is driven in large part by the need to make activities accessible and reachable, and how this might be achieved without needing buses, but have concluded that in practice it is likely that buses will be required in order to deliver the activities to the population in an equitable manner.

I have lifted the lid on some requirements of the access and bus networks so that you can have an idea of the needs before becoming involved in how they might be met. The science involved in understanding the details of these issues is covered in Part 2, where a number of the questions raised in this chapter will be resolved.

REFERENCES

Adhitya S and Tyler N (2014) It's the little things that count ... *Proceedings of the International Symposium for Next Generation Infrastructure*, Vienna, Austria, October 2014.

Akcelik and Associates (2001) *An Investigation of Pedestrian Movement Characteristics at Midblock Signalised Crossings*. Technical report. Akcelik and Associates, Melbourne, Australia.

Barham P, Oxley P and Shaw A (1994) *Accessible Public Transport Infrastructure*. Department of Transport, London.

Brown IEW and Tyler N (2001) Users' responses to the implementation of an innovative accessible bus service in a remote rural area. *9th International Conference on Mobility and Transport for Elderly and Disabled People*, Warsaw, Poland, 2–5 July.

Gibson, Baeza I and Willumsen LG (1989) Bus stops, congestion and congested bus stops. *Traffic Engineering and Control* **30(6)**: 291–302.

Hammond C (2013) *Time Warped: Unlocking the mysteries of time perception*. Canongate, Edinburgh, Scotland.

Kunaka C (1996) *Modelling Paratransit Services: A microscopic simulation approach*. PhD thesis, University of London.

LBHF (London Borough of Hammersmith and Fulham) (1994) *Unitary Development Plan*, p. 187.

Lerner J (2014) *Urban Acupuncture*. Island, Washington, DC, USA.

Low S (2000) *On the Plaza: The Politics of Public Space and Culture*. University of Texas Press, Austin, TX, USA.

Lynas JR (1998) *The Hackney Plusbus Scheme: Initial Monitoring and Review*. Working paper. University College London, Centre for Transport Studies, London.

Tadesse D and Islam M (1996) *Accessibility to Public Transport in Bloomsbury*. Project report. Department of Civil and Environmental Engineering, UCL, London.

TfL (Transport for London) (2014) TfL Planning Information Database. http://www.webptals.org.uk (accessed 31 December 2014).

TRB (Transport Research Board) (2000) Highway Capacity Manual. Transportation Research Board. Washington, DC, USA.

Zimbaldo P and Boyd J (2008) *The Time Paradox Rider*. Random House Group, London, UK.

Part 2

Science – What?

In Part 1, I argued that the prime reason for having a transport system was in order to enable people to carry out those activities they deemed would meet their aspirations to improve their wellbeing. In Part 2, we start to look at the science involved in meeting the requirements that result from that insistence on shifting our focus from the provision of transport to the provision of accessibility. How the science can then be put in practice in a city is then explored in Part 3.

Accessibility and the Bus System: Transforming the World
ISBN 978-0-7277-5980-1

ICE Publishing: All rights reserved
http://dx.doi.org/10.1680/aabs2ed.59801.115

Institution of Civil Engineers

publishing

Chapter 4
Reaching the bus

4.1. General considerations

In Chapter 3, I discussed the outline relationship between a person and the bus system. This chapter considers the process of reaching the bus in more detail – the journey along the footway to moving inside the vehicle. For completeness, I consider the footway to have the same needs and characteristics whether the journey is to or from the bus stop. In terms of the move into and out of the vehicle, these characteristics are actually quite different so these are considered separately in Sections 4.4.1 and 4.4.2 respectively. The emphasis in this chapter is to look at the issue from the perspective of the person. In terms of the person using the stop, I consider this in three phases – the pedestrian walking along the footway to or from the bus stop, the passenger on the bus and the intervening 'pedenger' phase as discussed in Chapter 3. I then consider some elements of the bus stop operation that create particular challenges for these processes in Section 4.5. Finally, I summarise the requirements for bus stop design from the perspectives of different people in Section 4.6.

4.2. Pedestrians

So the purpose of having a bus system in a city is to provide one element of the process of improving societal wellbeing by delivering people to activities that are too far away to be easily reached on foot and thus enabling people to realise their aspirations. Only in a very few cases will the bus actually deliver a person to their chosen activities – this is normally achieved by means of the pedestrian environment. Therefore, it is necessary to think about the pedestrian environment and its interface with the bus system. The point of interface is of course the bus stop, but in fact the pedestrian environment is very much a core part of the bus system so I am going to consider not only the bus stop itself, but also the means of reaching the bus by virtue of the pedestrian environment.

4.2.1 Functionality of bus stops

In Chapter 3, I discussed some of the issues around the distance it might be necessary to walk in order to reach a bus stop on the basis that the aim is to assure accessibility to the activities that people see as the way of meeting their aspirations to improve their wellbeing. This means that the emphasis for determining the distance is neither the actual number of metres nor the time taken to cover that distance (although, as discussed in Chapter 3, these need to be considered), but the ability of the walking route to deliver that accessibility – it is about the service of accessibility to the activities and the quality of the service being provided. This changes the way in which the distance between activities and bus stops should be calculated and evaluated.

So, how to conceive of accessibility in these terms? In Chapter 2, Table 2.1, I gave some examples of functionalities required of the bus system in order to meet the five cities requirements and thus generate the feasibility of achieving the aspiration of improving wellbeing by making the associated activities accessible. In Figure 2.2 I gave some examples of how aspirations and achievements in relation to the bus system itself could affect the requirements for a bus system. These tables need to be seen in the context of the five cities model as shown in Figures 1.7 and 2.1 so that we can see how we need to use our science to drive these requirements. Table 4.1 links these tables and figures so that one can see the relationships between these functionalities work.

4.2.2 My walk to the bus stop is enjoyable
As noted in Table 2.2, a requirement is that the environment is designed to be interesting, with rhythmic interactions with sensory stimuli, the bus network brings the buses reasonably close to the activities, there is good lighting, visibility, acoustic environment and pedestrians are prioritised over traffic.

4.2.2.1 The pedestrian space
Creating an environment which is enjoyable to use and adds the function of enjoyment to that of moving from A to B is a major part of making the journey to an activity attractive. Sometimes, 'enjoyment' comes from an immersion in nothingness – the de-sensing of the environment in order to 'clear the mind' is one of the reasons for activities such as meditation. However, for the most part, enjoyment comes from the presence of stimuli, and in the way in which stimuli are presented over time or space and related to different senses. A stimulus is only perceived as such because of the lack of stimuli around it. A lot of art is about the presentation of stimuli in this way – think of the spread of light or colour in a painting, the presentation of sound through rhyme and rhythm in poetry, the movement from dissonance to consonance in music, the use of vertical and horizontal lines in architecture and so on. An intensive and continuous stimulus rapidly becomes desensitising – some might say boring, others would say stimulating – because of the reduction in difference, Then, because our senses are evolved to detect and respond to change, they are ignored. The desensitising monochrome paintings of Rothko or compositions such as 4' 33" by John Cage, for example, use this evolved characteristic in that they remove the 'usual' stimuli and make the brain search for, and thus become more sensitive to, the unusual.

So the presentation of stimuli in a way that creates interest in making a journey is an artistic endeavour. Making access aesthetically attractive is a core part of ensuring not only that a journey can be made but that it is enjoyable to make as well. As the journey is a private endeavour in a public space, and the particular stimuli which create 'interest' will vary from person to person, it is necessary to resolve the issue of how to create interest in the journey for everyone. This need for universalism suggests that the stimuli could be provided in a number of ways and we should be open to combinations of stimuli as part of the process. For example, the 'Piano Stairs' set up in Odenplan Station in Stockholm enable people to create their own stimuli. London has a few 'edible bus stops' (see Figure 4.1), which seek to make the bus stop environment more pleasant for people using the bus stop and others.

Table **4.1** Functionality requirements, implications for the bus system, aspirations, satisfaction and potential impact on the five cities in relation to the Access Network

Functionality requirement for the bus system (Table 2.1)	Implication for the bus system (Table 2.1)	Aspiration (Table 2.2)	Satisfaction in the bus system (Table 2.2)	Success factors for five cities (Table 2.1)				
				Courteous	Active	Public	Healthy	Evolving
A wide choice of different activities to meet aspirations	Dense network designed on the basis of location and timing of activities and setting access points at suitable locations to provide equitable access to all activities	My walk to the bus stop is enjoyable	The environment is designed to be interesting, with rhythmic interactions with sensory stimuli	✓	✓	✓	✓	✓
			Bus network brings the buses reasonably close to the activities	✓	✓	✓	✓	✓
			Good lighting, visibility, acoustic environment	✓	✓	✓	✓	✓
			Pedestrians prioritised over traffic	✓	✓	✓	✓	✓
		My wait for the bus is comfortable	Provision of shelter from weather	✓	✓	✓	✓	✓
			Seating, lighting	✓	✓	✓	✓	✓
			Sufficient space for the expected number of waiting passengers and their baggage		✓	✓		
			Real-time information about the bus system performance, maps, available destinations etc.	✓	✓	✓		
			Bus service frequency sufficient to keep waiting times to an acceptable level	✓	✓	✓	✓	✓
			Bus service is reliable	✓	✓	✓	✓	✓

Figure 4.1 Edible bus stop in Lewisham, London

The responsiveness of people to this sort of opportunity can be seen by the change in the way people choose to move before and after the installation of the new stairs (after installation, many people preferred to use the stairs to using the adjacent escalator). Another type of event that provides a stimulus is the 'flashmob', for example where a public space is taken over by a group of performance artists. These examples are place-specific in the case of the stairs and time-specific in the case of the flashmobs and it might be thought that such stimuli are good for the moment or at specific places and thus not something that can be repeated frequently in the access network. However, stimuli can be quite different and can be changed in time in order to catch interest – after all, this is the basis for street advertising! The key point to make here is that accessible journeys do not have to be boring or devoid of aesthetic interest – indeed I would say they must not be so and that it is incumbent on planners and designers to ensure that journeys are both interesting and accessible.

What would make the walk towards an activity more interesting?

Jan Gehl has studied this issue in some depth in a variety of cities around the world, taking a view about urban planning that is based on the space between the buildings rather than the buildings themselves (Gehl, 2011). One of the things that make people feel that the space between buildings is attractive is the extent to which they can interact

Table 4.2 Distances and social interactions (Gehl, 2011)

Interaction	Distance	Comment
See others and perceive that they are people	500 m–1 km	
Determine human individuals	100 m	Gehl calls this the 'social field of vision'
Determine a person's sex, approximate age, what they are doing	70–100 m	Recognise a person already known
Detect facial features, hairstyle, age	30 m	Recognise people met only infrequently
Detect feelings and moods of others	20–25 m	
Hearing others	<7 m	
Detect the degree of detail generally necessary for human contact	1–3 m	
'Public' distance	>3.75 m	Quoted from Hall (1966)
'Social' distance	1.3–3.75 m	Quoted from Hall (1966)
'Personal' distance	45 cm–1.3 m	Quoted from Hall (1966)
'Intimate' distance	0–45 cm	Quoted from Hall (1966)

with people in that space. Gehl suggests a set of distances at which different types of personal interaction occur. These are summarised in Table 4.2.

To understand how this matters to us in considering the urban environment, it is helpful to have a brief description of how vision works. You might consider that the image you have of this book as you are reading it is a stable picture of the page. In fact what is happening is that your eye is moving very rapidly around the page, choosing points to stop for a short while. It is possible to track these movements using a technology called eye-tracking. Basically, the eye stops (this is referred to as a 'fixation') when it has a view of some point on the page, perhaps a particular word or group of letters, and stores the image that it sees. It then 'switches off' and moves to another point (the motion is referred to as a 'saccade') and repeats the process. Your brain stitches all these images together to give you what appears to be a full and stable picture of the page. You are quite unaware of the saccades because the eye is switched off while it is in motion. Sometimes, the eye repeatedly fixates on a particular point in the environment and using eye tracking equipment I can count the number and duration of repeated fixations. This gives a perspective on the relative importance of that point in the environment. The choice of fixation location is not ordered, so it does not, for example, start at the top left corner and progress along and down the page or anything like that. Neither is it random: the choice of fixation location is driven by some pre-conscious assessment of need, or interest.

The eye works in this way because high-resolution vision processing is very resource-intensive. You are actually looking at this page using a very small part of the retina –

less than 1% – in an area called the fovea. This provides a cone of high-resolution, high-colour-sensitivity radiating from the retina at an angle of about 3°, so this is a very small part of your visual field. The fovea contains as many receptors as the other 99% of the retina. The system works by means of the rest of the visual field, called peripheral vision, which is much lower resolution and has only poor colour sensitivity. Stimuli detected in your peripheral vision can, if considered to be sufficiently interesting, stimulate the eye – and, if necessary, the head – to turn to the site of the stimulus so that it can be examined by the high-resolution fovea. Research into peripheral vision in relation to the environment is scarce, so the relationship between peripheral and foveal vision is poorly understood at the moment, although researchers are starting to look at the actual mechanisms involved in this process. The outcomes of this work will be important for urban design.

Reading the page of the book does not make huge use of the peripheral vision – although it does make use of it to some extent – but when you are in a larger environment, such as a street, it is of huge importance to how you actually perceive the environment. The way to think about this is to realise that, rather than your eye 'looking at' the environment and seeing things, actually the stimuli in the environment are 'showing themselves' to your eye. Sometimes, a stimulus is picked up by the fovea, but most of the time the stimuli will be detected by the peripheral vision (even if only because it covers a much greater proportion of the visual field) and the fovea is directed on the basis of your brain's evaluation of what is received. You might not actually see the sky above your head – your fovea will only be drawn to it if an important stimulus is detected in the peripheral visual field (or you consciously choose to look at it). However, you will feel very differently about the environment if it is obscured by, for example, tall buildings. This is crucial to the whole issue of design: in terms of vision, there is a tendency to design for the fovea – what can be seen in high resolution full colour – whereas, in the urban environment, maybe the objective should be to design for the peripheral visual field so that the fovea is directed to the most useful stimuli. Maybe it is your peripheral vision rather than your foveal vision that suggests to you that a place feels either safe or creepy. This could be because the 'peripheral stimuli' are worrying, causing more calls for the foveal vision to scrutinise the scene, either because there are too many stimuli, or too few. I will discuss more about this in relation to the urban environment in Chapter 5. One consequence of this is that, apart from the issue of distance in front of us, we need to think about the visual field on either side and above us.

There are four main issues to consider about visual fields.

First, a person's visual field covers a range defined by an angle of about 200° (horizontal) centred on the central line of vision and about 135° vertical, although the vertical range is not centred around the central line of vision (all these angles are approximate and will vary between people). The vertical range can be described as ranging from the lower side at around 70–80° from the central line of vision to about 50–55° above the central line of vision.

Second, people do not have equally powerful vision across the whole of the visual field. The *fovea* has very high resolution in terms of sharpness (acuity) and colour. Peripheral vision operates at a much lower resolution in terms of acuity and colour, but is distinguished by being excellent at detecting movement. This area is broken down into two regions, the parafoveal, which is about 10° around the central line of vision, and the peripheral visual field, which operates above 20° around the central line of vision. It is also noteworthy that the foveal visual field is less able than the peripheral visual field to function well in low light conditions.

Third, humans, like many animals, are characterised by stereopsis – the ability to see objects in a way that allows for depth perception. This is because of our binocular vision, which arises because we have two eyes and a processing system that manages the data to deliver a 3D image. Our binocular vision does not cover the entire visual field. Essentially, the area that is covered by binocular vision is around 114° around the central line of vision. The remaining approximately 43° on either side of our visual field is covered specifically by either the left or the right eye. There is a view that stereopsis only kicks in at short distances between the eye and the object.

Finally, people tend to walk with their head inclined downwards by about 10°. This means that the vertical visual field is skewed downwards slightly – so the view of the ground is rather better and the sky rather less so. This is amplified by the design of our spinal column, which makes it easier to scan the ground and to rotate our head in the horizontal plane than to look upwards.

These characteristics of the human vision system have a profound effect on the way in which people see the world around them. Their visual field works well at eye-level and they can see quite a long way ahead, but the ability to see detail only really works up to 10 m ahead (a person can recognise someone 70 m away by physical aspects such as their height, gait and other clues, such as the type of clothes, etc.). The ability to see detail that is sufficient for recognising facial features well enough to recognise someone for sure (especially someone we do not know well), determine mood and so on is only really possible up to a distance of 'less than 10 m ahead' (Gehl, 2011).

So, it is possible to construct an imaginary visual field 'box', in which people can recognise their immediate environment at a level of detail that is sufficient for them to be able to feel comfortable, safe and secure. In a very simple way, people take the angles of their visual field and combine them with their ability to see detail at a distance to give a simple range in which they are open to stimuli and can operate comfortably with the visual information that is being delivered. The important conceptual principle is that the data being received by the brain, from which it makes its perceptual interpretations and decisions, emanate from the visual field set by the angular range (200° horizontal by 135° vertical) but only that from within this 'box' is supplied in sufficient detail to enable decisions based on detail to be made.

The 'box' extends about 12.5 m in front of a person, about 2.25 m either side of their central line of vision (before they have to rely on their lower-quality peripheral vision field), up to about 14 m above them (assuming a 10° inclination downwards of the head and a 50° upwards angular range) and between 4 m and 15 m downwards (assuming 10°

Figure 4.2 Lateral environmental field from which visual data are transmitted to the human brain

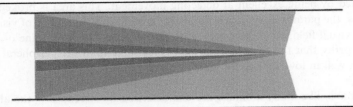

inclination downwards and a 70–80° downwards angular range) – although this is of course usually limited by the presence of the surface on which the person is standing to about 1.3 m below eye level.

Now, think of a street environment that you know. This 'box' suggests that, if you were in the middle of the street, the information you need to feel comfortable would be within an area defined by the building line on either side of a 4.5 m street (you will lose perceptual detail beyond a longitudinal distance of about 12.5 m, and closer than this you are relying on your peripheral vision), with lower-quality peripheral vision between a point on the building line aligned more or less with where you are standing, along the building line to about 12.5 m in front of you, about 2.25–12.5 m above you, including the use of your peripheral vision and 4–12.5 m in front of you along the ground. A street much narrower than this begins to feel a little threatening – especially if the boundary construction is tall (things usually feel better for people if they can see the sky without having to look for it). So the area most distinctive in terms of the visual data they receive falls within these limits – about to second floor height, a width of a narrowish street and about the length of a bus in front of us. The lateral and vertical fields of this 'box' are shown in Figures 4.2 and 4.3 respectively. In particular, Figure 4.2 shows the lateral extent of a 4.5 m wide street compared with the horizontal visual field and Figure 4.3 shows the narrow band of high quality vision applied to the footway surface and the reduced vertical field of view. Of course, people can look at things beyond the range of the box, but for the purposes of design it is necessary to consider that the data being received by the brain – especially that which is passed by way of peripheral vision, which tells people about the general circumstances in which they are (the presence of sky, wide or narrow fields of view, etc.) are, as they appear with the head held in its normal position for walking. It is also important to remember that the view changes as the person walks along, so the view is being updated for this reason at the rate of 1 m/s (or whatever the walking speed turns out to be). This dynamic – that people constantly change their perspective of the environment as they move through it – is a major force in the way I consider the design of the person-centred environment. The environment is not a static entity that never changes while people move around it: it is always being seen from a different perspective,

Figure 4.3 Vertical environmental field from which visual data are transmitted to the brain

Figure 4.4 Tango footway, Buenos Aires, Argentina

it influences how these perspectives turn into perceptions and it is these perceptions that drive the people's feelings about the place.

This emphasises the importance of having interesting space that is visible at ground level – above the second floor is not really perceived unless the person specifically looks upwards – and at a fairly small width – they need to feel confident that we can see and interpret danger lurking at the edge of their visual field. Bus stops, and the bus system in general, function at this level and I believe it is in a great position to contribute to that sense of excitement and interest being noted by Gehl. This can be achieved really quite simply – Figure 4.4 shows a delightful use of the phenomenon of looking downwards in Buenos Aires, Argentina, where a simple Tango lesson is provided in the footway surface.

123

Not all interactions are positive. Gehl describes a set of principles which cause environments to stimulate a sense of isolation or attraction on the basis of encouraging or discouraging contact. Table 4.2 shows environmental features that tend to encourage feelings of either isolation or an encouragement to make contact with other people.

Gehl also emphasises that if we want a place to be pleasant, it needs to allow for people to stand comfortably and informally, and to have good opportunities for sitting where it is possible to see what is happening – oriented towards activity. Thus, the rate of receiving stimuli, which I have indicated is driven by the speed at which a person passes through the environment, can also occur when the speed falls to zero. Standing, sitting or leaning enables a person to receive a vast amount of stimuli about the local environment without being distracted by having to move and is a great enabler for the generation of social living in the city (the courteous city). Capitalising on this is really important because it is part of the social scene – people need to be able to enjoy the activity of holding a conversation without raising their voice or being very close (5–15 cm) to the 'other' person. This requires background noise levels to be around 45–50 dB (the active city). The space needs to feel protected from crime and bad weather and to have good access to good weather (the city as public space). Overall this is a great stress-reducer (the healthy city). I shall discuss the benefits of stationary people and how and why the bus system can be an active player in this aspect of city living in Chapter 5.

So, when designers puts the issues of attractiveness of the access environment, social distances, isolation and contact and protection together, they can start to think about the characteristics of the access environment as a contributor to the five-cities model of city life. They are dealing with people in motion. Walking speeds vary, but they can start to design bearing in mind the time it takes to cover the social distances. Gehl suggests a walking speed of 5 km/hour, which is quite fast – as noted in Chapter 3, older people will struggle to maintain 1 m/sec (3.6 km/hr) and traffic planners even tend to work with 1.3 m/sec (4.7 km/hr). Thinking 'slower' is a good approach, remembering that in certain places the desirable speed could be zero: thinking hard about the rate at which stimuli are to be made available for sensing by the people in the area becomes a defining agent of the process of the design of the environment.

At 1 m/sec, the social field of vision at which it is possible to distinguish people as individuals (100 m) would be covered in 100 seconds. Thus, two people approaching each other at this speed would have 50 seconds from initial identification of 'a person' to meeting each other. During this time the information about the other person is increasing – at an increasing rate as the distance between the people reduces (see Table 4.3), requiring increasingly rapid processing of information about the other person, especially if the two people have not known each other before.

In terms of the physical environment, it seems reasonable to think that we should be able to see either the activity itself or an indication towards it within the social field of vision (100 m). It is fairly clear from research (e.g. Gehl, 2010) that people like to walk directly towards the destination and to take the shortest route, even if this means a change in level, although Souman et al. (2009) have good evidence that when external stimuli are

Table 4.3 Physical planning to encourage isolation or contact (Gehl, 2010)

Isolation	Contact
Walls	No walls
Long distances	Short distances
High speeds	Low speeds
Multiple levels	One level
Orientation away from others	Orientation towards others

not available people tend to walk in curves – even in circles. This work suggests that visual targets, or at least visual markers (e.g. the sun), are crucial for maintaining that direct trajectory and that if left to only 'internal' devices (such as proprioception or vestibular awareness), people lose the capability for following a direct path to their destination. Equally, there is a sense of making the route interesting – edges are more attractive than wide open spaces and places of interest along the way provide opportunities to stand, converse with other people and generally improve the overall experience. Walking alongside a blank wall is much more boring than walking along an edge that has different opportunities occurring, especially if it is also porous – so shopfronts are good and attract people even if they are not intending to enter the shop. The provision of benches every 100 m or so provides a good supply of opportunity to rest and take in the world – but the benches only really work if they are situated so that they have meaningful views of what is happening. This all suggests that we need to ensure that the space for pedestrians is adequate.

Gehl (2010) suggests that an upper limit for an acceptable density in streets and footways with two-way pedestrian traffic is 10–15 pedestrians per minute per metre of width. So a 10-metre wide footway would be able to have 100 people per minute walking along it. Above this level, however, people form into unidirectional streams and interactions are lost. Interactions are lost and the space ceases to be social. Dimensioning pedestrian space bearing in mind the way the senses operate means that 'big' is not necessarily 'better' and Gehl (2010) cites Venice as an example of a city with 3 m wide streets which provide 'room for a pedestrian traffic of 40–50 pedestrians per minute (p. 91). Gehl and Hall mention the issue of hearing, but the main issues around the hearing sense and the built environment are not considered as much as, for example, the issues around wheelchairs or vision. Work is starting in this area and there is an additional scope for excitement because realising the sensorial implications of hearing provides not only a way of thinking about space but also a way of understanding it from a person's point of view. Sara Adhitya (2013), for example, has looked at the relationship between city space and music, both in the sense of a musical interpretation of space and in the use of a musical form to determine the design of space. The great thing about each of these conceptualisations is the link between time and space and the representation of this link through music. This allows the delivery of stimuli as a person walks along a street, for example, to be perceived overtly in a form of rhythmic progress instead of as a static set of stimuli which can only be experienced in something like a map. Conceiving this dynamic and using it to design the sequence of stimuli is an exciting way to stimulate progress around the access network and make it a place where one would want to be.

Gehl's concept is that the human body has evolved to function at walking speed – the senses work on the basis of receiving information within distances – and therefore perceives time – based on moving at walking speed. The human sensory systems work on the basis of detecting change rather than stasis. Humans become adapted to their background and only respond to stimuli that indicate change. Too many stimuli and we become over anxious; too few and we seek more stimuli: the Rothko painting I mentioned earlier in this chapter stimulates the senses to seek out increasingly small stimuli because they are missing the stimuli that they would normally expect to receive. So there is a case for looking for some level of stimuli detection that lies between 'too many' and 'too few'. Gehl (2011) maintains that this suggests that the vision sense should be receiving new stimuli around every five seconds (although I have to say that I have not been able to find any direct neurological evidence in the literature for this – neurologists tend to concentrate on the stimuli as processed by the neuron, rather than the rate at which the person encounters them) and that, in the case of visual stimuli, they should be at eye level or below and within a reasonable horizontal range (e.g. the visual field box described earlier in this section). Stimuli received at around this rate signify that the surroundings are 'normal', 'safe' – in other words, the sensory system is working and there is nothing to worry about. The vertical edges between shopfronts, typical in older cities, mark the boundaries between different visual images presented by the different shop windows and their displays. Therefore, these are examples where the eye is stimulated by a new vista at a comfortable rate (approximately 20 per 100 m, or every 5 m) and at a reasonable walking speed this presents a new view or stimulus around every five seconds. Gehl contrasts this with a long monotonous wall of a supermarket, where there is no stimulus for several 10s of metres, in order to illustrate the difference.

Apart from the width and length of the footway, which has been discussed above, there are other characteristics that can make a walk to the activity difficult: the nature of the walking surface, and the range of height differences on the footway surface.

4.2.2.2 The footway surface

Footway surfaces tend to be made of a surface that is hard, uncompromising and more or less uneven. They are uncomfortable to walk on and give no support to the walking process – some present severe challenges to comfortable walking or wheeling. Although serious consideration is given to the nature of the surface of the roadway for vehicles, almost no consideration is given to that of the footway for people. A hard surface is tiring to walk on and is extremely unforgiving if a pedestrian has the misfortune to fall onto it. Deep study has been undertaken on the nature of the running surface in an athletic stadium – the London Olympic Stadium is a case in point – in order to make the surface as beneficial as possible to the athletes. This has been notably successful in improving performance. It would be useful to consider bringing some of the learning from that work into the domain of the pedestrian footway. A modern running track is not made of concrete or any other hard surface, but of a resin-based compound. The surface is laid onto a springy sub-base which is designed to respond to the rotation of the foot as it strikes the surface. Running tracks must deal with the forces applied by runners, which are rather higher than those applied by walkers, so it should be possible to adjust the design of the running track to produce a surface which supports the lower forces, but similar rotation of the foot, during the process of walking so that it becomes less tiring. The slightly springy nature of the surface would also be much more forgiving in the event of a fall. This type of surface would also be easier to maintain than the conventional surfaces as it would only require a respray if it is broken. A very similar material is commonly used in children's playgrounds in the UK, so the techniques and processes involved are not unfamiliar to local authorities and their contractors. The complexity of the sub-base would be newer to them, but it is not difficult to understand how to lay it properly.

The footway surface should be comfortable and smooth with no unexpected sudden changes in surface. Where such changes do arise, however, they should be clearly marked so that they can be perceived from a suitable distance away. This distance is determined by the time it takes to ascertain that there is something about the surface that requires a reaction – for example, changing the gait to raise the foot a little more than usual – and then to take the required action. Two of my students conducted two sets of experiments in the Pamela facility to explore what such a distance should be.

The experiments considered two aspects of the problem:

1   How far in advance of the change in surface topography is a response required (Cheng, 2015).
2   How well can a person determine some change in the footway surface (Wang, 2015).

Detecting a change in surface level
Tsu-Jui Cheng undertook some experiments which sought to determine how far in advance of a change in level of the footway surface people adjust their gait in order to accommodate the change. To do this he used eye-tracking technology to determine the first time that the eye fixated on the surface change, and pressure insoles (these are devices inserted as an insole in the shoe that measure about 200 pressure points exerted by the foot while walking). He recruited two groups of participants, a 'younger' group (25–40 years of age) and an older group (65–80 years of age). He asked each participant to walk along a straight path in the Pamela facility (at University College London (UCL), see below). The path could be adjusted so that the last 2.4 m could be raised or lowered relative to the rest of the path. He then analysed the eye-tracking data to see when the eye first fixated on the surface change and the pressure-insole data to see if and how the gait changed. The participants were unaware of whether or not there would be a change in the surface and the change could be to form a step up or a step down, or to leave it at the same level as the rest of the path.

The results are quite complex and I would recommend that if you need more information than is presented here you refer to Cheng's thesis (Cheng, 2015). Basically, participants fixated on the surface change when they were about 2.5–3.5 m away from it, rather less in the case of the downwards changes and rather more in the case of the upwards ones. There was little noticeable change in gait in the younger group until they encountered the actual surface change. However, the older group tended to make a very slight but significant change to their gait after the first fixation and this tended to prepare them for dealing with the surface change. It is important to note that this change in gait, although small, is made before the person is consciously aware of any need or benefit. It is a preconscious act stimulated by the reception of the data signifying the stimulus.

Detecting a change in surface type

Tianyu Wang conducted some experiments to find out how well people could detect changes in the surface profile, when this was set at the distance determined from Cheng's experiments (i.e. about 3.5 m away). She designed four surface profiles (one flat, one step, one saw-tooth profile and one profile with a pseudo-random design). Each profile (apart from the flat one) was provided with three height ranges, 12, 21 and 36 mm between the lowest and highest point in each case. The surfaces were all made out of the same material so there was no difference between them in terms of the base colour. The experiment was conducted under two lighting conditions, which related to two common street lighting levels – normal daylight (represented by 200 lux) and a residential street lighting level (4 lux). At the time of writing, only the initial pilot tests, designed to check the method being proposed for the full experiments, had been completed. Wang recruited a group of younger participants, all with 'normal' vision (i.e. no self-reported clinical vision impairment). Each participant was allowed to see the target surface for 3 seconds and then was asked to identify which, out of a set of 11 sample profiles, was the same as the one they had just seen. Their eye movements were recorded using the eye tracker. The outcome is that participants exhibited difficulties with recognising the height differences, especially at the low lighting level. The worst profile was the medium height saw-tooth design, which was often confused with the random surface. The significance of this is that the two profiles are in fact quite different; yet at a distance similar to the one at which they would be encountered at the critical point of first fixation, there is ample scope for confusion. Fixations tended to be higher frequency and shorter under the brighter high lighting condition than under the low lighting condition. There was a strong negative correlation for hit rate against measures such as visual acuity, contrast sensitivity and stereo acuity. This suggests that older people will find the detection of uneven surfaces much harder than younger people, especially under low lighting conditions, as their acuity tends to decline with increasing age. It will be interesting to see the full analysis of the full experiments, which involved a group of older as well as a group of younger participants. Initial reading of the data suggests that the older group found the exercise much harder than the younger group.

In both Cheng's and Wang's experiments, the responses were obtained from the participants at a preconscious level. This means that they were not being asked to interpret the solution in any way – the gait response was faster in Cheng's experiment than would have been possible with a conscious acknowledgement of the change in surface level and in Wang's experiment, the available time to see the target surface was too short to allow interpretation. These experiments were looking at the preconscious response to a stimulus, which is necessary before any conscious response can be started.

This is important because, in reality, walking is managed at the preconscious level – people only think about where or how to place their feet in extreme circumstances, yet for the most part they can manage changes in gradient, surface level, surface type and so on, without tripping or stumbling. It is a system that works extremely well in the main – the problem is that the processes that make it work so well are not well enough understood at present to allow us to design the environment (or train the person) to reduce the incidence of failures. These experiments are just the start of trying to improve that understanding.

Thus far, the conclusion is that footway surface detail needs to be easily perceivable at a distance of around 3.5 m under low lighting conditions and that increasing the lighting level in a way that helps to highlight the change in height would help. The good news is that this falls within the 'more detailed' visual box described in Section 4.2.2.1 and so is consistent with the distances and ranges discussed in terms of the perception of the space around the person.

4.2.2.3 Crossfalls

The second aspect of footway construction is the crossfall. This is a transverse gradient designed to allow drainage of water to the gulley and drainage system at the kerbside. Typically the crossfall gradient is 2.5%, but it is often greater than this and sometimes becomes reversed. In practice it is the slope required to reach the kerb height, which is determined by the roadway construction, from the boundary with the frontage of buildings or other boundary feature at the back of the footway. A change in kerb height or level at the rear boundary will alter the crossfall.

Most pedestrians are unaware of the crossfall – they are so used to it that they just do not notice it unless it is severe. However, a pedestrian who is propelling a wheelchair or other wheeled vehicle, or using a walking aid, will become acutely aware of the slightest crossfall. Holloway (2011) has analysed the impacts of crossfall gradients on wheelchair users and their attendants using the Pamela facility. Pamela allows detailed research of footway design under controlled conditions so it was possible to examine how the crossfall gradient affected people pushing wheelchairs. Figure 4.5 shows the forces involved in starting to push a wheelchair along a footway with crossfalls set at 0%, 2.5% and 4%. This was derived from experiments using instrumented wheelchairs. What Figure 4.5 shows is not only the amount of force required just to start moving the wheelchair (e.g. over the flat (0%) gradient), but how this becomes dramatically higher as the crossfall gradient increases, especially for the attendant-propelled wheelchair, to the extent that the force required exceeds the regulated maximum permitted for people employed to push trolleys (e.g. postal workers), even at the design gradient of 2.5%. Figure 4.5 shows only the starting forces. Sustained wheeling requires a variety of techniques – some people in self-propelled chairs push very hard on one wheel and steer up the slope, then repeat this as the chair rolls back under the force of gravity. Others provide lots of small pushes. Attendants have to maintain constant pushing contact with the chair and have to push constantly against the gradient in order to maintain a straight line. Obviously, journeys also require effort in order to maintain motion and a braking effort in order to stop, so it is easy to understand just how hard it is to push a wheelchair along

Figure 4.5 Forces required to start pushing a wheelchair on various crossfall gradients. Guidelines from Snook & Ciriello, 1991

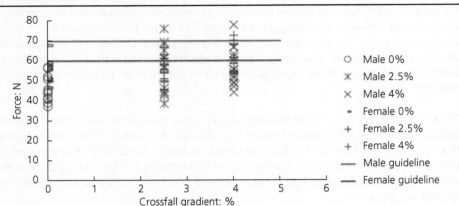

even a normal, well designed and constructed footway, let alone one which is not well designed or constructed or in a poor state of maintenance. Ambulant people also experience difficulties walking on crossfalls – the difficulty being taken up by the foot-ankle-knee-hip system – and this presents strain – and often pain – to one or more of these elements of the body's walking system.

Systems do exist for draining a surface which does not have a crossfall. These permeable paving systems are basically a surface (usually, but not necessarily, concrete) designed to have holes through which water can drain into a drainage system underneath the footway. The biggest problem with installing such systems is the means of managing the utilities which are often placed underneath the footway to avoid interrupting traffic when access is required, which would be the case if the utilities were placed under the roadway. On the other hand they could provide an excellent pedestrian surface quality in wet and dry conditions.

Another source of height change in the footway is the need to cross streets and other vehicle access roads which cross the footway. Increasingly, these are being redesigned to maintain the footway level by raising the level of the access road to that of the footway, but there are still many which have not yet been redesigned in this way. If a change in height is required it will be necessary to install a dropped kerb, where the footway surface is sloped towards the roadway so that there is no height change where they meet. *Inclusive Mobility* (DfT, 2005a) explains the requirements for dropped kerbs, including the maximum slopes, widths and other dimensions and the use of tactile paving to alert people with vision difficulties of the potential hazard. However, changes in height should really be avoided if at all possible and the pedestrians should be provided with an even, logical and continuous surface for their journey.

Lateral obstacles in the footway are also problematic – advertising 'A' boards, road signs, street lighting, parking meters, bicycle parking stands and so on, are all placed on the footway and each reduces the space available to pedestrians. In UK cities, footway width is at a premium anyway and these devices serve to reduce it. If we want to make the city for people rather than traffic, we need to redefine our priorities – including those about the use of space in the public realm – so that people are prioritised.

4.2.2.4 Lighting

It is also necessary to consider lighting. Street lighting is generally supplied for the benefit of motorists and they need to be able to see a long way ahead with a smoothly lit surface. This is best achieved by having the light source vertically above the road surface. Lenses and reflectors serve to spread the light over the road surface as evenly and widely as possible. Pedestrians have different priorities for lighting. They need lighting to cover the social distance, in particular where it becomes necessary to recognise facial features (Table 3.1 suggests that a person needs to be able to recognise an unknown person at a distance of 30 m). However, they also need lighting of a very different nature to recognise the imperfections in the walking surface, where, rather than a smooth unbroken bright light source, it is more effective to have an angled source which highlights unevenness in the footway surface at a distance of a couple of metres or so. In the main, if lighting is provided for the pedestrian footway, it is the overspill from the lighting provided for traffic and where additional lighting is provided for the footway it is usually installed vertically above the footway on the street lighting columns and no better at revealing trip hazards. Many possibilities are now available through the use of light-emitting diode (LED) technology and this should certainly be considered when designing the lighting for the pedestrian environment.

4.2.2.5 Noise

Noise and a person's ability to detect it are subjects of intense research at the moment, but, except in a few cases, the issue is still seen in the mode of the medical model of disability – the intention is to try to replace a 'failed' hearing system with some form of device. Even though some of these are extremely good, there are a number of important difficulties that affect how they might be able to help in the urban environment. Unlike vision, which has a visual field of around 200° (horizontal) × 135° (vertical), the hearing field is virtually 360° × 360°. Also, unlike vision, which is restricted to 'line of sight' – that is, unobstructed straight-line vision – hearing can detect stimuli through solid objects, such as walls, behind the person or around corners. In addition, our hearing system can follow lines of sound very accurately indeed (this is giving rise to the use of sound analysis to analyse large data). Very low (inaudible to the human ear) frequencies can be felt through our haptic systems – Evelyn Glennie has developed a highly successful career as a professional solo percussionist even though she is profoundly deaf, largely because of this capability.

Hearing is very definitely an undervalued resource. The human ability to detect even really quiet sounds amidst a plethora of other noises is well known (and something that even the most modern sophisticated hearing aids cannot replicate). The 'cocktail party effect' of being able to hear your own name being whispered at the other side of a noisy room is the hearing equivalent of the peripheral vision capability in vision. Walk into a room with your eyes closed, click your tongue or clap your hands and, with practice, you will be able to determine the size of the room quite accurately. Your stereophonic capability will enable you to locate a sound source to within a few millimetres even when it is further away than you could see the object that is producing the noise. You will modulate your voice automatically as background noise increases and if the level becomes too high you will pause your conversation without thinking – or even realising – until the noise has reduced. You will remember a musical tune, often more easily than you will remember lines of words or images, and associate it with past events – a phenomenon used to great effect by the advertising industry. Very often the idea is that if we need to hear something we should just make it louder – the current discussions about the low level of noise emanating from electric vehicles are a case in point, where the solution thus far has been to suggest creating a noise to make them more audible. Surely there is a better solution than this?

The world is noisy and the importance of hearing means it is necessary to design the soundscape of the environments people live in, including the pedestrian space.

With the emphasis on people, it is important that they can communicate easily in the space. This means thinking hard about the ambient noise. Conversation between people becomes increasingly difficult when the ambient noise level is more than about 60 dB (the UK government uses 57 $dBA_{Leq\ 16h}$ as the threshold for the onset of significant community annoyance (Lee *et al.*, 2011)). The impression to the human ear of increasing the noise intensity by 3 dB is that the noise level has doubled. By the time noise levels have increased to 75 dB it is difficult to maintain a conversation – these become reduced to short utterances of simple words in a raised voice. At 85 dB it is impossible to continue talking and people will simply stop the conversation until the noise level is reduced. How does this relate to a city environment? Well, a quiet urban street with no traffic has an ambient noise level of around 55–60 dB. As traffic increases, this rises to around 75 dB, with intense increases over short periods (e.g. there is one type of (older) bus in London that emits about 90 dB as it accelerates away from a bus stop (measured from 2 m away)). By contrast, Gehl found that streets in Venice, which are largely pedestrian, have an ambient noise level of around 52 dB (Gehl, 1978).

If the city is to be courteous, the ambient environment should enable people to converse without difficulty, and a maximum ambient noise level that permits easy conversation should be a criterion for design. Whether it is possible to bring the ambient noise levels in a city like London down to those of Venice is a good question, but ensuring they do not exceed 57 dB would be a good start. If it could be reduced to under 50 dB that would be fantastic. In Cat Street in Tokyo (Figure 4.6) for example, I recorded ambient noise levels of around 45–48 dB when there was plenty of activity – and no traffic. Cat Street displays many person-friendly features – the regularly changing shopfronts present new visual images very few seconds as a person walks along; the line of walking is not straight. Figure 4.6 shows that in the near-distance, planters are placed to encourage people to meander and, further away, the street curves into the distance. These add interest and stimulate curiosity to progress along the street. The one criticism here is the lack of encouragement to linger – seats, places to lean or stand and so on that add to the sense of people being able to stay in the place and enjoy being there.

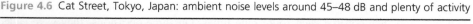

Figure 4.6 Cat Street, Tokyo, Japan: ambient noise levels around 45–48 dB and plenty of activity

With the quieter street space, it is possible to listen better to the city and its sounds, hear the rhythms as well as see them and feel the ambience as an environment that is fit for people. Creating 'talkscapes' in which people can stop and chat – whether with seating or with suitable places to stand and lean – encourages people to be in the pedestrian environment and the city begins to take on its active function.

One factor that has to be borne in mind is the prevalence of aural devices such as mobile phones, especially when used with earphones. These have an unusual effect. This is because they deliver sound in, or very close to, the ear ('near-field'). This means that exterior ('wide-field') sounds are almost excluded. The effect is to divert attention to the near-field stimulus and away from other stimuli. Some students of mine did an experiment to explore the effect of a mobile phone on their interpretation of the environment.

The students set up three walking routes in the Pamela facility. The three routes had the same number of left and right turns and were the same length so, although the sequence of turns was different in each case, the complexity was the same. This meant that there were six equivalent routes (each could be followed in two directions) but that learning them would be difficult. The routes were provided with ten objects to represent 'pieces' of information. The objects were different – a brightly coloured shape or a sign, poster or picture. Each participant was asked to walk along the routes and to recall the ten objects in each case. The participants were directed to each of the six routes in a randomised sequence and they covered each route nine times. On three occasions, they were called on their mobile phone and engaged in a scripted conversation with the caller, and on three occasions they received a text message and engaged in a text message interaction. The other three times they just walked along the route without interruption. The interactions were organised so that the participant could not predict which would happen prior to starting the walk but that each interaction arose three times in the experiment.

When the mobile phone call was made, the participants immediately slowed down and they were able to follow the conversation but were unable to recall about 40% of the 'information' along the route. In the text message situation, they slowed down more and lost about 60% of the information. An extra test was run where they were called on the phone but the ambient sound system was used to create an acoustic environment (a railway station) in which an announcement was made. None of the participants could work out what the announcement said. These outcomes were not unexpected – they were in line with previous work undertaken by, among others, the Transport Research Laboratory (TRL) on the use of phones while driving, where the ability to maintain task functionality was also severely compromised during a mobile phone call.

If society wishes to make its cities civilised, it is clearly necessary to think hard about the hearing environment. It is not easy to control noise though. It will depend a lot on a wide variety of factors, including the type of surfaces around the environment, but it is not impossible to do something constructive: for example, intelligent design of street frontages can help to baffle sound and particular attention could be paid to areas where we would like people to congregate and chat, so it would be interesting to include positive acoustic design in the design of a bus shelter. It is best to minimise it at source, hence the preference for electric vehicles – without added noise – as a great contribution to making the acoustic environment more civilised.

4.2.2.6 Coherence and the pedestrian space

So, how do the issues discussed in Sections 4.2.2.1 and 4.2.2.5 affect the access network? Well, they have a number of important implications. First, the access environment needs to lead towards the activities and these need to be within around 400 m walking distance. This distance needs to be broken up by spaces for standing and sitting – the former relatively randomly distributed and informal (e.g. opportunities for leaning) and the latter in the form of benches or other designed infrastructure convenient for sitting (the steps of the Sydney Opera House are a good example of informal seating) placed so that there is an opportunity to sit comfortably about every 100 m or less with a view of the world passing by (see Table 4.2). Figure 4.7 shows a case in Buenos Aires, Argentina, where the protective plinths around trees on the street had been adapted by local people to form a seat – so there was the potential to have a seat in the shade almost every 10 m without undue additions to the street furniture.

The activity needs to be signposted so that a person can detect the right general direction to follow around 100 m ahead, with greater detail as required as the person approaches key decision points along the route (the Legible London pedestrian information system

Figure 4.7 Tree seats in Buenos Aires, Argentina

provides information points at a series of nodes (monoliths) about 5-minutes' walk apart (~300 m) (TfL, 2015)). A key point as a starter for these directions is the bus stop, as it is here that people will be arriving from other parts of the city, without any sense of where they are or where they need to go to reach the activity they are seeking. Signs need to be easily identifiable and simple to understand. They need to be able to reassure the people who are unfamiliar with the local environment, so being able to see the 'next' sign while standing at another one is a very important guide for location and spacing.

Second, the access environment needs to have sufficient and not excessive capacity. In order to make the walk towards the activity attractive, it is necessary to accommodate sufficient numbers of people without them feeling that they are in the midst of a huge unpopulated space or that they are in an intensely overcrowded environment in which they are forced to interact with people at too personal a scale (see Table 4.2). This may mean rethinking the priority and scale of pedestrian space in relation to the space for vehicles (including bicycles).

Third, the access space needs to be interesting, with 'soft', porous edges (such as shop entrances) so that people can easily enter and leave and have interesting things to see and do around the edges. The access network should attract and not repel people. It needs to be inviting so that people are encouraged to be in it, activities are there for people to do and watch, it is easy to linger – a good measure for the success of an area is the product of the number of people and the amount of time they spend in the area – a larger value of this measure indicates a place which is more interesting and valued by people. Bearing in mind the comments about vision in Chapter 3, it would be good to ensure that vision stimulation is designed in at an appropriate rate and to ensure that the acoustic environment is amenable to people holding conversations.

Fourth, the access network needs to have a sense of rhythm within it so that it makes sense and feels comfortable and attractive to move around it. One example of rhythm is the presentation of stimuli at the rate of one stimulus every 5 seconds – where the stimulus could be just the introduction of a vertical alignment, a different shopfront, a new view: a difference for me, the stimulus should be attractive to the peripheral vision, rather than the fovea. This means emphasis on nuances of change and movement, rather than colour and specific objects. The vision system is quite capable of directing the fovea to important stimuli when necessary and over-provision of stimuli could lead to confusion for people with vision problems. Although the word 'rhythm' is used most commonly in relation to sound, it is about any repeated stimulus, so could apply to the regular (or not) presence of a visual or tactile stimulus, the rhythm of footsteps as a person walks is another example.

Thus far, I have been considering the access environment as the way to reach the activities, which are therefore the start or finish points of the journey. Some journeys will be completed entirely within the access environment near to the activity, but others will require the bus system to deliver a person to this point in order to continue their journey to reach the activity. The bus stop then becomes the portal between the access network and the bus, so I would now like to turn to the bus stop and how that can encourage us to reach our desired activities.

4.3.   At the bus stop
4.3.1   Basic principles behind bus stop design
There are six basic elements to be considered in the design of bus stop infrastructure and these can be grouped into three broad categories:

People:

1   The accessible phase-triality (see Table 3.1) between the pedestrian, passenger and pedenger environments and the infrastructure and information systems required to manage these.

Infrastructure:

1 The nature of the bus stop platform as the boarding/alighting point for the bus, including the vertical and horizontal gaps between the platform and the bus.
2 The nature of the bus stop as an element of the urban realm.

Vehicle:

1 The bus manoeuvre when arriving at or leaving the bus stop.
2 The bus characteristics – dimensions, design, capabilities – that pertain to its interface with the bus stop.
3 The dynamics of bus interactions with other buses and with other traffic.

The passengers' needs have to be brought to bear on these elements in order to obtain a design that is accessible, civilised, user-friendly and that minimises conflicts within the bus stop environment. The simple fact is that none of these can be met in isolation from the others. Yet, all over the world, public transport system implementers face real difficulties in achieving these synergies. Normally, transport or urban planners would handle the design of the people aspects, whereas vehicle designers and manufacturers deal with the vehicle, and highways engineers the infrastructure. This division is solidified in law – except in the most unregulated country, each of these groups of experts is constrained by legislation which sets specific requirements and standards – whether these concern the location of a bus stop, the specification of the vehicle or the traffic regulations with which the bus stop must comply. Even in less regulated situations, custom and practice yields habits and behavioural constraints, which prevent better performance. None of these regulations require a designer to deal with the person's needs. Design in this case means working simultaneously with people, vehicles and infrastructure. Given that the people who generally design urban systems are usually tied into one or another of these fields, this is a real challenge. It means that the design for boarding and alighting must be handled in the context of its complexity – as Einstein said 'A scientific theory should be as simple as possible, but no simpler' and design in this context is a good example where this way of thinking is essential. A major objective of this book is to show how the bus system's complexity can only be addressed by the coming together of these groups of participants in the design process.

At a superficial level, the design of a bus stop has three governors:

1 the laws of physics
2 the laws of the land
3 the needs of the people.

At this level and in the short term, the laws of physics trump everything – a bus cannot stop instantly – the laws of the land have to be obeyed (although they are changeable (unlike the laws of physics), changing them could take a long time) and the needs of the people will be met only insofar as the other two sets of laws allow. The needs of the people are often ignored in the face of the other constraints, or end up being met purely by luck. However, look at it the other way around. Once the other two have been met, the needs of the people are free to be realised and can then become the primary influence on the subsequent decisions.

To make the bus system accessible, it is necessary to turn the conventional governance system on its head. Accessibility means making the needs of the people – all the people – paramount and then resolving the laws which seek to prevent these needs being met. There is also the challenge that, although the Laws of Physics are immutable, it could be possible to devise ways of mitigating them.

So, what are the needs of the people?

In relation to direct users of the bus stop, there are two groups of people to consider: the people wishing to use the bus as a passenger and the people who are providing the service at the bus stop – the bus driver and other crew and, in some cases, other staff who are involved in the operation of the bus service.

In the case of the passengers, their needs in relation to boarding and alighting are that a person can make the transition between the three phases – passenger to pedenger to pedestrian and vice versa – easily and comfortably. To achieve this, they need to be confident that they are going through this process for the correct bus (when boarding) or bus stop (when alighting). Table 4.4 shows the three phases and their transitions in relation to the

Table 4.4 The needs of the people in the boarding/alighting process: phase transitions and stages concerned with boarding and alighting a bus

Phase transition	Stage
Pedestrian to pedenger	1. Confirm correct bus stop using information at the bus stop
	2. Wait
	3. Rearrange bags
	4. Find money or validation ticket
	5. Identify the correct bus
Pedenger to passenger	6. Locate the correct door
	7. Step onto the bus
	8. Initiate payment/validation
	9. Move inside the vehicle (free up space for the next pedenger)
Passenger to pedenger	10. Locate the correct bus stop
	11. Gather bags/belongings, etc.
	12. Move to the correct door
	13. Initiate payment/validation (this is rare but is the case in some countries, e.g. Japan)
	14. Step off the bus
Pedenger to pedestrian	15. Rearrange bags
	16. Orient themselves to the new environment, using information at the bus stop
	17. Move away from the bus stop (free up space for the next pedenger)

bus stop. Table 4.4 shows that there are 17 stages within the whole phase transition – nine in relation to the boarding process and eight in relation to the alighting process.

I will now discuss these stages in terms of the broad issues that pertain to each one when designing an accessible bus system.

4.3.2   Pedestrian to pedenger
4.3.2.1   Confirm the correct bus stop

This requires all bus stops in the city to have a consistent (but not necessarily the same) design so that they can be easily identified from a distance anywhere in the city. The usual approach for this is to place a 'flag' on a pole and for that flag to have an indication of the fact that it is a bus stop (see Figure 4.8). As the pedestrian approaches the bus stop it needs to become clear which bus stop it is and which buses stop there. It should also provide confirmatory information to indicate the direction of travel – this could be a

Figure 4.8 A London bus stop flag, showing services and route directions

Figure 4.9 A decorated bus stop in Buenos Aires, Argentina

broad description of available destinations and/or a significant milestone along the way. Maintaining the necessary consistency over all bus stops is important, but there is scope for local people to add a flavour if they wish. Figure 4.9 shows a bus stop in Buenos Aires that is consistent with the local standards but which has been decorated by a local shop. Consistency does not mean uniformity – as long as the bus stop is recognisable as such, this approach allows the system to have a strong local appeal. There will not be space for complex information on the flag or pole (and this must be available within the bus stop environment), but a quick indication is helpful. This summarised information should also link into other information systems, such as timetables, real-time bus information apps, travel information websites, local pedestrian information and so on, so that people feel that they are in a coherent system where all the information is supportive.

Information within the bus stop environment can be more comprehensive than is possible on the pole and must include information about the bus services available from that stop and the identity and location of other bus stops in the vicinity, together with the identity of bus services that are available there. This is particularly important where bus stops are split so that some buses travelling along a road stop at one and others, which are at this point travelling in the same direction, stop at another.

In terms of accessibility, it needs to be possible to see the information from the height of a person seated in a wheelchair, and for vision – or hearing impaired people, and it has to retain the consistency needed by people with cognitive difficulties.

4.3.2.2 My wait for the bus is comfortable

There is good provision of shelter from weather, seating and lighting; sufficient space for the expected number of waiting passengers and their baggage; real-time information about the bus system performance, maps, available destinations and so on; the bus service frequency is sufficient to keep waiting times to an acceptable level; and the bus service is reliable.

So I see the bus stop as not only the place where someone catches a bus, but also as one of Gehl's 'soft edges' in the pedestrian environment – similar to a shop window and doorway. The bus stop is in fact a place where one enters and leaves the pedestrian environment and it provides those useful characteristics of the soft edges: permeability, a place to sit, stand and watch the world go by, where information and activities of interest happen, and where the environment constantly changes yet remains reassuringly constant. This transforms the approach to the design of the bus stop so that it is an active part of the process of making the pedestrian environment a place of interest – a place to be – in its own right and not only a public transport interchange (although undoubtedly it must perform this function).

First I would like to consider how the soft edge links to the public transport function of the bus stop. Several attempts have been made to formalise bus stop design in recent years. Transport for London (TfL, 2006) followed a considerable amount of previous guidance on bus stop design, such as London Transport (1997) guidelines on bus stop and bus bay design as part of the London Bus Priority Network Scheme. This work was updated in 2000 with the publication of the guidelines for accessible stops published TfL's London Bus Initiative (London Bus Initiative, 2000). Barham et al. (1994) have also published guidelines for bus stations and other public-transport-related infrastructure. Parallel work in France has also begun to identify the space required for bus stops (Uster et al., 1997) and has resulted in guidance on the design of accessible bus stops (CERTU, 2001). COST 322 (European Commission, 1995) has included aspects of stop design as it relates to the design of low-floor, wheelchair accessible buses. Rogat et al. (1993) discuss various approaches to kerb design for bus stops. Tebb (1997) proposed a 'unistop' concept in which stops are standardised with higher 'bus-friendly' kerbs, using guide wheels to help align the buses with the platform. From empirical tests, Tyler and Caiaffa (1999) explain how much space before and after the bus stop is required to achieve an accessible service at the stop. Typical outputs from this body of work include the design of bus stop platforms and layouts to accommodate buses within the traffic systems often encountered in town centres. In all these cases, the emphasis is on providing solutions to the problem of the interface between the vehicle and infrastructure. In some cases attention is paid to the bus interface with the passenger wishing to board or alight. None considers the bus stop as an active part of the pedestrian environment.

The first edition of this book was one of the first attempts to change the perspective of the bus stop from that of the bus planner and operator to that of the users of the bus stops – namely the passengers and bus drivers, with some consideration of non-users who are affected by bus stops – pedestrians and traffic. In some ways bus stop design in London has improved since then, especially in terms of the information available at bus stops, but it is still challenging for people with little prior knowledge of the system or for those who have cognitive impairments to use the bus stop. Other aspects of design, such as the sense of it being a place to be or a soft edge, as discussed above, really have not surfaced, so in the present edition of the book I am making the opportunity to offer some new thought and perspectives.

Following the outcomes-based decision model discussed in Section 2.2.1, I can start to populate the model in relation to bus stops. The first step is to consider the desired outcome – what people would like the bus stop to be. Most people, if asked about what they would like a bus stop to be, would look fairly blank and think about its purpose as a place to board (sometimes they might think about alighting) a bus. So I would like to help to make the discussion more mature by thinking about what the bus stop should be.

I would like to start with the functionality of the bus stop. I see this in the context of the proposition that the bus stop is the portal between the pedestrian access environment with its activities and the bus system as a means of reaching a particular part of that environment from elsewhere in the city. It is in this sense that I see it is a 'soft edge' in the same manner as a shop doorway.

On one side of a shop doorway is the pedestrian environment and on the other is the shop with all its desirable contents. What functions does the doorway provide? Clearly, the most obvious is that it is the means of entering and leaving the shop. However, it is also the transition between the two environments: it needs to show what is inside the shop to those outside and what is outside the shop to those inside. So, a doorway that allows people to see the other environment helps – think of a shop with no window and a solid doorway and it is not really very appealing in the sense of inviting you to cross the threshold. Showing people what sort of produce is available in the shop, maybe with some element of pricing, is important as a means of enticing people into the shop. Similarly, it should be enticing to leave the shop and re-enter the exciting pedestrian environment.

It is interesting when examining shopping malls to see the extent to which it is difficult to find the exit – it is clearly the intention of the mall owner to keep people inside the mall

Table 4.5 Functions of a shop doorway

Function	Requirement
Allows entry to the shop and to the pedestrian environment	Accessible for all potential customers
Shows what is inside the shop	Either allows visibility of the inside of the shop or advertises the contents to potential customers on the outside
Shows what is outside the shop	Shows the weather, the volume of pedestrian activity and available space outside
Entices people in/out	Makes it look attractive to cross the threshold (going in: to conduct business; going out: to want to enjoy the pedestrian environment (having concluded the business inside of course)). Crossing the threshold in either direction means improving wellbeing just a little

for as long as possible in order to increase the footfall for the shop owners who are leasing premises inside. So it is unusual to find a clock in a shopping mall, the lighting is bright, exits are dark and not so easy to find. Windows to the outside world are few. In contrast, the high street shop wants the interplay of people entering and leaving the shop – the premises is too small to retain people inside for too long as this would reduce the custom – the commercial activity does not rely on footfall as such, but on the head or heart that wants to make a purchase and the hands that carry out the exchange. That means a movement of people in and out of the shop. The shop has to develop and maintain a duality in the doorway: of the world on the 'other' side being slightly more attractive than the world on 'this' side. This duality plays out in time: the 'other' side is the shop interior at one moment and the street environment at another. Table 4.5 shows some functions of a shop doorway and a simple description of the resulting requirements.

The shop window has a different function. This is to display products and entice people to linger and think about the prospect of wishing to buy something, but it also has a function as part of the soft edge – clearly not in the same way as a door in terms of entry and exit, but in terms of showing the world on either side. The window allows people to see what is, or might be, inside the shop, but if people turn around, it also acts as a lingering-place, where people can see what is going on in the world outside the shop, by offering a place to lean while watching the world go by. The shop owner might think that leaning against their window and looking at the pedestrian environment is stopping other people from having the opportunity to consider purchasing something inside their shop, but they would be wrong.

Table 4.6 shows some functions of a shop window and a simple description of the resulting requirements.

Table 4.6 Some functions and requirements of a shop window

Function	Requirement
See what is in the shop	Display with products or indications of products or simply to see inside the shop
Display some aesthetic activity	The window contains artwork or something of interest rather than products that might be on sale inside
Place to lean	The window is generally a vertical surface, but it would be good to have some horizontal leaning structure, such as a shelf or windowsill so that people can perch while looking at the pedestrian environment or place bags while looking into the window
Create an ambience of people being there	The window is a place to be, interesting, attractive

First of all, the presence of people per se is a sign of the place being active and that the shop is a great place to be. Second, actually the amount of time any one person lingers could be relatively short, so the opportunity would reoccur reasonably soon (and a lingerer would tend to move if someone showed that they want to look into the window). Pedestrian – and therefore potential customer – activity always increases in areas where there are people already, so the lingerer is providing a service to the shop owner as well as the environment by creating activity in the locality of the shop. Taking Gehl's measure of activity as the product of the number of people and time in a given space, it is possible to gauge the difference in activity resulting from a lingerer.

A person standing by the window for 10 minutes would yield an 'activity value' of 600 person-seconds and would occupy, let's say, 1 square metre of space. To achieve this value without them would require 60 people walking at 1 m/sec across the 1 metre in the same time – but they would not be looking in the shop window, they would certainly not be making a purchase and they would not be creating atmosphere other than the bustle of movement. Indeed, the lingerer would be using his or her peripheral vision and ability to turn his or her eyes, head and body, so that he or she could observe what is going on in a wide area around the place where they were standing. The walking pedestrian, on the other hand, would be tending to focus their foveal vision in front of them, and responding to the wider environment only through their peripheral vision. This is far better than if they were driving a car through the area, but it is still a lot less engaged than the lingerer. For the lingerer, the footway (shop window) is a place to be, but for a car driver it is simply a space to pass through. Think of Gehl's idea of a stimulus every 5 seconds. A lingerer will be obtaining these from the interesting goings-on in the place; the car driver will have passed some 50 m in the same time. This thinking connects with the 'link and place' approach to urban design – where a street is considered in terms of its use as a place – a destination – or as a link between two places. This leads to different approaches to design of both the urban realm and the traffic management systems.

However, the link and place concept applies just as much to pedestrian areas, which have no vehicular traffic. I call the options 'lingering' and 'walking' in such an environment. Just as with the more usual adoption of link and place, it is necessary to be sure to design facilities for whichever is the priority in the particular environment under consideration. Lingerers need sensitive and helpful design and so do walkers. Whereas a traffic 'link' (or even a traffic 'place') needs to be designed for vehicles, which follow mainly straight lines or predictable curves in a predictable direction, people do not follow these rules. People change direction, stop, walk sideways, walk in pairs or groups or alone and so on, so the urban design must take into account that a pedestrian space is almost certainly simultaneously both a 'link' and a 'place', with some people using it for each or both of these purposes. What is not good is where the assumption is that people do not linger but only walk, or the reverse. In fact, the very helpful levels of service introduced by Fruin in the 1970s are really only describing a fraction of the pedestrian activity (the 'link'), and urban design needs to be evaluated on the ability to deliver much more than flow.

I like the approach that follows the multicriteria analysis set out in Chapter 2 (see Figures 2.7, 2.8 and 2.9 and associated text for a description) using radar plots to establish the performance of various criteria, which could include flow, but also the ease of stopping and chatting, holding a conversation, resting, lingering, waiting, sitting, standing, turning in multiple directions, ease of turning and so on. Others could be brought into play depending on local circumstances, such as shade, warmth, air quality or humidity. The skill is thus not to use indicators, but to create criteria which describe performance in the circumstances that pertain and then 'measure' these in whatever is the most appropriate way for each criterion. Creating the criteria is driven by the vision – what is necessary in order to achieve that goal – using the sense of value (see Chapter 1) as achievement of aspiration – so the issue is what will help to improve the wellbeing of the people in the city?

Remembering that value is the achievement over the aspiration we can now use such a simple measure as an input in our estimation of value. The aspiration here is to generate an environment which is a 'place to be'. It stands to reason that such a place is one in which one would like to linger, because it is in some way interesting – there is something good to sense (not only 'see'). Such a pedestrian environment therefore delivers more stimuli to a stationary lingerer than to a pedestrian walking through it because stimuli for a moving pedestrian need to attract them to move through the space rather than to linger in it. However, even the moving pedestrian receives infinitely more stimuli from the place than would a car driver passing through the same space. If the desire is to enable the space to deliver interest to people – to make it a place to be – people need to want to stay there. In addition, the lingerer attracts others to pause in the space – look at how people aggregate around an event, whether it be a street musician, a building site – or a university professor measuring crossfall gradients! I think about bus stops in the same way as I think about the urban realm – as places where people should want to be. This affects the way I think about bus stops, in particular about the main activity that occurs at bus stops: waiting.

Waiting is a curious concept. Within the three-and-a-half pages of entry for the word 'wait' in the *Oxford English Dictionary*, the meaning of the word 'wait' most pertinent to this discussion is 'To remain in a place, defer one's departure until something has happened'. In terms of the bus system, normally the 'something' that 'happens' is the arrival of the bus and thus the concept of waiting would be to wait 'until the bus comes'; in a clinician's surgery, it is the revelation that the clinician is available. This implies that providing somewhere to wait and making this reasonably comfortable until that 'something' happens is all that needs to be provided – but also that, in fact, if nothing specifically directed towards waiting were provided at all, people would still wait for that event to occur. So some bus stops have shelters with seats and other facilities such as information to assist the waiting process, but others have nothing at all. People wait for buses whether or not facilities for doing so have been provided, and even where such facilities are provided, they often do not use them.

Observe a high street bus stop and see where the waiting people are. A few will be inside the protection of the bus shelter, but many will be dispersed around the pedestrian environment – they wait, leaning against the soft edges of the environment, such as shop windows, doorways and so on, leaning on railings, sometimes just standing in the pedestrian footway area. They are spread over a considerable distance – maybe 20 m or more along the footway – and only reveal themselves as a bus passenger when the bus comes and they move towards the boarding point. Figure 4.10 shows just such a situation. Here there are pedengers waiting in the shelter, near the bus stop flag, but also along the rear of the footway, allowing pedestrians to move freely. You can also see the real-time information. The pedenger is basically lingering in the vicinity of the bus stop and, in so doing, is providing an activity in the social space of the street. They may be looking at the shop window, reading a newspaper or a book, using their mobile phone, looking around, watching the world go by – until the bus comes and provides the 'something that happens' which defines the wait: in terms of the street environment, the lingering has

Figure 4.10 A London bus stop showing people waiting and the real-time information display

turned into a wait only at that point. Waiting has a stress component which is determined by the focus on the end point – the arrival of the bus – whereas lingering, which has no end point as such, is a much more relaxed affair. Converting waiting to lingering is a major reducer of stress in the bus system.

As mentioned in Chapter 3, real-time bus information systems, such as Countdown in London, are actually designed to de-stress the wait by improving knowledge of the projected end point. The key to this is to realise that it is not the wait per se that generates the stress, but the uncertainty surrounding the end point of the wait – the arrival of the bus. By making the end point better known to the waiting people, the uncertainty is removed and waiting has been turned into lingering. But this is just the period in which they are actually turning from a pedestrian who is only weakly associated with the bus system, through a 'pedenger' to a passenger who is quite directed towards engaging with the bus system by boarding a bus. De-stressing this process is a major part of enabling people to feel better about using buses.

These 'waiting' people are actually people whose lingering activity is positioned in space and time by the bus system – they are lingering in this place because there is a bus stop nearby, and at this time because this is associated with the timing of their activity in some other place to which the bus will link them once it has arrived. Because lingerers tend to aggregate, they create a common activity – a serendipitous collaboration – that creates an atmosphere of benign human (in)activity that yields benefits for society at large. The passive overview of the area provided by lingerers reduces opportunities for crime, supports people who experience calamitous events, and generates a sort of pop-up community in the space (see Figure 4.11 for an example of a good place for lingering, the Plaza Bolívar in Cartagena, Colombia). Another, smaller, example in Havana, Cuba (Figure 4.12), also adds a message about the sort of relationship people in the city can have with their local environment – part of the 'city as public space' concept and making the point that this is not only about the sense of ownership, but also the sense of responsibility to make the city a civilised place. The Havana case has a sense of shade and nature but also seats placed in a way that makes conversation convenient. Contrast this with a public space in Hartlepool, UK, Figure 4.13, where seats are few and far between and 'nature' is conspicuous by its absence – and the number of people and their corresponding activity is quite low.

The bus stop creates an opportunity for creating all this lingering. Yes, the Plaza Bolívar is a large space – much larger than a bus stop, but the same outcome emerges at the Angel in Islington, London, where in the mornings and for several years, a provider of coffee and croissants has had a lucrative business selling coffee from the back of his motorcycle-based espresso machine. The Angel bus stop is a major interchange between two broad corridors of bus services which cross – north-west to south-east, north-east to south-west. There is therefore a large amount of interchange at this stop and many passengers avail themselves of a coffee and a croissant while making the interchange. This is a progression from the Plaza Bolívar example – at the Angel, people are *in transit* and they are not staying for a long time. In this case their lingering takes longer than they need to change buses, but they do move on to take their ongoing bus after a short while.

Figure 4.11 Plaza Bolívar, Cartagena, Colombia; a place to linger

Figure 4.12 Parque Guayasamin: a quiet corner in Havana, Cuba – the sign reads 'Nature is life and health – look after the plants'

Figure 4.13 Public space in Hartlepool, UK – less than might be hoped to attract people's interest here

The bus frequencies are quite high, so they can take a subsequent bus if they are able to. Provision of real-time bus information means that they can estimate how the bus system is working that morning, so they can judge how long they may linger. They are of course changing from being pedestrians or passengers into a pedenger – and taking a cup of coffee while they do so. Nevertheless, in the context of a commuting journey, this pause is indeed a linger of some import and one they obviously enjoy.

In such a situation, the bus stop, although it must provide suitable waiting facilities for people who wish to use them, is acting as the focal point in time and space for assigning the collective lingering of people, stimulating them to linger 'here' and 'now', but then to disappear from this environment in an instant as soon as the bus arrives – only to be replaced by the next group of lingers. Can we design more of our bus stops to stimulate such a civilised activity?

The bus stop thus provides a dynamic canvas for the life of the street – constantly refreshed and energised by the arrival and departure of the buses, but realised by the temporary stay of people between the bus arrivals. The bus stop is therefore a place to be – temporarily – so it is necessary to think about its design in order to facilitate that. One aspect of that design is its location: in the list of success factors in our outcomes-based decision model, therefore, is the sense that the positioning of a bus stop could encourage street activity that we want in order to give life to the environment. This becomes one of the priorities in the location of a bus stop after the laws of the land and physics (see Section 4.3.1) have been satisfied. When we have a choice of places to locate a bus stop, this becomes a way of creating added value – and when we are trying to maximise the value of our accessible bus system through its contribution to the improvement of wellbeing, perhaps the facilitation of lingering is a good way of increasing value.

How to ensure that this activity is positive for pedestrians, passengers, pedengers – and lingerers – is a great opportunity for multifactorial design. How do we make sure that the lingerers are able to see the real time information while they are lingering, for example, so that they can time their transition to pedenger in good time, without feeling hustled? Places to lean, sit, stand, watch – and see the buses as they approach – provide a passive overview of activity in the area which encourages positive engagement and discourages less desirable activity, then help to make the place feel good – indeed a good place to be. These are all good aspects of the bus stop which help it become a positive focal point in the local area. Ensuring that this is positive is essential – and a key requirement of the design.

Making sure that lingering, which generally feels benign, does not turn into lurking or loitering, which are generally a little sinister, is a design objective for the area – and one that can be achieved – but is rarely thought of in bus stop design. The emphasis hitherto has been to respond to the negatives: remove the possibilities for loitering or lurking – by removing seats or making them uncomfortable, for example – but the danger is that in making lurking and loitering uncomfortable and unwelcome, it is all too easy to make lingering feel unvalued and unwanted. The bus stop then becomes a place for nobody, least of all those people who wish to use the bus system.

I want to change that!

When the bus stop is seen only as a part of the bus system, it is simply a 'cost centre' – one to be minimised so that its impacts on the bus system are as small as possible. Advertising companies have seen their potential though. Bus stops provide them with spaces for their advertising, often in prime city centre locations. They are not advertising to the occupants of the bus stop though. Their market is the car drivers who pass the bus stop, who are perceived to be a higher-spending fraternity than bus passengers (remember that 26-year-old at the start of this book ...). Therefore, there is no incentive to fill the bus shelter with people as these would obscure the advertisements.

Enrique Peñalosa, the Mayor of Bogotá who implemented the Transmilenio system in the city, famously said that the sign of an advanced city was not that the poor could afford to use taxis, but that even the rich used the buses. One part of reaching that situation would be to make the bus stop attractive to them, something that could be of interest to advertising companies as well as to the passenger/pedenger community – and one that should also be attractive to the pedestrians who pass by. This is important because it is a source of income for the bus stops, which could help support improvements to the infrastructure.

If bus stops were not the negative they are currently perceived by many to be, and the experience of being at one were more positive, the benefits could be considerable. Waiting pedengers will be at the bus stop for a maximum time of, say, 10 minutes (depending on the frequency of their bus service). A pedestrian will have the bus stop in view for maybe 20–30 seconds; a car driver will have it in view for perhaps 4–5 seconds. If the passenger's total experience of the bus stop is positive, the time spent there will be a positive backdrop to the advertisement, something that would be less effective for pedestrians and non-existent for car drivers. The additional viewing time then provides scope for advertisements to change, allowing for a wider range of advertisements and public service information to be displayed to the people in the stop.

In terms of value engineering, if we are aspiring to make the bus stop a place to be, the value (achievement over aspiration) will be much greater if we have lingerers than if we have pedestrians walking through the area. The car driver receives virtually no value from the place – and delivers less, as they are polluting and imposing congestion and other barriers. The use of resources to generate this effect is much smaller in the case of the lingerer because the stimulus generation space is so much smaller. The issue is how to ensure that the stimuli happen, but as many of the stimuli are provided by the other people in the area it is necessary only to use resources to encourage people to be there.

Sometimes it is sufficient just to have a space where lingering is encouraged by having places to stand comfortably (places to lean or sit are very helpful in this regard) (e.g. Piazza di Campo in Siena, the steps in front of the Opera House in Sydney or Covent Garden in London). Listening to the rhythms of the people and the space helps to define what would be needed. Watch people walking in step to the music of a street musician, or the different speed they adopt as they walk along a street of small shops compared with one characterised by having a single blank wall on both sides. Compare Figure 4.15 and Figure 4.14 and it is fairly easy to see which one is preferred by people (even though Cat

Figure 4.14 A pedestrian space in Cat Street, Tokyo, with only blank walls. Ambient noise is low but would you want to stay there?

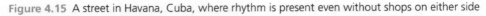

Figure 4.15 A street in Havana, Cuba, where rhythm is present even without shops on either side

Street has few places designed to encourage people to linger) and to imagine which one would be characterised by a higher walking speed. Another example can be seen in Havana, Cuba, where the street width is relatively narrow (about 5 m), but, even though there are few shops, the sense of rhythm is present. The interest is also enhanced by the placement of the trees in the roadway, thus causing the (mainly) pedestrians to move around them (see Figure 4.15).

So, to summarise. The bus stop is both the shop window and shop doorway between the bus and the activities in the pedestrian environment. It shows people what is there, enabling them to enjoy being in a 'place to be', and acts as the portal between the two environments. It is not a no-man's land between them and it is not the province of either. The bus stop is simultaneously in both environments and yet must perform well in each without being a detriment to the other. The person at a bus stop is rather like Schrödinger's cat: at an instant they are either a passenger or a pedestrian and it is impossible to tell which they are. I referred earlier to the concept of a pedenger which is the transition state between these two states, and one function of the bus stop is to facilitate that transition. It is this 'phase-triality' – the constant flipping between being a pedestrian, passenger and pedenger – that must be accommodated at the bus stop that makes it such a complex entity and thus so hard to design.

Tables 4.7 and 4.8 show how the bus stop requirements can be formulated from the phases identified in Table 4.4 in a little more detail, and highlight the transitions between the phases from the point at which the pedestrian has identified that they are at the

Table 4.7 Some possible functions and requirements of a bus stop as a waiting environment

Function	Requirement
Shows where the bus stopping point is	Clear and consistent signage (e.g. a flag), unique to the bus system, but integratable with the other elements of the public transport system (including the pedestrian environment)
Shows what the bus system can offer there	Good understandable and positive information about the bus system at that stop and elsewhere Real-time bus information about arriving buses and downstream travel time estimates (derived from the bus information systems) to act as an encouragement for people to use the bus service
Part of the urban realm	Attractive, accessible and appropriate for the locality. It could be a destination in its own right, comfortable resting point for tired pedestrians. It should be entertaining, aesthetic, interactive and provide a service (e.g. wi-fi) and information about the local area
Creates an ambience	People want to be there – the bus stop acts as a safe and secure place to be in the urban environment. It is a good place to be, interesting and attractive

correct bus stop to the point at which they move away from the bus stop in the pedestrian environment.

I can now construct a starter for the outcomes-based decision model. Recalling from Chapter 1 that the overarching vision is to improve societal and individual wellbeing and that the strategy is to adopt the aims of the five cities model, it is worth summarising the journey to this point.

Aiming to contribute to each of the five cities, I have singled out the bus system as one of the contributory systems to that end. I have argued that in order to have a bus system that can make that contribution, it is necessary that it is accessible and integrated with the network of activities and the associated access network, especially with the urban realm and pedestrian environment. As just one part of this, it is necessary to design the bus stop to be easy and attractive for passengers to use. This becomes a desired outcome for the decision model. Figure 4.16 shows how the requirements of Table 4.8 become the success factors of the decision model and the limitations are then defined on the basis of what might turn out to be factors that prevent success being achieved and thus which have to be eliminated as an issue or mitigated in some way. The desired outcome – that the bus stop should be easy for everyone to use – will remain as the key issue to achieve, and decisions about the actions necessary to activate the success factors while mitigating the limitations then become the issue for discussion with the people concerned.

Table 4.8 Bus stop requirements based on the 'phase-triality' of needs of pedestrians, passengers and pedengers

Pedestrian	'Pedenger'	Passenger	Bus stop requirement
1. Interacts with the pedestrian environment: walks along it, lingers in it – looks in shop windows, watches the world go by – goes into/emerges from doorways, arrives from or leaves towards the footway		Interacts with the bus environment: 2. Boarding: looks for bus services, timetables, arrival times, checks fares, payment methods, boarding protocols, queues, sits/rests/leans 3. Alighting: checks bus stop location, services and times for onward or return journey	1. Must not impede the pedestrian environment, Needs easy and fluid access from/to the pedestrian environment, needs space for people to linger around the bus stop with access to the information they need about bus arrivals, etc. 2. Provision of information about the bus services, fare systems/prices etc., indications of where the bus(es) will arrive, where to queue, provision of seating, leaning support, good lighting 3. Provision of information about the surrounding area, activities, routes, location of nearby bus services and stops, return service times, etc., good lighting in sympathy with the pedestrian environment

Interacts with the bus:

4. Boarding: arranges bags and payment/ticket validation ready for boarding the bus, moves to the doorway of the bus when it arrives

Interacts with the pedestrian environment

5. Alighting: arranges bags, balance ready for the pedestrian environment, checks which way to go, leaves the bus stop area

4. Sufficient space and facilities to enable rearrangement of bags, etc. to take place, clear pathway to the boarding point, clear arrival and onward journey information

5. Sufficient space to allow alighting passengers to stop and rearrange bags without interrupting flows off and onto the bus, clear simple information about which way to go to find local activities

Figure 4.16 Basic outcomes-based decision model for a bus stop based on Table 4.8

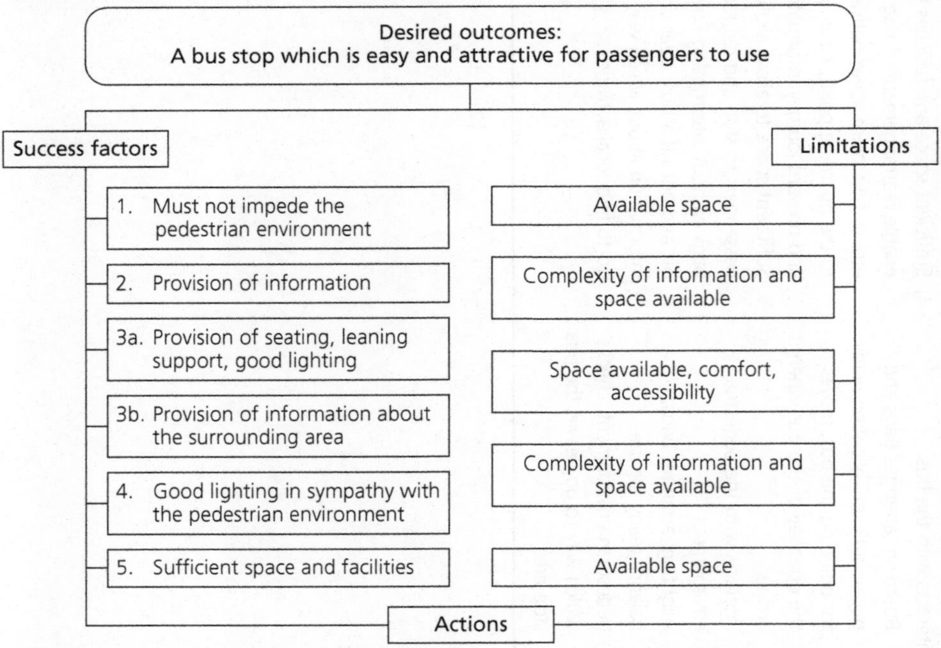

```
┌─────────────────────────────────────────────────────────────┐
│                     Desired outcomes:                        │
│   A bus stop which is easy and attractive for passengers     │
│                          to use                              │
└─────────────────────────────────────────────────────────────┘
```

Success factors	Limitations
1. Must not impede the pedestrian environment	Available space
2. Provision of information	Complexity of information and space available
3a. Provision of seating, leaning support, good lighting	Space available, comfort, accessibility
3b. Provision of information about the surrounding area	Complexity of information and space available
4. Good lighting in sympathy with the pedestrian environment	
5. Sufficient space and facilities	Available space

Actions

Wait

The intention is to provide a situation in the bus stop where the person's perception of time is altered so that it is at most equal to the elapsed time and if possible may become less than this, although allowing for sufficient time for the pedestrian-pedenger phase change. The bus stop should be comfortable and services such as wi-fi could be provided. The environment should be made acoustically pleasant. In Paris they are experimenting with different kinds of music, which can be changed by people waiting in the bus stop, but other soundscapes could be inserted, such as birdsong, which tend to be relatively unnoticed but are perceived by people (they would certainly notice if the sound were to stop) and, depending on the varieties chosen, are generally thought to be pleasant. A soundscape can be delivered without devices such as loudspeakers. Using the glass panes for this purpose is quite simple and they can be focused so that the sound can be contained within the bus stop area. This system could also be used to provide announcements to people in the bus stop about service changes, oncoming buses, downstream travel times and so on. The lighting in the bus stop could also be used to create a more relaxing feel to the place – warmer white (pink-tinted) lighting will tend to be more friendly than cooler blue-tinted light, for example: the availability of LED lighting systems makes this quite easy to achieve.

Rearrange bags

The way in which bags are carried while one is walking along the footway is often different from the way they need to be carried when one is boarding a bus. There are several reasons for this – the doorway of a bus is usually narrower than the available width on the footway, there could be several people also boarding the bus at the same time, there might be a need to pay or validate a ticket on entry to the bus, for example – but whatever the reason, it is often necessary to change the way that the bags are held. The space for doing this ranges from a small amount of space on the ground near to where the person is waiting, to the use of an available seat or bench – this has the advantage that it is not as low as the ground and this makes the process more comfortable, especially if the bags are heavy.

Wheelchair users often place their bags on their lap or hang them from the back of the wheelchair. Neither is particularly good or comfortable, but there is usually nowhere else to put them. Hanging a bag from the back of the wheelchair makes the whole chair extremely unstable – especially when moving up the sort of ramp angle often required to board a bus. When the wheelchair is moving along a flat footway the imbalance is less of a problem if the person can move their weight forward to compensate and the whole mass is more evenly distributed between the four wheels. When ascending a ramp, more of the weight is passed to the rear of the chair and, because the bags are hanging from the handles, higher up the chair. There is therefore a much higher risk of tipping over backwards when ascending the ramp with bags hanging from the back of the chair. It might well be necessary to move bags from the back of the wheelchair to the lap in order to have a less risky ascent into the bus if level access is not possible. Removing the need for a ramp by making access between the platform and the bus level would remove this problem.

Find money or validation ticket

Most bus systems require payment while entering the vehicle. Some systems – especially bus rapid transit systems – require payment or validation within the bus stop environment. If this is required, then suitable provision has to be made. It is often the case that this is woefully insufficient, causing queues that interfere with the pedestrian environment or leaving passengers frustrated and subjected to inclement weather. Especially where income levels are low or the local economy is essentially cash-based (often both of these apply), people will not be willing to buy large advance credit for their bus travel. Therefore, they need to pay for each journey separately or for a small number of journeys at a time and this means that they will visit the payment (rather than the validation) system more often. The number of payment points needs to reflect this. Standard queuing theory will give a reasonable estimate of the number of points required but it will only give an answer according to the data with which it is fed. So the arrival rate of paying customers used in the calculations needs to be realistic and future-proofed. Whether payment has been made in advance or only at the time of travel, there will need to be some form of validation process. In more sophisticated systems this can be some form of smart card (e.g. Oyster in London, Octopus in Hong Kong, Suica in Tokyo) or, as recently implemented in London contactless bank cards. In these cases the validation time is very short and can often be accommodated within the time taken to walk a couple of metres. So a ticket can be validated as the person enters the bus stop, but this requires a validation machine/reader which can prevent illicit travel. These tend to be cumbersome – they involve some form of gate which either needs to be opened to allow access (e.g. as in London) or closed to deny access (as in Tokyo). They also mean that the bus stop is segregated from the pedestrian environment, and present accessibility problems which need to be resolved (usually by having the gates sufficiently wide or (more commonly) an additional wide gate). So these are not really feasible for most bus stops outside a BRT-type system. However, most bus systems require payment or validation on entry to the vehicle (see Stage 8 of Table 4.4).

Identify the correct bus

Especially where there are several bus services calling at the same bus stop, it is crucial that it is possible to identify the correct bus. The first stage of this should have been completed in Stage 1 (see Table 4.4) – making sure that the person is waiting at the correct bus stop. The process of identifying the correct bus starts some distance away. Real-time information at the bus stop, such as London's Countdown system, is very helpful for this as it indicates the sequence of oncoming buses. However, the identity of the bus service – usually a number – and its destination should be visible from a considerable distance away. The gathering up of bags and so on, which were rearranged during Stage 3 of Table 4.4 and moving to the boarding point can only really start once the pedenger knows that their bus is arriving, and the more time they have for this the easier it will be for them. Better preparation by the person for the bus arrival will also mean a smoother operation when it arrives. So a combination of easy visual identification of the bus service (large, simple numbers and lettering), combined with easily read and understood real-time information at the bus stop are necessary.

It is also important to ensure that bus services are consistent. The problems arising from the short-turning of buses are discussed in Stage 10 of Table 4.4. As far as the pedenger at the bus stop is concerned, the difficulty arises because a bus indicating that it is a particular service number could arrive with a different destination from other buses which otherwise look identical. This is really confusing, especially for people with cognitive difficulties, vision impairments, poor knowledge of the local (or not so local) geography and others unfamiliar with the system, such as tourists and visitors. Bus services should never have more than one destination except in the case of emergency, when significant information must be made available at all bus stops that are affected so that confusion is avoided.

In terms of accessibility, identifying the correct bus needs to be possible from the height of a person seated in a wheelchair, and for vision – or hearing-impaired people – and it has to retain the consistency needed by people with cognitive difficulties.

4.4. Boarding/alighting the buses
4.4.1 Pedenger to passenger

So, the bus arrives at the bus stop. At the bus stop, the pedenger is in the final stages of becoming a passenger and is now ready to board the vehicle. Inside the bus, the alighting passenger is finally emerging as a pedenger. We therefore have to think about how to complete the process of transition so that the pedengers become a passenger on the bus and a pedestrian in the bus stop. This occurs during the boarding and alighting process. These actions must be accommodated in an accessible way so that the bus is genuinely available to all members of society.

Locate the correct door

Many urban buses have more than one door and therefore it is necessary to know which door(s) are available for boarding. This should be clearly indicated at the bus stop so that people who are unfamiliar with the system can understand how it works and what they should do – including which door they should use to board the bus. It is also essential to be clear about where the bus will stop. Making this consistent is essential for people with visual impairments and those who find it difficult to manoeuvre. Boarding the bus is difficult enough without having to walk up and down to find the door. Marking the surface of the bus stop platform with clear information about the location of the door, in such a way that helps the driver to be consistent (see Chapter 5 for more details), helps people feel more comfortable and reduces the pressure on them to cope with the boarding process in a crowded situation and under severe time constraints. If the number of services is sufficiently high, these can be separated into two bus stops. In these cases, the different stops must be easily identifiable – with signage at each stop to indicate which services stop at which and where the 'other' stop is located – this is part of facilitating successful completion of Stage 1 of Table 4.4.

It is also essential that the bus service can be identified easily when the bus is at the stop. This means having the service and destination indicated on the side of the vehicle in such a way that people at the bus stop can see them and on the back of the bus (it seems to have escaped some bus manufacturers that prospective passengers do sometimes approach the bus from behind).

In terms of accessibility, this needs to be possible from the height of a person seated in a wheelchair, and for vision – or hearing-impaired people – and, it has to retain the consistency needed by people with cognitive difficulties.

In some cases, wheelchair users must use a particular door (because of the availability of a ramp, for example) and this must be made apparent in plenty of time before the bus arrives. This might place them in a different position in relation to the rest of the bus queue and therefore the bus driver needs to be alert to the presence of a wheelchair user as they approach the stop.

There needs to be some communication between the person in the wheelchair and the driver to establish that the ramp is required – this is much easier if the bus stop-vehicle design has achieved level access, of course, but they might need to board the bus at a different door from other passengers. Other people with disabilities may have similar problems – if they are unable to see the bus coming it might be difficult to establish communication with them.

Step onto the bus

The main activity of the boarding process is of course to step onto the bus. The previous stages simply prepare the person for this stage and insufficiency in any one of the previous six will make the process of actually stepping onto the bus more difficult. This process is the focal point of the interface between the bus and the platform infrastructure.

In terms of the requirements, what is needed is clear and unambiguous space on the platform adjacent to where the door(s) will be when the bus stops. 'Clear' means that the space should be unobstructed and easily accessible so that wheelchair users, visually impaired people, and people with locomotory limitations can arrange themselves comfortably in relation to the door to provide them with the most accessible entrance. 'Unambiguous' means that this space should be obviously identifiable as being available for this purpose.

The bus needs to be designed in such a way that the doorway is wide enough, with sufficient supports, to enable easy boarding. The bus floor needs to be delivered at a level that is sufficiently low to allow step-free entry to the vehicle and sufficiently close to the platform to enable entry to the vehicle without an excessively large step over a horizontal gap. Although all buses should be equipped with a ramp, deployment of ramps is problematic. It takes a long time to deploy and the space requirements for the platform are extensive. If the bus delivery can be achieved so that a ramp is not required (i.e. the vertical and horizontal gaps are sufficiently small) the design of the bus stop environment would be easier and smooth and quick boarding would be much easier to achieve.

When standing or walking on a flat surface, normally the human body's centre of mass is normally located slightly forward of the physical body at about the height of the midriff. This is because the body naturally leans slightly forward. The action of stepping upwards, as on entering a bus, works quite well with the body's equilibrium systems because the shift of balance can be accommodated easily by the fact that the leading foot encounters the stair earlier than they would have encountered the ground when walking along a flat surface, thus correcting for the imbalance. Stumbles and trips while climbing stairs are rarely the result of imbalance. Usually they arise from an underestimate of the height of the stair and thus the amount by which the foot should be raised in order to clear it. This is affected by the extent to which the person is aware of the position of their foot relative to their ankle (older people often have a condition, peroneal nerve injury ('drop foot') which means that the toe is not as high as they think it is). Stairs are normally tackled as a set and a slight difference in height of one stair in a flight can also cause the person to trip.

In the case of a wheelchair user, this will often require a ramp between the bus stop platform and the bus. The manoeuvre required is a huge amount of work (which is why it really is worth finding a way of not needing a ramp for this purpose) and requires a large amount of space at the bus stop platform – for the appropriate ramp length and the space required for the wheelchair before the ramp – and the space required by the wheelchair user (or their assistant) to gather enough momentum to make it up the ramp.

Initiate payment/validation

Payment or validation is often done by paying the driver or paying into or validating a machine located near to the boarding point. This imposes a massive delay – experiments in Pamela suggest that merely validating a smart card on entry to the bus reduces the boarding flow rate by as much as 15%. Where payment is made is a question of trust. The further into the boarding process it occurs, the more potential there is to evade payment or validation. The more courteous the city becomes, the less of an issue it would be to have the payment/validation separated entirely from the boarding process. During the period when articulated buses were in use in London, several Oyster Card readers were placed inside the vehicle so that ticket validation could occur after boarding had been completed and the bus was in motion. This was a contributory factor to the high boarding and alighting rates obtained with these vehicles. There was, however, a perception that there was a high level of fare evasion. In fact, these buses were not any more prone to fare evasion than other buses; the problem was that passengers with multitrip tickets, such as Travelcards or bus passes, were not required to validate their Oyster Card and so it appeared that many people were not paying for their journey. As approximately 95% of passengers had such tickets, the appearance of non-payment led to the widespread belief that the buses were a licence for free travel. The simple solution would have been to require all passengers to validate their Oyster Card. Separating the validation from the boarding process has a very positive impact on the boarding rate, thus on the bus dwell time, thus on the journey time and thus to the operating cost of the service. It is therefore an essential element of making the service accessible.

Move inside the vehicle

The final stage of the transition from pedenger to passenger and the final element of the boarding process is the move into the vehicle and release of the space for the following person who wishes to board the vehicle. This needs to be rapid in order to maintain an appropriate and comfortable boarding rate. The process requires the space between the boarding space inside the vehicle and the pathway to the passenger saloon to be free of obstacles, including other passengers. So standing in that area should be limited and the physical design needs to permit a smooth flow. This can be complicated by the physical needs of the vehicle – for example, wheel arches – which narrow the available space. The New Bus for London has a problem with this space at the rear door, where the entry to the lower passenger saloon is only 60 cm wide, and involves a sharp turn to the left and negotiating the space between the door edge and the stairs (and the conductor whose standing position is also between the stairs and the entry to the lower saloon. This means that the boarding platform can only contain two, possibly three, people before stasis occurs and thus the rear door becomes extremely slow in terms of its rate of boarding. This in turn becomes the restricting element on the bus dwell time at the stop. As a result, there is a risk that operating buses of this design places a space requirement – to accommodate the queuing people on the bus stop platform until this process is completed.

Once inside the vehicle, the passenger needs to be able to find their travelling position – seated or standing – so that the vehicle can move off without causing a loss in balance. Xenia Karekla's experiments (see Chapter 5 for more details on these) show that the ability to respond to a change in acceleration (jerk) is much harder for older participants compared with younger people. Younger people can absorb these through their ankles, knees and hips in order to maintain their equilibrium, whereas older people are less able to achieve such an outcome – sometimes amplifying rather than absorbing the effect – and have to resort to grabbing hand rails or grab poles in order to avoid falling. Making sure that the bus design allows for seats near to the doors to reduce exposure to this risk is helpful. Controlling the bus accelerations is also a requirement, although how this can be achieved most successfully is still under investigation.

A wheelchair user will need to be able to find and position themselves in the appropriate space in the vehicle. This requires sufficient space, not only for the wheelchair to be parked while the bus is moving, but also to reach and manoeuvre into the space. This depends on the arrangements of grab poles, seat designs and so on in the area approaching the wheelchair space.

With this stage completed, pedengers are finally converted into passengers. To convert them back again we need to consider the alighting process.

4.4.2   Passenger to pedenger
Locating the correct stop
One of the biggest criticisms of bus systems is the sense that the passenger does not know where they are, or where they have to alight. If there is a member of the crew available to help passengers that can be one way of reducing this problem. However, in many cases this is not possible. If the bus is a one-person-operation vehicle, it is neither reliable nor reasonable to expect the driver to remember to advise passengers of the current location of the vehicle. Modern location systems, such as the i-Bus system in London, provide location information which is sufficiently accurate for information to be provided to passengers visually and audibly so that forthcoming bus stops are announced. It is also helpful to have a service map which indicates where the bus is (such a map is beginning to become more common in metro systems). Some cities, London included, have mobile applications that provide this information to those passengers who have access to a smartphone.

An important problem that affects people who are less familiar with the local geography, and people who are likely to be confused by the unfamiliar, is when a bus is being diverted from its normal line of route. In such a circumstance, it is essential that passengers are advised that the bus is on a diversion, which stops will and will not be served, and how these changes will affect the service to passengers in terms of their delivery to their chosen bus stop and activities. It is simply not enough just to say that the bus is on diversion. This also applies to operational changes to the service, such as the turning short of a bus at some point short of its destination. This is an extremely undesirable practice, which arises out of a belief that it will repair damage to the bus service in the opposite direction (which is a highly contentious idea) or to other operational failures, such as the attempt to avoid overtime payments due to the late running of a bus causing the driver to over-run their working shift. This is a practice that should be discouraged as it is confusing to passengers and extremely troublesome for people who find it difficult to cope with the process of engaging with the bus system, including older and disabled people. Issues for people waiting at downstream bus stops (if the bus is still in operation as it approaches those stops – of course, if the bus has been turned short before those stops all they will notice is the lack of a bus) were mentioned in Stage 5 of Table 4.4. For passengers on the bus, this frustrating exercise means that they have to consider how to proceed to their destination. This could be simply waiting for the next bus on the same service, or it could mean taking other opportunities to complete their journey. To make this choice, the passengers need sufficient information – about when the next bus will arrive, what other opportunities will be available, how fares might be transferred to the new service, and so on.

Informing the driver that a passenger wishes to alight at the next stop is essential. This should be possible before leaving their seat so that people can remain seated for as long as possible to reduce the risk of falling over as the bus moves. This means that there should be a means of communication (usually a bell push) within easy reach of every seat.

On-bus information, whatever the reason for needing it, must be accessible for everyone. Visual and audible announcements are obviously a necessity, but they must be visible and audible from the seats which older and disabled people might be using. Bearing in mind that, in some buses, wheelchair users and some passengers will be facing backwards, this means that visual signage also needs to be mounted at the rear of the vehicle where it would be visible to someone seated in a wheelchair and facing backwards.

Many bus systems now have systems that update passengers on the next bus stop but it is also necessary to know where the bus is in relation to its route as a whole. In London, this information is easily obtained through various smartphone apps, but so far it is not available on the bus itself. It should not be too difficult to incorporate this information dynamically and display it in the bus.

Gather belongings

Similar to the process involved in preparing to board the bus, alighting means having to shift from the in-vehicle environment to the outside. If the passenger is seated, this will mean collecting their belongings – possibly this involves standing up and moving to collect them, or more often it means simply being able to pick up the bags and make them ready to be carried through the vehicle. A similar process will be required for a standing passenger and this involves different issues. For example, bags placed on the floor of the vehicle (e.g. between the passenger's feet) need to be retrieved, which means bending down, for which movement there might be insufficient space because of the positions of other passengers.

Move to the correct door

Having retrieved the bags it is necessary to move to the door. This is a tricky manoeuvre because almost certainly the bus is in motion at the time, likely to decelerate and turn towards the kerb in order to arrive at the bus stop. This is discussed in more detail in Chapter 5. One of the great advantages of having more continuous information available to passengers than just the name of the next stop is that passengers can begin to prepare earlier for their departure from the bus. The announcement of the next bus stop does not usually say how much time there is before arrival, so the assumption tends to be that arrival is imminent and people start to prepare while the bus is in motion. If there were a continual display of the bus location along the route as well, the passengers could decide more calmly when they needed to start gathering their bags etc. If it were possible to avoid people having to move inside the vehicle while it was in motion that would be a really good answer, but this is unlikely to be achieved. Good information systems could help to reduce the problem though. Knowing which is the correct door to exit from is an important issue around familiarity (or rather, lack of it) with the system and so needs to be indicated clearly throughout the vehicle. This applies even more strongly to wheelchair users, who are often restricted to using only one particular door because of the ramp or other facilities located there.

Initiate payment/validation (this is rare but is the case in some countries, for example Japan)

In some countries, in order to reduce delays in the boarding process, fare payment/ validation is done on exit, rather than entry. The rationale is that the 'slow' part of the process – the transaction – takes place on the vehicle prior to the bus arriving at the bus stop and therefore will not delay the alighting process. This is quite rare in prac- tice and only really works when the passenger flows are quite low because it still requires the passengers to reach the validation or payment point. This results in a need to start the process of moving towards the door rather earlier than might otherwise have been the case and thus the increased risk of being unbalanced by the movements of the vehicle.

Step off the bus

Leaving the vehicle is often underplayed, if not ignored, in the bus operational process, yet it is one of the most complex manoeuvres we require of the passengers. In Stage 7 of Table 4.3 I raised some issues that arise when stepping upwards. When stepping down- wards, however, the centre of mass is too far forwards, resulting in a tendency to fall forwards. This is made worse if the person is wearing varifocal lenses as the best viewing area within the lens for the relevant distance is around the centre. This makes the person instinctively tend to rotate their head downwards, and this in turn tends to cause them to lean slightly forwards, thus pushing their centre of mass even further forward. Alighting with a step downwards is therefore a complicated affair. It is therefore necessary to reduce the height of any downward step as far as possible.

In relation to wheelchairs, the comments above about boarding the bus apply also to the process of leaving the bus. Of course in this case the issues around a lack of balance do not apply in relation to tipping over backwards, but they do apply in relation to moving down a ramp. It is important that this manoeuvre is made under control so that the des- cent to the footway level is properly managed without risk to the wheelchair occupant, their assistant or anyone else in the vicinity.

4.4.3 Pedenger to pedestrian

Rearrange bags

Having stepped off the vehicle, the pedenger then needs to rearrange their bags and belongings because they are now in a much wider space than they were when inside the vehicle and they are less constrained – and less supported – by their surroundings. The usual reaction in such circumstances is to stop, sort out the bags and then proceed along the footway. This impedes the following pedenger and thus creates a hiatus in the alighting process.

Orient themselves to the new environment

Before the pedenger can proceed, they need to know which way to go. At a familiar bus stop, that might be easy to do, but it can be much more complicated at a stop which they do not use very often. This causes them to pause in order to find their bearings. Clear signage at the bus stop, which is easy to locate and see, is therefore a vital part of the process of maintaining the flow of passengers away from the vehicle.

In terms of accessibility, this needs to be possible from the height of a person seated in a wheelchair, and for vision – or hearing-impaired people – and, it has to retain the consistency needed by people with cognitive difficulties. Keeping the form of this information consistent throughout the city makes this much easier. The Legible London project in London is achieving this with great success, incorporating the same information style throughout the entire pedestrian network and transport systems (e.g. in stations). Some employers are also adopting this in relation to their own premises, particularly when they expect members of the public to pass through.

Move away from the bus stop (free up space for the next pedenger)

The final part of the whole process is therefore to move away from the bus stop, for which it is necessary to ensure that the pedestrian environment has suitable capacity and is of sufficient quality to make this as effortless as possible for people whatever their capabilities.

This discussion has set out the sort of needs arising from the whole process of interacting with the bus stop. Now I will turn to how to approach these challengers.

4.5. Interfaces at the bus stop

If we really want public transport to be fully accessible, we must learn how to design all the elements of the system to meet the requirements indicated in the previous section. This means placing people's needs at the forefront of the design process. Too often, current design processes satisfy the engineering, planning and commercial requirements, and the people who will be using these – or having to deal with them being used by others – are only considered afterwards. Accessibility works the other way around: the engineering and commercial decisions should really be about how to meet the users' needs. The approach advocated in this book is to learn what people aspire to do to improve their wellbeing and that of society, and what is needed from the bus system in order for them to do that. We then determine how the bus system can meet those needs by enabling the whole population to use the bus system. One element of this is to work out how to ensure that a bus stop can be designed to play its part in reducing barriers to travel.

It is necessary to plan to meet the people's needs first, then to adjust the project according to technical and economic restrictions, bearing in mind that each element that is removed as a result of these restrictions will affect group(s) of people and might exclude them from the public transport system. With this process, decision-makers know what they can offer and who will suffer as a result. Where they cannot offer suitable accessibility within their project, decision-makers must know what alternatives they will have to provide so that genuine access is available to everyone.

Converting people's needs into bus stop design requires detailed consideration of four groups of interactions:

1 between the people in the pedestrian environment and the people at the bus stop
2 between the people and the bus stop
3 between the people and the vehicle
4 between the vehicle and the bus stop.

It is important to include all four in the design of a fully accessible bus stop as the exclusion of one could negate the benefits from the others.

In the first edition of this book, Martha Caiafa and I described the Excalibur project, which was set up in 1998 to investigate what was required of bus stop infrastructure in order to enable a greater number of disabled people to use the bus system. We started by exploring the interfaces between users, bus stop and vehicle, and converting these into a specification for the design of an accessible bus stop. The Excalibur project studied the following three basic areas:

1 Physical access to the vehicle:
   (a) to ensure consistent ease of access for passengers between buses and bus stop platforms
   (b) to avoid the need for specialised equipment to enable boarding and alighting from buses
   (c) to enable buses to reach the bus stop platforms at all times.
2 Use of space at the platform:
   (a) to have adequate shelter, seats and space for passengers at bus stops
   (b) to promote comfort, security and safety.
3 Information provision:
   (a) to provide clear, understandable and appropriate information to bus passengers.

We carried out a number of experiments on a specially constructed site in the Royal Docks in London to help us to determine ways of addressing these problems in a controlled environment before adding the complications of in-service operation on-street. Excalibur explicitly studied bus stops and not the pedestrian footway – this followed later.

Before discussing the various elements of an accessible bus stop it is useful to be clear about the terminology we shall be using. Figure 4.17 shows a conceptual bus stop, indicating the various terms we shall be using.

1 The *footway* is the space used by pedestrians by which they reach their desired activities from the bus stop (or vice versa).
2 The *roadway* is the space used by vehicles (including buses) and is usually bounded by a footway on either side.
3 The *kerb* is the boundary between the *footway* and the *roadway*.
4 The *bus stop platform* is the surface of the bus stop which is used by people waiting for the bus – or by other pedestrians using it as a 'good place to be'. The platform might be indistinguishable in physical terms from the footway in many

Figure 4.17 Glossary of terms of an accessible bus stop

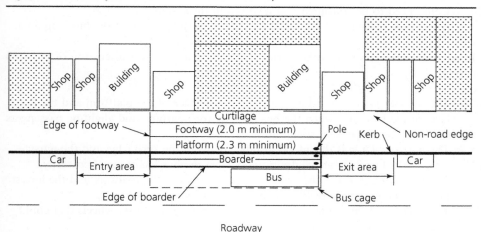

cases, but we need to design it specifically to be part of the accessible interface between the buses and the pedestrian space on the footway. Every bus stop has a platform, even where it is not identifiable as a physically separate infrastructure: the platform constitutes the area from which they board buses and at which they arrive when alighting buses.

5   The *edge of the footway* is usually delineated by a kerb in an urban area, but this may not be the case in a rural area (if there is a footway at all) or in shared space schemes. The edge of the footway is therefore the boundary between the *footway* and the *roadway* used by traffic or the *bus stop platform*.

6   The *entry area* is the space defined by the distance required by a bus to move from the driving line (the line it follows along the roadway in normal driving conditions) to the kerb. This depends on the approach angle required to reach the bus stop.

7   A *boarder* is a *bus stop platform* (or part of one) that has been constructed into the roadway. These can be either *full boarders* (extended into the road by at least 2 m) or *half boarders* (extended by about 1 m).

8   The *exit area* is the space defined by the distance required by a bus to move safely from the stopping position to the driving line.

9   The *edge of the pedestrian area* is the physical limit of the space between the roadway and the building line, fencing or other boundary of the street space.

10 The *curtilage* is a term under UK law which describes the space between the *edge of the pedestrian area* and the legal limit of the public footway. The boundary between the curtilage and the *edge of the pedestrian area* marks the edge of the part of the footway that is under the control of the highway authority and may be coincident with the *edge of the pedestrian area*, but might not be. The curtilage may be owned by a building owner and, as such, is not technically part of the footway. This is important if it is necessary to make changes to the

footway in order to make the bus stop accessible, as the owner of the curtilage would need to be consulted and involved in the scheme.

11 A *bus cage* is the set of markings on the roadway that delimit the bus stop area.

In addition, there are some other terms that will be used in our discussion of bus stop design.

12 The *vertical gap* is the distance between the surface of the platform and the floor level of the bus door when the bus is ready for boarding and alighting passengers (i.e. with the suspension system lowered).

13 The *horizontal gap* is the lateral distance between the kerb edge and the outside edge of the bus floor at the doorway(s) when the bus has stopped correctly.

14 The *ground clearance* is the vertical distance between the roadway and the lowest point of the underside of the bus overhang areas at the kerb edge.

15 The *front overhang* is the area of the bus in front of the front wheels that could overhang the platform as the bus approaches the kerb.

16 The *lateral overhang* is the gap between the side of the bus body and the outside surface of the tyre.

17 The *rear overhang* is the area of the bus behind the rear wheels that could overhang the platform as the bus leaves the kerb.

18 The *skirt* is the lower body panel along the nearside of the bus between the wheels.

The key objective for the interface between users and the vehicle is to ensure consistent ease of access for passengers between buses and bus stop platforms. Passengers have problems when the gap between the bus and the platform is too big. There are two gaps to consider: vertical and horizontal. This is often mitigated by the use of a ramp, but this is quite inconvenient for both people in wheelchairs and operators so it would be helpful if we could find a way of eliminating the need for a ramp while increasing the accessibility of the person-vehicle interface.

In 1997, the German government published some research which showed a relationship between horizontal and vertical gaps, which is illustrated in Figure 4.18. This suggests that the maximum horizontal gap should be 50 mm and the maximum vertical gap should be 100 mm, although problems increase with the latter as the gap increases from 50 mm to 100 mm.

However, more recent experience in London Underground has indicated that there are significant problems with small vertical gaps. This follows the introduction of low-floor trains where the vertical gap between the train floor and the platform is between 5 and 10 mm (see Figure 4.19). It has been observed that the number of trips and stumbles on these trains is some six times the number on older trains with higher floors. I believe that the reason for this follows from the way vision has evolved. As discussed in Section 4.1.2, the major part of our vision system used for high quality vision – such as reading this book or looking out of the window – is undertaken by the central fovea, which is a very small part of the retina dedicated to high resolution, high quality colour/contrast vision. The rest of the vision system is dedicated to lower quality peripheral vision, which is

Figure 4.18 Gap dimensions recommended by the Federal Ministry of Transport in Germany (Bundesministerium für Verkehr, 1997)

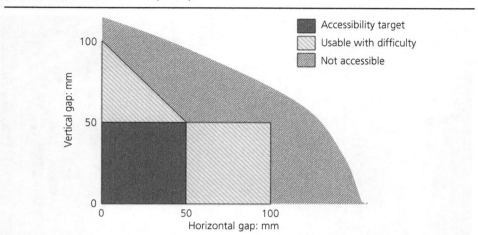

capable of detecting movement, but not shape or colour to the same extent as the foveal vision. The location of the train floor and platform – and thus the vertical gap – is found in the lower area of the peripheral vision field – a very poor area indeed – so there is only very poor quality vision available to alert the brain of a potential hazard. Unless there is a real stimulus to alert the brain to the need for action, no action will be taken – so there would be no action to raise the foot to clear such a small gap. What is needed is a way to alert the brain of the gap without doing this by increasing the size of the gap to a level which would be unattainable for wheelchair users without the use of a ramp.

Figure 4.18 shows that there is some tolerance towards the vertical gap if the horizontal gap is smaller. Thus, a vertical gap of 75 mm could be tolerated if the horizontal gap were 25 mm. However, if the horizontal gap is more than 50 mm, the vertical gap can be no more than 50 mm. In no case should either gap be more than 100 mm. Our findings broadly support this view in relation to wheelchairs, but we have noticed a problem for other people in relation to the visibility of the vertical gap when it is small.

Another issue for many passengers is the location of the door of the bus when it arrives. Uncertainty about this changes people's perceptions of where to wait to be ready to board the bus. This is a particular barrier to people who need to prepare more carefully to board the bus or for whom the doorway is less obvious (e.g. people with low vision).

As buses become longer and have more doors for the driver to oversee, the rear-view mirrors need to be larger and positioned further away from the vehicle body. Figure 4.20 shows the mirror cluster on a bus in Kassel, Germany. Three mirrors are provided to assist the driver in positioning the bus. The main mirror is the standard rear-view mirror used for locating the rear corner of the bus. A second mirror enables the driver to check the position of the side of the bus relative to the platform so that it is easier to see how

Figure 4.19 Circle Line train in London, showing reduced vertical gap between the train and platform

Figure 4.20 The mirror cluster used in Kassel, Germany

well the centre and rear doors are aligned with the platform. Finally, the third mirror allows the driver to see exactly the position of the front door relative to the platform. However, the cluster, and in particular the large rear-view mirror, is very large and presents a potential obstacle. Figure 4.20 shows the position of the cluster relative to the height of a passenger standing on the platform. Current buses in London have four cameras on the outside of the vehicle to make it easier for the driver to see what is happening all around the vehicle. These do not preclude the use of well-positioned mirrors, but they do represent less of a hazard to people waiting at the bus stop. There is a good case for examining how cameras could be better deployed on the exterior of buses. This not only applies to helping the driver at the bus stops, but also for avoiding other obstacles, including cyclists, on the rear side of the vehicle.

4.5.1   Problem: Gaps between the bus and the platform
Vertical gaps

The vertical gap is a design issue related to the design of buses and platforms and, as indicated in Figure 4.21, is an issue of concern both to highway engineers and the bus operators who purchase the vehicles. One way to tackle this is to raise the platform level so that it is nearer to the height of the bus floor at the doorway. If the platform is raised above the 'standard' kerb height, the stop must be designed so that the bus can always reach the kerb with a small horizontal gap. If a passenger has to step down to the road level in order to walk to the bus, the higher kerbs will make this harder rather than easier than would be the case with the current kerb heights. However, increasing the kerb

Figure 4.21 The elements of a bus stop and their interactions

Vehicle characteristics	Platform characteristics	Bus stop layout	

• Type
• Overall length
• Front overhang
• Lateral overhang
• Wheelbase
• Ground clearance
  (ride height and lowered)
• Door positions
	• Length
	• Width
	• Height
	• Crossfall
	• Kerb profile
	• Connection to footway
	• Drainage system
		• Kerbside
		• Full boarder
		• Half boarder
		• Bay
		• Single berth
		• Multiple berth
		• Parking/traffic
		  implications
			Interests of highway and traffic engineers

	Interface: gaps	Interface: manoeuvres	
	• Vertical gap • Horizontal gap	• Approach • Alignment • Stopping • Exit	Interests of bus drivers
Vehicle	Vehicle–platform interface	Platform	Vehicle–bus stop layout interface	Bus stop layout	Interests of the users
• Comfort • Security • Cleanness	• Safety • Easy access	• Width • Crossfall • Even • Consistent	• Any, as long as it is accessible	• Shelter • Information	

height could cause problems for buses as they approach the stop, and therefore care is needed to design the bus stop infrastructure to eliminate any such problem. Simply increasing the kerb and platform height by raising a standard kerb is not an option, as this will cause problems for both buses and drivers (I will consider the bus–kerb interface in more detail below). At this point, however, we are considering the effects on the passenger side of the bus stop, including the effects on footway design and construction and the aim here should be to minimise the vertical gap as far as possible and to try to achieve level access. This is likely to be achieved only by making the bus more adaptive to the kerb height offered by the bus stop.

Horizontal gaps

In order to reduce the horizontal gap, it is necessary to be able to bring the bus very close to the kerb. It is important to recognise that the position of the bus when it is stopped at a bus stop is the focal midpoint of a series of actions taken by the bus driver, starting many metres upstream of the bus stop and ending many metres downstream. A difference in the driving line before or after the bus stop, the approach angle, the point at which the driver begins to turn towards the kerb, or the driver's view of their exit path from the stop determines a difference in the horizontal gap and longitudinal position of the bus when the driver has brought it to a stop. The horizontal gap, as indicated in Figure 4.22, is a design issue for bus drivers and involves the detailed design of the kerbs and the approach to the bus stop. Apart from being a matter of infrastructure and bus design it should also be a major element of drivers' training programmes. In our experiments, we were looking for consistent stopping positions and small horizontal

Figure 4.22 Footway markings for a bus stop in Leipzig

gaps, and therefore we had to find ways of making the bus approach path more consistent.

The vehicle using a bus stop has to have a floor height that is sufficiently low in order to obtain a satisfactory vertical gap. It also needs the ground clearance to be high enough to pass over the kerb without causing damage to either the kerb or the vehicle. The most satisfactory results will be attained when the floor height and platform height are set to produce a vertical gap within the limits indicated in Figure 4.18. However, this requires a degree of co-operation between the purchaser (and manufacturers) of the vehicles and the designers (and manufacturers) of the infrastructure that has hitherto been all too rare.

The need for a small horizontal gap means that the driver has to bring the bus close to the kerb without damaging either the vehicle or the kerb. Drivers are normally trained to stay away from kerbs because of the damage that can arise as a result of a moving steel object striking a stationary concrete one. In addition to designing the infrastructure (and vehicle) to ensure that no damage occurs, it is necessary to counteract many years of experience and habit before a driver will feel confident about bringing a bus so close to the kerb. It is also essential to bring the bus parallel to the kerb. This requires a platform length which is rather longer than has hitherto been expected at a bus stop.

We found in the Excalibur experiments that the approach to the bus stop was highly critical and needed to be determined several metres upstream of the stop. This supported the findings of the research done in France by Uster *et al.* (1997). The special kerbs used to help the driver align the bus required a very specific approach angle to work properly, and this proved difficult for the drivers to maintain without some form of guidance.

4.5.1.1 Gaps: approaches to resolving the gap challenge
Floor height: Step
The EU Buses and Coaches Directive 2001/85/EC followed the UK Public Service Vehicles Accessibility Regulations (2000) (PSVA, 2000a, 2000b), which stipulate that the entry floor height of a bus at a bus stop should be 250 mm above ground level, but this does not take into account the need for a small vertical gap and the consequent constraint on platform height (the UK regulation was subsequently amended in 2005 (DfT, 2005b) to offer the alternative of compliance with the EU Directive 2001/85/EC). The vertical gap can be reduced by using a lowering mechanism within the suspension system. This mechanism allows the bus to have a relatively high floor height while travelling, and can lower the bus to provide a floor height that will provide a better interface with the platform. Thus the platform height can be increased, while still allowing the ground clearance to be practical for buses under driving conditions. Modern lowering and raising systems take a very short time to operate and do not materially affect the dwell time. Many drivers lower the bus at every stop because they feel that this speeds boarding (in some countries this is a requirement).

One issue that arose during our Excalibur experiments was the variability of the ground clearance between different vehicles and even for the same vehicle over the course of a day. Accessibility requirements now make it necessary to keep this issue under constant review. This could be done by moving the control of the regulator valve to the driver's cabin and ensuring that the appropriate height is set before starting on each journey, or by making it adjustable to the bus stop in each case, as is the case with aircraft and jet-ways at airports.

Whereas reducing the vertical gap is an issue of infrastructure and vehicle design, the reduction in the horizontal gap is largely a matter of enhancing driving skills. Nevertheless, it is possible to assist the driver with the help of a number of aspects of the design of the infrastructure. The most obvious of these is the kerb profile, which needs to be able to accommodate the tyre or wheel of the bus in such a way that the vehicle is always able to stop at the same point relative to the kerb edge. Cooperation between vehicle manufacturers and infrastructure designers would enable the kerb to be designed so that it can accommodate the tyre at road level and the bodywork of the vehicle at platform level. We discuss these profiles in more detail below.

Sufficient platform length is necessary. It has been found that reductions in platform length beyond a certain threshold result in poor and inconsistent performance in terms of being close and parallel to the kerb.

The accuracy of the approach can be improved dramatically if a guidance system is incorporated in the design of the bus stop.

One of the features of accessible bus transport is that it makes greater and more detailed calls on the manufacturers of both vehicle and infrastructure to produce designs geared to work with the detailed requirements of the interface between the vehicle and platform. I have already made some comments with respect to the suspension height. Another essential change is to regularise the lateral overhang so that the infrastructure which guides the wheels or tyres always delivers the bodywork (and thus the horizontal gap) to the same place with respect to the kerb edge, whatever the type or manufacturer of the bus.

Height: Ramps
Vertical and horizontal gaps can be bridged by means of a boarding device. The UK Public Service Vehicles Accessibility Regulations (PSVA, 2000a, 2000b) specify that buses should be installed with a boarding device such as a lift or a ramp. If the bus stops are well designed and the drivers well trained, these should only need to be used *in extremis* (e.g. when the kerb cannot be reached properly for some reason, or if a wheelchair user has a particular difficulty at the stop in question). Ideally, the design of the bus stop should be geared towards providing the best assistance to the driver and the wheelchair users to be able to achieve fully accessible operation without the need of a ramp. This is better for everyone, as it is less stigmatising for the users and reduces the dwell time.

Nevertheless, designers also need to check the likely distance of the bus from the kerb. If a boarding device is required ramps are easier and quicker to deploy than lifts, especially if they are organised so that the driver can operate them without having to leave the cab.

Even so, a powered ramp takes some 15 s to extend or retract once activated by the driver. In addition and prior to starting the ramp, the driver has to ensure that no obstacle or person could obstruct the ramp movement and that the operation will be safe. This is a lot easier (and quicker) if the ramp is situated at the front door of the vehicle, because the driver has a clear view of the ramp, its operation and use. Even so, use of the ramp could easily add 30–60 s to the dwell time at the bus stop. Where a centre door is provided, it is usually easier to enter and leave the bus by the centre door because this means that they do not have to negotiate the space between the front wheels on their way to the wheelchair space in the bus. This is more difficult for the driver to manage and places the ramp mechanism in one of the most damage-prone parts of the vehicle. There is no easy solution to this issue (other than designing so that a ramp is unnecessary): the important point is to make sure that whatever is done is consistent so that people understand how they are expected to enter and leave the bus when it arrives at the stop.

A ramp to cover a vertical gap of 125 mm at 7° (12.5%) needs to extend about 1 m from the bus. As noted above, the key constraint here is the need to accommodate a wheelchair user leaving the bus. A wheelchair user cannot begin to turn the chair until all its wheels are free of the ramp, so there needs to be a distance of at least 1.5 m (ideally 2.3 m) beyond the end of the ramp before any obstacle (e.g. the back of the shelter, a wall, passengers' feet, shopping) is encountered in front of the wheelchair. The amount of space required on the platform as a result of this depends on the size of the horizontal gap. To cover all eventualities, assume that the bus has pulled up with a horizontal gap of 0 mm, and therefore we need to allow for the full extension of the ramp from the expected floor height to the platform height at the correct gradient. Example ramp lengths for a variety of vertical gaps and ramp gradients are given in Table 4.9.

Table 4.9 Ramp lengths (mm) given selected gradients for different vertical gaps

Vertical gap: mm	Gradient of ramp*			
	5%	8%	12.5%	14%
50	1000	625.0	400	355.8
75	1500	937.5	600	533.7
100	2000	1250.0	800	711.5
125	2500	1562.5	1000	889.4
140	2800	1750.0	1120	996.2
150	3000	1875.0	1200	1067.3
160	3200	2000.0	1280	1138.5
175	3500	2187.5	1400	1245.2
180	3600	2250.0	1440	1280.8
200	4000	2500.0	1600	1423.1
220	4400	2750.0	1760	1565.4

Note: 5% = 1 in 20 = 2.86°; 8% = 1 in 12 = 4.6°; 12.5% = 1 in 8 = 7.13°; 14% = 1 in 7 = 8°

Ramp angles are a problematic issue: many wheelchair users would like to have smaller gradients, but, as Table 4.9 shows, the resulting ramps would often be very long. It should also be noted that the balance of a wheelchair can be quite eccentric: the weight distribution is often thought about only with respect to travelling along a reasonably flat surface. Moving up an incline can make the wheelchair unstable, a condition that is made worse if additional weight (e.g. shopping) is placed at the rear of the chair. As with the buses, there is an urgent need to review wheelchair design, taking into account the conditions in which people wish to use them to go about their daily lives, including the use of public transport.

It might be tempting to think that a ramp (or other boarding device) reduces the need to bring the bus close to the kerb: after all, the ramp could be deployed to bridge quite a large gap. However, it should be remembered that there are many people who find it very difficult to negotiate a ramp, especially one as steep as 12.5% or 14%. This applies to many elderly people and those using sticks or other walking aids in order to walk. For these people there is no alternative to a small horizontal gap.

Thus, even with ramps available on the bus, there is still a requirement to bring the bus close to the kerb in order to make the service accessible. A much better solution is to design the bus-stop interface so that a ramp is unnecessary.

4.5.1.2   Gaps: Excalibur outcomes

A major part of the experiments was therefore to make sure that the bus could approach the stop easily and stop at a given stopping point with a consistent horizontal gap. We found that this was largely a matter of obtaining a correct approach to the stop. To obtain this consistency we have to ensure that the bus drivers can stop their buses in such a way that the access door is always at the same place in relation to the bus stop, irrespective of the vehicle design. This would be a lot easier if all buses had doors in the same place, but this is unlikely to occur in practice. The solution is to provide the driver with an easy way of making sure that (at least) one door is presented to the passengers consistently at the right place. This might mean providing different stopping markers for different buses. These would be similar in nature to the indications at railway stations or airport terminals which show the correct position for the vehicle to stop, depending on its type or length. Jaime Lerner recounts the way that bus drivers achieve this level of accuracy in Curitiba, by fixing a marker on the bus that aligns with another on the bus stop when the position is correct (Lerner, 2014). Of course, these buses operate in a segregated busway, so the deviation necessary to reach the platform is much smaller than in the mixed traffic case.

The Excalibur experiments showed that the process is largely deterministic. If the bus is positioned in a certain place in relation to the kerb at a certain point upstream of the bus stop, it will end up being in a deterministically defined point at the stopping point. Excalibur showed that, with Kassel kerbs, the bus should be at an angle to the kerb of between 9° and 12°, with the nearside wheel touching the kerb (the Kassel kerb is designed to permit this) at a point 21 m upstream of the stopping point. The issue is therefore how to ensure that the bus is at the correct alignment at this point. Excalibur tackled this challenge by means of a combination of physical markings in the roadway and a differently coloured kerb stone set to guide the driver towards the correct point where the wheel should touch the kerb at the correct angle, a guideline along the bus stop platform to assist in maintaining alignment and a clear indication of the stopping point. Although this worked, it was difficult to implement – the guideline required a change in regulations, the explicit definition of the actual length of kerbside required in order to enable this manoeuvre to take place scared many highway engineers as it would reduce parking space, and there was a general difficulty in maintaining the skills levels of the drivers to undertake this manoeuvre – which still required care and attention – under the conditions of 'normal' bus operation, when other requirements (e.g. adherence to schedule) were often considered to be more important.

4.5.1.3 Gaps: recent advances

However, technology has moved on. Recent technology in cars has resulted in rear-view closed-circuit television (CCTV) cameras showing the rearward path of the vehicle in terms of both where it is actually facing and as a projected path given the alignment of the steering wheels. Such a device could be configured to work for the forwards view of the bus in relation to its approach to a bus stop. The facing and projected path combination would then align with the oncoming kerb so that the driver could then adjust the approach path to ensure positioning at the correct point once stopped. The algorithm can be adjusted for speed and could even indicate appropriate speeds for the manoeuvre. Placing this in a heads-up display would help the driver considerably and act as a real help towards making good positioning at bus stops the normal thing to do. So the principle is to design the platform and approach as described by Excalibur, but to install a heads-up display for the driver as the main way of helping to guide the bus. A clear path should be indicated to other road users to show where the bus path will be – this is both important (in order to make sure it remains unobstructed) and made easier by the better control over the approach path because of the guidance system.

Mirrors and wheels are a matter for vehicle design, but some thought could be given to encouraging passengers to wait away from the kerb edge so that drivers are not discouraged from making a closer approach to the kerb because of a fear of colliding with people who are waiting on the platform. This can be achieved easily using a yellow line or other visual contrast (see Figure 4.22) set back from the kerb edge by 500 mm: people instinctively stand behind such a line and are accustomed to doing so.

4.5.2   Problem: Interface between people and the bus stop

As stated earlier in this chapter, people need to know where the bus stop is and be able to recognise a consistency in the appearance of bus stops so that they know how to recognise them. However, bus stops will always look different from each other, even if the basic design is standardised so that their appearance is consistent. In the UK, it is fairly common (but not universal) practice to indicate bus stops by means of a pole with an indication that it is a bus stop (usually called a 'flag'). Leipzig, Rouen and many other cities have adopted a contrasting paver with a roughened surface which is detectable by a long cane (Figure 4.22) as a means of marking the bus stop area. Another indication is the shelter. Whatever the means of displaying the presence of a bus stop, it will be necessary to ensure that the same method applies to every bus stop. This does not mean that every bus stop has to look the same – each one should reflect and be in sympathy with its immediate pedestrian area – but they should be identifiably consistent. So the flag and pole should always be the same, the shelter should always convey the same relevant information but might not always be the same design. The surrounding area will morph into the footway area and so could be different. Nevertheless, the overall object should appear to be a bus stop within the same network as all the others.

Whether the indication is a pole or the shelter or markings on the footway surface, the indication must take account of the fact that if the bus stop were a boarder the indicator would still have to be identifiable from the footway. A simple example of this problem would be that a person would know when they had reached a kerbside bus stop because of the presence of the pole and flag and the shelter (if there is one) within the footway. However, if the stop were a bus boarder, the pole and flag will be located near the kerb and the shelter would be located towards the edge of the footway, almost at the 'normal' kerb line. Such a bus stop could easily be missed by someone looking for poles, flags or shelters in the footway.

The bus stop shown in Figure 4.23 is an example of the confusion that can arise when it is not clear where a bus stop is actually located. In the photograph, the bus has stopped at the bus stop pole, at the end of the half boarder platform where the elderly man is sitting on the bollard. The bus stop pole is obscured from pedestrians and passengers

Figure 4.23 A confusing bus stop: neither passengers nor bus drivers know where the bus should stop

by the telephone box. The shelter is located several metres downstream from the boarder – a long way away from the bus stop – yet you can see passengers waiting in the shelter. The confusion is increased because the bus stop cage markings in the road continue to the end of the kerb line in front of the shelter. Passengers are confused by the arrangement and bus drivers have a real problem in deciding whether to stop at the bus stop or at the shelter where the passengers are.

The passenger–pedenger–passenger transitions take time. The whole bus stop area is a place where many different people undertake many different actions and we want to increase the opportunities to make the bus stop attractive to more people in the urban realm, so we can expect this to increase. People need to negotiate the horizontal and vertical gaps; they have to rearrange their bags, cases and pushchairs in order to board the bus, to look for information, and to find their money or ticket to pay or show to the driver on entry. A similar process occurs when a passenger leaves the bus: they have to change from being a passenger to being a pedestrian. People, after alighting from a bus, commonly take one or two steps and then stop to rearrange their bags, pushchair and so on, before proceeding along the footway as a pedestrian. This can cause delays to other alighting (and sometimes boarding) passengers. One purpose of infrastructure such as a bus stop is to organise time for these processes by providing them with a convenient space. A bus stop is not just a place where people wait to catch a bus – we have also to design the physical space to facilitate their arrival at, and departure from, the bus stop as pedestrians and the lingering space which characterises the way people wait for buses. It is therefore important to include the space required for these activities in the overall dimensions of a bus stop in such a way that it does not interfere with the continuing activities along the footway.

The bus stop design must ensure sufficient space to make sure that accessibility is maintained in the bus stop area. The main – but, as we shall see, not the only – basis for measurement for this is the manoeuvrability of a wheelchair. This is because a wheelchair needs a continuous and smooth surface in order to move on its wheels and is constrained by the space needed for turning with the wheels remaining in contact with the ground. A wheelchair user should be able to leave the bus and move away from the stop, enter the shelter and gain access from the shelter to the bus. The space required for these manoeuvres determines how much space should be made available for the bus stop area as a whole. This provides one of the conditions under which a boarder might need to be considered, as this would relieve the constraint where the footway is narrow. The space available for a bus stop will also influence the choice of shelter.

4.5.2.1 Finding the bus stop

As stated earlier in this chapter, the means of identifying a bus stop should be clear and consistent, including information about the services that call at the stops. This is often done using a bus stop pole and flag. Some places have done away with the bus stop pole and flag to indicate the location of a bus stop, preferring instead to place the flag on the shelter (Figure 4.24). The main point is to help passengers and drivers identify the location of a bus stop from a distance. However, the size of the service numbers on the bus stop shown in Figure 4.24 is far too small and requires passengers to approach

Figure 4.24 A bus stop flag incorporated in a bus stop shelter

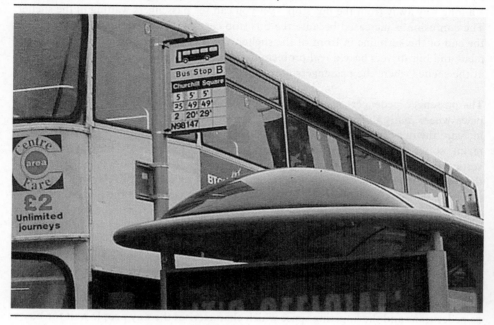

too close to the stop when attempting to find out if their bus calls there. Consistency is extremely important: whatever means are used to identify a bus stop, they should always be in the same place with respect to the boarding point for the buses. This will be helpful to both passengers and drivers, by indicating where the main part of the activity will be when the bus arrives. Identifying such a point within the bus stop environment provides a location from which other elements of the bus stop can be measured (e.g. for legal reasons).

The bus stop pole can be a good way of telling the driver where to stop the bus. By common consent, this was felt by drivers in London to be easier if they were required to stop the bus with the front of the bus level with the pole. The pole should therefore be set so that the bus doors will be aligned with the access point when the front of the bus is aligned with the pole. Placing the bus stop pole anywhere further along the platform will obstruct passengers trying to board the bus.

4.5.2.2 Boarding and alighting

Another objective of the Excalibur experiments was to establish exactly how much space is required at bus stops in order to enable people with mobility difficulties to use the stop in comfort. This enabled us to work out how much space should be reserved for passengers at a bus stop and where obstacles and street furniture would need to be excluded in order not to disable people. We also looked at the needs for shelter design, given the interaction between the bus and the bus stop and the needs with respect to the provision

Figure 4.25 Obstacles at a bus stop make it difficult for passengers as well as the driver

of seating. We also investigated information needs at bus stops and the extent to which these affected bus stop design.

The first issue is to have enough uncluttered space. The passenger area of the bus stop should be kept free of all obstructions so that passengers are free to move easily onto and off the bus and to enter or leave the bus stop area without undue hindrance. The obstacles make it extremely difficult for passengers to find their way around the area, but also make it difficult for the drivers. I have commented on this above (see Figure 4.23). Another example is shown in Figure 4.25 where the bus driver finds it difficult to locate the front door near to the bus stop without obstructing it at the shelter and the rear door being obstructed by the litter bin. Figure 4.26 shows the bus stop illustrated in Figure 4.23 after it had been redesigned to make it more accessible. Comparing Figure 4.23 and Figure 4.26, you can see the difference between the original cluttered and confusing bus stop and the new arrangement installed as part of the Excalibur project.

It is very useful for boarding passengers to know where to expect the bus entrance doorway to be when the bus arrives. This enables them to form a queue or group so that they are ready to board the bus when it arrives. Where different types of bus arrive at a bus stop, and where some of these have doors at different positions (e.g. some at the front and some at the rear), it is important to make sure that in every case the doorway appears at the same place at the bus stop. This avoids confusion among the passengers and helps to speed the boarding and alighting process.

Figure 4.26 The obstacles have been cleared away to make the bus stop more accessible

Where alighting passengers are concerned, it is important that they can leave the bus stop area as quickly as possible. If boarding passengers are milling around the entrance door, the alighting passengers should be able to leave the bus stop, either by turning towards the rear of the bus, or by walking around the boarding passengers towards the front of the bus.

The bus stop shown in Figure 4.26 leaves ample space for passengers to leave the bus stop area and disperse along the footway. This is made a lot easier because the platform length ensures that the platform width is maintained towards the rear of the stop, and thus the dispersal from the bus stop onto the footway can take place over a reasonable distance. The platform length also helps to draw alighting passengers towards the less congested space towards the rear of the bus, and therefore away from boarding passengers. If the platform is too short, this cannot happen and the result is congestion on both the platform and the footway, which can prevent passengers from alighting in some cases.

Where buses have more than one door, it is usual in the UK to require passengers to board through the front door and to alight through the other door(s). The new bus for London allows boarding and alighting through all doors. In such cases, in addition to the identification of the entry door position, it is useful to identify the area where alighting passengers could be expected to step onto the platform. This helps to keep the area clear so that they can leave the stop quickly and without obstructing boarding passengers. This is even more important where wheelchair users are required to use the rear door of the buses: they need to know where to wait in order to have an easy route to the bus when it arrives.

4.5.2.3 Waiting

There is also an issue about the way in which people wait for buses at a bus stop. Historically, people have been expected to queue ahead of the bus stop so that they can face the bus as it arrives at the stop, and this has dictated the location of the shelter (e.g. see Figure 4.23). However, such queuing practice is now very rare and people tend to wait in the area around a bus stop as well as within the confines of the shelter. This means that access to the entrance door of the bus is from all directions – upstream, downstream and straight in front of the door. The group of people attempting to board the bus must sort out who goes first, and how people with wheelchairs, buggies, shopping or young children are accommodated. The resulting approach to boarding the bus can have a substantial effect on the dwell time. Obstacles anywhere near the expected location of the bus doorway will obstruct passengers and should be removed.

As part of its contribution to being a good place to be, the bus stop should be designed to accommodate people waiting for the bus away from the actual bus stop. This helps to enliven the area and draw in people – to the shops and other activities near the bus stop. This needs to be designed properly though. People waiting away from the bus stop area could easily be obstructing the footway area, including entrances to shops, while they wait, and are also quite likely to obstruct alighting passengers as they attempt to leave the stop area. We need to ensure that this form of waiting is properly accommodated in the design so that its benefits are maximised and the potential problems are minimised.

4.5.2.4 Seating

People need to feel comfortable while waiting for the bus and although this is often achieved by providing spaces to sit down, this is not always the solution. Many elderly people and some with spinal problems cannot wait for the bus without sitting down, but for others, sitting down – or rising from the seat afterwards – presents a major problem. The amount of waiting time depends on the frequency and reliability of the buses. However, there are upper limits to an acceptable wait. We have found that among people with arthritis, for example, 10 minutes is the most they can tolerate in one position. Appropriate shelter and seating is therefore essential. The shelter needs to be large enough to accommodate the likely number of waiting passengers, and including wheelchairs, pushchairs and shopping. However, a suitably sized bus stop shelter can be yet another obstacle on the footway. The shelter should also be located far enough away from the kerb line that people leaving the bus can vacate the stop area quickly and easily. Bus stop shelters should be highlighted so that they do not cause problems for visually impaired people. However, one of the benefits of the lingerers is that they do not need to be accommodated inside the bus shelter as they are lingering elsewhere in the footway area. Attracting them to do so, by making the 'lingering area' attractive, will reduce the pressure for space in the bus shelter itself.

People need different seat heights – we concluded that three heights would accommodate most needs, and two would be better than one. Seats should be placed in the shelter so that people sitting on them can see arriving buses and do not obscure information panels. They should also be positioned so that people can see what else is going on in

Figure 4.27 The 'sciatica seat' in Buenos Aires, Argentina

the area. This includes the people in the shelter within the local area and it also helps to make them feel more secure. Arranging seats to encourage conversation (e.g. by placing benches at an angle to each other) would also help to make the area more friendly, but this does take up space which might be limited. Some people find it difficult to sit down – for example, people with arthritis or sciatica (remember that there are some 7.5 million of them in the UK). Their difficulty is that it is painful to stand for any time and it is very painful to get up from a seat. One approach to this has been adopted in Buenos Aires. Their 'sciatica seat' (Figures 4.27 and 4.28) allows a person to lean against and be supported by the structure rather than sit on it. This was designed after considerable ergonomic research with sciatica sufferers, and the dimensions are set very precisely. It would be interesting to see what adjustments might need to be made if it were to be introduced to the UK. Other examples of seats which are designed to make resting, rather than sitting, easier are shown in Figures 4.29 and 4.30, where more of a profile has been incorporated in the design than in the Buenos Aires example.

4.5.2.5 Information
Information needs to be presented in different formats so that people with vision and hearing difficulties are not disadvantaged. Audible announcements must be produced to match any information provided visually and should take into account the background noise expected at the bus stop. Announcements should also be available for the lingerers waiting away from the bus stop itself. The availability of apps means that there is an opportunity to develop apps to provide real-time information to people who have suitable mobile phones and have downloaded the app. Apps which provide real-time bus arrival information for every bus stop in London are available and these are based on the

Figure 4.28 The 'sciatica seat', side view

Figure 4.29 The leaning seat in Kassel, Germany

Figure 4.30 The leaning seat in Leipzig, Germany

same information as the TfL Countdown system so the information they provide is the same as that displayed at the stops.

The obvious information to have at a bus stop is a timetable. However, although a time-table is necessary, it is not sufficient to act as the only available information at a bus stop. It is essential that the timetable is printed clearly and shows times for all buses calling at the stop. However, people also want other information at bus stops. A large-scale map of the surrounding area, including where other bus stops and other means of transport (railway stations, taxis, etc.) are located, is helpful. The bus stop name should be read-able from inside the bus. This could be addressed by ensuring that the name of the bus stop is shown on the shelter in print that is large enough to be seen from inside the bus. The identity of the bus services using the stop should also be displayed clearly, large enough to be seen easily and in a consistent location at the stop. This information should be repeated in tactile writing (including, but not only, Braille) for visually impaired people on the footway and on the platform. Real-time bus information should also be provided – this reassures passengers that a bus might be coming (although it would be even better if the buses could run to the published schedule as well!). Information could be provided aurally – this can be done using the glass panes of the shelter as amplifiers.

4.5.2.6 Pedestrian activity at the bus stop

As I have stated several times already, the bus stop is an important element of the urban realm and thus pedestrians are important actors in the bus stop environment. Ensuring that pedestrian activity is available to everyone means that footways must be clear of obstacles and sufficiently wide. Footways should have an uncluttered minimum width of 2 m. At pinch points this could be reduced to about 1 m, but this should be treated as an exception to the general rule. As with other aspects of accessible design, any reduction from these minimum dimensions results in a reduction in accessibility and should be avoided. As noted in Section 4.1.2, the pedestrian space has to be coherent, the footway as smooth and predictable as possible, lateral obstacles avoided and lighting appropriate. However, the pedestrian space around the bus stop has other opportunities.

It is necessary to find out how much of the pedestrian space around the bus stop is actually used by lingerers who are actually waiting for a bus. This will vary between cultures, climates, environments and operating conditions (e.g. frequency) – and will also vary over time, for example, between peak hours and off-peak hours, days of the week, weather conditions, and so on. However, as there could be a greater number of people lingering than people waiting in the bus stop itself, it is essential that we take this into account when considering what space we have to include in our consideration when designing a bus stop. Attractive and interesting shop windows and doorways will attract people, benches, perches, supports for leaning and so on are all good for lingering – and if we design these into the bus stop area we can make sure that we retain the coherence of the pedestrian space so that the area functions as a space for lingering, walking and waiting as well as providing access to the activities in the immediate vicinity, without losing the vital functionality of any of these.

Bus stops have to be made fully accessible, and this means responding to the needs of the people using them. The engineering aspects of the design must be based on an approach directed to satisfying these needs as far as possible and working with the public on the compromises that are sometimes required. Many of the features that are necessary to deliver accessibility are very detailed: it is essential that attention is paid to these details, or the ability of the design to deliver accessibility will be compromised.

We have briefly reviewed some of the problems encountered when trying to improve accessibility at bus stops and have indicated some of the possible ways in which these difficulties might be countered. We now discuss how the design of the bus stops can incorporate a lot of these requirements and features so that accessibility can be enhanced at this point in the accessible journey chain.

4.6. People-centred approach to definition of bus stop design
4.6.1 Requirements

I am concerned with the accessibility at bus stops from the users' point of view and between the bus stop and buses. One thing that is quite clear is that there are many 'users' of the bus stop. Several of these were considered in the first edition of the book, but now it is important to reconsider these and see if they remain, should be changed or whether we should be considering new issues. In this edition, we are therefore exploring bus stop design from a slightly different perspective. What do we expect a bus stop to be? What is its Value? The answer to this question changes according to the respondent's point of view.

4.6.1.1 Pedestrians/pedengers/passengers
In the first edition of this book, we stated that 'users of the bus stop' like a place:

1A where they can wait comfortably and safely for a bus service to which they will have easy access, that will arrive within a time that is reasonable enough to wait and that is going to take them where they want to go
1B which they can identify easily
1C where they can find out about the bus service (arrival and departure times, destinations and other information)
1D where they can find out about the area around the bus stop so that, on alighting from a bus, they can find their way from the bus stop to their destination.

Little has changed in this regard during the intervening decade. Looking at Table 4.8 and Figure 4.16, it is possible to see that there is a greater emphasis on who the 'users' are and how they will use a bus stop. One of the main differences is that we are now much more particular about considering 'people' rather than just 'users'. The bus stop is the portal between the bus and pedestrian environments and can act as a great place to be within the urban realm if it is also convenient for the pedestrians who pass by and do not wish to use the bus stop. So the provision of seats and shelter, opportunities to stand and lean – to linger – and the orientation of these can help or hinder the use of the bus stop in this way (where are the interesting stimuli?). The provision of a wide range of information – about both the bus services and the local area – means that the bus stop becomes a place to visit to discover things. So a bus stop can deliver functionality in terms of the place in which it is located as well as being the entrance to the bus system: it should act and have the characteristics of both the shop doorway and the shop window (see Table 4.5 and Figure 4.13). We should also consider the stimulus-generation space around the bus stop – how large is it? What opportunities are there for being in the bus stop and observing stimuli? I can therefore add some more requirements to the list of what our Pedestrians/Passengers/Pedengers need from a bus stop:

2A a place to sit or stand comfortably and observe the surrounding space
2B orientation of the seats/standing facilities so that it is easy to linger
2C provision of a wide range of information in addition to the bus service information
2D good lighting which is in tune with that in the local environment (including consideration of sun angles)
2E a place where it is easy to converse – or not – with other people
2F a place where it is easy to transition between being a pedestrian, passenger and pedenger – space for arranging bags, orientating oneself without causing an obstruction
2G a place which delivers these functions equitably to everyone – all these functions are accessible.

188

Such a list might come as a surprise, especially to those who think of a bus stop as simply something to do with the bus system.

By way of example, Figure 4.30 shows how one of the items shown in Figure 4.19 might translate into a second level of decisions (see Figure 2.4 for an example of a series of decisions that are nested at different levels) – in this case in relation to the space availability. The desired outcome at the second level is in effect an action resulting from the combination of success factors and limitations in the first level of decision. The nested nature of the model means of course that the overall desired outcome – of improving well-being – is carried through and still acts as a major criterion in the decisions actually made in the second level. This of course passes down to subsequent levels in the nested decision model – the actions of one level becoming desired outcomes of the subsequent level.

Being a 'place to be' is, of course, only one of the functions of a bus stop. A bus stop is multifunctional and we must also consider other functions.

4.6.1.2 Bus drivers
In the first edition we stated that 'Bus drivers want a place:

1E   that is easy to identify in the street space
1F   that is easy to stop at
1G   that is devoid of parking and delivery-vehicle problems
1H   where passengers can board and alight as quickly as possible
1I   that has no obstacles that can be struck by the bus on arriving or leaving the stop
1J   that is consistent in its design so that all bus stops feel the same
1K   that is easy to leave and re-enter the traffic stream
1L   where it is easy to see passengers boarding and alighting from the bus'.

As with the passenger functionality discussed earlier, although all of these issues still stand, the world has moved on since then. The Excalibur bus stop described below (which was also described in the first edition) always raised a problem with the owners of public spaces – in particular the owners of the highway and shops with frontages near to the bus stop. The latter issue, which also arose in Bogotá, led to attempts to impeach the Mayor of Bogotá in 1999 because shop owners felt that by removing car parking from the space in front of their shops their business would be adversely affected. Similar arguments arose in our work in London and Brighton – and have also been raised on almost every occasion where such ideas have been proposed.

The world has moved on. Schemes to reduce traffic in cities have abounded – some more extreme than others (the London Congestion Charge scheme being one example) – and it is no longer surprising to see systems to pedestrianize street spaces. The science behind the Excalibur designs still stands – buses still require space to manoeuvre and this has not changed in the last 10 years – although the number of buses has in many cases (London has increased the bus fleet by about 30% since the introduction of the Congestion Charge in 2003), which makes it all the more important to accommodate them properly.

Two of the items in the previous list are of interest here. Item (1F) 'a bus stop is a place that is easy to stop at', is a case where we can now be much more specific. Now it is not only desirable, it is also essential to be more particular about some of these issues. For example, bringing the bus close enough to the kerb to enable near-gap-free boarding and alighting, which is helped considerably by the Excalibur design, requires consummate skill of the bus driver. This is still not emphasised enough in design specifications, driver training or in professional skills updates. It is difficult to achieve, even with designs such as the Excalibur one which provide some help. However, now technology is available that could assist the driver to a much greater extent. High-end cars and trucks have video-based reversing aids which help a driver know exactly, not only what is near the rear of the vehicle, but also the implications of the present position of the steered wheels. There is no reason in principle why such technology could not be developed to operate in the forward direction so that it could assist a bus driver to position the vehicle perfectly for the best boarding and alighting conditions at the bus stop.

Item 1G, 'a bus stop is a place that is devoid of parking and delivery-vehicle problems', really needs to be emphasised as well. This is difficult, particularly where the local environment contains activities, such as shops, where there is a need for loading and unloading. Of course having such activities is part of our 'Ideal City' and we need to encourage this. However, changes in logistics systems have often meant an increase in the number of delivery vehicles serving a shop – the use of high frequency deliveries to replace storage space and thus increase the commercial space inside the shop is a good example. A fairly small supermarket can easily have as many as 30 deliveries per day (you can see one of these in Figure 4.14). If the shop is within the operational umbrella of a bus stop there will be frequent interference with the bus operation and with the ability of passengers to be able to access the bus system – especially for people with accessibility problems. Such a shop-delivery practice dramatically increases the capabilities required to board and alight the bus and this will render some people no longer able to use the bus system. It therefore needs to be addressed as a matter of urgency. As far as the bus system is concerned, however, it is essential that we maintain the consistency required to enable the bus driver to deliver the near-gap-free environment for the passengers and this basically means that parking and loading is not compatible with bus stop operation if it is within the area defined by the Excalibur design – around 44 m for a kerbside stop, for example. So, in order to keep the activity, it is necessary for all parties to think about the challenge: the bus operators about the location of the stop, the shop owner about the delivery schedule, planners about the location of the delivery bays. Ultimately, the goal is to deliver a bus stop that contributes to the ideal city – the bus system negating the activity of shops is no more a benefit than the shops negating the activity of the bus system. What is needed is an intelligent conversation about the issue based on the achievement of the overall objective of improving wellbeing of society (see Figure 4.31).

4.6.1.3 Bus operators

In the first edition, we stated that 'Bus operators want a place:

1M where the bus can stop without problems
1N where the bus can re-enter the traffic stream as easily as possible
1O which imposes the least possible delay on buses'.

Figure 4.31 Basic outcomes-based decision model for a bus stop, 2nd level for item (1) of the model shown in Figure 4.19

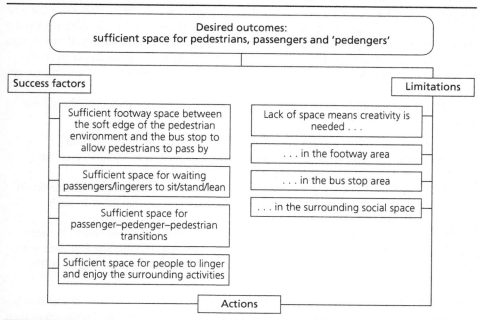

In order to provide a suitable bus service, it is necessary to be able to provide predictable arrivals. Bus stops are key to this in that they provide one of the main opportunities for conflict in the bus system. Guaranteeing consistency at bus stops is a matter of using a combination of frequency, good design of both the bus stop and bus to regularise boarding and alighting and intelligent approaches to management of the bus operation in real-time.

Better bus stop operation can be gained if the bus is well-designed. Having more doors reduces problems of congestion and thus variability in boarding times. However, just putting more doors in the bus is not sufficient. For example, the New Bus for London, has three doors, which should increase the overall boarding rate. However, there is a problem if more than a small number of people attempt to use the rear door. This is because there are two flows of passengers who wish to leave the bus – one from the staircase and the other from the lower saloon. The platform can only hold three or four people at a time. Therefore, first of all there is a delay while the alighting passengers leave the bus, then, once the boarding passengers must negotiate the small space in order to reach the stairs or the narrow gap to enter the lower saloon. Thus the platform quickly becomes congested and boarding stops, causing a delay to the bus. It is essential that the dynamics of passenger movements between the bus and the bus stop are studied in much more detail so that the design can be more accommodating. The new bus for London has two modes of operation for the rear door. During peak hours it operates with a member of staff present on the rear platform and the door is left completely open even when the bus is moving. The rest of the time there is no member of staff on the platform but the door only opens partially so that only one person can move through it at any one time. Doors need to be wide enough to permit two channels of flow and this means door widths of some 1.6 or 1.7 m to allow for the fact that people do carry bags onto the bus. The whole process of entering the bus must be taken into account in this work so that the passage of the passenger onto and off the bus is incorporated in the design. Better design means more consistency in the performance and this in turn means easier operation – and easier operation leads towards our goal of a bus system which everyone wants to use.

Therefore I should add to the previous list for bus operators, that they should put in place:

2H Procurement of bus designs that match the bus stop infrastructure and technologies to assist the driver to provide the highest quality service to the passengers.

2I Procurement of bus designs which encourage smooth consistent performance in boarding and alighting, based on proper research on people flows in such confined spaces and constricted times.

2J Consideration of the delivery of a frequency which reduces variability between buses in terms of the number of passengers boarding and alighting at each stop.

2K Design of the frequency to provide an attractive and acceptable service to the passengers.

Figure 4.32 shows a simplified version of the outcomes-based decision model for bus operators to consider their actions in light of the overall city objective by directing their objectives to improving the access to achievement of aspirations.

Figure 4.32 Outcomes decision-based model for bus operators

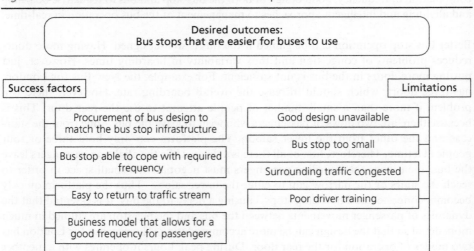

4.6.1.4 Traffic planners

In the first edition we stated that 'Traffic planners want a place:

1P that is safe for buses to stop with a minimum disturbance to traffic
1Q that is cheap to install and maintain
1R that will incur minimal opposition from users, nearby residents and businesses and bus operators'.

Again, this stands up today, but it is also necessary to think about how this will fit with the wellbeing objective. The priorities of a twenty-first century city require a mature understanding of how to ensure that the commercial needs need to meet with the societal requirements. Traffic does not mean a thriving city – it indicates a society which is characterised by individuals who are isolated from each other and have some dissatisfaction with the relationship between where they are and where they want to be – and, in particular, who want to cross that divide in their own environment rather than be exposed to the city on the way. The question is whether a city with a goal of increasing societal wellbeing can see the encouragement of private traffic as a priority. What therefore are the traffic planners' actions for creating the traffic environment in which the economic needs of the city can be supplied yet not at the cost of an improvement in societal wellbeing?

The courteous city requires us to think about how we make the city more polite and less prone to inducing stress in its inhabitants. Traffic is a major inducer of stress. It is possible to design a junction in such a way that, because of poor sight lines, bad traffic signal timings, inadequate provision for pedestrians or bad signage (among other things), the only way for any person to pass through the intersection is to act aggressively, forcing their way into the flow (vehicles or pedestrians) because not to do so would mean being delayed for an unimaginable time. It is also possible to design the same junction in such a way that people and vehicles move freely and without the need for forcing their way into or across the flow. It is the responsibility of the traffic planner to design in the latter way in order to contribute towards the overall vision.

The creation of a courteous city also means creating a city in which people are able to trust each other. Achievement of this aim would provide the traffic planner with an opportunity. For example, if it were possible to deliver goods and not have to deliver them into the actual destination building with the need for signed acceptance on the part of the client, it would be much more feasible to organise commercial deliveries during hours which do not impart negative effects on the rest of society, including the traffic system – and of course, as discussed above, on the bus system and its passengers.

In the main, this means moving towards traffic planning on the basis of people rather than vehicles as the prime measure. The sense of lingering, discussed in Section 4.1.2, might also be relayed to traffic in the sense that if society is more accepting of the benefits of lingering, it would place less priority on the reduction of delay, increase in speed and journey time reduction that currently drive much of the traffic planning culture. That 'civilised' stress-free junction described above would be much easier to achieve if the pressure to reduce delay were itself reduced. Traffic planners do understand this issue – the point behind variable speed management on motorways is that in order to reduce delay it is better to reduce the speed of the traffic so that vehicle arrivals at congested points occur at a more feasible frequency and thus the congestion resulting from too high an arrival rate does not arise.

There has been a move in recent years to shift from vehicle-oriented development, where the transport planning is directed to maximise the flows of vehicles, to transit-oriented development, where the transport planning is directed to ease the use of public transport. This carries through to the way traffic planners work – more bus priorities for example. More recently, particularly on the east coast of the USA, there has been a move towards neighbourhood-oriented development, where transport planning is used to encourage the activity and quality of a local community. However, even this does not really go far enough. The real driver for transport planning should be people-oriented development. This emphasises that the real gain in wellbeing comes from improvement in the quality of life – the achievement of aspirations – of the people in the neighbourhood community. Allowing organised parking might help improve a neighbourhood, but not if it prevents some people from being able to reach the activities they need in order to achieve their aspirations. Neighbourhoods are for people – neighbours – not for cars!

Figure 4.33 shows a simple approach for traffic planners to consider their actions in light of the overall city objective by directing their objectives to improving the access to achievement of aspirations.

Figure 4.33 Outcomes-based decision model for traffic planners

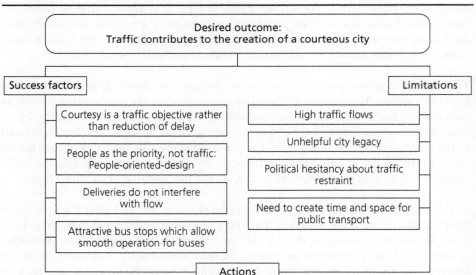

4.6.1.5 People living near to bus stops

In the first edition we stated that 'People living near to bus stops like a place:

1S   that is not too far from their home
1T   that is not outside their home
1U   that is not unsightly'.

Most people would probably still agree with these three principles, but, given the discussions in Chapter 3, it is important to expand on what exactly is meant by 'not too far', 'not outside their home' and 'not unsightly'. In terms of distance it seems that it is important to keep the journey to or from the bus stop to less than 400 m and to ensure that there are plenty of benches and other resting points along the way. This is crucial to ensuring that the bus stops are accessible to the widest range of people. The usual objection to a bus stop being outside someone's home is the behaviour of people waiting for the bus. This is clearly an issue for the courteous city but it does also impinge on the sense of the public 'owning' public space – and thus taking a responsibility for it. So the design of the bus stop becomes a crucial issue. Apart from it not being unsightly, it is a question of the design actively encouraging good behaviour. If the bus stop is a place that people want to be, this is something that should be a positive matter and should encourage people to behave in a courteous way. A high standard of design is a good start, especially when it is one that is accepted by the local people.

So the key to the acceptability of the bus stop lies in its ability to support and contribute to the five cities. Figure 4.34 shows a simplified version of the outcomes-based decision model which can guide bus stop designers to think in terms of the needs of people living near to a bus stop and which contributes to the achievement of an improvement in well-being. So I could add some more features to the list:

2L   that encourages the people using the bus stop to be courteous
2M   that promotes a sense of the place around the bus stop as a good place to be
2N   that is in keeping with the local surroundings so that it does not look out of place
2O   that creates an atmosphere that society owns and welcomes this use of the public space as a positive social asset
2P   that promotes good health – for example, the way it uses energy, reduces stress and infection transmission
2Q   that promotes a positive sense of the future and how it can evolve for the benefit of future generations.

Many of the items in this list reflect that a person living in the neighbourhood will, in the 'ideal city', wish to assure a good and positive future for the community as it evolves. The bus stop, as a relatively permanent asset, will be a part of that future until it evolves into something else. The idea that the bus stop is one of the positive examples of society's resources for the good helps to maintain the area as a good place to be. Figure 4.34 shows a simplified representation of how these factors can be structured into the outcomes-based decision model.

Figure 4.34 Outcomes-based decision model in relation to the perspectives of people living near a bus stop

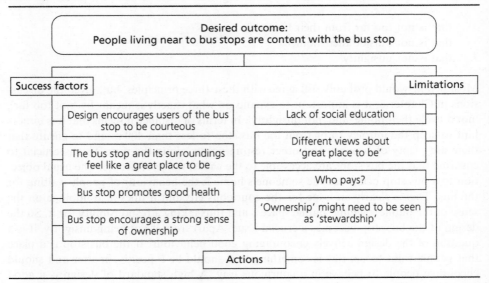

4.6.1.6 Traders based near a bus stop

In the first edition, we stated that 'Traders based near to a bus stop like a place:

1V that is close to their business (if they believe that bus users are core customers)
1W that is far away from their business (if they believe that bus users are not core customers)
1X that does not obstruct views of their premises
1Y that does not obstruct access for delivery vehicles and customers'.

Traders (and of course I include the owners/providers of activities in general so other activities such as sports, leisure, arts, education, entertainment and so on are all of interest here in this category) provide one of the major activities of the active city. Thus they are crucial to the overall intention of creating an ideal city in which wellbeing is continually improving. We therefore have to ensure that their activities are supported.

I discussed in Section 4.1.3 the way in which shop doorways and shop windows perform as examples of soft edges in the pedestrian environment and, when it comes to their inter-action with bus stops, it is important to remember that in the end their direct interaction is with the pedestrian, rather than the bus, environment. In addition, there is also the need to remember that the soft edges I am talking about here not only involve shops but also include the interfaces with an art gallery, gym, football stadium or whatever. The bus stop is placed in the pedestrian environment in order to deliver and receive people who wish to undertake activities and so it is necessary to think about the concept of how the interaction between the bus stop and those activities works in practice. Making all these activities accessible is a crucial element of making the active city truly available to the whole of

Figure 4.35 A street in Cartagena, Colombia, showing people making a soft edge

society. Rawls' difference principle, discussed in Section 1.2, shows that in order to maintain social justice and fairness the soft edges would need to be designed in a way that ensures that the worst-off – in whatever context (i.e. whether this is considered in terms of, for example, wealth or capability) – are able to avail themselves of the activity.

The need to interact with the bus system suggests that the bus stop needs to be within a reasonable distance of the activity. 'Resting places' should be made available and these could be benches or seating areas, but could also simply be places to lean. One of the downsides of the recent move to eliminate guard rails separating traffic from pedestrians is that, although it opens up the environment and removes a barricade between pedestrians and traffic, it has also removed a source of opportunities to lean. However, thought around the design of soft edges could remedy this and thus make the activities more available from the bus stop; informal soft edges can also work well. Figure 4.35 shows an example in Cartagena, Colombia; Figure 4.36 shows the use of a statue to encourage lingering in Havana, Cuba and Figure 4.37 shows people using bollards for having a chat in Buenos Aires, Argentina.

The nature of the activity will also affect the relationship. On the one hand, the small shop will tend to have smaller numbers of people visiting it at any one time and, depending on the nature of the merchandise, they will emerge with smaller or larger bags of merchandise. On the other hand, other activities might be recipients of people mainly in groups: these people might arrive and leave in groups (necessitating thought about this in the design of the bus stop) or might form the groups outside the venue before entering (necessitating thought about the pedestrian environment around the activity).

Figure 4.36 Using a statue to encourage lingering in Havana, Cuba

Figure 4.37 Using bollards to make a space for conversation in Buenos Aires, Argentina

Something that should change, though, is the prevailing idea that a customer for an activity would not arrive on a bus. First of all, as traffic restrictions increase in relation to private traffic, it is likely that more people will arrive by bus – and, as noted right at the start of this book – the concept that only losers use buses is so off the mark that it is a nonsense to pursue in this belief. Second, the actual arrival at the activity will be via the pedestrian network, and where people have come from in order to join the pedestrian environment near the activity is irrelevant for this purpose. Third, even if the providers of some activities might believe that a bus stop in close proximity might harm their trade – and it is hard to see that they would be correct in this – the likelihood is that there are other activities around that would benefit from having a bus stop close by – perhaps it should be the activity that should move in these circumstances, rather than the bus stop?

There is no value in the view of an activity being obscured and it is important that the bus stop is seen as the way to reach the activity rather than something that hides it. This is largely a question of the information being provided at the bus stop about the local area and the extent to which it is able to perform as a soft edge in its own right. There could also be scope to provide information inside the bus about local activities.

The most complex problem with the interface between activities and the bus stop is that of deliveries. The bus stop requires adequate space for the buses to manoeuvre so that they can reach the bus stop properly (see Section 5.3.4) to provide an accessible interface for the passengers. Parking of any sort, including delivery vehicles, within the manoeuvring envelope will prevent this from happening and members of society will be disadvantaged as a result. Therefore it should not happen.

The first approach to this problem is to see if it is possible to move the deliveries. Perhaps rescheduling them so that they do not occur during operation hours of the bus system is a possibility. Simply keeping them off-peak does not work, because this is the most likely period when people with reduced mobility choose to travel. This might require night-time deliveries so it is necessary to consider all the implications – for the activity and the local area – of such a solution. Another alternative is to move the deliveries physically to another place which does not affect the bus system. It might be possible to consolidate delivery bays for a number of shops so that the problem is confined to an area which does not affect the bus stop. Or, as a last option, it may be necessary to move the bus stop. However, before this is considered, there is a question of how deliveries are made, particularly in city centres. Over the years there have been a number of attempts at delivery consolidation, but these have a tendency to fail – businesses like to deliver in their own vehicles, for example. However, with modern logistics technologies becoming more widespread, it is beginning to become more feasible to imagine a consolidated delivery system, which would reduce the number of delivery vehicle visits to an activity to a group of activities in the same area. It is worth exploring this possibility in order to maintain an adequate accessibility for the bus passengers who will become the pedestrians who will become the customers/visitor/attendees of the activities being served by the bus stop.

Figure 4.38 Outcomes-based decision model for design that supports traders and activity providers near a bus stop

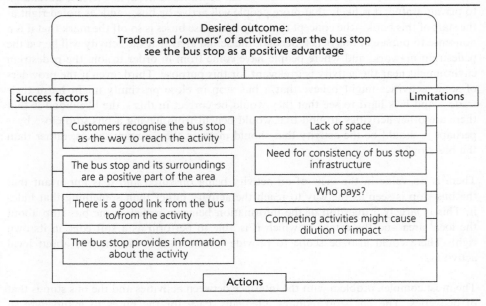

All the issues raised in the preceding paragraph would be transformed if we could invoke the 'courteous city' approach (see Section 1.4). This is because part of the courteous city could be the sense of having a city where goods could be left safely for later collection without fear of theft or damage.

So I can add to the list of requirements that, first of all, we should not think only of traders but more of a wider group of activity providers.

Activity providers therefore need the bus stop to be a place which:

2R provides an attractive portal to their activity
2S provides good quality and relevant information about their activity – this could be a source of revenue of course. Figure 4.38 shows the associated decision model for traders and activity providers.

4.6.1.7 Pedestrians
In the first edition, we stated that 'Pedestrians want a place:

1Z   that does not obstruct their use of the footway
1AA   that does not make them feel insecure'.

I have discussed at length in Section 4.3.1.1 the importance of the interface between the pedestrian and the bus stop activity and I have shown that it is important that the

Figure 4.39 Outcome-based decision model for design that includes pedestrians

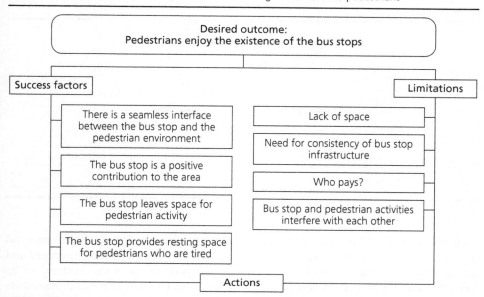

bus stop delivers a positive interaction rather than simply being a passive obstacle to pedestrian activity that has to be minimised. Importantly I have emphasised the need to incorporate the pedestrian environment explicitly in the bus system and to seek to join the two together in a seamless way, using the bus stop as the point of contact.

I can therefore add:

2T   that celebrates the interface between the pedestrian environment and the bus system
2U   that can be enjoyed by pedestrians whether or not they intend to use the bus system. The decision model for pedestrians can be seen in Figure 4.39.

4.6.1.8 Car drivers

Finally, in the first edition, we stated that 'Car drivers want a place:

1BB   that does not interfere with the traffic system in any way
1CC   that does not eliminate or reduce parking'.

When considering car traffic it is necessary to consider the transport hierarchy – the order in which priorities are settled. Over the past 100 years or so, and in particular in the last 50 years, the priority has been to accommodate car traffic (and some cities and countries still adopt this priority). However, as congestion has increased, the generation of noxious emissions from traffic has both increased and become a political issue, this priority has had to change.

Figure 4.40 The shift from a car-dominated transport hierarchy to a person-oriented transport hierarchy

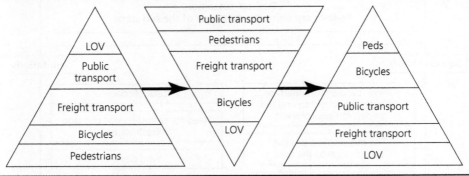

Figure 4.40 shows how the 'old/present' hierarchy works. The left-hand pyramid represents vehicle-oriented development and is geared towards increasing movement and leaves slower-moving entities such as cyclists and pedestrians at the bottom, to be considered only when all the others have been satisfied. The central pyramid represents transit-oriented development, where the hierarchy is geared around an accessible public transport system. The right-hand pyramid shows how in person-oriented development, accessibility rather than movement has pedestrians at the top, as these are the people who actually require accessibility and thus whose needs must be satisfied before moving down to the other elements of the transport system.

In an integrated society, car drivers fall to the bottom of the hierarchy because they impose the most unnecessary obstacles to bus stops and thus to the person-centred nature of the new approach. In the past decade, many city centres have reduced traffic access and increased parking restrictions. As we reverse the transport hierarchy so that pedestrians are the first priority, cars should be accommodated when all the others have been satisfied and in such a way that they do not interfere with the higher-order needs in the environment. The decision model for pedestrians can be seen in Figure 4.39.

4.6.1.9 Putting the requirements together

First of all, I must point out that the example outcomes-based decision models shown in Figures 4.30–4.38 and Figure 4.40 are just simple possibilities. You should create your own models to respond to your own situations. The main point is to include all of these issues in the overall decision, to link them all to the overreaching vision through the desired outcomes and to consider carefully the limitation as well as the success factors. Needless to say, many of the wishes expressed by stakeholders are mutually incompatible, and the task of the bus stop designer is to achieve a compromise that will satisfy as many of these desires as possible. The 'phase-triality' discussed in Section 4.1.3 makes it very difficult to determine where the priority should lie when dealing with conflicts between pedestrians, passengers and pedengers, and it is clear that these need to be met

Figure 4.41 Outcomes-based decision model to take car drivers into account

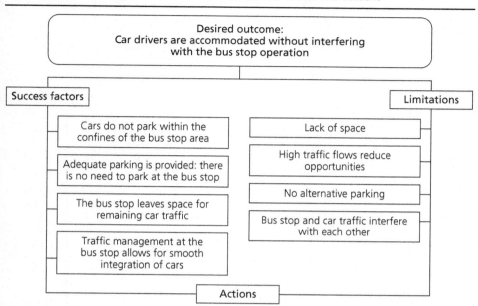

before starting to try to address the issues for other elements of the system as described here. The outcomes-based decision model provides the way of resolving this problem by making it explicit that it is the desired outcome that drives the choice of priorities: the choice must be made depending on how successfully the decision promotes and achieves the desired outcome. This brings us back to the evaluation of the attainment of the outcome and thus to the concept of value engineering, which will be how we can evaluate the various options in terms of how well they help us attain the desired outcome.

Figure 4.42 shows a typical schematic arrangement of the potential participants in the bus stop design process, together with their paths of communication. Figure 4.43 shows how the same groups would be involved in a more participative structure, including the associated communication routes.

The relationships I have been discussing provide the means by which the inputs to the design process should be brought to the attention of the bus stop designer. As can be seen from Figure 4.42 and Figure 4.43 the sources of these are varied and come from agents with very different priorities. The bus stop designer has the difficult and important task of taking these inputs and generating a design that seeks to minimise the conflicts between the differing priorities and accentuating the opportunities for achieving good outcomes for society as a whole. Bus stop designers need a high level of knowledge of the techniques and opportunities available to them as well as a good knowledge of accessibility needs to enable them to make good decisions about the inevitable

Figure 4.42 Current participation in the bus stop design process

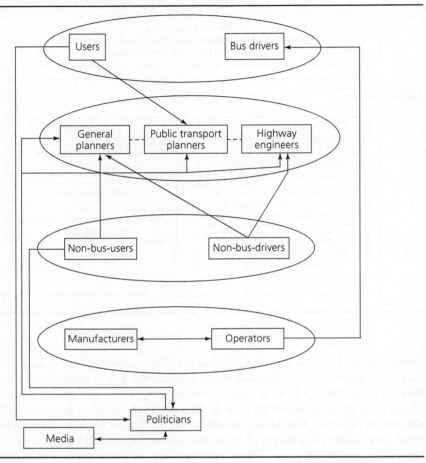

compromises that have to be handled. Figure 4.41 shows the decision model for the consideration of car drivers.

4.7. Conclusions

In this chapter I have tried to bring together some of the thoughts about how to consider the process of reaching and using the bus stop in the context of contributing to making the city help people to improve their wellbeing.

I have made a number of suggestions about how to view bus stops in this context, and also about how to frame the decision processes that would help to put improvements in place.

The next chapter takes these thoughts and applies the design process in order to consider how solutions could be devised.

Figure 4.43 Participative approach to the bus stop design process

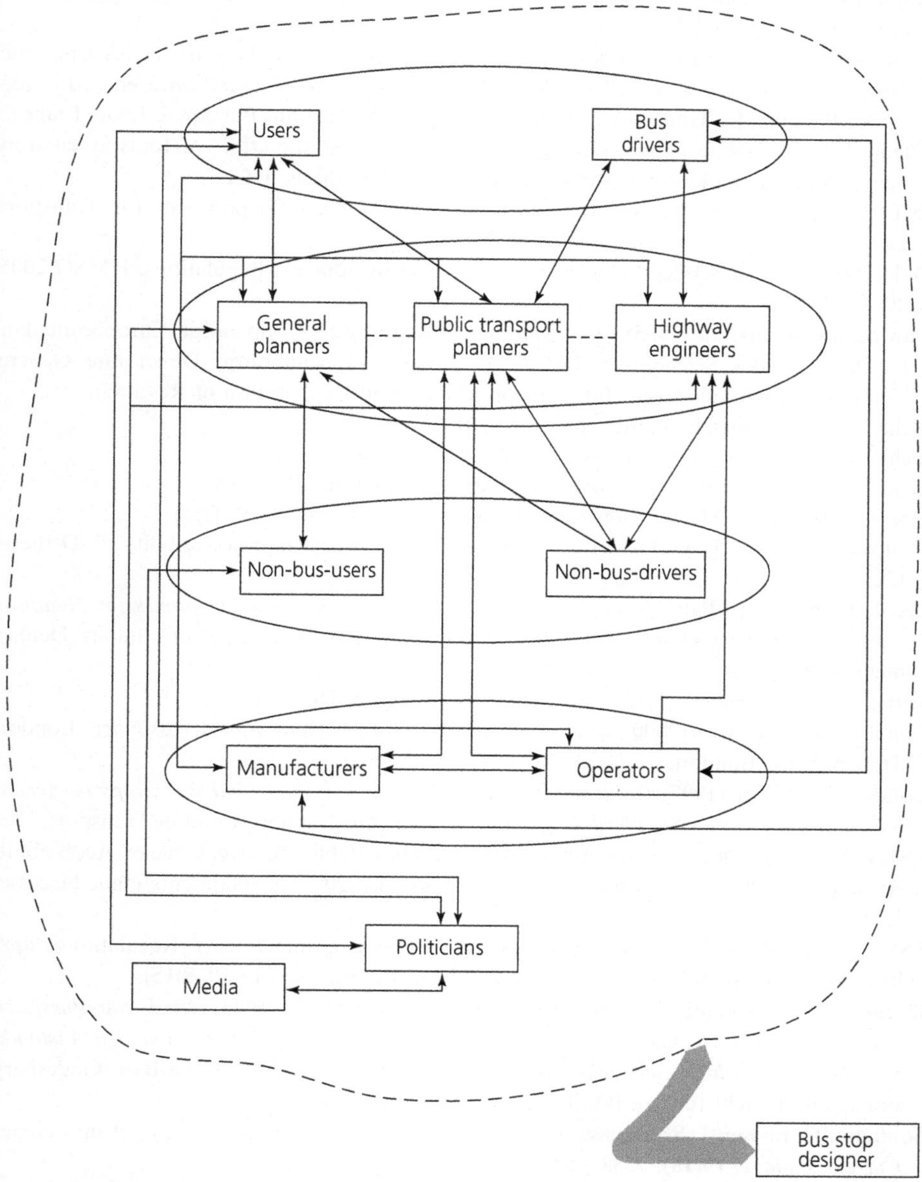

REFERENCES

Adhitya S (2013) *Sonifying Urban Rhythms: Towards the spatio-temporal composition of the urban environment*. See http://rice.iuav.it/400/ (accessed 27/10/2015).

Barham P, Oxley P and Shaw A (1994) *Accessible Public Transport Infrastructure*. London: Department of Transport.

Bundesministerium für Verkehr (1997) *Bürgerfreundliche und behinderten-gerechte Gestaltung von Haltestellen des öffentlichen Personennahverkehrs*. Bonn-Bad Godesberg, Bundesministerium für Verkehr, p. 51.

CERTU (Centre d'Études sur les Réseaux, les Transports, l'Urbanisme et les Constructions Publiques) (2001) *Les Bus et leurs Points d'Arrêt Accessibles à Tous*. Centre d'Études sur les Réseaux, les Transports, l'Urbanisme et les Constructions Publiques, Lyon, France.

Cheng T-J (2015) Use of gaze and gait analysis to assess the effect of footway environmental factors on older pedestrians' accessibility. PhD thesis, UCL.

DfT (Department for Transport) (2005a) *Inclusive Mobility*. Department for Transport, London.

DfT (2005b) Public Service Vehicles Accessibility (Amendment) Regulations. HMSO 2005/2988.

European Commission (1995) *Low Floor Buses*. Report 322, Cooperation Européenne dans la Domaine des Sciences et Techniques (COST). Luxembourg: Directorate General (XIII) Telecommunications, Information Market and Exploitation of Research.

Gehl J (1978) Studier I Burano, *Arkitekten*, **18**.

Gehl J (2010) *Cities for People*. Islands, Washington, DC, USA.

Gehl J (2011) *Life Between Buildings*. Islands, Washington, DC, USA.

Hall ET (1966) *The Hidden Dimension*. Doubleday, New York, NY, USA.

Holloway C (2011) The effect of crossfall gradient on wheelchair accessibility. PhD thesis, UCL.

Lee J, Edmonds L, Patel J and Rhodes D (2011) *Noise Exposure Contours for Heathrow Airport 2011*. ERCD report 1201. Environmental Research and Consultancy Department, London, UK.

Lerner J (2014) *Urban Acupuncture*. Island, Washington, DC, USA.

London Bus Initiative (2000) *Bus Stop Layouts for Low Floor Bus Accessibility*. London: Transport for London.

London Transport (1997) *Guidelines for the Design of Bus Bays and Bus Stops to Accommodate the European Standard (12 metre) Length Bus*. London: London Transport.

PSVA (Public Service Vehicles Accessibility) (2000a) Public Service Vehicles Accessibility Regulations 2000. http://www.legislation.gov.uk/uksi/2000/1970/contents/made (accessed 15/10/2015).

PSVA (2000b) Public Service Vehicles Accessibility (Amendment) Regulations 2000. http://www.legislation.gov.uk/uksi/2000/3318/made (accessed 15/10/2015).

Rogat U, Blennemann F, Grossmann H and Krämer T (1993) *Niederflur-Bussystem Anstandshilfen: Untersuchung von Möglichkeiten zur Erhaltung eines minimalen Anstandes zwischen Niederflurbussen und Haltestellen*. FE No. 387/92. Bonn-Bad Godesberg: Forschungsbericht für den Bundesministers für Verkehr.

Souman JL, Frissen I, Sreenivasa MN and Ernst MO (2009) Walking straight into circles. *Current Biology*, **19(18)**: 1538–1542.

Tebb R (1997) *The Unistop: Towards a fully accessible bus stop*. Discussion document. Firstbus Development.

TfL (Transport for London) (2006) *Accessible Bus Stop Design Guidance*. Transport for London, London.

TfL (2015) Maps and signs. https://tfl.gov.uk/info-for/boroughs/maps-and-signs (accessed 15/10/2015).

Tyler N and Caiaffa MM (1999) *EXCALIBUR III Experiments: Performance of the Guidance System with Different Low Floor Buses*. Working paper. London: University College London Centre for Transport Studies.

Uster G, Kaplan S, Dessaigne M and Dejeammes M (1997) Le développement d'une aide à l'accostage. *Recherche Transport Sécurité*, **54**: 43–51.

Wang T (2015) Perception of unevenness in the footway environment. Upgrade Report, UCL Accessibility Research Group (unpublished).

Accessibility and the Bus System: Transforming the World
ISBN 978-0-7277-5980-1

ICE Publishing: All rights reserved
http://dx.doi.org/10.1680/aabs2ed.59801.209

publishing

Chapter 5
Design of accessible bus stops: Transforming the world

5.1. Design in the decision-making process

In this chapter, I consider how the design process can be brought to bear on making the bus system accessible and helpful in achieving the visions raised in Chapters 1, 2 and 3, and to meet the challenges put forwards in Chapter 4. To start, I present a brief discussion about the nature of the design process and how this is evolving given these challenges.

5.1.1 Design

One of the core elements of the decision-making process is the design of potential solutions. I see conventional design as a combination of (1) a result of and (2) a process that encapsulates curiosity. The main design process – brief → conceive → test → consider → make → use – is complemented by other processes (identifying the desired outcomes, identifying and understanding the functionality required, determining the functions being made available and learning from these how much the process is meeting and extending the desired outcomes). It is also characterised by a number of iterative processes. The iteration between 'conceive', 'consider' and 'brief' is crucial in determining whether the conception can meet the brief and if any or all of these needs to be revised before proceeding to testing and making. This relates to the outcomes-based decision model, with its desired outcomes, success factors and limitations (encapsulated in the functionalities required and the functions delivered) leading to actions (the final design).

In the case of a bus system as a whole or just an element of it, the scale suggests that the process would involve some sort of pilot implementation – perhaps one or two exemplar bus stops (as demonstrated in the Excalibur project (see Chapter 4)) – so that an evaluation of the performance of the design could be made, including its acceptability to the public and bus operators and other actors (see Section 4.6). The evaluation should include an estimate of the overall functionality which would determine how the design could, should or would be used and this could then be tested in a wider implementation if the pilot example were considered to act as desired. The functions could be tested again to see if there are any more that were unintended – these additional functions could be either positive (e.g. people enjoy using the design in an unintended way) or negative (e.g. people seek to abuse or destroy the design) and lessons could be learnt from this step which would influence the consideration of the performance of the design in terms of the

Table 5.1 Public participation in the design process

	Action	Who is engaged in the action		
	Stage in the design process	Public	Decision-maker	External experts
1	Problem identification (set desired outcomes)	***	****	**
2	Conceptualisation of the problem	**	****	***
2.1	Legal responsibilities and constraints	*	****	***
2.2	Technical constraints ('laws of physics')	*	****	***
2.3	Other issues	****	**	***
3	Development of the brief	**	***	****
4	Conceive possible solutions	**	***	****
5	Test solutions	***	**	****
6	Consider the results of the tests	***	****	**
7	Implement a pilot trial	***	****	**
8	Test functionality in the pilot trial	***	***	****
9	Implement more widely and use the solution(s)	***	****	*
10	Consider functionality, including unexpected functions	***	****	***
11	Learn from the implementation and functionality tests	***	****	***
12	Set new desired outcomes	***	****	**

Key:
**** = leads the process and is responsible for the outcome; *** = important role;
** = important interest in the outcome; * = concerns and opinion need to be noted

desired outcomes. This could then lead to an adaptation to the brief for subsequent design applications.

In terms of public participation, the key is where the public enters the process. The simple answer is 'throughout', but the level of involvement changes as the process evolves. Table 5.1 presents an example where three players are considered: (A) the public, (B) the decision-maker and (C) the external experts who could provide independent technical advice to either the public or the decision-maker. In Table 5.1, 'External experts' also include stakeholders such as the transport operators, the Police and other bodies with technical (and possibly legal) knowledge which could concern the outcome. The 'public' does of course include a large variety of entities and these all need to be considered throughout the process.

The participation process for public decision-making has been ratified by the United Nations (UN). The United Nations Economic Commission for Europe (UNECE) Convention on Access to Information is the codification of what was formerly known as the Aarhus Convention (UNECE, 2014a, 2014b). It was adopted on 25 June 1998 in Denmark. The UNECE Convention is important because it sets out the principle that the public must participate in all decisions that relate to the environment. The associated Protocol empowers people with the right to have easy access to information to participate effectively in the decision-making process and to have access to justice if these rights are denied.

It is also important to determine who has the final decision at each stage and this is indicated in Table 5.1. For most of the stages this will be the decision-maker, but at some critical points this is not the case – for example, the conceptualisation of the problem other than the legal and technical issues is something that, with appropriate advice, could be 'given' to the public to decide as part of their participatory contribution.

It is also important that the decision-maker does not act as the prime interpreter of the outputs from tests and evaluations as well as being the arbiter of what should be done. They should act on the basis of what these outputs mean rather than what they are and the actual testing and evaluation should be undertaken by independent experts. This prevents (or at least reduces) the perception of the outputs being skewed to support the case being proposed by the decision-maker, and the maintenance of this level of credibility and confidence is an important element of the public participation process. Inclusion of all parties throughout the process in this way ensures compliance with the UNECE Convention, the inclusion of both technical and emotional competence in the decision process and, possibly most important of all, a sense of ownership in the outcome on the part of the public who will use and/or have to live or work with the resulting design.

5.1.2   Composition

The design process, as seen in Section 5.1.1, is a conventional way of considering design. However, it does not, of itself, ensure that all things are considered, especially in relation to space, time and sensorial interactions, so it is poor at incorporating the dynamics of life as it is lived by the population of a city. The world changes all the time and the way in which events happen involves an important relationship between constancy, repetition and change. A daily commute seems, at first sight, to be a repetitive experience and the infrastructure involved appears to be constant and unchanging. However, the reality is that this is not the case at all. As Heraclitus said, 'A man cannot jump into the same river twice', by which he was referring to the fact that on each subsequent attempt the water would be different and the man would have changed. So it is with something as routine as engaging with the bus system. A person cannot use the same bus stop (or bus) twice: the environment around the bus stop, including the people nearby, will be different, the person will be different and so on. Time is constantly repeating, although never repeated. Repetition is thus a rather poor way of describing using the bus system on different occasions. As I want buses to transform the world, I had to find a method that embraces these concepts.

The concept of 'repeating but never repeated' is the essence of music. Sara Adhitya (2013) has been thinking about this problem in her consideration of how cities relate to music – for example, the rhythms of the city and its people – and has developed the concept of 'composition' as an approach, rather than 'design'. This can be thought of in terms drawn from bringing disparate elements, concepts and movements together in an outcome that responds in and to space and time, which allows for constancy and change, inspires creativity – and which includes the audience as an explicit part of the performance.

In terms of rhythm, music works by challenging repetition – the sense of a regular pulse – by applying different rhythms which compete with that pulse. The resulting tensions and resolutions provide a satisfying outcome. Of course music also works in a harmonic sense – by creating harmonic dissonances, which are then resolved. Combining the rhythmic tensions with the harmonic dissonances to delay final resolution of both is one of the ways in which a piece of music attracts us. Without the sense of pulse or harmony (usually culturally defined), music would just be noise. However, even if following a written score, a musician does not adhere precisely to the required rhythm and melodic instructions as set out by the composer. Every time a piece of music is played, it will be slightly different – each time, just as with Heraclitus, the musician is different and the environment around them is different: the tension between pulse and rhythm and pitch, dissonance and consonance will be unique to a particular performance. In an art form like music the performer will respond to the changes in the environment as well. The same applies to other performance art and this is indeed what we expect in a performance. Viewing the urban realm – and within it, a bus stop – as a performance rather than as a static unchanging object brings great opportunities for making it a better place to be. Composition is the skill of bringing a variety of components together to create a performance and it is this aspect of creating a bus stop environment that I will discuss now.

Composition is the bringing together of what are often discrete opportunities in order to achieve a unified outcome – in this case, a contribution towards the attainment of the vision. One common use of the word 'composition' is in relation to music: we speak of music as being 'composed'. Music, however, does not actually exist until it is performed and this can be a highly multisensorial experience – it includes different sounds in space and time, but can also include actions and visual settings. It is also something that speaks simultaneously both to the individual person and the collective crowd. Whether we are talking about some historical piece of music, a contemporary composition or an extemporised 'jam session', the music does not exist until it is performed and the audience is part of the performance just as much as the players: every performance is different, even though the piece of music – as written in the score – itself might be the same. Thus, the music is simultaneously both a product (the piece of music) and a process (the performance). These are very interesting characteristics to apply to the composition of our environment – including the composition of the bus system. To have a generic definition, I like Sara Adhitya's definition of composition as 'multisensorial design in space and time'.

The product-process duality, which is exemplified in performance and central to composition, means that the composition evolves over time, so the 'product' can change over time and in space. The multisensorial nature of the 'process' means that the composition can affect all senses, and interacts with all people in a multidirectional way – just as with a musical performance, the individual person can respond to the composition and the composition can respond to the individual. With this as the basic principle, Sara and I have been working on developing composition as a way to create outcomes which are explicitly about, by, with and for, people, consider multisensorial approaches to space and time, allow for interactions to happen in all directions and adapt over time and place. We are trying to build a method to ensure that we can create solutions that can answer questions such as: How will the solution feel, sound, look like, evolve, adapt in relation to individual people? – as well as (in this case) how it provides the working solution necessary to enable the bus system to function in delivering accessible mobility for the city (Adhitya and Tyler, 2014).

However, composition cannot be seen in isolation from the rest of the decision process. So composition is the central element of a process, in which other processes are also required in order to generate actual changes to the world: if I want the bus system to transform the world, I need to make sure that the process is sufficiently comprehensive. So I have had to rearrange the design process a little, to be sure that the process incorporates transformation.

Sara Adhitya and I have come up with a seven-stage transformation process, which is a slight adaptation of the composition process that Sara has been working with for some years. The transformation process starts with the *realisation* of the problem. This is the determination of the vision and the identification of the problem to be solved in order to attain that high level expression of the purpose of the city. Next, we take this as a starting point to *envision* the ways in which we might be able to solve the problem. This is the equivalent of developing the brief in the conventional design process. Then we *compose* solutions to meet the challenge set out in the envisioning process, bringing people-centred, multisensorial, spatio-temporal, operational opportunities to bear on the way in which the challenge could be met. Then we *implement* the composition, followed by a process of *evaluation* to check whether or not we are reaching the goals we are seeking. Next, we reconsider the whole outcome in order to understand how to *translate* it to other places/times, not only in order to spread the outcome in space and time, but also to see how to adapt it to other cultures and opportunities. This is also the way in which we consider what could be done differently in order to learn more for the future about how the composition could meet the vision.

We characterise the whole process as a transformation, in the sense that even if we retain much of what existed before the process, it will be seen in a different way and as such will help to transform the cultural as well as the operational functionality of the system and the people who engage with it. The whole process culminates in transformation and the whole transformation process can be seen in Figure 5.1, in which relevant terms from the conventional design process have been inserted for comparison. Composition is a core element of the process and has to include a more direct inclusion of the high-level vision because the adaptation over space and time implicit in composition requires direct association with the vision, not only with a brief (which would be more specific to time and place than the envisioned challenge). It is this relationship with its original vision that makes the composition approach so much more suitable for applications such as the development of an accessible bus system in order to transform the world.

5.1.3 Composing bus stops
The design of a bus stop to achieve all the points raised in Section 4.6.1 is always going to be difficult in the real world. However, the Excalibur project provides a starting point for the design of an accessible bus stop. This section deals in some depth with how to meet

Figure 5.1 The transformation process

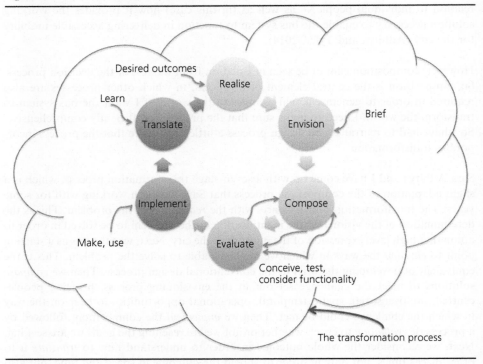

the requirements outlined in Section 4.6.1. What is highly critical, however, is the way in which the bus stop and its accoutrements act as part of the way people live in the urban realm. This was not considered in the Excalibur project, as the scope was to explore only how to respond to the accessibility needs. Although the technical aspects of delivering the requirements are important, it is also essential to consider the aesthetics of the bus stop and its surrounding area. These are not an add-on, but a core part of how the bus stop is a contributor to the life of the community, whether this is in its function as an interchange facility between the pedestrian and the bus or as part of the community realm. It is important to realise that whereas the bus passengers and pedestrians move past the bus stop, the bus stop remains in its place within the community space. This is all part of transforming the world rather than just the bus system.

The actions described in Sections 4.6.1.1 to 4.6.1.9 are what has to be done to generate a suitably accessible bus stop for the community and its bus service. These need to be collated into a set of functions that are required of the bus stop. Each of these can be measured using the value engineering techniques discussed in Section 1.4 (see Table 5.2).

Every bus stop site is different and, therefore, the basic design might need to be altered in almost every case. It is therefore important to understand why the basic design is the way it is so that the inevitable compromises can be made with a minimal loss to the

Table 5.2 Functions of a bus stop

Function	Evaluation criteria	Section(s) where this is discussed
Being a 'good place to be' within the urban realm	Use of the space by people whether or not they are using the bus system	4.2, 4.3, 4.5
Delivery of a sociable interface between the bus stop and the pedestrian realm	People find it easy to move between the pedestrian realm and the bus realm	4.2, 4.3, 4.5
Delivery of accessible information about the locality	People use the bus stop as a source of information about the locality	4.2
Delivery of accessible information about the bus service	It is easy for people to understand how the bus service works, including real-time performance of the service	4.2, 4.3
Delivery of easy access to/from the bus for all passengers	Measurement of capabilities and determination of who is not able to use the bus at each bus stop	4.4
Delivery of sufficient capacity for the buses using the stop	Minimised operational delay for buses at the stop	4.3
Delivery of sufficient capacity for passengers using the stop	Comfortable waiting in and around the bus stop area	4.3, 4.4

accessibility, functionality (including the function of aesthetics) of the bus stop. Another reason why a clear understanding of the principles underlying the basic design is necessary is that this will help to identify those people who will be excluded from the service as a result of any compromise to the design. This will highlight the difficulties that would be caused by a change to the design and make it easier to determine suitable alternative arrangements in the unfortunate cases where such exclusion is unavoidable and thus help to ensure that these are eliminated – or at least mitigated in every case.

The basic designs provide the ideal (i.e. what is theoretically necessary to obtain an accessible bus stop), and it must be remembered that any diminution of these fundamental principles means a reduction in the amount of accessibility on offer. This would result in some people being excluded from the bus service and thus from the activities they wish to pursue. Each reduction in accessibility must be considered in light of how it can be compensated for through other measures (and the associated costs and problems that might result). It is also necessary to design the bus stop for the function of being a good place to be, to fit within the urban realm and to be an active and accepted part of the urban realm. For these, the aesthetics are crucially important. The designer must therefore work out how to combine the accessibility functions of the bus stop, performance with the bus services and the community function of the bus stop as a core part of the delivery of a vibrant community.

The following discussion concentrates on the analysis of the decisive elements and steps that will define an accessible bus stop. They are:

1   the aesthetics of the bus stop
2   dealing with the vertical gap
3   dealing with the horizontal gap
4   balancing the crossfall
5   setting the design of the surface and passenger area
6   helping the driver with a guidance system
7   locating the entrance door position
8   safety measures
9   the shelter.

These are not set out in any particular priority order. The bus stop is a portal to being able to move around the city beyond the area that can feasibly be covered on foot. As such it has a permanence in the environment which means that the statement it makes is everlasting – yet each bus stop needs to be able to evolve over time. It must therefore appeal to the senses of the people who interact with it – even if they are just walking past it – and then deliver accessibility to the bus services for those who wish to use it as the point of entry to the bus system. However, we need a successful outcome in every one of these design categories in order to achieve an accessible bus stop.

5.2.   Aesthetics

Aesthetics is the (attractive) appearance or sound of something (OED, 1989). There is a view that is too often expressed which states that once you incorporate accessibility, aesthetics are irrelevant. This is wholly wrong. The art of the urban space in all its forms – sculpture, music, poetry, literature, dance, the urban form itself and the way in which it operates – are all part of the way in which a city can be a good place to be. And people will respond warmly to the stimulus of an aesthetic environment. The key is to involve people in the aesthetics as well as everything else.

5.2.1   A word about senses

In order to consider the aesthetics of a place, a person must use their senses, so I am going to spend a little time on discussing senses before going on to consider aesthetics. Western cultures tend to think in terms of five senses: vision, hearing, smell, touch, taste. In other cultures there is a greater range of senses. Senses are the mechanism by which we detect our environment, which is necessary in order to determine whether or not it is threatening, whether it is pleasant to stay in or better to leave. I like to think of the senses in three broad groups: physiological (those related directly to the bodily functions), environmental (those which relate to characteristics of where we are) and interpretational (those which we use to judge a situation or context in which we find ourselves). Table 5.3 shows a selection of such senses, categorised into these three groups. You may well be able to consider more – just think of completing the sentence 'I have a sense of ...' and see how many you can come up with!

Physiological senses are those contained and processed within the body. We have a variety of sensors linked to the nervous system – the taste buds in our mouth, the hairs in our ears,

Table 5.3 Senses we use to understand our surroundings

Physiological senses	Environmental senses	Interpretational senses
Sight	Rhythm	Ownership
Sound	Harmony	Justice
Smell	Colour contrast	History
Taste	Spatial awareness	Culture
Touch	Direction	Politics
Balance	Pitch	Wellbeing
Proprioception	Place	Fear
Vestibular Awareness	Time	Care
Pain		Safety
		Experience
		Emotion
		Pride

the photoreceptors in our eyes, for example – and these deliver signals to specialised areas of our brain which then converts these into recognition and then, if necessary, stimulates a response. The sense of balance for example detects first that a person is out of balance, causing them first to feel insecure but then to respond instinctively as the stimulus-response system kicks in and, by some means or other, equilibrium is restored.

The environmental senses are those by which we process what we see, hear, feel and so on in order to make sense of them. So a sense of rhythm enables us to walk in step with others around us, whether this is instigated by music we hear, a sight we see or just the sense of walking 'in step' with someone near to us. This is how crowds can move without people colliding into each other. However, the sense of rhythm is also used to keep us alert. It is why we find a street with many small, different shops more interesting than a street with only a blank wall on either side, or the positioning of objects in a painting – as well as the more familiar rhythms associated with music. The presence of a discernible rhythm therefore reassures us that the world is working, that things are in order and we can move onto pay attention elsewhere.

Interpretational senses are those we use to assess the context. The sense of fairness signals to a person that some act is appropriate or not and is important because then he or she can determine whether a situation is making some people worse off than a fair society would deem satisfactory. Although not everyone will see it this way, the Congestion Charge in London has remained in place through a number of mayoral elections largely because there seems to be some justice in using the proceeds from a charge on private driving in the central area solely to improve the public transport service. If the money were not hypothecated in this way, it could just be seen as a rather unfair tax on a certain part of the population, with no benefit to the population as a whole.

We can separate these categories in terms of the degree of processing involved: physiological senses are essentially natural processes of the body designed to sustain survival, environmental senses are sensitivities to aspects of the environment where the raw material for these senses is derived from the physiological senses of seeing, hearing etc. but applied to another construct, such as time (in the case of rhythm for example). People will have greater sensitivity to some of these constructs than others, but most of the time none is crucial to survival. Interpretational responses are learnt and are responses to what is seen, read, heard, according to a set of 'rules' derived from education and experience (from whatever source) and could change from time to time.

Interpretational and environmental senses can affect changes in physiological senses and this is important when considering capability changes in people. Changes in capabilities are often observed in older people and these are often considered to be some form of decline – in vision, hearing, balance, etc. I think it is incorrect to consider them in this way. For example, typically, visual acuity changes as a person ages, but instead of seeing this as a decline, it can be viewed as favouring long distance rather than short distance acuity. This is a change, not a decline, and can be compensated by changes in other senses. For example, the experience gained over a lifetime means that the person can compensate for the change in vision by using their learnt experience to seek out relevant signs and indicators earlier in the process. The experiments undertaken by Cheng, described in Section 4.1.2.2, showed this taking place – the fact that this was a preconscious response shows that the sensorial system was adapting naturally to the change. This, as with the finding of Karekla (see Chapter 6) in relation to moving around inside a moving bus, that lifetime experience is a way of compensating for age-related changes in order to improve stability in readiness for the inevitable as the change in surface level approached.

The importance of all this is that when designing something to be a great place to be for the people who encounter it – indeed to encourage people to want to encounter it – it is important to provide sensory stimuli for as many of these senses as possible. Or at least to be deliberate in declining to stimulate them: I mentioned Rothko in Section 4.6 where the absence of visual stimuli is used to heighten sensitivity to other stimuli. Another example would be John Cage's 4'3", in which 'silence' is used to heighten sensitivity to ambient noises (including those inside one's head). Understanding senses in this functional way is what I call the science of senses, or just 'aesthetics'.

5.2.2 Aesthetics in action

Aesthetics – derived from the Greek for 'to perceive, feel or sense' – is really about how we perceive the world around us. When creating this world, it is important to realise that our mind will act to perceive. If it finds this impossible it will tend to ignore or downgrade its importance, resulting sometimes in the response to destroy or damage it, or simply to treat it as if it had no value. People often treat the bus system in this way – quite possibly because we have a habit of designing it to have no aesthetic value. If we believe that a person who is over the age of 26 and (still) using a bus is a failure, then we will be subconsciously designing 'down' systems for such 'failures' and there is no desire to design 'up' to people who are successes. Think of the difference in the design approach adopted to create the I-phone compared with that of a bus stop, or the lack of care when designing the interior of a bus which results in the need to put signs saying 'Mind your head'.

Similarly, the beauty and elegance of driving taught to chauffeurs of high-end limousines is quite different from the more prosaic skills taught to drivers of buses, as is the highly programmatic approach to 'driving' an aeroplane which is taught to airline pilots. In all three cases the emphasis is on driving safely. However, in the case of the chauffeur, the objective is to provide movement without the sense of motion (i.e. to control acceleration, deceleration and turning so that the passenger does not perceive the change in motion). In the case of the bus, the emphasis is on ensuring the vehicle keeps to time and is not damaging the bus or its passengers in the process. The complexity of an aircraft and its operation means that the only way for a human to engage with it is to learn the discipline of following instructions exactly, whether these are provided in the form of a manual or from air traffic control instructions.

Even in emergency situations, aircraft pilots resort to checklists and follow these because the complexity of the operation is so high. This does not preclude the use of human judgement of course and checklists are only as good as the assumptions on which they are based. Nevertheless, pilots have to have frequent and routine visits for simulator training so that they can maintain the skills of flying the aircraft safely under a wide variety of circumstances – and to provide as comfortable a ride as possible to the passengers in their care. In the three cases – the chauffer, the bus driver and the airline pilot – the issue of 'care' is crucial to a high quality performance and at its most prosaic, that sense of care is the difference between a comfortable and an uncomfortable ride.

The carriage of people in a vehicle is an unnatural experience – humans have not evolved for this even though it is now a relatively common occurrence. Therefore, the perception of the experience is all-important. Making a ride so that it is perceived to be safe and comfortable is the responsibility of the person, systems and management providing the service. Driving a bus is as aesthetic an experience as performing a piece of music or painting a picture of a landscape – it is a multisensorial performance in space and time.

How should a bus stop appeal to the senses? Interestingly, the linking together of aesthetics and railway systems has been a strong feature of many transport systems around the world. Paris with its art nouveau Hector Guimard entrances, London, with Leslie Green, Charles Holden and more recently Norman Foster, and Moscow (architect/designer unknown, but much of the engineering and design work was done by engineers from London Underground) are all famous examples. An attempt some years ago to encourage innovative design for London's bus stops failed to find a winner, so there is great scope for thinking about how the aesthetics of a bus stop could help to transform the urban environment in London. I wonder what a Gaudí bus stop would have looked like? His lamp posts in Plaça Reial, Barcelona, are early examples of his work (actually his first commission), but the luscious curves of his later buildings could be really interesting if applied to a bus shelter.

However, aesthetics could take other forms, including performance art – the stairs at Odenplan station in Stockholm, artwork such as the murals of the opportunity for a flashmob orchestra in Barcelona, 'Poems on the Underground' and so on. Tokyo associates a different tune to each station on its Yamanote line. Aesthetics is all about making the place seem a good place to be by communicating directly with the senses. A bus stop, as part of the physical environment, should certainly contribute to such a sense. The 'piano stairs' at Odenplan station encourage people to want to 'play the piano' and use the stairs rather than the escalator – but the people on the escalator are also enjoying the experience as they watch the stairs go by. By all means have music at bus stops – providing that it is acceptable to people living nearby – or we could generate a playlist of pieces related to each stop and its locale that people could pick up when near the stop using their smartphones.

It is no surprise that most of these examples are to be found at railway stations – these have long been associated with statements in architecture and design – so why should bus stops not also have such a statement? London has almost 20 000 bus stops and the statement about the environment that these make is highly important. These have shifted from being simply a marker for where buses stop, sometimes with a shelter, to something for waiting, with information about the bus system and the surrounding area and maybe other health-giving properties such as a garden or clean air. However, bus stops are designed to discourage lurking and loitering, so are deliberately made to be uncomfortable! They have yet to progress to being a place which is good for people to be – where the distinction between lingering and lurking is encouraged so that the bus stop becomes a place to enjoy.

The bus stop is part of the public space and thus contributes to the cultural and aesthetic environment. We should therefore ensure that this contribution is positive. In 2014, as part of an exercise to change perceptions about bus stops, the UCL Universal Composition Laboratory set up two bus stops on Regent Street in a way that would challenge people to look at them in a different way. Taking advantage of a special event run by Transport for London (TfL) for which Regent Street was closed to traffic for a day as part of TfL's 2014 Year of the Bus celebrations, we converted one bus stop into a range of settings related to rooms – an office, a bedroom, a lounge, a garden – and the other as a musical bus stop, which people could play like a musical instrument. You can see the result in 'The bus stop: London's agent of change', a short film we made about this which won the Best Urban Design film at the New Urbanism Film Festival in Los Angeles, USA where its innovative approach to changing perceptions was recognised. What we learn from this is that it is both possible and acceptable to revise our view about what a bus stop should be like.

This requires an appraisal of the functionality of the bus stop. Table 5.4 shows some possible functions for a bus stop, where the difference is highlighted between a bus stop which is intended to be 'just' a good working design for the bus system and one in which the primary function is to be an active part of the public space and secondary functions are related to the operation of the bus system. Perhaps the biggest difference between the two is that, in the first case, the bus stop is specifically designed for bus users and buses whereas, in the second case, because the bus stop is perceived as part of the public space, it is designed for the public as a whole, with additional features for people who wish to use the bus system. The bus stop is therefore a part of the public environment which is also providing a service to the bus system – it will still be there, contributing to community wellbeing, even when the buses are somewhere else.

Table 5.4 Possible functionality of a bus stop

Function	Bus stop as an element of the bus system	Bus stop as an element of public space
Primary	Identification of a place where buses stop to set down or collect passengers	An accessible place that provides an aesthetic element in the public space that is easy to enjoy and conveys the quality of the area
Secondary	A place which is safe, accessible and with sufficient capacity for both passengers and buses	A pleasant place to be, which is safe and accessible for passengers and where people can enjoy lingering, sitting, watching activities, conversing with others
	A place which provides accessible information about the bus services	A place where artworks can be displayed, performed, enjoyed
	A place which provides accessible information about the local area	A place which provides accessible information about the local area
	A place which provides accessible real-time information about oncoming bus arrivals	A place which provides accessible information about the bus service
	A place which provides accessible shelter from the weather	A place which provides accessible real-time information about oncoming bus arrivals, visible from outside the actual shelter area
	A place which provides accessible seating for waiting passengers	A place which provides accessible shelter from the weather
	A place which provides good access to the buses	A place which is safe, accessible and with sufficient capacity for buses
	A place which provides good access to/from the surrounding area	A place which provides good access to the buses
Tertiary	Seats should be accessible, comfortable and provide a good view of information and oncoming buses	A place which provides good access to/from the surrounding area
	A place designed to be a consistently identifiable part of the bus system	Seats should be accessible, comfortable and arranged to provide both a good view of oncoming buses and other activities in the surrounding environment
	A place designed with the participation of the local community	A place designed with the participation of the local community

In both cases the bus stop must provide sufficient capacity for both passengers and buses and must provide information and so on, but in the public space version there are more functions concerned with how it works as part of the public environment to provide opportunities for people and a recognition that the bus stop might be of use as a bus stop to people who are not actually in the shelter and thus should provide information to the

Figure 5.2 Edible Bus stop, Landor Road, London (Source: William Sandy)

wider audience. The shelter needs to provide protection from the weather, but can be an environmental statement at the same time. Real-time information needs to be provided in a way that enables people to know about the oncoming arrivals even when they are not actually in the shelter. Seats should be designed so that people can enjoy sitting in them and can chat, read a book, enjoy watching the world go by – whether or not they are waiting for a bus. This suggests that the orientation of the seating should be considered to promote relaxed conversation, activities which might or might not involve one or more people, as well as to enable waiting pedengers to see the information they require. The point is to design the public space element in such a way that it also serves the bus system and vice versa. All the functions in Table 5.4 need to be seen as design requirements. Primary, secondary and tertiary do not imply differences in importance – just their relationship to the overall functionality of the service. The question is: how should the design deliver all of these functionalities?

One of the outcomes of the 'bus stop as a public space' approach is that its incursion into the non-bus stop area is more acceptable because it is a part of that area as part of the public space – and needs to be designed as such.

The 'edible bus stop' movement engages with local people and studies how they approach the bus stop so that they can design a garden around the paths chosen by the community (see Figure 5.2). The raised beds (constructed using recycled granite kerbstones) provide a 3D element to the space, thus breaking up the normally flat perspective, and the garden provides welcome colour. The garden is maintained by the local community and provides an example of a 'pocket park', a small local green space that helps contribute to making the city green. The bus stop still makes use of a 'standard' London bus shelter though. This means that someone sitting in the shelter would be facing away from the garden and thus less able to enjoy its benefits. How would this be if the bus shelter were aligned differently so that (a) people could sit in the shelter and enjoy the garden as well as see the oncoming buses, and (b) people could enjoy sitting and chatting in the garden and still be able to see the information about oncoming

Figure 5.3 New concept bus stop, Gare de Lyon, Paris, France

buses? If the shelter could be replaced with one that is a better aesthetic fit with the garden it would be even better.

RATP (Régie Autonome des Transports Parisiens), the Paris public transport authority, has designed a new concept bus stop which illustrates some of the ideas addressed in this section. The bus stop at Gare de Lyon in Paris, France, is an example of extending the bus stop into the community environment. It includes a community book-swapping scheme, recharging for electric bicycles, information about the local area, first aid equipment and a coffee bar (although this has to compete with a café next to the bus stop!). Figures 5.3 shows some of the bus stops in use and Figures 5.4 shows the care with which the seat at the bus stop was designed, including the material from which is was made.

Having achieved the aesthetic quality required for the bus stop within its locality, I now turn to the business of making the bus stop work for the community who wish to use it to access the buses. It is my contention that the two foci are completely compatible and mutually beneficial.

5.3. Operations
5.3.1 Dealing with the vertical gap: Choice of kerb height
The height of the platform above the level of the roadway affects the vertical gap between the platform surface and the floor of the bus at the entrance and/or exit door(s). One of

Figure 5.4 Ceramic seating at the Gare de Lyon bus stop, Paris, France

Figure 5.5 The profile of the Kassel kerb (dimensions in mm; *R*, radius)

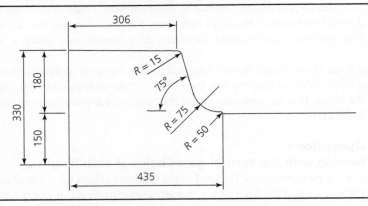

the most useful things to do with a bus stop is to increase the height of the kerb so that the vertical gap can be reduced. There are a few kerbs available that are higher than normal kerbs but that have been designed to allow buses to approach them without damaging the tyres or bodywork. The best of these is the Kassel kerb, originally produced in Germany. This is designed with a 75 mm radius curve at the interface with the road level to match the tyre profile and a face set at 75° to the horizontal so that the edge of the bus body just fits beside the kerb edge. The combination of these two design elements means that the kerb can 'steer' the bus along the platform without damaging the tyre or body. Kassel kerbs are available in two heights (160 and 180 mm) in the UK, although they have been used in Grenoble, France, with a height of 210 mm. The Kassel kerb profile is shown in Figure 5.5.

There are other designs in use in Germany – for example, the Aachen kerb, 180 mm high and a 65° face with a straight edge at road level; the Herten kerb, which is 165 mm high, with a 65° face with a small (15 mm radius) curve at the bottom; and the Dresden kerb, designed for use with bus or tram stops, which has a cut-out at the top to allow for the different body-width characteristics of the two vehicle types. Another development in France is a stepped kerb for use with optically controlled buses.

When the vehicle eventually stops to collect passengers, the vertical gap can be reduced by lowering the bus. This can reduce the floor height of the bus door from its 'drive height' of around 320 mm to a 'knelt height' of about 250 mm above the road level, although I have found that this could be as low as 200 mm in older buses (where the suspension has settled over time). The ground clearance is typically about 80–90 mm less than the floor height (i.e. by the thickness of the floor and any chassis parts and other equipment installed underneath the front quarter of the bus). At present, the difference between ride height and knelt height seems to be of the order of about 80–100 mm. Thus, a bus purchased to deliver the Public Service Vehicles Accessibility Regulations' 250 mm floor height, may have a ground clearance of 160 mm when knelt and 240 mm at floor height (PSVA, 2000a, 2000b). This becomes important when we consider the dynamics of the bus motion as the vehicle approaches the kerb.

As the bus approaches the kerb, it is decelerating and application of the brakes tends to cause the bus to rotate slightly around the front axle, thus lowering the front edge of the vehicle. As the driver steers the bus towards the kerb, the vehicle will be moving down the camber of the roadway, which will tend to rotate the vehicle towards the kerb. The combined outcome is that the front of the bus is some 40–50 mm lower as it approaches the kerb than it is when stationary and parked on flat ground. This gives an upper limit to the height of a bus stop kerb – and thus the platform – at the bus stop. Allowing for some leeway, this suggests that a kerb higher than about 180 mm is at risk of being struck by the underside of the bus as it approaches the kerb. With a platform thus set at 180 mm above the roadway, the kneeling of the bus to a floor height of 240 mm means that there will be a vertical gap of 60 mm between the platform and the bus floor (see Figure 5.6). A 60 mm gap without a ramp will be a problem for some wheelchair users. Unlike the bus shown in Figure 5.6, which only has one door, most buses in London have a ramp fitted to the centre door.

Figure 5.6 The height of the bus floor when lowered at a Kassel kerb 180 mm high

The kerb profile, another important feature of the special kerbs, affects the horizontal gap. Whereas the vertical gap is largely a matter of the relative height specifications of the bus and the kerb, the horizontal gap is a result of the way drivers approach the bus stop area (this is considered in detail in the following section). To make a good decision about which kerb to use I will consider what happens in the dynamic situation (i.e. when the bus is moving towards and against the kerb).

The objective needs to be to obtain level access. This is quite possible but it would need a smarter approach to the suspension system and how it can be controlled at the bus stop. For example, a transponder at the bus stop could inform the bus of the height of the kerb so that the suspension system would lower itself automatically to that height. This would require manufacturers to increase the feasible range of movement of the suspension system and install appropriate communication and control systems (these can be very simple).

5.3.2   Dealing with the horizontal gap

The delivery of a small horizontal gap depends strongly on the driver's ability to bring the bus close and parallel to the kerb. In looking for a small horizontal gap, I am asking the driver to bring a rigid object 12 m long and 2.55 m wide to a stop within a few milli-metres of a concrete platform. The driver's view of the bus stop is limited to what can be seen from the driver's position. In practice, this is restricted by a number of factors. The nearest point on the road surface that can be seen from the driving position is about 4.5 m in front of the vehicle. The nearside is obstructed by the corner pillar of the vehicle. Often the front doors have a curtain about 30 cm high at the bottom. Perhaps the most

Figure 5.7 A bus stopped ~400 mm from the kerb at an Excalibur bus stop in London. The passenger alighting at the rear door is having some difficulty in reaching the platform

important outcome of all this is that the driver cannot see the kerb near to the bus (i.e. less than 4.5 m from the front of the vehicle) from the driving position. The colour of the road and footway surfaces, which are often in various forms of grey, gives the result that once the nearside of the vehicle is within about 500 mm of the kerb, the driver has no feedback to advise where the vehicle is in relation to the kerb. Thus, the driver is unsure whether the vehicle is about to mount the kerb or if it is half a metre away from it. Caution means that the tendency is to stay away from the kerb rather than strike it, so the result is that drivers have a tendency to bring the vehicle to a stop about 400–500 mm away from the kerb (see Figure 5.7). This is difficult for many passengers and impossible for some.

The driver's view of the rear of the vehicle is restricted to what can be seen in the rear-view mirrors. The rear steering pivot of the vehicle is the rear axle, which could be located some 6 m behind the driver (or more if the bus is articulated). This means that steering the bus towards the kerb cannot be done until that point is clearly past any obstruction (e.g. a parked car) on the nearside. Asking a driver to position the vehicle with the level of accuracy required for the accessible operation of a bus stop means expecting him or her to achieve a highly skilled and precise control over the vehicle in extremely difficult circumstances.

So the effect on the horizontal gap of a car parked upstream of a bus stop is profound (see Figure 5.8).

Figure 5.8 This bus is constrained to stop a long way away from the kerb because of the combination of the car parked upstream, the closeness of the shelter to the kerb and the position of the bin. The driver has done as best as he can in these circumstances, but this will be quite inaccessible to many people

Meeting the users' need for a small horizontal gap is therefore concerned with helping the driver overcome these difficulties. This requires an understanding of how the vehicle interacts with the infrastructure, so I will now discuss the characteristics of the vehicle-platform interface which affect this interaction.

5.3.3 Vehicles and the bus stop

As mentioned in the previous section, I found a wide variation between buses in relation to ground clearance. The difference between ground clearance and the vertical gap depends on three factors:

1 the kerb height
2 the difference between the ride height and the boarding height of the bus
3 the depth of the floor on the bus.

It is essential that bus operators, bus manufacturers and bus stop designers agree on these aspects of bus design and kerb height. Generally speaking, the higher the kerbs, the more difficult the problem is to resolve, but the better the potential outcome. The greater the difference between ride and knelt heights, the longer it takes to kneel and raise the bus at a bus stop, and this could eventually impose an increase in the dwell time. At present, however, the time taken to lower or raise a bus 80 mm or so is about 1–2 s and does not affect dwell time because it occurs while other actions are happening: for example, opening or closing the doors.

Bus manufacturers can help by thinking hard about the area concerned – under the floor on the near-side front of the bus, in front of the front wheel – and what they can do to increase the ground clearance without increasing the vertical gap. On examining the buses, I found a number of parts attached to the underside of the bus in this area (chassis members, compressors, and various bolts and other extrusions) that reduced the ground clearance on particular buses. The fact that some buses had nothing in particular fitted underneath the bus floor in this area indicates that these features could be removed or placed elsewhere where the clearance is not so critical.

Differences in performance of the suspension mean that the kneeling mechanism has different effects. In addition, there are different kneeling systems: some buses are equipped so that the kneeling mechanism works on all wheels, others can only lower both axles on the nearside, front axle only or the front nearside only. Examining different buses, I found that the amount by which the bus lowers varied from 70 mm to 100 mm. There is also a wide variation in the lateral overhang: at the front axle, this varied between 35 mm and 95 mm; at the rear axle I encountered a range from 25 mm to 70 mm. The rear axle was placed at different places along the bus length, and the rear overhang varied from 2.2 m to 3.3 m. The front axle was also quite variable, with the front overhang ranging from 2.175 m to 2.67 m (all the buses I examined had the front door in front of the front axle). Given the degree of accuracy required by the passengers' needs it is clear that the drivers are given a very difficult job to do by the manufacturers.

When parked with the wheel against the kerb, as the special bus stop kerbs are designed to work, the horizontal gap then depends on the relationship between the wheel and the body-work. In general, a Kassel kerb will deliver a smaller horizontal gap than either of the other kerbs, for two reasons. First, its profile allows for a steeper face than the other kerbs (75° to the horizontal rather than 55° or 70°) so the top edge of the kerb is nearer to the vehicle when the wheel is positioned properly against the bottom of the kerb. Second, the round profile at the contact point between the tyre and the kerb supports the profile of the tyre and thus makes it easier for the tyre to remain in the correct position as it moves along the kerb and does no damage at all to the tyre. However, the 180 mm height will deliver a larger vertical gap than the 200 mm or 220 mm of the other kerbs unless the suspension system is designed to allow a greater range of movement. In principle, with a current suspension system, a vertical gap of 60 mm can be obtained with a Kassel kerb, with a slight overhang which gives no horizontal gap. The access kerb has a horizontal gap of some 37 mm, but the vertical gap would be 40 mm. The Marshall kerb brings the bus close to the kerb, with an overhang, and thus the vertical gap would be the same as the floor depth (around 80 mm, i.e. about the same as for a Kassel kerb). Dimensions can vary a lot depending on the type of vehicle using the bus stop and the effect of the road camber at the bus stop. However, the way in which these kerbs perform in practice is rather different, as I shall discuss below.

Dresden kerbs work in a similar way to Kassel kerbs, but present a higher platform to help reduce the vertical gap. They also extend the footing to accommodate the whole tyre. These were designed for the situation where both buses and trams used the same infrastructure. The cut-out at the platform level allowed the tram body to clear the kerb edge. A similar design could enable the bus body to drop to provide a flush level between the floor of the bus and the platform with virtually no horizontal gap. This needs to be provided at least at the door used by people in wheelchairs. The extended foot of the kerb unit was to enable it to abut the tram track without the need for an awkwardly small in-fill between the kerb and the track, which would be difficult to install and maintain. The Dresden design would allow for the platform height to be as high as desirable.

With such infrastructure in place, it becomes possible to install a parking guidance system that would provide feedback to the approaching driver about the vehicle's proximity to the kerb – similar in principle to the parking systems used by aircraft at airports. This could be displayed to the driver at the bus stop or in the driver's cabin – perhaps using heads-up display technology. This could be a specially-adapted version of current technology used in cars to aid reversing.

The difference in lateral gaps between the wheel and the exterior of the bus body is also a matter for the manufacturers. There are two reasons why wheels are set so far inside the bodywork. First, the chassis is in effect too small for the body but this is the combination that has been procured for some reason. Second, the wheel nuts are exposed and the risk of injury and damage caused by these if the wheel is too close to the outside of the vehicle is considered to be too high. There is a case for the providers of the bus stop infrastructure to discuss suitable vehicle dimensions with bus operators and manufacturers. The dimensions of interest for accessible bus stops are not normally of much concern to an operator when specifying a vehicle, as they tend to believe (incorrectly – see Chapter 6) that they affect neither operating costs nor passenger capacity and neither is there an incentive for the manufacturer to take this into account. However, they can make a lot of difference to the ease with which accessibility can be delivered at bus stops. More compatibility between bus and bus stop design could also reduce damage to both infrastructure and vehicles. Recent discussions with one bus manufacturer revealed a blank refusal to redesign the chassis to reduce the lateral gap problem on the basis of the investment cost that would be incurred. A manufacturer with this sort of view will only be persuaded to change by pressure from potential purchasers. This will only be forthcoming if bus operators and infrastructure providers combine forces to produce a consistent requirement for such elements to be included in vehicle specifications. Thinking in terms of a whole bus system in which bus stops and buses are procured to complementary specifications would be a great step forward in improving the accessibility of the bus system.

The rear overhang of the bus is also important. If the bus turns too sharply on leaving the stop, the rear of the bus will overhang the kerb. I found examples of buses with a rear overhang of over 3 m (measured from the rear axle). In order to help ensure the safety of passengers on the platform (who will, by and large, not be visible to the driver as the bus leaves the stop) the exit angle needs to be reduced. Improved arrangements for rear and side view mirrors would make the driver's job a lot easier. Figure 4.20 shows the nearside mirror cluster used on buses in Kassel, Germany. Modern buses are routinely supplied with a number of internal and external cameras (the London bus specification is for

12 internal and four external cameras) so these could be deployed to simplify the safety issue. As mentioned in Section 4.6.1.2, there is a great opportunity to help the driver on the approach to the bus stop as well as when leaving it, through the use of more recent video-based guidance software.

Quality contracts and partnerships would seem to be a good opportunity simultaneously to improve the buses and provide the corresponding accessible infrastructure. It would certainly be interesting to see the horizontal and vertical gaps obtained in operation being measured as one of the performance measures in such a partnership.

5.3.4   Helping drivers: Guidance systems

The physical aspects of the design to help drivers discussed in this section, especially the profile and height of kerbs, bring implications for the design of the platform surface at the bus stop. Some of these are opportunities for improvements; others are challenges, which need to be resolved.

There are several pressures on bus drivers: they are required to oversee boarding and alighting passengers, sometimes to oversee the collection of fares and deal with change, oversee the display of electronic tickets and passes, oversee the safe carriage of people in their wheelchairs, supervise the discipline of passengers, drive the bus safely and with the safety and comfort of passengers as a priority, maintain the schedule and cope with the other traffic on the road. Given all these other pressures on drivers, actually driving the bus is quite a small element of their job. To all these pressures must be added the requirements of an accessible bus system. Accessibility means that the driver has to bring the bus sufficiently close to the kerb at the correct point in each bus stop so that people can board and alight easily, safely, comfortably and quickly – whatever their accessibility needs. As described in Section 4.5, a number of very detailed manoeuvres are required on the approach to the bus stop in order to meet the passenger needs.

For a kerbside bus stop these manoeuvres start some 15 m upstream of the bus stop. So the driver has to be encouraged to think about the detailed positioning of the bus well before arriving at the stop. I will now discuss how the driver could be helped to achieve the level of accessibility required at the bus stop.

Helping the driver with a guidance system

Accessible bus operation relies very heavily on the skills and performance of the drivers.

1   The driver needs to be able to bring the bus close to the kerb at a consistent position in relation to the bus stop: consideration needs to be made of the physical limitations of moving a rigid vehicle within the appropriate limits.
2   The driver needs to see the kerb edge: some sort of feedback on the position of the bus relative to the kerb is required.
3   The driver needs to see that he will be able to manoeuvre the bus into the bus stop from the 'driving' position and to re-enter the traffic stream when leaving the bus stop: bus stops need to be cleared of parked vehicles for a suitable distance before and after the stop.

4   Drivers are sensitive to the dangers of approaching a platform with obstacles (including people) near to the kerb edge: the platform should be maintained free of obstructions near to the kerb edge.

It is therefore necessary to do whatever is possible to help drivers perform as consistently as possible. The issues to be tackled in the design are:

1   How does the bus react to the 'stimuli' from the infrastructure?
2   What is the best approach path that will enable the bus to use the infrastructure correctly?
3   How can we ensure that this approach path is attained accurately and consistently?

Buses cannot move sideways, so in order to stop precisely enough at the bus stop it is necessary to approach at an angle. As stated in Section 4.5, the experiments in the Excalibur project showed that the approach angle has to be between 9° and 12°. This is extremely difficult for a driver to judge, given all the other calls on his or her attention. This angle shows how far in advance of the bus stop the driver has to start the turning manoeuvre. The point at which the manoeuvre has to start depends on where the bus is in relation to the kerb line as it is driving along the road. If it is passing parked cars, for example, the nearside of the bus will be something in the order of 2–3 m away from the kerb line. The point at which the turning manoeuvre must start identifies the distance upstream of the bus stop where parking has to be prevented. It is highly unlikely that a driver would be able to approach every bus stop within this range without some form of assistance, given the traffic and other conditions that he or she has to deal with.

One of the outcomes from the Excalibur experiments was to paint a guidance line on the roadway, running from the offside position of the bus at its driving line a little upstream of the stop and directing it towards the kerb at an angle of 10°. This helped the drivers attain an accurate, consistent and accessible stopping position at the stop. The guidance line was positioned so that it aligned with the offside of the bus as it was driving along the road and passing cars parked along the kerb before the bus stop. The starting point for this line was set so that it allowed 2.3 m for a parked car and a further 2.8 m to the position of the offside of the bus. The starting point was therefore set at 5.1 m from the kerb, 13 m upstream of the point at which the front wheel was expected to strike the Kassel kerbs at the bus stop platform. The actual path of the bus as it approaches the kerb is actually an 'S' bend, with a steep approach to the kerb which is steered out as the bus approaches the kerb so that the angle of the vehicle when the wheel contacts the kerb is correct. The performance of the drivers in this respect was that they tended to start steering earlier than they did without the guidance line and at a less sharp angle to the kerb. The whole process was therefore smoother and more comfortable.

Drivers asked for a target kerb to be provided in a contrasting colour to help them steer the bus correctly, and this is positioned at a particular point along the platform. We tested the positions for the target kerb and located it on the basis of drivers' performance. Once the drivers had become acquainted with the idea of letting the kerb steer the bus, they found it relatively easy to come to a stop with a horizontal gap of 0–70 mm.

Another problem for bus drivers is that they will not stop close to the kerb if they cannot see a clear exit from the stop. It was therefore necessary to determine a clear exit path for them. When asked, all bus drivers said that they could turn the bus to leave a stop to avoid a parked vehicle within about 2 m of their stationary position. Some drivers remarked that this could leave a problem at the back of the bus, and this is undoubtedly true. Some of the buses tested in the Excalibur project had a rear overhang of some 3 m. This poses a safety hazard, especially under acceleration as the bus leaves the stop. Therefore a second guidance line was introduced at the exit end of the stop. This was set at 14° to the line of the platform, which was steep enough to reduce the kerb-take of the stop, but not so sharp as to cause a problem for people standing on the platform. The exit taper is designed to indicate the point downstream of a bus stop up to which a car can park without affecting the performance of the stop. The two angled guidelines were joined by a line parallel to and 2.6 m away from the kerb. This was deliberately tight (the width of a bus is 2.55 m) because we noted that, although drivers denied being influenced by the demarcation line of the bus stop cage, when it was moved their parking position changed. The position of the guidance line (at 2.6 m instead of the standard 3 m) brought the bus, on average, about 100 mm nearer to the kerb.

A set of guidance facilities was tested and converted into a form that could be used on-street. The guidance system incorporates three major parts, which are then divided into seven elements:

1 *Entry taper*: this varies according to the chosen layout and is the distance necessary to pass a parked car before the bus has to turn towards the kerb.
   (*a*) The guidance line is painted in the roadway at 10° to the line of the kerb, starting upstream at the nearest point that a parked car could be to the bus stop (the actual distance depends on the type of bus stop layout and the width of the parked vehicle being considered) and 5.1 m from the kerb edge at that point. The entry taper must be kept clear of parking. This will require a rigid and effective enforcement system. The distance from the beginning of the entry taper to the end of the exit taper defines the extent of the bus stop environment.
2 *Platform*: in addition to providing the space for passengers, the platform is an essential part of the guidance system as it provides the basis for steering the bus towards the correct stopping position, close and parallel to the kerb.
   (*a*) The platform length is a function of the vehicle dimensions (front overhang, wheelbase, total length, distance between the wheel and the side of the bus).
   (*b*) One kerb unit is coloured and is positioned precisely to act as a target kerb on the nearside.
   (*c*) The bus stop cage width is reduced to 2.5 m along the platform between the entry and exit tapers.
   (*d*) The guidance line along the platform is 500 mm behind the kerb edge.
   (*e*) There is an indication of the stopping position.

3 *Exit taper*: like the entry taper, this varies according to the layout and is the distance necessary to pass a parked car.

   (*a*) The guidance line on the offside from the stopping point is at 14° to the line of the kerb to the nearest point that a parked car could be to the bus stop without affecting its operation (the actual distance depends on the type of bus stop layout and the width of the parked vehicle being considered) and 5.1 m from the kerb edge at that point.

The length of the bus stop environment is the sum of these three parts. It is important to note that the guidance system is a complete set. Each of the seven elements noted above is required because each contributes to the driver's ability to perform adequately at the stop. Removing one of these detracts from the performance. The only exception to this general statement is for full boarder bus stops, where the exit taper is not really necessary because the platform is already built 1 m into the roadway. The special nature of the bus stop within the road space should be indicated by a special surface colour or other road marking. The more controlled approach path of the buses means that the entry taper is effectively a track over which all buses will pass. The special colour emphasises this to other road users as well as to bus drivers.

Table 5.5 shows the dimensions of the physical lengths required for the physical manoeuvre of the bus from its driving line in the road to a position close to the kerb at the bus stop. Table 5.5 also indicates the position of the target kerb.

The next issue is how to help the driver manoeuvre the bus with this level of precision so that the desired accessibility can be delivered at the bus stop. Performance at the on-street Excalibur stops has shown that a skilled driver can bring an otherwise incompatible older bus to a stop at the correct stopping position without causing damage to the bus or platform. For the Excalibur stops, the driver positions the bus in line with the guidance line and steers towards the kerb to achieve the correct angle at the strike point.

Table 5.5 Summary of dimensions for Excalibur stops (all measurements in metres)

Layout type	Strike point (exp.)	Platform (total)	Entry taper	Exit taper	Bus stop (total)	TfL
Kerbside	3	21.5	13	9	43.5	37
Bus bay	–	20.5	24	20	64.5	53
Half boarder	2	20.5	7	5	32.5	27
Full boarder	5	23.5	2	–	25.5	9–17
Multiple bus stop, second build-out 0.5 m	2	20.5	15	10	45.5	41
Multiple bus stop, second build-out 1.0 m	–	21.5	15	8	44.5	35

Exp. = experimental; TfL = total length for a bus stop given in TfL (2006)

234

He or she then allows the kerb to steer the bus along the platform. The bus will be aligned correctly as the bus reaches the correct stopping point (indicated by the orange tactile surface). The driver then kneels the bus in order to reduce the vertical gap. When this is achieved, there is often no need for the ramp to be deployed for a wheelchair user as the vertical and horizontal gaps are small enough for many wheelchair users to cross.

The guidance system was explained to drivers and illustrated in two forms. The first was as a diagram showing where the bus should be at various points during the approach, docking and exit manoeuvres. The other was a set of photographs showing buses carrying out the manoeuvres as described. These were part of a set of posters which were left for drivers to look at and comment upon as part of the training exercise.

I now turn to the basic designs for the Excalibur bus stops that resulted from our research. The overall dimensions of each of the four basic bus stop layouts (kerbside, full boarder, half boarder, bay), together with a sketch drawing for each case, are given in the following sections, for both single-berth and multiple-berth bus stops.

5.3.4.1 Excalibur bus stop layouts
Kerbside bus stops
The most successful guidance system for a kerbside layout at the London Docklands experiments is illustrated in Figure 5.9. It can be seen that we can conclude that a kerbside bus stop with a platform length of 22 m would satisfy the needs of all the bus types. The total length of a single-berth kerbside stop (i.e. including entry and exit tapers) would therefore be 44 m.

Figure 5.9 Generic design for a kerbside bus stop (dimensions in m)

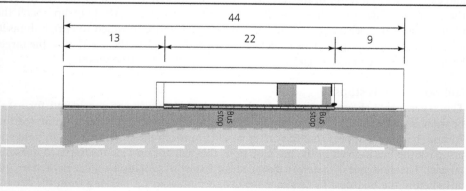

Entry taper: 13 m
Strike point: 3 (contrasting-colour kerb at position 3)
Platform: 22 m
Exit taper: 9 m
Entry angle: 10°

Exit angle: 14°
Speed before guidance system: 25 miles/h
Speed within guidance system: 10 miles/h
Speed at strike point: 5 miles/h

Figure 5.10 Generic guidance system for a half boarder bus stop (dimensions in m)

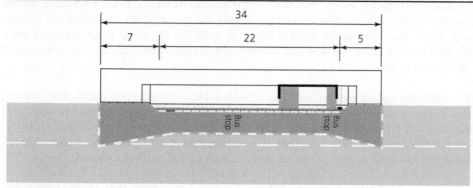

Entry taper: 7 m
Strike point: 2 (contrasting-colour kerb at position 2)
Platform: 20 m
Exit taper: 5 m
Entry angle: 10°

Exit angle: 14°
Speed before guidance system: 25 miles/h
Speed within guidance system: 10 miles/h
Speed at strike point: 5 miles/h

Half boarder bus stops

The half boarder guidance system follows the same principle of the kerbside system. The main difference is the reduction on the entry and the exit taper as the lateral movement is reduced to 1.3 m, because of the presence of the boarder. The most successful guidance system for a half boarder layout at the Excalibur experiments in the London Docklands is illustrated in Figure 5.10.

For half boarder single-berth bus stops, the total bus stop length is 32 m. The difference, compared with the kerbside layout, arises because less distance is required for the entry and exit tapers as a result of the reduced lateral manoeuvre required by the bus to reach the platform. The driver has less space to manoeuvre and so tends to approach the platform at a sharper angle, but he has less lateral distance in which to correct himself using the guidance system. This is the reason for the change in the position of the target kerb – it allows for inaccuracies in touching the kerb at the strike point.

Full boarder bus stops

The experiments showed very clearly that the lateral movement considered for a full boarder is small (about 500 mm in practice), but it does exist and it must be allowed for. Although it might appear that the driver would approach the stop in a straight path and just park the bus in front of the bus stop pole, this will not provide the required horizontal gap. The guidance is therefore designed for the worst situation – a car parked irregularly before the boarder. In this case the distance allowed for steering from the driving position to the platform is short, with the result that it is very difficult for drivers to strike the kerb at the correct angle.

Therefore, the platform has to be slightly longer in order to allow the vehicle to straighten before it comes to a stop at the correct position. The most successful guidance

Figure 5.11 Generic guidance system for a full boarder bus stop (dimensions in m)

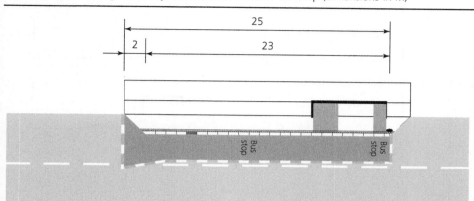

Entry taper: 2 m
Strike point: 5 (contrasting-colour kerb at position 5)
Platform: 23 m
Exit taper: none
Entry angle: 10°

Exit angle: 14°
Speed before guidance system: 25 miles/h
Speed within guidance system: 10 miles/h
Speed at strike point: 5 miles/h

system for a full boarder layout at the experiment is illustrated in Figure 5.11. It can be seen that the platform length is rather longer than that for a kerbside or half boarder stop. However, as the entry and exit tapers are very small, the total distance required for the bus stop is considerably shorter than that required for the other designs. The total distance required for a bus stop with a full boarder is therefore 25 m.

Bay bus stops

The most successful guidance system for a bus bay layout in the Excalibur experiments is illustrated in Figure 5.12. The bus bay requires a very large distance to be reserved to guarantee access to the stop. In this case the buses require about 65 m for the stop. This is because the guidance must bring the driver in from the driving position (i.e. outside parked cars) into the bay. The consequences of bus bays are severe in terms of parking constraints and should therefore be avoided.

Multiple-berth bus stops

As discussed in Chapter 4, bus stops must be designed with sufficient capacity: an over-saturated bus stop will not be able to deliver the required accessibility because the buses will not be able to reach the kerb. One of the ways of increasing the capacity of a bus stop is to increase the number of berths. I consider here the infrastructure requirements of constructing a bus stop with multiple berths. We will consider the two base cases:

1   *Two adjacent berths*: (1) a bus cannot enter the front berth unless the rear berth is empty; (2) a bus cannot leave the rear berth unless the front berth is empty (see Figure 5.13).

Figure 5.12 Generic guidance system for a bus bay bus stop (dimensions in m)

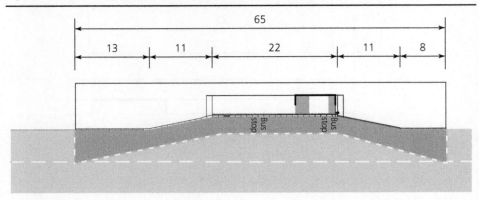

Entry taper: 24 m
Strike point: 3 (contrasting-colour kerb at position 3)
Platform: 24 m
Exit taper: 19 m
Entry angle: 10°

Exit angle: 14°
Speed before guidance system: 25 miles/h
Speed within guidance system: 10 miles/h
Speed at strike point: 5 miles/h

2   *Two independent berths*: (1) a bus can enter the front berth even if the rear berth
    is occupied; (2) a bus can leave the rear berth even if the front berth is occupied
    (see Figure 5.14).

Although bus stops can be much more complex than these simple cases, the complexity
will always be a variant of one or other of these or a combination of both.

Figure 5.13 A bus stop with two adjacent berths (dimensions in m)

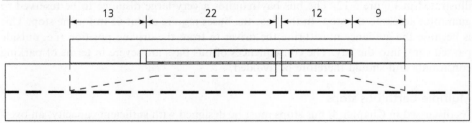

Element	Longitudinal dimension (m)
Entry taper	13.00
Platform	22.00
Gap	2.00
Platform	12.00
Exit	9.22
Total	58.22

Figure 5.14 A bus stop with two independent berths (dimensions in m)

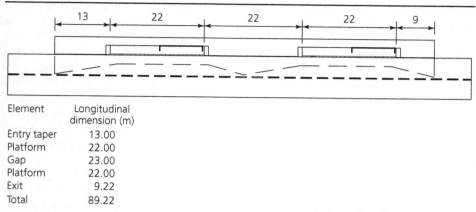

Element	Longitudinal dimension (m)
Entry taper	13.00
Platform	22.00
Gap	23.00
Platform	22.00
Exit	9.22
Total	89.22

Adjacent berths

The arrangement in this case requires that the platform is long enough for two bus lengths and a sensible gap between them, plus the length of platform required to straighten the bus for the rear berth. This will ensure that the bus occupying the second berth will be able to stop close and parallel to the kerb. It might be tempting to think that the rear berth could be squeezed in by adding the length equivalent to the distance between the front of the bus and the rear of the front doorway, plus 1 m for the gap between two stopped buses. However, neither bus would be parallel to the platform in these circumstances and the rear bus would find it very difficult to obtain the appropriate horizontal gap. A two-door bus requires the full-length platform in order to ensure that the rear doorway is parallel to the kerb, so that a ramp fitted to the second door can be deployed safely. The platform surface markings (tactile surface and any markings for a second door) must be repeated for the second bus in the appropriate positions. The yellow line is required along the whole platform.

The entry taper should be provided to guide the bus driver towards the rear berth. The driver approaching the front berth will have enough space to make the lateral manoeuvre without an additional guidance line. A second target kerb placed 20 m upstream of the stopping point for the front berth will help the driver make the correct approach at the right place. The exit taper leads from the front berth in the same way as for a single-berth stop. A two-berth bus stop with two adjacent berths is, therefore, some 58 m long.

Independent berths

The situation is slightly more complicated if the required capacity means that berths have to be independent of each other. In this case the buses must be able to manoeuvre around each other in such a way that the presence of one bus does not affect the other. The key point is the gap between the two berths. This is calculated on the basis of the entry taper for the front berth. This is not quite the same as for the entry taper for the rear berth, which is the same as that for a single-berth stop. The reason for the difference is that the bus arriving at the front berth must be able to pass around a bus stopped in the rear berth: the entry tapers described above are calculated on the basis of a parked car and so we have to calculate using a wider vehicle. This allows for the bus to be close to the kerb plus two rear-view mirrors plus a gap between them. This is $2.55 + 0.5$ (offside wing mirror of front bus) $+ 0.5$ (gap) $+ 0.5$ (nearside wing mirror of rear bus) $= 4.05$ m. The entry taper required to allow the bus to reach the kerb from this distance is 23 m. This is the length of the gap required between the stopping point of the rear berth and the target kerb of the front berth in order to maintain independent and accessible operation of both berths. A multiple-berth stop with single independent berths can, therefore, be designed as a single-berth bus stop with an additional platform length and gap for each additional berth, but with suitable taper lengths associated to each berth as appropriate.

The lengths of each element of the bus stop are shown in Figure 5.13. A two-berth bus stop with independent berths is therefore some 89 m long. A four-berth bus stop, laid out in two pairs of adjacent berths, would require 115 m of sterilised kerb, the difference between this and the dimensions shown in Figure 5.14 being the length of the two additional berths.

I used this approach when we produced the bus stop part of the award-winning design for an intermodal interchange in Buenos Aires, where we needed to ensure that buses could not enter the bus stop at the rear berth and just travel along the whole of the platform. Drivers were tempted to do this because of the possibility of collecting 'extra' passengers on the way. The gap between the berths was filled with a platform, angled at $14°$ on the exit side of the rear berth and $10°$ on the approach side of the front berth. This profile matches the exit angle from the rear berth and the approach angle to the front berth. Although that design was never implemented, more recent systems in Buenos Aires do contain markings that are based on that thinking and are in operation on the Metrobus BRT system in the city centre.

One possibility is to park the rear bus at an angle to the kerb in order to reduce the width from the kerb line that is necessary to avoid on entry to the stop. This could not be tested in practice, but the idea behind an angled bus stop is to try to make it easier for a bus arriving at the front berth (although it will still have to negotiate around the rear offside corner of the stationary bus in the rear berth) and to reduce the amount of kerb space required. The bus will still need enough platform to allow the bus to come close to the kerb, so the platform length required for these berths is the same as would be required for single berths (i.e. about 22 m).

The first question to resolve is the correct angle to use for the angled berths. If the angle is large, the total longitudinal length of the stop would be reduced, but it could be harder for buses to reach and (more particularly) leave the kerb. If the angle is too small, the length of the stop would be increased and the buses would find it harder to avoid other buses on arrival or departure. To demonstrate the principles, an angle of $8°$ allows the front of the bus to be contained within the bay area at the front of a 22 m platform and the back of the bus to protrude only about 1 m into the roadway. The entry taper is set at

10° to the line of the angled kerb (i.e. 18° to the driving line) and starts 7.1 m before the first of the angled kerbs. As mentioned above, the platform length is 22 m. The target kerb is the third unit (i.e. 2–3 m after the start of the angled kerbs). If the angle is 8°, the kerb line at the front of the berth will be 3.05 m from the original kerb line. The exit from the platform has to be 14° to the line of the platform (remember that this is set because of safety and damage problems with the rear overhang). The platform should continue for 5 m to permit the bus to start the turn and then the kerb line needs to be designed so that it remains clear of the bus as it manoeuvres.

My desktop study suggests that about 16 m is required from the end of the rear bus stop to the beginning of the front platform at the original kerb line. The dimensions and angles for the front berth and exit are the same as those for the first berth. An exit taper required to avoid the nearest parked car needs to be added downstream of the stop. The overall length of the bus stop in this analysis is about 89 m.

Perhaps the most surprising element of the angled bus stop is the distance required between the two berths. This is because the exit angle has to be calculated with respect to the platform and not with respect to the roadway. The gap between two berths at a multiple-berth stop is determined by the manoeuvre that requires the most space: exit or entry.

At a bus stop where the two berths are in line (e.g. as shown in Figure 5.14), the entry manoeuvre determines the length of the gap because it occurs at a greater speed and smaller angle than the exit. In the case of the angled stop, the exit manoeuvre defines the gap because the bus has to turn through a greater angle in order to leave the stop, thus requiring more space to regain the traffic lane.

The additional space required for exit at the angled stop is more or less compensated for by the reduced space needed for entry so the bus stop requires about the same kerb length as the straight kerbside version shown in Figure 5.14. Increasing the angle of the platform relative to the kerb line might be tempting on the grounds that it would reduce the amount of kerb space required for the bus stop. However, as the angle increases, the entry manoeuvre becomes more difficult because it necessitates a sharper turn from the driving line. If the platform angle is reduced, the entry and exit become easier, but the effect on the kerb space is less. Placing the bus stop at an angle in this way does little for saving kerb space and it has implications for the safety of the buses at and around the bus stop.

The bus driver has to look in the rear-view mirror when he is about to leave the stop. However, the view from the mirror is worse at an angled stop than at a 'straight' stop because the bus is stopped at an angle to the traffic and the mirror cannot show the traffic conditions upstream of the bus stop. The bus driver cannot really see approaching traffic until he has moved away from the stop and straightened the bus up (when the mirror would be better aligned to show the oncoming traffic).

Basically, I believe there is little to be gained from an angled bus stop and quite a lot of disadvantages and I would not recommend them.

Another option is to extend the platform into the front berth by 1 m. This reduces the lateral movement required to reach the front berth, which in turn reduces the length of the gap between the two berths. With this arrangement the lateral manoeuvre would be 3.05 m instead of 4.05 m and the entry taper would become 17.3 m instead of 23 m. However, the rear bus would have to clear $1 + 2.55 + 0.5 + 0.5 = 4.55$ m on exit and this would require an exit taper of 18.25 m. However, the bus stopped at the front berth would be sufficiently far forward that it would not interfere with the exit from the rear berth. A two-berth bus stop with independent berths and a platform build-out for the front berth is therefore some 80 m long.

All other things being considered, if a bus stop with two independent berths is required, the design requiring the least amount of kerb length has the platform build-out for the front berth. The worst design with respect to 'kerb-take' is the angled bus stop. A bus stop with two adjacent berths requires about 58 m of kerb, but will have significantly lower capacity than the bus stops with independent berths.

It is hugely important that the distances required to attain accessible performance at a bus stop are fully understood. As with the designs for single-berth bus stops, any reduction from the dimensions discussed here will inevitably result in a reduction in accessibility at the bus stop. Undoubtedly, compromises will have to be made in many cases which will result in such a loss. Each compromise must be considered with the people who will be excluded from using the bus stop as a result, and a suitable alternative must be provided.

It is worth noting that the guidance line is set at 10°, but the buses tend to arrive at a much sharper angle. This is because of the way in which bus drivers manoeuvre the vehicle: they take quite a sharp turn (towards the target kerb) which is then adjusted in response to the guidance system to obtain the correct approach. The distance allowed for the kerbside and bus bay arrangements allows this correction to be made within the entry taper. However, the much shorter entry taper for the boarders does not provide enough space for this. The result is the additional length of platform needed to straighten the bus. We know from the initial experiments that without the 10° line the approach starts much later and is much steeper. We therefore recommend that the line be kept to 10°. If the driver approaches the platform at a much smaller angle, the straightening-up process is less severe than for a sharper approach. However, it is much harder to strike the target kerb correctly, and so an additional platform length is required to allow for undershooting the platform. The outcomes from the experiments were the definition of four designs for bus stop guidance for drivers.

Ten years on and technology has developed. This provides new opportunities to help the driver deliver good accessibility at bus stops. However, the research to refine the basic ideas is yet to be done – some ideas are discussed briefly in Chapter 6.

There are some standards to be adopted in the platform design process. These standards (Table 5.6) reflect a commitment between users' requirements and technical engineering restrictions. In a survey phase they might indicate what to look for in a bus stop environment in order to improve the area.

Table 5.6 Principal elements to consider at a bus stop environment

Element	Measure	Comments
Layout	Generic types: kerbside, half boarder, full boarder, bus bay	Any layout option should respect the free space for pulling in and out without any kind of obstruction. Bus bays are therefore not a good idea in most cases
Footway width	2000 mm	Minimum 1800 mm
Footway crossfall	Aim for 0.57° (1%) 1°30'–2° (2.5–3.5%) is possible, but the compromise would exclude some people 2°–2.3° (3.5–4%) will exclude more people and an alternative solution should be sought 2.3°–3.5° (4–6%) should only be attempted in extraordinary situations >3.5° (6%) is impossible and an alternative must be sought	It may be impossible to achieve a satisfactory crossfall. If this is so, accessibility can only be maintained if suitable support is provided along the footway Difficulties with crossfalls may be a reason for considering a boarder
Platform width	2300 mm with an L-type shelter 3400 mm with an enclosed-type shelter	Any reduction in this measure will affect wheelchair users' ability to manoeuvre to and within the bus stop environment Insufficient platform space may be a reason for considering a boarder
Platform crossfall	Aim for 0.57° (1%) 1°30'–2° (2.5–3.5%) is possible, but the compromise would exclude some people 2°–2.3° (3.5–4%) will exclude more people and an alternative solution should be sought 2.3°–3.5° (4–6%) should only be attempted in extraordinary situations >3.5° (6%) is impossible and an alternative must be sought	It may be impossible to achieve a satisfactory crossfall. If this is so, accessibility can only be maintained if suitable support is provided along the footway Difficulties with crossfalls may be a reason for considering increasing the width of the footway
Kerb height at platform	160–220 mm	Kassel, Charcon and Marshall kerbs for bus stops are available in the UK. These are designed to permit buses to stop close to the kerb without damaging the vehicle

Table 5.6 Continued

Element	Measure	Comments
Transition kerb	–	Should be provided with a non-slip surface
Main surface	Pavers	Natural grey, small (4000 mm × 400 mm) pavers are preferred. Asphalt is not a good surface for a bus stop platform
Warning line	A strip of contrasting-colour surface blocks must be set 500 mm back from the kerb edge to warn about the possible bus overhang along the platform	Blocks provide better durability than a painted line. Reflective blocks work well in this case. Yellow is a preferred colour
Tactile surface	Coloured tactile surface to indicate where the bus door will be	The only tactile surface to be used at a bus stop is the 'information surface'. This should be laid, in accordance with inclusive mobility (DfT, 2005), from the warning line to a point 400 mm before the back of the shelter
Other surface	Coloured pavers to indicate where the rear bus door will be (if buses are fitted with more than one door)	Buff pavers are suitable for this purpose. The exact location of the pavers depends on the design of the buses using the stop. The 'worst' case should be incorporated in the design
Shelter	This should be designed in accordance with the bus stop characteristics. It should be large enough to accommodate the expected number of waiting passengers. Space should be provided for wheelchair users and people with shopping or other encumbrances. Information for people with vision and hearing impairments should be provided at a consistent location within the bus stop environment. An adequate, accessible information system is necessary for all users. Different heights and types of seat should be incorporated	The dimensions and type of shelter will demand on demand (number of passengers waiting) at the bus stop, available space and climate. However, accessibility for wheelchair users to enter and leave in a forward direction is probably the major design constraint (this consideration will generally include other encumbrances, such as baby buggies)

Table 5.6 Continued

Element	Measure	Comments
Guidance system	Guidance line before bus stop Target kerb Guideline on platform Reduced width of bus stop cage Stopping position Guidance line after bus stop	Starts upstream of the bus stop to help the driver position the bus correctly to carry out the stopping manoeuvre Located at the correct point along the platform 500 mm from the platform edge, along the whole platform 2.5 m from the kerb edge, along the platform length Must be consistent in design and position for all stops. Can be indicated adequately by the coloured tactile surface Encourages driver to pull out without the rear of the bus sweeping over the platform

5.3.5 Balancing crossfalls at the bus stop platform and footway

It is usually impossible to increase the height of the platform without having to adjust the drainage in some way. *Inclusive Mobility* (DfT, 2005) states that the maximum acceptable crossfall on a footway should be 2%; other literature about disabled users' needs asks for 1%. In the Excalibur experiments, we found that people in wheelchairs and, more particularly, people who need mobility aids such as sticks to walk, began to detect a difficulty with crossfalls approaching 4%. The work of Holloway (2011), mentioned in Section 4.2, shows that this is not merely a difficulty – wheelchair users and especially people pushing wheelchairs face a real additional amount of work to cope with this feature of our pedestrian environment. A 2% crossfall might be a best compromise, but it is important to realise the difficulties in achieving this in many cases. A crossfall as steep as 4% is acceptable only if this means that otherwise there would be no accessibility at all at the bus stop. However, most people do not perceive the crossfall and assume that the footway is in fact flat. This could lead to a different problem: a wheelchair or baby buggy parked with no brakes applied because it is assumed that the footway/platform is flat can easily start to roll towards the kerb edge. Examples of such an event have been detected at railway platforms that have adverse cambers towards the platform edge (this is not the normal situation, although it is the case in a number of stations) and some accidents have resulted in passengers rolling onto the track – in the UK and a notable case in Melbourne, Australia. The slopes involved in these incidents have been as low as 2%. Incidents of this nature have not been widely reported in relation to bus stops, but this is not to say they do not happen, rather that the impact of the incident and the consequent reporting (and investigation) requirements are not as great as they are for the railways.

Given the practicalities of constructing crossfalls with small gradients, it is likely to be difficult to achieve crossfalls less than 2% except that is probably easiest to construct a footway with a completely horizontal gradient of 0% – as long as the drainage is resolved in some way (e.g. using permeable paving). Whatever the chosen crossfall gradient, the complexity of arranging it so that the bus stop has an appropriate gradient in practice is complicated. Following is a practical guide on how to set about dealing with the problem of footway and platform crossfalls.

It is essential for the design process that a horizontal datum be set and this is helpful in the discussion of the effects of relative kerb and platform heights:

1 Set a datum coincident with the road surface level at its boundary with the kerb.
2 Check the width of the footway from the non-road edge to the edge of the road at various points along the proposed bus stop environment (also note the ownership of the curtilage). The aim is to have a minimum of 2.00 m for the footway and a minimum of 2.30 m for the platform if a one-sided shelter is to be adopted so that a wheelchair user can leave a bus safely and manoeuvre onto the footway. So the total width equals 4.3 m. Where there is less than 4.3 m available, an alternative bus stop layout should be considered. The most common case of this sort is where a kerbside layout needs to be changed to a half or a full boarder. It is important to note that if a bus shelter with an end panel is required, this will increase the necessary width of the platform because of the need to maintain access to the platform for people with pushchairs or in wheelchairs. This is discussed further below.
3 Check the heights of the existing kerb relative to the datum in the whole area of the proposed bus stop environment.
4 Check the current crossfalls. This will enable you to calculate the heights of the footway from the datum line at the non-road edge. Consider installing permeable paving at 0% crossfall, of course with its associated drainage system.
5 Calculate the crossfalls for both the footway and the platform as a result of using a raised kerb at the edge of the proposed platform (common heights: 160 mm, 180 mm and 220 mm).
6 Then:
   (a) If the proposed crossfall is positive (i.e. sloping towards the kerb edge) and less than 2%, the proposal can go ahead and there should be no need to install a new drainage system for the footway.
   (b) If the proposed crossfall is positive and greater than 2%:
      (i)   Consider introducing a full or half boarder.
      (ii) Check if the non-road edge could be adjusted so that the crossfall is reduced to 2% or less.
      (iii) Consider if a step (with the necessary safety measures) could be placed between the footway and the platform, thus improving both crossfalls in order to achieve 2% or less.
   (c) If the proposed arrangement is to arrange drainage along the footway-platform interface:
      (i)   Check that both positive and negative crossfalls will be satisfactory.
      (ii) Check that drainage into and from the gully can be accommodated without causing ponding or other problems.

    (iii) In some cases it will be impossible to provide satisfactory crossfalls without a step between the footway and the platform. In this case, check pedestrian and passenger flows and movements and, if appropriate, install a step. This will have to be protected by a handrail in order to avoid becoming a trip hazard. Check that the transfer from the platform to the footway is smooth and safe at each end of the platform.

  (d) If the proposed crossfall is negative the non-road edge must be examined:

    (i) If the non-road edge is a wall (rather than a building) or vegetation and the proposed crossfall is less than 2%, check if it is possible to leave the crossfall as it is.

    (ii) If the non-road edge is a wall (rather than a building) or vegetation, check if it is possible to make the crossfall positive by increasing the height of the footway at the non-road edge.

    (iii) If there are buildings with frontages at the non-road edge, then it is better to leave the non-road edge as it is and concentrate on the platform side.

7   A solution with a step between platform and footway might be necessary (see 6(b)(ii) above) along with the alterations to the drainage system.

8   Consider reducing the height of the new kerb, even though this will reduce accessibility to the buses. Consider who would be excluded from the bus service as a result and how they could be accommodated.

9   If other road works are being undertaken at this point, consider lowering the road level (this was done in one case where a major rebuild was in progress, but normally this would be far too costly).

Balancing the crossfalls is not an easy engineering task but it is an extremely important part of building an accessible bus stop. Kerbside bus stops generally attempt to fit an accessible bus stop into an existing space. A full or half boarder bus stop adds to the width available for the footway and platform at the expense of space within the roadway. At one level, the decision about which of these solutions to adopt is a matter of policy (e.g. the preference for public rather than private transport). However, the problem could be a physical issue: it might be impossible to construct an accessible bus stop within the existing space and thus additional space must be created or the bus stop moved to a more accessible location. The latter possibility needs to be considered in the light of overall effects on the accessibility of the network as a whole (as discussed in Chapter 3). Bus stops which only provide restricted accessibility should be announced as such in all network and service information, including announcements in the vehicle (as is currently the case with stations on the London Underground). The best solution is to remove the problem by only having fully accessible bus stops – remembering that this includes having them suitably close to the desired activities.

5.3.6   Surfaces in the passenger area

Bus stops need to have sufficient space for people to arrive and leave them, whether they are intending to board a bus or have just left one, or are using it as a resting place or are just passing by. Here I am going to discuss practical issues such as:

1 locating the entrance door of the bus along the platform
2 adopting safety measures (the need for a warning line or railings)
3 establishing the position and shape of the shelter.

5.3.6.1 Locating the entrance door

In the Excalibur project, a common complaint from users was that they did not know where the bus door would be. It is only possible to advise where the entrance door of the bus will be if the bus stop has been designed to enable bus drivers to stop consistently at a certain point along the platform. The issue for the drivers is discussed in Section 4.5.1. As far as the passengers are concerned, a number of cities have attempted to provide such an indication. This is usually done by using paving with a contrasting colour, or a painted symbol or painted line on the platform surface, which can be used by both drivers and passengers as an indication of where the door(s) will be. In Grenoble, France, one line of pavers in a colour that contrasts with the platform surface marks the front door and two lines mark the centre door (where wheelchair users are expected to board and alight). In Rouen, France, the location of the door intended for use by people in wheelchairs is indicated on the platform by the international symbol for disabled people. In BRT systems, the door positions are often extremely clear as these are indicated by the platform edge doors which only open when a bus is in position. This requires extreme consistency in driver performance and is achieved successfully in all cases. They do of course have the advantage that these are generally not in a mixed traffic environment and they do not have to contend with inconvenient parking upstream of the bus stop.

For bus stopping point indicators to work credibly, drivers must have some indication so that they know how to deliver the doors to the correct points along the platform. I mentioned Jaime Lerner's approach to this issue in Chapter 4. The Excalibur project explored the needs of bus drivers with respect to controlling the stopping position of the bus in the course of the experiments. We found that the bus drivers could stop their buses within ± 200 mm of a given stopping point, whatever means of indicating the correct position was adopted (e.g. a conventional pole, line on the roadway, line or other markings on the footway). BRT drivers tend to perform better than this (± 50 mm) – even when having to make a turning manoeuvre towards the kerb – but do not have to contend with parked vehicles or other traffic. They also have the advantage that all the bus stops have the same design detail – something that ought to be the norm for all bus stops.

It is also necessary to indicate the door positions to people other than users of wheelchairs, so ways of communicating this information to others (e.g. blind or partially sighted people) were investigated. The tactile *information surface* (PSVA, 2000a, 2000b) to indicate the location of the front door to passengers worked extremely well. The surface in question is made of the rubberised material used in children's playgrounds as a safety surface because of its slightly soft feel. Blind people can detect this change of surface so it indicates to them where the doorway will be. The surface is a highly visible orange colour in order to help partially sighted people and this also helps the driver position the bus correctly. Taking into account the ability of drivers to stop within ± 200 mm, the surface is 400 mm wider than the doorway to allow for this variation.

Using the tactile surface in this way helps everyone, but it is of special interest to blind and partially sighted people. It enables us to designate this part of the bus stop as the place where tactile and audible information is available. It is also really helpful as a marker for drivers, who can use this surface to indicate their stopping position.

Where buses have a second door, the platform surface around the expected location of the second door can be marked with pavers of a contrasting colour so that people can leave it clear for alighting passengers. TfL requires wheelchair users to use the centre door for boarding and alighting, so the area in front of the centre door also serves as an indicator for people in wheelchairs. As the contrasting colour surface indicates the likely location of the centre door it also serves to indicate to people in wheelchairs where to wait in order to be conveniently positioned to board the bus when it arrives. This is also a good place to put information at a convenient height for someone sitting in a wheelchair. It is also good to ensure that the shelter reaches at least as far as this point so that wheelchair users can wait near the doorway with the benefit of the shelter. This has proved problematical in practice, as it is felt by local businesses in particular that the resulting shelter is too long and by the advertising company to be too expensive. This is a very good reason for adopting a more aesthetic approach to shelter design. Working with local businesses, the shelter can be designed to be a positive element of the urban realm and accepted as such. This also joins up with the aesthetics issues discussed in Section 5.2.

The position of the area corresponding to the centre door will vary according to the type of bus using the stop. As a result, the area to be identified needs to accommodate buses with the centre door nearer to the front as well as those with the centre door placed nearer to the back of the bus. In the Excalibur project this was 2.4 m long in order to accommodate the range of buses using the bus stop at the time, but this could be reduced if the number of bus types is reduced or the position of the rear door relative to the front of the bus is standardised.

The rest of the platform surface area should have a surface colour which contrasts with the surfaces that indicate the doorways. Tactile paving is not appropriate at bus stops because the limited information that it provides already indicates very specific situations within the street environment (e.g. pedestrian crossings, stairs, guidance paths). It is felt by organisations such as the Royal National Institute of Blind People (RNIB) that the difference in kerb height at a raised bus stop platform is not a hazard that warrants another specific tactile surface. However, there is a lot of sense in using non-slip paving on the lateral ramps between the footway and the (higher) platform surface.

The upper surface of a Kassel kerb is characterised by a non-slip surface with a diamond pattern. This is not a tactile surface, but it does present a definite, regular and rougher surface than a standard concrete paver. By adding a diamond-surface paver behind the Kassel kerb we could continue the diamond surface for 500 mm behind the kerb edge. We then placed the yellow warning line behind the paver and started the main platform surface behind the line. The warning line is therefore distinguishable as being the boundary between a rough and a smooth surface.

Figure 5.15 The general arrangement of the platform at an Excalibur bus stop (half boarder)

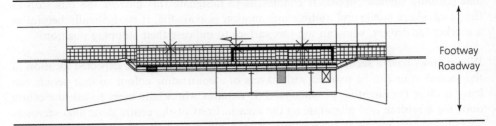

Footway
Roadway

The warning line has another purpose. It provides visual feedback to the bus drivers so that they can judge where the vehicle is positioned relative to the kerb during its final approach to the stopping point. If the line is made using special blocks, a localising transponder could be installed and this could be a neat way to provide information to the bus about the location and height of the kerb.

Figure 5.15 shows the general arrangement of the bus stop platform at an Excalibur bus stop, including the various surfaces. This is shown for a half boarder arrangement, but the platform surface is identical for all bus stops, giving a consistency to the bus stop area that is helpful to passengers and drivers.

5.3.6.2 Adopting safety measures

The experiments we carried out in the Excalibur project showed that the approach manoeuvre of the bus will result inevitably in its overhanging the kerb at some point. As a result of this overhang, the clearance between the underside of this part of the bus and the ground needs to be sufficient to be sure that the bus will not come into contact with the top of the kerb. Figure 5.16 shows the region of the bus that needs to be considered in this respect.

Figure 5.16 The overhang region for a bus as it approaches a kerb (dimensions in mm)

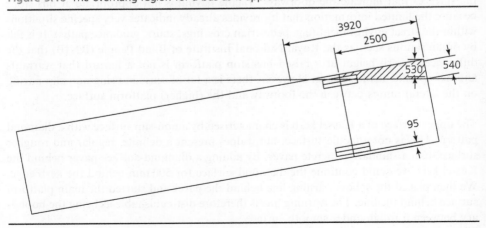

For safety reasons, a line was provided along the platform, behind which people should stand while they waited for their bus. In the Excalibur project this line was made from 100 mm wide yellow blocks on the platform, 500 mm from the kerb edge. This seems to work well – as long as it is maintained in good order. However, the line must also be able to warn people who cannot see it – and be made from something which could be sensed by blind people but that would not confuse them about its meaning.

This is not easy because the way in which a person using a long cane sweeps with their cane could easily miss the warning, especially if they are walking parallel to the line. We looked at an attempt to do this in France, which involved a block paver with a groove cut along it. The problem with this was how to make it large enough to distinguish it from, for example, the gap between lines of pavers, yet not so large that it could constitute a trip hazard in its own right. We were not convinced that the blocks we saw were really able to achieve this. My doubts were confirmed in work undertaken in relation to the shared space project in Exhibition Road in London, where the ability to detect a variety of tactile surfaces with sufficient reliability was really quite poor.

Craig Childs set up some experiments in the Pamela facility to test a wide range of tactile surfaces to see how they performed. Participants included visually-impaired people, wheelchair users and ambulant elderly people. In all, 54 different tactile surfaces were tested. We were interested in whether they acted as an indicator to prevent people from crossing it and if they could serve as a guidance path that could be followed. Put simply, if a visually-impaired person could detect the surface, wheelchair users and ambulant elderly people found it hazardous. The surface that was installed performed about as successfully as many of the others which performed much better than some.

Exhibition Road was redesigned to be a shared space – in the sense that kerbs, railings and other segregation paraphernalia were removed, thus allowing free access to all parts of the space between the buildings to both pedestrians and traffic. Concern was expressed by visually impaired people about the safety of this arrangement and the Pamela facility was asked to examine what form of tactile surface might be deployed to give confidence to visually-impaired people while maintaining the appearance of physical-barrier-free design. 54 different possible tactile surfaces were tested and none performed particularly and noticeably well. In the end a corduroy surface, coloured to match the surrounding surface, was selected and installed.

In the end, pedestrians tend to avoid the part of the street used by traffic and thus the 'shared space' element of the scheme might be less 'shared' than intended. The point for the present discussion is, however, that the tactile surfaces were not particularly good performers unless they were sufficiently large that they also caused problems to other pedestrians, notably ambulant elderly people and wheelchair users. It would therefore seem unsuitable to rely on tactile paving as a warning in the case of bus stops, although it could help some people.

Kerbside railings near bus stops are quite common, but are often obstructions to smooth operation at the bus stop. These should be removed. If they cannot be avoided, they

Figure 5.17 Railings can cause limitations to the accessibility of a bus stop (and to its capacity)

should be set so that the requisite number of buses can use the stop without the passengers being impeded by the railings. At the very least they should enable both doors of the number of buses expected to be at the stop at the same time to be used without any of the buses having to move. In the example shown in Figure 5.17, the gap between the end of the bus and the start of the railings is about 3 m: it would be just enough for passengers wishing to board a second bus (although it would be easier if the rubbish bin were moved) if the first bus stopped in exactly the right place. However, passengers would not be able to leave the second bus by the centre door, which would be obstructed by the railings. Buses often have to stop twice at this bus stop as a result, thus doubling the dwell time. This causes needless problems at peak times when more than one bus arrives at the stop at a time – especially important in this case as it is an interchange where passengers from a number of bus lines alight to enter a commuting railway station.

The points made above apply with respect to different buses using the same stop. The main point is to design the stopping points in such a way that the driver of each bus knows where to stop in order to deliver the entrance and exit doors to the correct places along the platform. To have any realistic chance of achieving this, it is essential that drivers can, and do, treat every stop in the same way. The idea is not workable if drivers have to remember that different stops have to be approached differently or that if there is a wheelchair user at the stop they should make a different approach. Just as drivers have to start preparing their approach to the stop several metres upstream, so the designers must prepare the stop to accept the bus in a way that presents a consistent approach for the driver. We discuss this later in this chapter.

5.3.6.3 Establishing the position and shape of the shelter

One of the key elements to improve the area of bus stop is the shelter. A bus shelter is multifunctional. It is considered to be the place to:

1   Protect: consideration needs to be given to the prevailing wind, rain, sunlight and heat.
2   Inform: the shelter is also the location for information about the bus services and the local area. It is the point where people have continuous access to information to proceed on their journey, whether they are waiting for a bus or have just left one.
3   Provide comfort: all bus stops should have seats, preferably located within the shelter. Space for wheelchairs, pushchairs, shopping and luggage must also be included.
4   Promote safety: shelters must enable people to feel secure and safe while they wait for a bus.

In light of the discussion in Section 4.1.3, additional features for a bus stop include:

5   Enable the transitions from pedestrian to pedenger to passenger.
6   Provide a 'good place to be' in the local area: it needs to be a positive element of the urban realm.
7   Support people who are waiting for a bus, but not inside the shelter itself.
8   It needs to be aesthetically pleasing.

These needs should be met for all users of the pedestrian environment, so a shelter must be an attractive element of the public realm and be able to accommodate people with wheelchairs, pushchairs, shopping and young children, as well as elderly people. The shelter should enable people to wait for the bus and to enter the vehicle in comfort, but it should also enable people to use it as a place where they can rest comfortably without impeding the operation of the bus stop. Once a minimum length has been reached, the only real way to increase the capacity of the shelter is to increase its length or width if possible, or increase bus frequency to reduce the number of people who have to be accommodated at one time.

In London, the usual length for a bus shelter is three or four panels. Each panel is 1.3 m long, thus giving a shelter length of 3.9 m or 5.2 m. As noted above, the use of centre doors for boarding for some people means that the shelter should really extend to the rear of the centre door. Depending on the position of the centre door on the buses using the stop, this could require a minimum shelter length of 8.725 m (seven panels), as in some cases this is the minimum length from the front of the bus to the back of the rear door. The reason for this determining the length of the shelter is that wheelchair users

Table 5.7 Acceptable minimum internal dimensions of four-sided shelters and associated space requirements

Description of the space inside the shelter	Minimum dimensions	
	Length: m	Width: m
Internal shape of shelter	4.0	2.4
Entry to shelter	–	1.2
Manoeuvring space for a wheelchair	–	1.2
Seating area per person	0.5	0.5
Legroom per person	0.5	0.5
Area for luggage or shopping	0.5	0.5
Space for pushchair	1.2	1.0
Space for wheelchair (marked on ground)	1.2	1.2
Essential: all-round visibility for wheelchair users; minimum zone of visibility 0.9–1.2 m above finished floor level	Full length of shelter; full width of shelter at both ends	

can wait comfortably in the shelter near to the door at which it is intended that they should board the bus. This avoids the stark choice between (a) having to move along the platform to find their entrance door after the bus has arrived and (b) waiting in the rain.

Resulting from these tests, a summary of the minimum shelter and platform dimensions deemed acceptable to the wheelchair users is given in Tables 5.7 and 5.8.

Some shelter designs are not able to accommodate wheelchair users because their entrances are too narrow. A shelter with two or more sides and a bus stop pole (or some other similar obstacle) aligned at one end needs 3.5 m of platform width in order to ensure that the shelter is accessible to people in wheelchairs. If a ramp is expected to be deployed the width required would be 3.5 m plus the appropriate ramp length.

Table 5.8 Acceptable minimum dimensions of footways on free-standing platforms for four-sided bus shelters

Type of shelter	Footway	Minimum dimensions	
		Length: m	Width: m
Front entry	Front (including ramps and/or stairs)	Equal to length of shelter plus either two ramps @ 8% incline, or one ramp and one flight of steps	1.5
	Side	No footway required	–
Side entry	Front (including ramps and/or stairs)	Equal to length of shelter plus 1.5 m, plus either two ramps @ 8% incline, or one ramp and one flight of steps	1.5
	Side	Equal to width (front to rear) of shelter	1.5

Modern shelters make a lot of use of glazed areas, which is good from the point of view of increasing ambient light in them, but can make them a hazard for people with impaired vision. Where glazing is used, a bold brightly coloured band 140–160 mm wide should be placed on the glazing about 1500 mm from the ground.

All shelters should be set with their solid side(s) away from the road edge. This provides much more space for passengers to board and alight from the buses and helps to separate the bus stop area from the footway space. It also avoids the problem for bus drivers in bringing the bus close to the kerb – a shelter positioned close to the kerb edge will tend to 'push' the driver away from the kerb and thus increase the horizontal gap. It is also a lot harder to see on-coming buses from seats with their back towards the roadway. It is necessary to turn about 120° to see an arriving bus from this position. A shelter position with the back away from the kerb means that buses can be seen by turning about 30°. The difference is considerable, and is important for people with back or neck problems.

There is no reason why the shelter has to be straight-sided. For example, it could have a curved shape, which would have several advantages. It could allow some of the seats to be facing more towards the oncoming buses, and have seating which is more amenable to conversation. However, care needs to be taken to ensure that such a design is positioned correctly to permit a good view of oncoming buses.

There is a potential problem with shelters because of the way in which they are currently funded as advertising panels – an activity that does not always fit neatly with an accessible bus stop. A challenge that has become increasingly difficult with the advent of the need for accessible bus stops is that the needs for accessibility are often seen by the advertising companies as counter to their needs. The problem arises in the following way. The advertising company provides a number of bus shelters for the local area on the basis that the cost will be recouped through the sale of advertising. The value of the advertising sales depends on the position of the advertising panel. To maximise revenue from a panel, the panel needs to be near the roadside and visible for the maximum amount of time to the intended audience (i.e. car drivers). We have shown that, in order to be accessible, a shelter should be set away from the road edge, so one conflict is the actual positioning of the shelter on or near to the platform. Secondly, the advertising panel is worth less if it is likely to be obstructed by waiting passengers, so a busy bus stop could well be unattractive to the advertising company. It is therefore essential that a local authority intent in making its bus stops accessible exercises a strong control over the type, positioning and general layout of the bus shelters provided in this way by advertising companies. Many local authorities have met problems in this area as a result of other pressures (e.g. conservation areas in which advertising is not welcome). However, an inaccessible shelter can render the bus stop inaccessible even if all the other accessibility features are included in its construction.

The answer is not to ban advertising in bus shelters, but to consider how to use it more effectively as a great opportunity to have better shelters. As noted earlier, the attraction for advertisers is currently the traffic driving past the bus stop rather than the people waiting inside it. This is because the advertisers see bus passengers in the way mentioned at the very start of this book – that they are low-spend, low-interest consumers – so the advertising revenues for products that would interest bus passengers would be too low to be worth the investment in the bus shelter as an advertising panel. However, if the bus system were to be more attractive, this would change, just as it does when the urban environment is made more traffic-free and the bus system becomes used by a wider section of society. If higher-spending people use the bus system, then the advertising in the bus stop – where people might be waiting for a few minutes rather than passing by in a few seconds – could be made more interesting and appropriate for bus passengers. The opportunity is to use the accessibility improvements in bus stops to improve the aesthetics and attractiveness of the bus system in order to increase the number of high-spend people using the bus on a regular and frequent basis – as a pleasure rather than as a chore.

Where the bus stop construction is contracted to an advertising company, often the choice of shelter design and its position are both fixed by the advertising company in order to improve the advertising impact and thus its profitability. This can all too easily compromise the level of accessibility at bus stops. This sort of activity has to be changed and there is an urgent need to revise the relationship between local authorities and the companies that provide bus shelters and other facilities at bus stops so that such decisions do not obstruct accessibility objectives. The lack of discussion between advertising companies and local authorities is not a problem found only in the UK. Unfortunately, similar inappropriate behaviour has been observed in France and Germany.

However, the interest shown by advertisers is a great opportunity. If the bus shelter is an active element of the public realm and the bus stop environment as a whole is seen to provide an attractive and positive feel for people who encounter it, then instead of mitigating for the disadvantages of having to have a bus stop, it could be a positive contribution to the local life, businesses and community. This more positive approach could be better for the advertisers and open up new opportunities for their interaction with the public.

In some cases it is necessary to provide protection against a prevailing wind which comes from the direction of the roadway. In this case, the shelter should be four-sided. This causes other problems for shelter design, as discussed above, which need to be resolved so that accessibility is assured.

One common reason for placing the shelter with the back along the kerb edge is that it reduces splashes from passing traffic. This is a drainage problem and should be treated as such – it is not an excuse for making the shelter and its seating arrangements less accessible.

There are lots of different types of seating, some being more suitable than others for people with different kinds of needs. *Conventional seating* should be 480–500 mm high to the seat surface with a back angled between 95° and 100° to the (horizontal) seat surface. The seat surface should be 420 mm deep. Seats should be provided even where it is not possible to install a shelter, and only in exceptional circumstances should a bus stop not have seats. Whether in a shelter or not, seats should be available in two or more different heights to cater for children and older people.

Conventional seating should be complemented by *lower seats*. These should be 300 mm high and with the seat surface 300 mm deep. The angle of the back should be angled between 95° and 100° to the (horizontal) seat surface. The choice of seat height is to accommodate people who have difficulty in sitting, getting up or down to high or low seats. Armrests should be provided at least to pairs of seats, so that people have some support when leaving the seat. These also serve to discourage people from sleeping on the seats. Armrests should be approximately 200 mm above the seat surface.

Higher, *perch-type seats* are designed for a passenger to lean or 'half sit' for a short period of time. They take up very little space and are attractive to some passengers with arthritis, stiff joints or back problems who find it difficult to get up from a low seat. However, for perch seats to be effective for people with back problems or who find it difficult to use lower seats, it is necessary to construct them at a higher level. In Chapter 4 I mentioned the sciatica seat in Buenos Aires (Figures 4.27 and 4.28). Perch seats should be provided in conjunction with other seating. The seat is designed to provide support without the need for downward pressure, thus is a 'supportive leaning device' rather than a seat.

Tip-up seats in shelters are typically too small and are difficult for elderly people to use. The *bench seat*, with end armrests, should be set about 480–500 mm from the ground for sitting. As such, this is generally felt to be comfortable by those people who can use seats at this height. Bench seats are often found in a plastic variant with a slippery surface and without armrests. In this form they are almost uniformly unpopular with passengers. A newer version is now available that is made from two or three 'banana-shaped' pieces, set to form a seat. However, these seats still lack armrests, which provide the means for getting up for many people, and the dimensions are odd (e.g. the back is too low to provide support).

A brightly coloured coating that contrasts strongly with the background helps visually impaired passengers both to find the seat and to avoid it when they are not looking for it. Seat surfaces should be covered so that they are not cold or slippery.

Seats should be arranged so that a passenger can see oncoming buses without the need for excessive movement. It is usually impractical in this respect to set the seats so that they actually face oncoming buses, but they should be set so that their occupants face the roadway. This has been discussed above in terms of the positioning of the back of the shelter and is an important accessibility issue, especially for elderly people and people encumbered with luggage and shopping. This is because such people need early notice of the bus arrival so that they have time to prepare themselves to board the bus.

If space permits, it is a good idea to set seats in such a way that people can see what is going on around the bus stop and can engage with each other. Making seats that are actually comfortable to sit in would be a major step forward in making the bus system more attractive to more people.

5.4. Information and communication along the journey chain

Information is central to accessible bus systems. Whether an information system is good or bad depends to a great extent on the way in which it allows people to make appropriate and timely decisions about their journey. I now consider what is meant by 'appropriate' and 'timely'.

Accessible transport is irrelevant if the potential user does not know that there are activities to do and how the transport system enables these to be reached. Other issues might make the system inaccessible, even if everything else were known in advance (e.g. cost and fares systems might make the journey too expensive or too complicated, and thus impossible). Even if the journey is thought to be possible and the costs are within acceptable limits there is still the issue of ensuring that the journey takes place as planned and, if not, that the journey can still be made by an alternative route without undue stress on the traveller. Each of these issues can be a potential barrier for different users. The information role is to minimise the impact of these barriers.

Learning to identify what can represent a barrier is necessary, but not sufficient. To deliver the information successfully it is also necessary to understand how the users think. This cannot be achieved without the active involvement of users: it is necessary to incorporate what they think and not what we think they think. This task involves learning not only how users acquire knowledge but also how they process it. Users need information that is consistent, clear and complete. More than that, it needs to be available at the right place and at the right time, so good strategies for diffusion and dissemination of the information must be formulated.

Identifying how users think is not enough either. We need to understand why the system that we have designed, considering all the recommendations to suit people with special needs, still does not work for some people. Understanding this will help us to design a truly accessible information system. Of course, just as with other accessibility issues, there will be a need for compromise when applying the thinking in practice. This means that we must judge what can or cannot be adapted or cut in order to know who will be affected by the resulting barrier and what this might represent to the community.

5.4.1 Specific users' needs

Information is needed at every stage of the journey chain:

1 pre-trip information, to help the user plan routes and connections
2 in-trip information, which assists users at each decision point during the journey
3 supportive/confirming information, which repeats and informs data and decisions and helps users feel more confident while progressing towards their desired destination(s).

The first issue is to decide what information is needed at each point. Following Ackermann's approach (Ackermann, 1995), we can separate information into two basic types: *specific information* related to each stage of the journey and *orientation information* which directs people along the journey.

A person who wishes to make a journey must first identify where they will start and where they want to go. They will need to find the correct bus stop and bus service, board the right vehicle, alight at the right stop and find their way to the destination. However, this simple view of a journey oversimplifies the information needs. A lot of information is required in order to make a journey, and if the traveller has particular requirements (e.g. is a deaf person) their information needs are even greater. A more comprehensive view of a user's information needs at various points in the journey chain is given in Table 5.9.

Table 5.9 shows the information needs in terms of both specific and orientation information in relation to various stages of a journey: pre-trip, the walk to and from the bus stop, the wait at the bus stop, the ride on the vehicle, and interchanges. A very important point we can draw from the table is the need to explain the functionality of the environments around a bus stop, inside a bus and at an interchange point. Knowing how a bus stop works, for example, means that a user can feel more confident, and thus more comfortable, about using it. We have seen in this chapter that a well-designed bus stop places certain functions at certain places in the bus stop environment, and defines these very clearly (e.g. the boarding point, the alighting area). These definitions are useless if users do not understand what they are for and how to make use of them. It is essential that this information can be found at the bus stop. The same applies to other elements of the journey chain. For example, in a bus, information about which doors to use, where to pay the fare, where it is possible to stand, how to request the bus to stop and how to know where the bus is along its route would make it easier for passengers to make better use of the facilities in the vehicle.

Interchanges provide a more complicated environment in information terms because they consist of a convergence of different transport systems. Different bus lines or different modes could have different operational rules and different types of fare discounts for specific groups (e.g. elderly people, families, children). These 'rules' need to be explained so that people do not become confused while attempting to change from one service to another. Confusion translates into exclusion if the lack of understanding results in some people finding the system inaccessible.

I pointed out earlier in this chapter that a bus stop should provide information for people arriving on a bus. This information should indicate useful places within the local area, and the accessibility level of the pedestrian routes to local destinations. We have included this point in Table 5.9. The provision of such information is not only helpful to arriving bus passengers: it can also help other people, and for this reason the bus stop can become a valuable source of information about the local area. The area concerned should be large enough to include a reasonably comprehensive selection of likely facilities, but small enough that these could be easily reached from the bus stop. Indications of distances and accessibility levels would help people decide how best to continue their journey.

Balcombe and Vance (1998) suggest that the information upon which the majority of bus users depend is inaccurate and restrictive. Public transport information is usually provided by the operator or transport authority. Their perspective of the provision of

Table 5.9 Information needs of the accessible journey chain

Objectives of stages of the journey	Pre-trip information	The walk	The wait at the bus stop	The ride in the vehicle	Interchanges
Specific information system	1. Locate the origin 2. Locate the destination 3. Identify the line services. 4. Locate the nearest bus stop 5. Verify the need for interchange 6. Have a preliminary view of the departure time, waiting time, duration of the trip and costs 7. Check accessibility of the vehicle 8. Verify the accessibility of the walk to the bus stop/ terminal/station	1. Identify and check the correct bus stop platform	1. Be reassured of the bus lines that serve the stop 2. Have an estimate of the time to wait for the service 3. Be informed how the bus stop works – expression of the functionality of the bus stop environment 4. Be informed about the bus(es) number as it approaches the platform 5. Have access to a service centre to ask for more specific information	1. Identify the number of the bus line and destination 2. Know how the bus environment works	1. Have reassurance about the onward service 2. Have an estimate for the time to wait for the onward service 3. Be informed how the interchange point works – expression of the functionality of the interchange environment 4. Have access to a service centre to ask for more specific information

Orientation system				
	1. Have access to information to reinforce the chosen path with important points (supermarket, hospital, churches, etc.) 2. Be alert to any kind of situation that might represent danger (crossing point, cycle lane) 3. Know locations of any resting facilities along the path 4. Confirm a unique identification for bus stop in use	1. Be informed about the distance between the adjacent bus stops (upstream and downstream) 2. Be informed about the kind of service facilities offered within a convenient radius of the bus stop (medical, educational, entertainment, food, market services) 3. Be informed about the condition and access level of the infrastructure within a convenient radius of the bus stop (footway condition, rest facilities, etc.)	1. Follow the route along the journey by announcement of bus stops and route map 2. Have a general view about where the important destinations are along the route 3. Know where to get off the bus 4. Be informed about modal interchange points	1. Leave the arrival point and reach the departure point 2. Be informed about access to facilities (toilet, information points, lifts, help)

information is often more to do with advertising their service and not really what is appropriate for users. The legislation discussed in Chapter 2 places a duty on the local authority to find and judge what is meant by 'appropriate'. This begs the question: what is 'appropriate'?

The users' information needs as described in Table 5.9 make up a list of what, where and when information is required, but we have not yet indicated how it might be made available. If the users' needs identified in Table 5.6 are to be met, it seems clear that all four of these requirements must be satisfied before any information can be considered appropriate. The first step towards this is to determine what methods are available for presenting each type of information listed in Table 5.9. Ackermann *et al.* (1995) suggest that information should be provided in the form of an information chain, which runs parallel to the accessible journey chain. This makes a useful starting point because the information chain concept emphasises the need for information to be provided throughout the journey. Some methods that could be adopted by the providers of information at each point in the journey chain have been suggested by Ackermann *et al.* and are shown in Table 5.10.

Tables 5.9 and 5.10 are linked. For example, the users' need for information about a bus line and its departure times (from Table 5.9) could be provided by a timetable (from Table 5.10). Table 5.10 is beginning to express the fourth requirement – the 'how' – but it does not show how we can be sure that the information, having been sent, is actually received and understood by the users. Whatever means of providing the information is chosen, everyone must be able to receive and make use of the information that is provided. For instance, a map which might be ideal for displaying a network diagram excludes blind people simply because it relies on visual capability in order for the user to be able to use it. In order for the bus system to be accessible, the information must also be accessible for everybody. Hence the information provider must be sure that their information is not only provided, but is also received, processed and understood by the users.

Table 5.11 is adapted from a guidebook on passenger information services for passenger transport systems in the USA (Transportation Research Board, 2000). The guidebook underlines what different kinds of information may and may not be provided. We have expanded their approach to include more specific types of information and two other classifications:

1 the time and point of access to the information
2 a description of the people who could be excluded by the use of each information type.

There can be many interferences between the source and the receiver of information. These interferences could be caused by the media (e.g. where information is presented only visually or aurally), the format (e.g. the way a timetable is laid out) or the content (e.g. the information is confusing). The interference problem permeates the entire information process and just one lapse can destroy the accessibility of an otherwise adequate

Table 5.10 Elements of a continuous information chain*

Stage of a journey	Previous Information (e.g. at home)	Way to/from the bus stop	Bus stop area	On/inside the vehicle	Interchanges
Information system	Timetable Network diagram Telephone service		Arrivals and departures board Network diagram Tariff information Announcement Service centre		Arrivals and departures board Network diagram Tariff information
Orientation system		Pre-orientation Signposts Guide strips (markings on the surface)	Signposts Map of bus stop and the environment Guide strips (markings on the surface)	Announcement Pictogram	Signposts Map of bus stop and the environment Guide strips (markings on the surface)

Source: COST 322 (European Commission, 1997)

Table 5.11 General issues about forms of information

Information type	What they could provide	What they do not provide	Time or point of access	Who is excluded
Maps (including network diagrams)	Spatial relationship of landmarks, routes and connections Schematic view of the whole journey An overall picture of the transport system Flexibility for changing trip plans Supportive information during the trip Portable information useful both pre-trip and in trip	Easy availability (the map is a physical object that must be obtained before trip planning can begin) Straightforward information (map reading presents difficulties for many people)	Pre-trip In-trip At interchanges	People with vision difficulties (unless provided in tactile form) People having difficulties with spatial representation People with learning difficulties
Timetables	Temporal relationship of bus stop locations; services schedule Simple and narrow view of the specific route Portable information	Easy availability (the map is a physical object that must be obtained before trip planning can begin) Straightforward information (reading tables presents difficulties for many people)	Pre-trip In-trip At interchanges	People unused to timetable information People with vision difficulties (unless provided in tactile or audible format) People with learning difficulties People with dexterity problems

Oral instructions (telephone services)	Straightforward information	An overall picture of the transit system Reference material for future continued travel Flexibility or easy error correction	If equipment available, anytime, anywhere (including during a journey)	People with hearing difficulties People with learning difficulties People whose first language is not the local tongue
Sign	Supportive information Easy availability Straightforward information Permanent information	Detailed information and explanation An overall picture of the transit system Dynamic information Portable information	During the walk to and from bus stops and at bus stops	People with vision difficulties (unless provided in tactile or audible format) People with learning difficulties
Signposts	Directions and/or distance of specific points Supportive information Easy availability Permanent information	Detailed information and explanation An overall picture of the transit system Dynamic information Portable information	During the walk to and from bus stops and at bus stops In-trip, seeing from the vehicle	People with vision difficulties (unless provided in tactile or audible format) People with learning difficulties
Fare table	Detailed information about the price of the journey, type and discount Supportive information Portable information	Easy availability (the table is a physical object that must be obtained before trip planning can begin) Straightforward information (reading tables presents difficulties for many people)	Pre-trip In-trip At interchanges	People unused to fare information People with vision difficulties (unless provided in tactile or audible format) People with learning difficulties People with dexterity problems

Arrival and departure board	Detailed information about specific services Supportive information Easy availability Dynamic information Straightforward information	An overall picture of the transport system	At interchanges	People with vision difficulties People with learning difficulties
Variable messages, signs or oral announcements	Information about short-term changes: emergency or operational changes Easy availability Straightforward information Dynamic information Supportive information Stimulation for users' action	An overall picture of the transport system	At interchanges	People with vision (signs) or hearing (announcements) difficulties People with learning difficulties People whose first language is not the local tongue
Tactile surfaces (guide strips)	Permanent information	An overall picture of the transit system Information for people who are untrained to use it	At interchanges The walk (crossing)	People with poor sense of touch
Service centre	Detailed information about specific services Straightforward information Information about short-term changes (emergency or operational changes)		In theory, that is the place where all information should be available	In theory, nobody should be excluded

Figure 5.18 The arrivals board at Euston Station

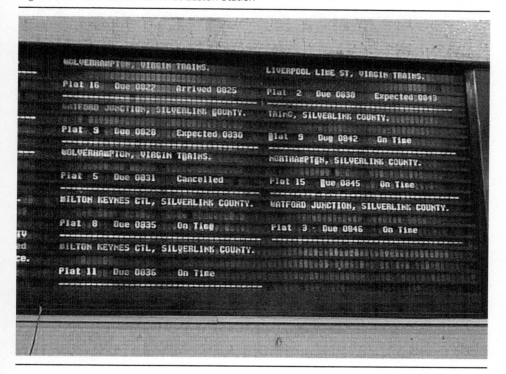

information system. Much of the effort employed in designing an accessible information system needs to be directed towards the elimination of interference from other information, such as advertising. Hiding a timetable in the centre of a panel so that it is barely visible amongst the more colourful and eye-catching advertisements is not a good way of making the information accessible.

Whatever the type of information, the provider has to suppose that the user has a certain level of knowledge about the system. This presupposition can easily exclude some people. Some information requires the user to know so much about the system in order to be able to understand it, that one wonders why the information needs to be provided at all. Figure 5.18 shows the arrivals indicator at Euston Station. This makes it difficult for people meeting someone from one of these trains to know which one to wait for unless the traveller started their journey at the station where the train started its journey. Even this does not help if the journey in question actually started at another station, with an interchange onto the train which is expected at Euston. In this case, there is no telling which train the traveller will arrive on, without a great deal of prior knowledge on the part of the person who is waiting to greet them. It is unlikely, for example, that a passenger will know in advance of making their journey where the train has come from (unless, knowing that it could be an issue, they ask when they book their ticket). Apart from this, the information shown in Figure 5.18 indicates the platform at which the train will arrive, the time it is due to arrive (both scheduled and expected) and the train operator. Unless they have prior knowledge of the train routes, a person intending to meet someone at this railway station would need to seek further information in order to be able to know where they should wait. People for whom this sort of uncertainty is difficult will find this sort of experience frightening, and as a result they may decide not to meet anyone at the station. If the passenger needs to be met, either alternative arrangements would have to be made or they would not be able to travel. I discussed in Chapter 1 the difficulty encountered when trying to use a transport system which relies on personal assistance at a particular point in the journey. This is a simple illustration of the sort of problem that might be encountered due to a poor information system.

Table 5.11 identifies the people who would be excluded as a result of choosing a particular way of providing information. Combining the information in Tables 5.9 to 5.11 gives an insight into the need for providing information, not only at specific points in the journey chain, but also in suitable formats so that everyone can obtain the information they need in a way that they can understand. Ideally, information should be available in a variety of formats so that users can select the one which best suits their own needs. Table 5.12 illustrates some examples of users' groups and their media preferences. The table was constructed based on the advice given in Gregory (1996).

5.4.2   Examples
We have used the concepts described above when delivering information within a number of our projects. The following three examples show how we approached the problem of communicating information in an accessible way.

5.4.2.1 The Hackney Plusbus timetable
When the Hackney Plusbus service started it was necessary to produce a timetable so that people would be able to find out about the route and schedule. One of the potential user groups for the service consisted of people with learning difficulties, so it was important to make sure that a timetable was produced in a way that would be helpful to them.

Two issues are important in the production of a timetable: the names of the places for which times will be supplied and the representation of time. The first issue was to identify the points along the route that would appear on the timetable and how these should be described. The places named in the timetable also appeared in the standard one, so that they would be compatible. We drew a number of simple symbols to represent the various places along the route, taking care to maintain consistency (i.e. all the health centres were denoted by the same symbol) yet trying to maintain differences (i.e. each health centre was framed by a different shape, such as a circle, square or triangle). An example of the timetable entry for two of the health centres is shown in Figure 5.19.

Shopping areas were indicated in a similar way (a shopping basket with the name of the area in clear text). The hospital was indicated by the conventional hospital sign (a capital 'H' in white on a dark background). Using this symbol meant that street signs near the hospital would match with the timetable information and thus help identify the location.

Table 5.12 Users' groups and their media preferences

Users group	Preferences
People with literacy problems	Television and radio Video and audio tape CD (multimedia) Telephone
People with hearing disabilities*	Text: printed information is acceptable, but English text must translate to BSL Television Video CD (multimedia) Television and video subtitling (with BSL) Teletext Textphones Typetalk Videophones
People with vision difficulties	Large clear print Tactile diagrams Braille Moon Television, video, audio description Radio Audio tape Electronic aids Telephone help lines CD (multimedia)
People with visual and hearing difficulties	Braille Large print Moon Tactile diagrams Clear speech in cassette Sign communications on video
People with learning difficulties†	Illustration Symbols/Makaton Television, video Audio tapes CD (multimedia)
Older people‡	The above, as required, plus oral and written information provided together

* Many learn and use British Sign Language (BSL) as their first language
† Repetition of information (visual or factual) is an important factor
‡ Less likely to pick up information casually

Figure 5.19 The Hackney Plusbus timetable

 ⏰	10:02 am	 🚶	Athena Health Centre
 🕐	10:15 am	 🚶	Clapton Health Centre

Some places could be identified by an icon that represented their appearance (e.g. blocks of flats or a church).

The people with learning difficulties involved with this project asked for the times to be printed digitally in large type in addition to a clock face. They had two reasons for this. First, the digital representation added further information for those who could understand time in this form; and, secondly, they felt it was less stigmatising because other people would not know whether they were reading the clock face or the digital version. Both text and symbols were used to represent places, for the same reason.

The symbols (and names) used in the timetable were repeated in a simple line diagram of the route which accompanied the timetable. They were also reproduced inside the bus on a display which lit each symbol successively as the bus passed the associated point on the route. A user could therefore follow their progress along the route using the combination of the timetable, the route map, the information inside the bus and the view of the world outside.

5.4.2.2 The Excalibur timetable

We moved on to more complicated timetables in Newham, associated with the construction of our Excalibur accessible bus stops. In this case, the bus services are not given as exact times, but as frequencies (e.g. 'every 8 minutes'). Working with people with learning difficulties, we devised a way of conveying frequency using the idea of a circular clock and its hands to mark a segment which indicated the interval between buses (Figure 5.20). The circle is placed on a black surround to indicate evening services. Clock face (and text) times are provided to indicate the times between which different frequencies apply.

The Excalibur information also includes a simple route map showing the whole route with the bus stop names, the journey times between the stops, and interchanges with other modes. The current bus stop is identified with a 'you are here' arrow. The journey times between each stop from the current bus stop are presented inside a bus symbol to reinforce the direction of travel. Another important point is the box that delivers information about intra- and intermodal interchanges available at the current bus stop. This information shows whether or not the onward service is operated with accessible vehicles. This way of representing frequency was developed working closely with a

Figure 5.20 The Excalibur timetable

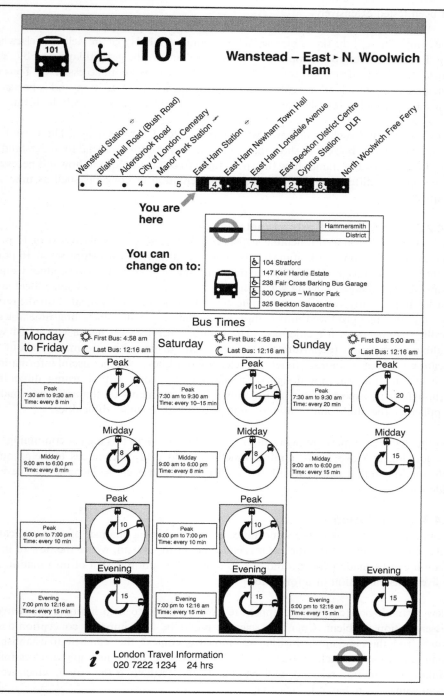

worker from Change (an organisation of people with learning difficulties), but has not yet been tested extensively.

The composition of the timetable tried to incorporate symbols that are well used elsewhere (e.g. London Underground roundel, 'you are here' arrow, the general layout of bus stop timetables used by Transport for London) with information about accessibility. Thus the timetable contains a level of detail that is appropriate for different users and is presented in a way that makes it easier for people who prefer information in symbolic form.

It is unlikely that such a timetable would be adopted for regular use. The reason for including it in this book is to show that involving user groups is crucial to understanding how they understand things, how they need them to be presented, and how it is necessary to be open to different perceptions of the presentation of concepts such as time and frequency.

5.4.2.3 The Cumbria Plusbus timetable

In Cumbria we produced timetable leaflets in a format with a standard text of 12 point Lucida Sans Unicode (or Optima), with timetable displays at bus stops set at 16 point. Although there was a simplified route map with the timetable, we also produced simple maps of each village, showing where the bus goes, where it stops and some local land-marks. Importantly, every bus stop indicated where the bus stop is located for the return journey. We also produced information about the bus service, including timetables in Braille together with a tactile map. The Cumbria service also had a CD-ROM with audible information (departure times from each village, with information about the location of the stop, journey times to a selection of places and other useful information). The information was not designed specifically for people with learning difficulties, although many aspects of the information are improvements on the usual information supplied to the public and will help some people with learning difficulties.

All the above examples are 'work in progress'. Our work in this area is continuing. We are looking at video maps, audible timetables and other techniques to help convey information so that people with learning difficulties can begin to increase their level of independence.

5.4.3   Conclusion

I cannot over-emphasise the importance of establishing a channel of communication between the designers and the various end users of the system, where the flow of infor-mation can be made two way and at two levels: conception/design of information and delivery/dissemination of information.

New technologies (e.g. mobile apps) are now available to help improve the delivery/dissemination problem. Cognitive sciences might be able improve conception/design issues. Together, and applied within an innovative context, they can help to establish the communication channel, putting the users at the centre, and thus improve accessibility. Making information relevant, understandable and aesthetic is the way in which we are progressing our research in this area.

TfL has taken a really innovative approach to information. In addition to the Legible London programme which makes information aimed for pedestrians available across the streets of London, it has opened up all its real-time public transport data to app developers so that they can develop the apps for the markets the app developers believe are relevant. The result is a number of apps, with slightly different intentions and applicability. There is an opportunity for people to develop apps which are directly applicable to people with different capabilities. In addition, a number of researchers are exploring how best to make this sort of technology useful for people with particular challenges. For example, Catherine Holloway and Steve Hailes are developing an app that will help wheelchair users understand the challenges of the street network, based on information from other wheelchair users in a kind of citizen science approach to data collection and dissemination.

5.5.   Putting it all together

Having discussed the various elements of the bus stop I can now turn to considering how to put it all together.

5.5.1   Aesthetics and operations

The emphasis in this book is that the bus system needs to be made for people – all people – so that they can achieve all the activities they need and in which they desire to participate and that anything less will make the city less civilised. This means that accessibility and aesthetics need to be brought together in a creative and practical way – the bus stop must be a great place to be and a marvellous element of the city environment, and it must also work. I am always astonished that some people still think that accessibility and aesthetics do not mix – that, as someone once said to me, 'if you want accessibility, aesthetics goes out of the window'. What nonsense!

Accessibility designers need to understand more about aesthetics and the artists, architects, planners, designers involved in the urban realm need to understand much more about accessibility. This book is intended to be a contribution to that discussion. In the previous sections I have tried to show that it is possible to be really creative with the concept of the bus stop and what it is intended for if there is a clear vision for what the city is trying to achieve and there is an understanding that this vision has to be made available to everyone in the city, whatever their capabilities.

Many of the operational requirements could be made much more aesthetically pleasing. The incorporation of technology can also help – creating a better air, acoustic and lighting environment is not that difficult in the space of a bus shelter and its environs, and not that expensive. LED lighting can offer a vast range of lighting which can be adjusted to suit the environment, time of day and the people affected by it, with almost no additional cost. Acoustic environments can be improved through the incorporation of low-cost baffling and sound projection systems to provide both an aesthetic acoustic background and the opportunity for audible information. Thought about the tactile nature of the bus stop is also possible – look at the ceramic seating in the Gare de Lyon bus stop (see Figure 5.4).

5.5.2 The bus system and the five cities

Having discussed how it is possible to increase the aesthetic and operational attributes of bus stops and to emphasise their positive role as part of the urban realm in its attempt to generate a better society for the future, I would now like to discuss how the bus stop can help transform the world towards the principles enshrined in the five cities as described in Chapter 1.

5.5.2.1 The courteous city

The courteous city is about how people live together in a societally cohesive and collaborative domain, with Sennett's 'differentiating exchange' at the centre. Bus stops are crucial players in this exchange – they form the theatre in which such exchanges should be encouraged to happen. Yet they rarely achieve such an outcome. I have outlined in this chapter how I think that the bus stop could – and why it currently does not – provide the incentive for such a civilised place in society.

The first point is to ensure that the bus stop is seen as something of society, that it belongs in the public realm as part of the urban environment intended for people. Too often the bus stop is seen by the passenger as a rather inconvenient part of the bus system, signifying only where it might be possible to catch – or, usually more memorably, to miss – a bus. To the bus operator, the bus stop represents one of the more problematic elements of the operation. To a planner it is an inconvenient necessity that messes up traffic flow or parking and to an urban designer it is an ugly eyesore in the urban environment. If these views are changed to one where the bus stop is actually a 'people start' – a place where people can come to do things, see others, participate in societal acts such as lingering, listening, chatting, communicating with others and also, perhaps, to catch a bus – then its impact on society is considerable. Factor that by the large number of bus stops that should exist in a city and with good composition along the lines suggested in this chapter, you have a transformative force for the benefit of society.

Civilising the bus stop therefore starts with civilising its design – improving the aesthetics, making it nicer and easier to use, making it a great and safe place to be – and considering how that civilising process could actually work. Seeing it as a positive element of society is just the start.

Angling seats to make it easier to converse with people, making the seats comfortable, having better information about oncoming buses and downstream journeys, what is in the local area and how to reach these activities are all a part of making the bus stop a convenient point in the public environment. It is also important to make sure that the bus stop works, both as the place where the transitions between pedestrian, passenger and pedenger can take place easily and comfortably and as the place where buses arrive to bring and take away passengers. It is this joining together of aesthetic and operational performance that singles out the bus stop as a location which influences how people treat each other on a daily basis and thus is a massive contribution to the courteous city.

5.5.2.2 The active and inclusive city

The bus stop is the portal between the activities and the rest of the city. This is where people arrive from distances too great to have walked and set off to destinations in other parts of the city. The activities do not exist if people cannot reach them and thus the inclusiveness of making sure that everyone can use the bus stop and its surrounding pedestrian environment is essential. Some activities are only of interest to people who travel there on a regular basis, but many will be attractive to people who are unfamiliar with the area. This requires good information about the local area and bus services, a space that is suitable for enabling people to wait while others are discovering how to proceed to the local activities.

Ensuring that the bus stop is accessible in relation to the buses is crucial for ensuring that access is equitable. Making sure that the footways and other aspects of the pedestrian environment are also sufficiently accessible so that the activities are accessible from the bus stop (and *vice versa*) is equally important. A lack of accessible bus stops simply means that the activities will not be accessible to many people in society, thus preserving the benefits only for those who are able to use the facilities on offer.

5.5.2.3   The city as a public space
I have made reference in Section 5.5.2.1 to the importance of the ubiquity of bus stops and how this can help to deliver the ability to develop a courteous city. The city as a public space also benefits from the omnipresence of bus stops. Bus stops should deliver a sense of ownership to the people in the city. This means that it is important to ensure that the local community is engaged in the design of the bus stop, that it is a good source of local information, that it entertains and reflects the 'personality' of the local area. The edible bus stop is a great example of community engagement in their local public transport system, yielding a better bus stop and greater cohesiveness in the local community at the same time. All bus stops should both reflect and feel as though they are a part of their locality, yet provide a city-wide consistency so that it is easy to know that it is a bus stop. The bus stop should be safe and secure and feel welcoming to its users, whether or not they intend to use a bus.

With the sense of ownership comes the sense of responsibility. Making sure that the local community feels that they are responsible for the bus stop – that it is not something that someone else deals with – should help to make sure that it remains clean, functional and locally relevant. It is also essential to make sure that bus stops are distributed appropriately around the city so that everyone is within reach of the buses they need to use. It is highly important that the community is engaged throughout the design and planning process, so that they feel a sense of ownership – and thence responsibility – for it. As with the active and inclusive city, people cannot feel ownership or responsibility for a system from which they feel excluded.

5.5.2.4   The healthy city
The bus stop can contribute greatly to the healthy city in a number of ways. It can be the source of good quality health and healthcare information. The bus stop – and associated bus system – is a major means of enabling people to access healthcare should they need it. It therefore needs to be designed to make this easier. Comfortable and appropriate seating for people with mobility difficulties is a must. There are possibilities for ensuring

that the bus stop is a healthy environment. Edible bus stops, for example, are great ways of delivering positive health outcomes. The health gains to be had in creating small but ubiquitous 'pocket parks' is just becoming established – transfer of microbes from the soil of such parks to the human body has great potential health benefits (Rook, 2013; Rook *et al.*, 2014). Bus stops provide a great location for such interventions and thus are net contributors to the health of the population. Making sure that the bus stop works well in operational terms means that buses will spend less time there, thus improving emissions and energy use. The availability of multicoloured LED lighting systems means that the lighting in the bus stop could be made to be attractive and to ensure that it is bright enough for people to read if necessary without becoming too expensive or making it difficult to see the oncoming buses.

5.5.2.5 The evolving city

Bus stops can stay in the same place for a very long time, even if the hardware of shelters, seats poles – or even the bus services – changes over time. One of the neat things about bus stops is that they can deliver all these societal, aesthetic and health benefits, whether or not they are active. However, if it is necessary to move a bus stop and shelter, this can be done relatively easily. So bus stops, like the bus system as a whole, provide a great way to enable a city to evolve, allowing it access to respond to changes in the activities while always being courteous, with that sense of ownership and responsibility on the part of the local community and delivering those valuable health benefits, over time. The present bus stops – or their successors – will be in place for many years into the future and will (if designed appropriately!) still deliver the five cities benefits to those succeeding generations.

5.6. Conclusions

Basically, as a bus stop becomes more attractive, more people use it and it becomes more congenial and safer due to the presence of people. There is clearly a balance to be struck: a bus stop which is so popular with non-bus users that its primary function – of providing shelter, information and access to and from the bus for bus passengers – loses out to the various secondary functions it can provide to others in the area, is likely to cause problems for the bus system and its passengers. Returning to the point made at the start of this section, a bus stop should be an aesthetic contribution to the environment and a place where people feel that they wish to be.

It is therefore necessary to design bus stops to be an aesthetic advantage to the community and to make them accessible to all sections of the population. Bus stops should be a great place to be in their own right, places where people want to be and want to be a part of society. There is a whole world of things to do to bus stops to make this a possibility and I have discussed only a few here. The main thrust of both this chapter and Chapter 4 is really about how to think about bus stops and to open up ways of thinking differently about their role in society and not just within the bus system. Once the thinking has changed, then the differences can be implemented – it is just a matter of making the decisions based on the right desired outcomes and linking to that overarching vision for the city. Many of the ideas suggested here about linking the bus stop to its urban environment and society in general are not expensive to implement – they are matters of detail inspired by new and creative thinking rather than mega projects costing millions of pounds.

In order to assess the performance of the bus stop design we need to adopt the functionalities considered in value engineering: in particular, those outlined in Section 1.4 where the specific issue of aspirations and achievement are incorporated into the concept. This will ensure explicit inclusion of all the aspects of design considered in this section in terms of their performance – achievement compared with our aspirations – and the resulting value this provides to the community. It is in this context that the value of lingering, attractiveness, contribution to the urban realm, integration with both pedestrian and bus facilities can be included in establishing the worth of the bus stop as a constituent element of the public realm.

REFERENCES

Ackermann K (1995) Low floor bus stops taking into account the situation in Eastern Germany. In *Low Floor Buses*. Report COST 322. European Commission, Luxembourg.

Ackermann K, Blaschke M and Feller G (1995) *Nutzungserleichterungen des ÖPNV für Ältere und Behinderte durch bessere Informations und Orientierungs-systeme*. 70 444/94. Bonn-Bad Godesberg: Federal Ministry of Transport and Digital Infrastructure, Berlin, Germany (in German).

Adhitya S (2013) *Sonifying Urban Rhythms: Towards the Spatio-temporal Comosition of the Urban Environment*. See http://rice.iuav.it/400/ (accessed 15/10/2015).

Adhitya S and Tyler N (2014) It's the little things that count. *Proceedings of the 2nd International Symposium for Next Generation Infrastructure*, Vienna, Austria.

Balcombe RJ and Vance CE (1998) *Bus Passenger Information: a Study of Needs and Priorities*. TRL Report 303, TRL Limited, Crowthorne, UK.

Brown IEW and Tyler N (2004) Community-run rural bus services: can theoretical cross-sector benefits be realised in practice. *Proceedings of the 10th International Conference on Mobility and Transport for Elderly and Disabled People*, Hamamastu, Japan.

DfT (Department for Transport) (2005) *Inclusive Mobility*. DfT, London.

European Commission (1997) *Low Floor Buses*. Report COST 322. European Commission, Luxembourg.

Gregory W (1996) *The Informability Manual – Making Information more Accessible in the Light of the Disability Discrimination Act*. Central Office of Information, London, UK.

Holloway C (2011) The effect of crossfall gradient on wheelchair accessibility. PhD thesis, UCL.

OED (1989) Oxford English Dictionary. Oxford University Press, Oxford, UK.

PSVA (Public Service Vehicles Accessibility) (2000a) Public Service Vehicles Accessibility Regulations 2000. http://www.legislation.gov.uk/uksi/2000/1970/contents/made (accessed 15/10/2015).

PSVA (2000b) Public Service Vehicles Accessibility (Amendment) Regulations 2000. http://www.legislation.gov.uk/uksi/2000/3318/made (accessed 15/10/2015).

Rook G, Raison C and Lowry C (2014) Microbial 'old friends', immunoregulations and socioeconomic status. *Clinical and Experimental Immunology* **177(1)**: 1–12, http://dx.doi.org/10.1111/cei.12269.

Rook G (2013) Regulation of the immune system by biodiversity from the natural environment: an ecosystem service essential to health. www.pnas.org/cgi/doi/10.1073/pnas.1313731110.

TfL (Transport for London) (2006) *Accessible Bus Stop Design Guidance*. TfL, London, UK. See http://www.tfl.gov.uk/corporate/modesoftransport/1548.aspx (accessed 04/01/2014).

Transportation Research Board (2000) *Passenger Information Services: A Guide Book for Transit Systems*. Transportation Co-operative Research Program Report 45, Transportation Research Board, Washington, DC, USA.

UNECE (2014a) See http://www.unece.org/env/pp/welcome.html (accessed 27 April 2014).

UNECE (2014b) See http://www.uncece.org/fileadmin/DAM/env/pp/documents/cep43e.pdf (accessed 27 April 2014).

Accessibility and the Bus System: Transforming the World
ISBN 978-0-7277-5980-1

ICE Publishing: All rights reserved
http://dx.doi.org/10.1680/aabs2ed.59801.279

Chapter 6
Travelling in the bus

6.1.   Introduction

The bus is the part of the bus system that people in general – and quite a lot of transport professionals – see as being 'the' bus system. It is everywhere; it works on our streets and should take us close to where we want to go. It is the primary means by which movement beyond the walkable can be achieved in a way which does not require capital investment on the part of an individual in order to use it. It is primary because it can be the most equitable means of motorised transport – but only if we design the vehicles to be accessible to all, not only in the sense of physical, sensory and cognitive capabilities, but also in terms of being affordable. It also only works properly for society if it is designed, operated and managed in combination with the associated infrastructure of bus stops and roadways.

The bus, like the associated systems discussed in previous chapters, is an agent of change. Every city in the world has some form of bus system and usually a large number of buses. Buses can therefore be highly influential in determining how people live their daily lives, whether they encounter them as passengers, pedestrians, vehicle drivers, city officers or employees. If the bus system is right, other aspects of life quality enhancement can fall into place more easily. For example, to reduce the amount of private vehicle driving, encourage healthier physical activity or develop a better sense of involvement in society, the community needs to have a good, affordable, easy-to-use public transport system in place to provide the movement necessary to live a twenty-first century life.

In Chapters 4 and 5, bus stops and the pedestrian infrastructure were discussed, and the way in which these should blend together was emphasised. The bus itself integrates with the pedestrian environment through the bus stop, so it is also a constituent of the blend, its contribution being (1) at the bus stop, by being the means of transferring bus passengers to and from the pedestrian world, (2) the appearance of the bus in a multisensorial way within the urban realm, and (3) the provision of civilised transport which is available and attractive to everyone. The key is that a bus is the means by which people are transferred from one part of the pedestrian realm to another. The bus is not the object of the exercise – it is another element of the means of enabling people to achieve their aspirations by being able to undertake the activities they wish or need to take on.

6.2.   The bus and the five cities

The five city model, described in Chapter 1 and Chapter 7, is the high-level driver of a city vision and the bus is one of the tools at the city's disposal in order to make that vision happen. How can we make the bus contribute more to these aspirations?

I shall consider this question in relation to a number of different characteristics of the bus:

1   its physical properties such as motion, energy, noise
2   its aesthetic characteristics
    (*a*) externally in terms of its appearance, visual intrusion, presence in traffic, priorities, infrastructure requirements
    (*b*) internally in terms of its comfort, 'feel' and satisfaction for passengers
3   its ability to serve passengers in terms of ease of entry/exit, seating/standing, circulation, and
4   its control, including both the driving involved in each vehicle and the operational management of the service as a whole.

It is then a matter of examining how each of these affects the potential achievements of each of the five cities.

6.2.1   The courteous city
The courteous city is all about mutual respect. The bus can contribute to this in all four of the characteristics.

6.2.1.1   Physical properties – motion, energy, noise
One of the most frequent passenger complaints about buses is about their acceleration. Xenia Karekla has been examining this issue in a series of highly complex experiments in the Pamela laboratory, involving our double-deck bus, which had been instrumented to record accelerations in three dimensions, and participants who were instrumented with pressure insoles, grip sensors and accelerometers. She could therefore study how the bus accelerations affected people as they moved inside the moving bus, as they walked along the bus or moved up or down the stairs. These effects could be measured by studying any changes in gait and grip following accelerations by the bus. By comparing the participants' performance in following the same moves (1) in an open space, (2) how they moved inside the bus while it was parked and (3) how they moved inside the bus under acceleration conditions, she could establish the extent to which their motion was affected by the physical design of the bus (comparing (1) and (2)) and by the motion of the bus under acceleration conditions (comparing (2) and (3)).

Karekla and Tyler (2015) show that even when the bus is stationary, there are distinctive changes in gait compared with the gait observed in an open platform and 'normal' stairs. These changes seem to be due to the more constricted space inside the bus and the steep and narrow stairs. The data show that just being in a bus presents a challenge, even when it is not moving.

The analysis of the massive amounts of data from these experiments is still ongoing, but it is already becoming apparent that there are important changes in gait following an acceleration, sometimes supplemented by an intense grip (as the participant grabs a handrail), with the gait patterns becoming irregular and additional pressure applied by the foot between the initial heel-strike and toe-off as the participants struggle to maintain balance while the world around them is moving. At one level, this is not surprising – we know that people are thrust backwards as the vehicle accelerates, and forwards as it brakes – but it is useful to know precisely how much acceleration is needed for balance to be lost and how much acceleration can be tolerated by a person before they have to make compensatory movements. It is also apparent that the thresholds for these forces, where people lose control of their balance, are different for people of different ages. From this work we will be able to establish what should be the maximum acceleration rates for buses. With this knowledge we can then work out how best to establish that maximum in practice – through better driver training, vehicle control systems, or better driver feedback from the vehicle.

If more appropriate rates of acceleration could be established (in particular, more suitable rates of change of acceleration (jerk)), the bus would become more civilised for the passengers, especially older people who tend to have more difficulty than younger people in responding to the changes in acceleration. It would also contribute to less aggressive driving practices in cities. Bus drivers have to maintain schedules and therefore are often under intense pressure to move quickly, but this need not result in harsher driving performance. Training can enable bus drivers to drive better, thus providing a good influence on the other vehicle drivers and pedestrians in the city. So this is a step towards a more courteous city.

The courteous city requires that buses are driven gently, within the constraints imposed by a person's capability to maintain their balance under conditions of multidirectional acceleration. This will cause the bus to consume less energy and reduce emissions. As a major component of the traffic system, this will have a strong impact on overall transport-induced greenhouse gas emissions, thus helping towards the healthy city. Energy and emissions are linked, but they are not the same thing at all. The bus used for Xenia's experiments is a series hybrid bus (one that uses the diesel motor to generate electricity for the electric motor that actually drives the wheels), and we use it for research in two areas, bus–passenger interactions, for example the effects of acceleration on passengers, accessibility issues of boarding and alighting, and energy and emissions. The bus follows the Transport for London (TfL) specification, so when it is not being used for 'laboratory work' it is operated on one of the TfL services by Hackney Community Transport. The fuel consumption obtained by this bus is reduced by between 30% and 50% compared with a non-hybrid version of the same bus model operating with the same diesel motor. The amount of fuel saved depends on the driving style and nature of the service being considered.

The amount of fuel saved increases if the bus has to stop more often. This is because the main fuel saving comes because the major consumption of energy occurs when the bus accelerates – something it does a lot in comparison to, say, a private car, because of the need to stop at bus stops. The amount of energy required to accelerate the bus at a given rate is of course the same whatever type of fuel is used – it is a matter of forces, the main components of which being, in this case, the mass of the vehicle and the rate of acceleration.

In a vehicle driven by a conventional internal combustion engine, potential energy is stored in the vehicle in the form of a fossil fuel. The amount of potential stored in the vehicle is sufficient to move the vehicle over a distance sufficient to enable the vehicle to operate in commercial service for a day, plus some spare. Our bus can store around 275 litres of diesel, which is considerably more than is required for the typical 300 km or so operated in a normal operational day – a conventional bus of this type consumes about 56.5 litres per 100 kilometres, so it would need refuelling about every 4 days. The concept to capture here is that in effect the bus is filled with potential energy, which is consumed over a period of time, depleting the store of potential energy by converting it into kinetic energy, which is then realised in the form of motion measured in terms of distance travelled. A series hybrid vehicle does not work in this way.

A series hybrid vehicle is based on a time-based view of energy consumption. Potential energy is placed in the vehicle in the form of fossil fuel as with the conventional bus. The difference in the case of the series hybrid vehicle is that the energy used to accelerate the bus is not this potential energy, but the conversion of this energy, not into motion, but into electrical energy. Initially, this is stored in the vehicle in the battery. However, the amount of potential energy that can be stored in the vehicle in the form of electricity is only sufficient to drive the vehicle for a few tens of kilometres. Instead, the fossil fuel is used to provide energy to the diesel engine, which then converts this energy from the chemical energy in the fossil fuel to electrical energy. The electrical energy is then converted into kinetic energy to enable the bus to move. The key is that the conversion from chemical to electrical energy can occur at any time and at any rate, as long as there is enough electrical energy available in time for the demand imposed by the required movement of the vehicle. This introduces the concept of time into the energy production process, something not normally considered with internal combustion engines. The question is not so much about how much fuel is in the tank, as it is, now, about how much energy the vehicle has available at a given moment in time.

As a result, in a series hybrid vehicle the consumption of the fossil fuel is separated from the motion of the vehicle. Instead of consuming the fossil fuel at the same time as the period of acceleration, the electricity required to fuel acceleration can be generated over a much longer period. The diesel motor can therefore operate at a constant speed, making it much more fuel-efficient. The diesel motor in most hybrids operates at just two distinct speeds depending on the state of charge in the battery or other storage device on the vehicle. This means that the motor can be optimised for fuel efficiency, emissions production and noise.

Another device that helps with the fuel consumption is also made possible because the bus is driven using electrical energy. This is the capture of kinetic energy during the braking process. Normally, when brakes are applied, the kinetic energy is converted into heat and noise energy. By using a regenerative braking system, the kinetic energy can be stored as electrical energy in a capacitor. Perhaps the most common use of a capacitor is in a camera flash system. Here, the camera's battery supplies the capacitor with energy over a relatively long period of time and, when the shutter is released, the capacitor releases the energy at a very high rate to produce a very bright (highly energy intensive) light over a very short time. The capacitor in the bus is much larger, of course, but the principle is the same. Capacitors can work in both directions: the camera example is a case where the energy is loaded slowly and released quickly; a capacitor can also receive energy quickly and release it slowly. This is important for bus operation because batteries are not particularly good at receiving or delivering energy quickly. So, during the braking process, the capacitor can be filled with the energy released by the conversion of kinetic energy to electrical energy, which occurs over a very short time. It can then store this and replenish the battery at a slow rate so that the battery is not damaged. Another option is to allow the capacitor to supply the energy directly to the electric motor, which would save storing it in the battery. The capacitor therefore provides a second source of electrical energy for the bus.

The series hybrid bus can therefore save fuel during both the acceleration and deceleration phases of its operation. This is the reason for the difference in fuel consumption between the series hybrid and the conventional bus and why it improves if there are more stops (this means that there are more accelerations and decelerations, where these gains are maximised).

Emissions reduction could be obtained by changing the fuel used, whether the vehicle were a hybrid or purely driven by an internal combustion engine. However, the ability to manage the main energy consumption modes of motion (acceleration, idling, etc.) by running these with electricity rather than directly by a fossil fuel is crucially important in the effort to reduce carbon, $PM_{2.5}$ and NO_2 emissions in the urban transport system. Using electricity in this way also allows other possibilities for reducing fossil fuel use. We are currently working on a way to use a combination of other on-vehicle energy sources to supply the electric motor without the need for an internal combustion engine, and thus to remove the need for fossil fuel in the vehicle.

The advantage for accessibility of this technology (and why it is described in such detail here) is that the fact that the bus is driven by an electric motor means that its motion can be controlled more accurately by software, rather than through mechanical control through a set of gears. Earlier in this section thresholds were spoken about. These can be encapsulated in software to manage the acceleration of the bus.

However, it would probably be better to stimulate the drivers to drive more accessibly by giving them feedback on their driving. Some buses are already equipped with a device which indicates to the driver how hard the accelerations are. These are quite simple – a set of LEDs, three green, two yellow and one red – and they are lit successively as the acceleration rate increases. These have been installed as a fuel-saving measure and it seems that drivers do respond to this feedback by reducing acceleration to acceptable limits. Xenia Karekla's work could supply the thresholds for the lighting up of the LEDs based on accessibility criteria so that acceleration is maintained at a level with which passengers could cope. Implementing the control in this way (rather than through control software) is better for the courteous city because it encourages the driver to drive in a more civilised manner as a conscious endeavour.

The gentler driving regime required by the courteous city also affects the energy consumption and emissions production produced by the city.

6.2.1.2 Aesthetic characteristics

If the function of buses is considered to be only that of moving people from A to B, the aesthetic characteristics of the vehicle are not very important. However, our consideration of aesthetics as an important quality of the function of the bus system means that one of the functions of a bus is to enhance – or at least not to make worse – the aesthetic qualities of the city. London has some 8000 buses and their continuous presence in the London environment means that they have a dynamic and permanent contribution to make to the whole image of what London looks like. If you look at a city such as Lima, where there are some 30 000 buses, the potential is even greater, yet at present their contribution to the visual aesthetic image of the city is not a function that comes readily to mind when one thinks of the city and its appearance. London has, since the 1930s, taken some sort of pride in the appearance of its bus fleet, but the concept of a uniform vehicle that was distinctive to London came about much earlier, in the 'B type' bus familiar in London before World War I. Paris has also had very distinctive vehicles, whose appearance has been one of their functions alongside the actual carriage of passengers.

In the last 40 years or so, operational convenience has tended to dominate the decision-making about bus design, especially as the need for cost reduction became dominant. Perhaps the most obvious example is the removal of the conductor as the means of collecting fares and their replacement by fare collection/checking machines and associated operational procedures. As bus design stimulus moved away from the people who had in mind a distinctive fleet of vehicles for their city, towards the bus operators (who wanted a vehicle that was cheap to buy and operate) and the vehicle manufacturers (who wanted a vehicle that was cheap to produce and buy), the vehicle design converged towards a more uniform entity. Ultimately, a uniform box (cheap to produce) emerged with one or more doors for passengers designed around the principle that the person driving the vehicle could also supervise the fare collection and supervision of passengers (cheap to operate). The emphasis has been on satisfying the objectives of the operators and manufacturers rather than pleasing the passengers and thus the potential for the bus to contribute to something as ephemeral as the image of the city has been rather lost. It is certainly much harder to see this style of operation contributing strongly to the courteous city.

The design of the New Routemaster in London is an attempt to reverse the trend in terms of the bus image. Certainly, it is a bold attempt to provide an image – it was intended to be an icon for the city and it is true that it has a distinctive appearance, which, for the moment at least, signifies 'London'. Whether its appearance is a positive contribution to the quality of life and sense of stress reduction that is the core of the courteous city remains to be seen.

Externally its distinction is apparent. Internally this is less impressive. A lot of thought was given to elements of the design details, but perhaps rather less to the comfort of the passenger. For example, in order to maintain a clean external line for the vehicle, the ability to open the windows has been removed. The internal air quality – surely something of interest to the passengers – is therefore at the mercy of the air conditioning system, which is woefully inadequate. The heat inside the vehicle in summer easily reaches 37° or 38°C, which is intolerable for many, and the lack of air circulation means that the vehicle feels stuffy even when the temperature is not so high. In order to have a 'retro' feel (part of the idea was to think back to the design of the Routemaster bus, first initiated in the 1950s), the upper deck in particular feels as though it is lacking in height (exacerbated by the attempt to provide some sort of air circulation through ceiling-based circulation channels, which reduces the internal height over the seats) and the large windows that have become a characteristic of the conventional buses have been reduced in size, which also contributes to the sense of smallness inside the vehicle.

There is a sense that it is trying too hard to be an icon and, in doing so, it has left some of the passengers' needs rather too far down the agenda in the design – even the psychological boost of feeling that one could open a window to improve the atmosphere has been refused. If we want the bus – like the bus stop – to be a great place to be, rather than a chore that has to be endured, these issues need proper attention. For what it is worth, my memories of the original Routemaster bus are those of freezing inside it on the way to school in the winter, scraping the ice off the windows to see where we were, and unbearably hot, sticky and smelly in the summer – hardly consonant with the current nostalgic feel for the vehicle that gave rise to the desire to have a new version! Certainly, having a bus that is uncomfortably hot and airless for the passengers is unlikely to contribute positively to the courteous or healthy city, even if the external appearance does provide an element of uniqueness that might give a sense of pride about the city.

Xenia Karekla's work shows that the ability to be able to grab a pole as a means of resisting falling inside the vehicle is important. The New Routemaster for London has many poles and these have a pleasant feel which is relatively non-slip so that the compromise between being so slippery that it is hard to grip and being so non-slippery that it is difficult to slide the hand along it (important for providing continuous support while moving inside the vehicle) has been very successfully achieved. The difficulty is that the poles are also used for attaching devices such as the Oyster card readers, which are inevitably set at the height where a person might need to grab the pole and thus preclude this possibility. Also, the in-bus information panel is attached to the pole at the bottom of the front stairs so that the pole cannot be held at a convenient height while completing the descent to the lower floor.

6.2.1.3 Ability to serve passengers

Another issue that relates to courtesy is the way in which buses are designed to accommodate boarding and alighting. The usual pressure on designers is to enable boarding and alighting rates to be as high as possible in order to minimise the time that a bus spends at bus stops. There are several issues to consider when trying to achieve this, some of which relate to the design of bus stops and have been discussed in Chapters 4 and 5. However, the design of the vehicle is a part of the 'boarding/alighting' system and there are design opportunities to be explored in the vehicle which could help to improve the situation for passengers on the vehicle and those waiting for the vehicle further along the route as well as those boarding and alighting at the stop. I will start with the bus doors.

The first question is 'how many doors do we need?'. Thinking in terms of urban operation, I would recommend that the bus should have as many doors as possible. The constraints which go against this are three-fold: relating to:

1 the effect of doors on the internal space of the bus, including the inevitable reduction in the space available for seating and complications with the circulation of passengers who have boarded or are about to alight from the vehicle
2 the implications on the structure of the vehicle of having a number of holes cut into the monocoque structure of the vehicle in order to accommodate the doors, and
3 the safety implications of having a number of doors away from the direct line of vision of the driver.

The reason for encouraging the use of as many doors as possible to enable as many people as possible to board and alight at the same time. The resulting flow rate is reduced if, for example, a passenger has to carry out some action during the boarding process, such as pay a fare, show a ticket to the driver or even touch in a smartcard ticket. Passengers with mobility difficulties that are not catered for in the design of the bus door area will take longer still. If a wheelchair ramp has to be deployed, this can take quite a long time. The ramp takes about 15–20 s to move to or from its extended position. However, the doors have to be closed during the deployment, so these might need to be closed before and then opened afterwards as well (about 4 s in each case). In some cases it is necessary for the driver to manoeuvre the bus into an appropriate position to be able to deploy the ramp at all (one of the reasons for making sure that there are no kerbside restrictions at the bus stop platform). Thus ramp deployment is time-consuming. A much better solution would be to design the bus–platform interface so that a ramp is only necessary in emergency. This is better for accessibility and operational efficiency as well as encouraging a more civilised city.

Having more doors available for entry and exit means that delays are spread between the different doors, thus reducing the dwell time at the bus stop for both the bus and passengers. For example, six passengers boarding a bus with one door would take around 12 s; the same six passengers boarding a bus with three doors would take 4 s – if the design of the bus allowed for two people to board at the same time at the same door and there was no congestion within the vehicle.

However, experience in the Pamela laboratory with mass loading of trains has given us the chance to study boarding and alighting in details. This suggests that boarding rates are not constant. There is a sharp increase in flow rate after the door opens, up to a maximum, which is followed by a rapid decline towards a much lower rate, which tends to decrease slightly over time (see Figure 6.1). The graph in Figure 6.1 shows 120 people boarding a train as quickly as possible and of course this is unlikely to happen at a normal bus stop. However, it is significant that only 15 people boarded the empty train in

Figure 6.1 Mass boarding of a train at the Pamela facility

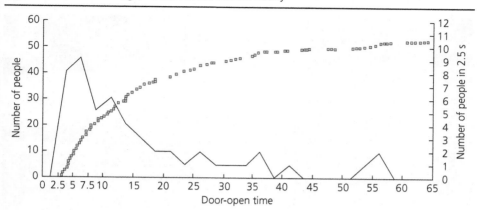

Door-open time

the first 7.5 s before the flow rate started to decrease. In this particular example, the unobstructed width of the open doors was 1.7 m (which is much wider than the effective width of most bus doors, which are sometimes less than 1 m) and the seats nearest to the doorway were perch seats. In this case, the immediate rush was to the central (fixed) seats and so there was a draw of the passengers into the vehicle, which helped to maintain a better flow rate for longer. When the perch seats were replaced with tip-up seats, these were occupied first, which tended to increase the rate very early in the process as people rushed for these, but then slowed it down as these people presented an obstacle to those attempting to board the train after that.

There are two things for us to learn from Figure 6.1. The first is that the design of the interior of the vehicle affects the speed of boarding – the overall benefit of perch or tip-up seats changes according to when the observation is made, although overall there is not much difference. We would not want to design a train system at which one train would be expected to board 120 passengers per carriage in these circumstances – and certainly we would not want to design a bus system like this – but understanding what happens in those first 20 or so seconds is crucial to how we should be thinking of the bus design. Second, it is clear that the reduction in flow rate after around 10 s suggests that we should be designing the bus system in such a way that we would not require the bus to accept more than the number of passengers that could be accommodated in such a time. The experiment illustrated in Figure 6.1 and in the photograph in Figure 6.2 was a test to see how quickly a train could be filled up. The rate decreases dramatically if the train is already occupied, especially if the density is greater than around two people per m². It also reduces rapidly if passengers are alighting through the same door, when, typically, boarding is delayed until much of the alighting has been completed. Figure 6.3 shows this scenario, where there were 20 alighting and 20 boarding passengers at the same door. You can see that there is a delay of about 11 s before boarding commences, by which time 11 passengers had alighted. Alighting continued in parallel with the boarding process until the remaining 19 passengers had alighted. This is because the door was wide enough in this case to permit multiple streams of passengers. The presence of the

Figure 6.2 A full boarding experiment for a mock-up tube train at the Pamela facility

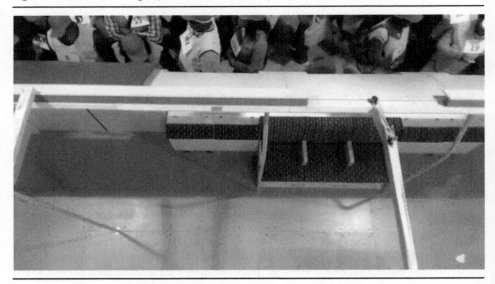

alighting passengers serves to limit the boarding flow rate, which only reaches a maximum of three passengers per 2.5 s period in this case, compared with a maximum of nine per 2.5 s period in the boarding-only case shown in Figure 6.1.

The rule of thumb in Santiago, Chile, is that passenger movements in excess of three–four per door make the service become unreliable. Examination of Figures 6.1 and 6.3 shows how this might be correct because of the uncertainty about how the tail of the flow distributions over time. The situation would be worse for a bus because of the narrower doors, but the key point is that if the door is kept open for an additional passenger, it

Figure 6.3 Flow rates for a train with both alighting and board through the same door

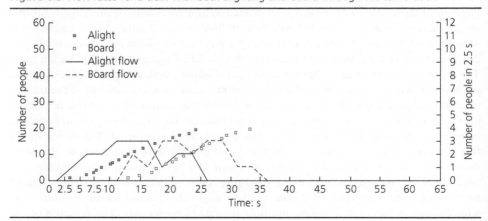

could take a disproportionate amount of time for him or her to board after the peak boarding rate has been passed (about 7 s in this case, but this was a wide door).

In the case of a three-door bus following the Santiago rule, this would allow, say, two alighting and boarding passengers per door, giving a maximum of six alighting and six boarding passengers per stop before the service lost its reliability. If the bus had only one door, this would limit the offer to a maximum of two boarding and two alighting passengers (or a different combination, but with the maximum of four movements overall). The New Routemaster for London has three doors, the front and centre ones having an effective width of 1100 mm. However, the front door is not used much for alighting (partly from habit and partly because it is not particularly convenient to use for alighting). The rear door is not so wide but takes advantage of being at the back of the bus by opening a small part of the rear face of the vehicle – but these benefits only apply when there is a member of staff in attendance, who occupies a part of the rear platform. The rest of the time (i.e. apart from some of the morning and afternoon peak time) only part of the door is opened so that the effective width (550 mm) does not permit two streams of movements. Therefore, the boarding/alighting capacity for the bus according to the 'Santiago rule' might be estimated to be four movements (probably boarders) at the front, four movements (alighters and maybe boarders) in the centre and maybe two at the rear. However, often there are many more passenger movements being attempted, especially at major bus stops, and this is why this discussion is so important for the courteous city. Scrambling to board a bus, or having to wait for the next one, are not conductive to being courteous.

The total passenger service time depends on the door that takes the longest time to cope with the number of passenger movements, so it is important that passengers are spread as evenly as possible between the doors. Three doors give more options than two for this to occur, so this is a good development. The main problem is that it is operationally inconsistent. The reason for this is legal and is a result of having an open rear platform (which was the Mayor's dream): the rear door is designed to remain open all the time so that people can board and alight even when the bus is not at a bus stop; the safety considerations mean that the law requires there to be a member of staff in attendance on the rear platform when it is in this 'hop-on-hop-off' mode. In addition, the driver cannot see passengers attempting to board or alight through the rearward-facing part of the rear platform and this is why when the member of staff is not in attendance the door only opens over the side-facing part of the platform. The current TfL specification for buses (TfL, 2013) is that they should have three doors – it remains to be seen whether a manufacturer comes up with a solution which has three doors but not an open platform – in this case, the legal problem would disappear and the benefits of more rapid boarding and alighting might be realised.

So the amount of time the bus stands at the bus stop is dependent not only on the number of boarding passengers, but also on the number and design of the doorways, the immediate interior space of the vehicle and the likelihood of meeting a contraflow of alighting passengers through the same door. However, there is another aspect that we need to consider, namely the design of the vehicle beyond the space near to the door (see Figure 6.5).

Figure 6.4 Boarding scenario 1: 13 s after the doors opened, passengers are accumulating in the door space even though there is space further inside the vehicle

Figure 6.4 shows the situation 13 s after the doors were opened in the experiment illustrated in Figures 6.1 and 6.2. In this case, people are crowding in the door area even though the central area is relatively clear of passengers. Even 21 s after the doors were opened, when people started to shift into the central area as a result of pressure from people trying to board the train, Figure 6.5 shows that the density is still far lower

Figure 6.5 Boarding scenario 2: after 21 s people are moving further inside the vehicle, but the density in the central area is still much lower than that around the door

in the central area than in the door area in the experiment illustrated in Figures 6.1 and 6.2.

Interestingly, London Underground's formula for calculating passenger density shows the reverse. This is because they allow a continuous area 500 mm wide and the length of the seating on either side of the central gangway for the feet of the seated passengers; in reality, the standing passengers occupy that part of this area that is not actually occupied by the feet of the seated passengers quite freely. As a result, the area used in the calculations for passenger density is far smaller than it is in reality, hence the higher density figure in their calculations. This is an example where the assumptions made in even quite simple calculations can make the outputs misleading.

Some buses have an upper deck. This has the advantage that they can accommodate a larger number of passengers with a small overall vehicle footprint. A typical London bus can legally carry 88 passengers, of whom about 20 are standing (on the lower deck), with a vehicle footprint of about 27.5 m^2, whereas the articulated buses used in London a few years ago could carry 149 passengers with a footprint of 45 m^2. The average density in the two cases is about the same – ~3.3 passengers per m^2 – but the footprint in the street is nearly twice as large for the articulated bus (which was one of the difficulties of operating these vehicles in London). Two double-deck vehicles can accommodate 176 passengers and with a gap of, say, 5 m between them would occupy a total of about 67.5 m^2 – but they can separate easily if necessary, so they do not present such a problem. They would also have four doors between them (six for the New Routemaster, if all doors are available), rather than the three on the articulated bus, and this should make boarding and alighting easier and quicker.

However, the benefit of the upper deck comes with disadvantages as well. It is necessary to have a staircase to reach the upper deck and this occupies space which might otherwise be occupied by passengers on the lower deck. It is also a further point of congestion in the vehicle. First, the increased number of passengers in the vehicle means that there are more passengers to alight. This means that the condition illustrated in Figure 6.3 would be made worse as the number of alighting passengers would increase the delay to boarding passengers attempting to board through the same door. If the bus has two doors, the problem is little better, as if there are more boarding passengers than can be accommodated in the vehicle before the alighting passengers have completed their journey from the stairs to the door, boarding will pause until that manoeuvre has been completed. The New Routemaster for London aims to resolve this issue by having two staircases, one associated with the middle door and one with the rear door. However, the situation is slightly worsened at the centre door for two reasons. With this design, there are two boarding flows that can be impeded by the passengers descending the staircase and in addition there is the possibility that the two boarding flows conflict with each other at the foot of the staircase. The rear staircase also has the problem that it has to be freed of alighting passengers before any boarding passenger can start to ascend, thus acting as a source of delay and the platform area near the door is too small to accommodate the conflicting boarding/alighting flows in relation to both the lower and upper decks. The truth is that these buses work well with relatively small numbers of boarding and alighting passengers, but once the numbers increase beyond the holding capacity of the door areas, they can be delayed at bus stops for a considerable time. The courteous city would require a higher frequency to reduce the numbers of boarding and alighting passengers at each stop.

So there is a very good case for making sure that the entry to and exit from the bus is as smooth and easy as possible and the design of the vehicle – including its interface with the bus stop – is crucial both to the operation of the vehicle and to the sense of comfort and civilised behaviour experienced by the passengers. This means that the service frequency should be designed around maintaining the number of boarding/alighting passengers for each bus to a level that can be accommodated without causing frustration and stress to the passengers – and the consequential delays to the system.

Buses in the UK tend to have more seats in them than their counterparts in other countries. This means that the passenger densities they can accommodate are lower than those in other countries. There is a bus in Italy with a capacity of 45 passengers – 11 seated – in a vehicle 8.5 m long (approximate passenger density therefore about 5.3 passengers per m^2). If we look at the provision of bus capacity in other countries, such as India, or in Latin America, the densities are much higher still. The passenger density is important in the courteous city because of the implications for adjacency of people to each other and thus to the sense that the journey is more or less pleasant.

The problem in the UK is that our lower density is not evenly distributed. The passenger density in the seated area is much lower – of the order of one passenger per m^2 – so that the actual density of standing passengers can reach much higher levels (not forgetting of course that standing is not permitted on the stairs or on the upper deck). Apart from the discomfort, this is an operational issue. The space in which people stand is also the space needed for passengers to circulate around the vehicle and thus contributes not only to the general sense of comfort and ease while the vehicle is in motion, but also to the ease with which people can board or alight the vehicle, and thus its performance at bus stops. In Panama City, people will wait for a bus with a vacant seat rather than stand. This causes them to complain that they have to wait up to an hour for a bus. Interestingly, this is not (yet) a problem for their new metro system, although they have relatively few seats and standing is routine, even in off-peak periods. The crowding on the metro is a problem though and additional carriages are being procured ahead of schedule to increase the carrying capacity by two-thirds.

There has been a tendency over the years to think of bus design as the creation of a static object, rather than as a dynamic process, with the result that the actual performance in operation in terms of the passengers has not really been considered enough. The circulation space is a case in point – it is simply not allowed for, yet is crucial to how well a bus can operate as well as to how the passengers feel. In effect it means that the operational system should be designed on the basis of the lower passenger density that arises from having a circulation space that is sufficient for proper movement within the vehicle – which has implications for the service frequency that is required in order to meet the passenger demand in a civilised – and courteous – manner.

Boarding and alighting would be a lot easier for passengers if the bus floor were at the same level as the bus stop platform. In Chapter 5, it was discussed what could be done to achieve that interface by rethinking the design of both the bus stop and the bus.

So the courteous city has implications for the design of the vehicle, for the associated infrastructure and for the operational regime in which it operates, but it is clear that the bus has some serious contributions to make towards this ambition.

6.2.2 The active city
How does the bus contribute to the active city?

The main way is that it provides the means of taking people to and from their chosen activities, so much of this aspect of the active city is served by the planning and design of the bus system as a whole.

Having taken on board the discussion about the location of and access to activities made in Chapter 3 and the need for the design of bus stops to be accessible to everyone discussed in Chapters 4 and 5, the next link in the chain is the bus. Considering of the location of activities and their way and times of working, it is almost inevitable that there will be peak periods when most activities of a similar nature will be starting or ending for the day. The normal working day for most people starts in the morning and ends in the late afternoon – although this is a trend that is changing rapidly and ought to be questioned in the future. More part-time working, either occupying fewer full days per week or the same number (or more) part-days, means that there can be peaks other than the traditional morning and afternoon periods. In many countries there is a substantial peak in the middle of the day as well. Other activities, including related employment, occur in the evening or at night. The civilised city needs to ensure that people working in these activities as well as those attending them can reach their chosen activities and return home using public transport, and this means thinking a lot harder about when and where the bus system needs to be supplying the capacity to meet these needs.

Notwithstanding the change in working patterns, it is also important to think about the difference in needs during the non-peak periods. Many bus systems are predicated on the home–work–home journeys anticipated by the 'normal' working day. However, there are many activities taking place in the city during other periods and these might require the provision of services to link areas that are not necessarily of interest to the peak period network. One of the beauties of the bus system is that it can be very flexible in terms of its service provision, including the route network, but how does this affect the bus itself?

One immediate consequence is the provision of seats and standing space. Peak period buses can provide greater capacity by means of having a larger number of vehicles to provide greater frequency; in principle, they could also do this by reducing the number of seats in the vehicle and increasing the space for standing passengers. This arrangement might not be suitable for the off-peak service, but severe differences would mean having more than one type of bus so the cost implications would need to be considered. It is also important to recall the number of passenger movements that can be accommodated in a bus at a bus stop without losing the reliability of the service.

Buses come in many sizes and configurations and, in order to provide a suitable network density, this is likely to be the norm in many cities. It is important to ensure that the vehicles are accessible to everyone, not forgetting that more older people and people with different capabilities will be working – some, but not all, part-time – and thus the peak hour schedules should include consideration for the characteristics of a wide range of people in such matters as boarding/alighting rates and the availability of seats. Of course, what would be standing space in the peak hour can easily become space for baggage or shopping in the off-peak, but people are often unwilling to be separated from their baggage on buses, especially if this would mean that the baggage is downstairs while the passenger is upstairs. Buses are not terribly good at handling lots of baggage and shopping and it would be useful to think about options that could serve both the peak and off-peak needs in terms of non-seating space.

However, the bus itself also has a contribution to make. In Chapter 5 the issue of passenger density – crowding – was discussed, and when this is too high this is a major disincentive to using the bus to reach activities. The design of a UK bus, typically with more seats than in some other countries, not only lowers the number of people that a bus can carry, but it also reduces the amount of space for circulation within the vehicle. How easily people can move around the vehicle is crucial to good performance at bus stops, for both boarding and alighting passengers. Carrying a number of standing passengers in a relatively small space simply makes circulation worse. In fact, the number of standing passengers a vehicle should carry is really limited, not by the available floor space and some notion of acceptable density for the standing passengers, but by the ability to move easily between the seats and the doors. The New Routemaster for London has the advantage of three doors, so there is less of the cul-de-sac feel of buses with one or two doors, whereby passengers who have gone towards the rear of the vehicle feel trapped when it comes to trying to alight. However, what was not taken into account in the design of the New Routemaster was the tendency of people to leave their seats and move in the direction they were facing whilst seated. As there are both forward- and rear-facing seats, this provides a point of conflict between the two directions, where people try to pass each other in order to proceed to the door they wish to use. All of this makes it harder for the bus to meet its duties as required by the (or courteous) active city.

Many activities require people to carry things – a briefcase, the shopping, sports gear, luggage, a wheelchair and so on – so the vehicle needs to be designed to accommodate these as well as the people who are travelling with them. Obviously the city bus is not going to be able to have a separate luggage space, as is possible on long-distance coaches, as this would make the boarding and alighting process impossibly long. So how should the designer allow for this issue? Similarly, travelling in inclement weather could involve wearing a coat, carrying an umbrella and so on, all of which takes up space. Wearing a coat adds about 2 cm to the breadth and depth of a passenger, an increase of about 10% in the floor area covered by each person, which gives a reduction of two passengers who can be carried in a bus in London in the winter compared with the summer!

Where do passengers put their bags while travelling in the bus? Space is limited and the need to keep passengers and their belongings together, which is important for making it easier and quicker to alight the vehicle, suggests that options are not plentiful. Luggage racks are difficult to accommodate because of the restrictions on height and a single space for baggage yields the problem of passengers being unhappy about being separated from their property and slowing down the boarding and alighting process. Where space is an impossible constraint, it is necessary to think in terms of time: just as the bus stop needs us to convert a time requirement into the provision of space, so the space constraints of the vehicle mean that we need to think how to convert this into the provision of space in time – in other words more buses operating at a higher frequency so that the number of passengers per bus is reduced. This is just a case of realising that bus passengers travel with things that must also be accommodated. Just thinking in terms of the space requirements of the person leaves unaddressed the issue of how to accommodate what they must travel with. Failure to allow for this means that the bus is restricting the availability – and accessibility – of the activities that people choose in order to reach their aspirations to improve their quality of life.

In the UK, the Public Service Vehicles Accessibility Regulations 2000 (PSVAR (PSVA, 2000a, 2000b)) define what buses need to do to be legally accessible to people who experience difficulty in moving around. The regulations specify all sorts of details, including the maximum angle of a wheelchair ramp, the minimum space required for a wheelchair space, the number of seats designated for people with reduced mobility, the colour contrast afforded by elements of the interior, such as grab poles and handrails, the provision of information and so on. Any new bus built for use in the UK must meet these Regulations before it may enter service. These Regulations mean that buses in the UK are generally accessible – which is a great achievement – but only to a point.

Currently in the UK, there is only one wheelchair space in a bus and this is a space that is also used by people with other legitimate claims – for example, buggies for small children, heavy luggage – and this can cause friction between passengers at busy times. One of the reasons that disabled people like the New Routemaster for London is that there is a member of staff in attendance (because of the open platform design). However, the attendant is not always present and in their absence the vehicle might be harder than other vehicles to use.

The active and inclusive city places a requirement on buses to be accessible to everyone so that activities are truly available to everyone. The PSVAR (PSVA, 2000a, 2000b) establish a minimum level of accessibility, but, like all regulatory standards, the temptation is to level down to their requirements. In many cases, although the wheelchair space meets the PSVAR dimensions, manoeuvring into and out of the space can prove extremely difficult (the New Routemaster is an example of such a case). How understandable is the ticketing system? This is not included in the PSVAR and in many cases it is almost impossible to understand how a system which is there for everyone to use manages to be so complicated. Outside London in the UK, many cities have a range of operators who operate a completely different fare system and structure from each other, often with no ability to transfer between services operated by different companies.

Even in London, where there is a single transport authority and a unified fare system, this breaks down when it is necessary for operational reasons to offload passengers from one bus and expect them to continue their journey on another. If the continuation happens to be on a bus on the same service, that can be achieved easily enough (if you know what to do) by obtaining a transfer ticket from the driver of the first bus; however, if the continuation is made on another service which is following exactly the same route but is operated by a different operator, the transfer ticket does not apply and a new fare has to be paid. Why should the passenger have to understand the commercial and legal niceties that give rise to such a stupid situation? Making it difficult to understand means that activities – including employment – are closed off to some people. This makes the active city much harder to achieve.

The active city also places a requirement on the bus system to be able to carry enough people to enough places in order to maintain – and possibly expand – its activities. Usually, this is thought of as providing sufficient capacity along sufficient routes in the peak period. Services in the off-peak are often slimmed-down versions of the peak service and some cities have a different service operating throughout the night. I think there are good reasons to reconsider this approach to the design of bus *services* rather than bus *routes*.

The point I raised when discussing the bus and the courteous city about the need for circulation space on buses is important for the active city. The capacity of a bus is not simply the number of seats plus the number of passengers who can fit into the rest of the space in the vehicle. It is the capacity to perform that is important, and this includes the performance of the bus at the bus stops. This includes the need for easy circulation within the vehicle and this in turn means that the space for standing passengers is reduced. Therefore, a bus should not carry so many passengers and this can only be remedied by increasing the size of the bus or the service frequency, so that the passengers are spread between more vehicles, thus reducing the number in each one to a level that can guarantee adequate performance at bus stops. The question is then how many people can a bus accommodate?

To estimate this, it is necessary to think about the way people pass each other in a narrow space. Remembering that the upper body is generally wider than the feet and legs, it is necessary to accommodate the combination of two upper bodies, where forced contact is not a desirable state. People also carry bags, shopping and so on, so these also need to be accommodated, thus thinking simply in terms of the anthropometric measurements of a person, or the person only in plan, would be a big mistake.

It is also necessary to consider that the people are moving in time – in relation to each other and the bus, but also as the bus moves towards their destination. This means that the sense of urgency, which increases as the bus approaches a bus stop, increases the sense of need in an alighting person to move towards the door, rather than just moving around another person. That sense of movement towards the door gives the alighting passenger a direction in which to move and this means that they would generally prefer to move forwards, rather than sideways, which places their wider profile across the narrow aisle space, rather than their narrower sideways-on profile. This means that the preferred movement would be to present a body width of some 700 mm (at shoulder level). Arms may be stretched forwards to grab a pole at slightly lower than shoulder level, so the profile in the forward-direction could be some 800 mm on one side at slightly lower than shoulder level, with the other arm hanging from the shoulder at 700 mm width down the body, possibly carrying bags, which can mean that the profile becomes wider towards the lower hand. Feet generally want to point forwards and move where they can – given that, especially in crowded situations, it is not always possible to see where they should be placed relative to other passengers' feet, and older people tend to have a wider (and less stable) stance than younger people. So the dynamic shape of an on-bus pedenger is quite complicated. Given that the width of an aisle in a bus is some 650 mm at hip height, the manoeuvre around another standing passenger is likely to be a spatially challenging process – even if the bus is stationary. The difficulty of doing this is one of the reasons why people resist moving towards the inside the bus – the difficulties of leaving the bus from that position are just too hard and unsocial.

Therefore, I would argue that the bus capacity should not really include the possibility of passengers standing in the aisles. This leaves options of reducing the number of seats or using other space, such as a wheelchair space when it is not occupied by a person in a wheelchair or buggies. This leaves a provisional space of some 1.3 m^2 for standing passengers, which translates into a few standing passengers – I would say a maximum of about five people (current norms in the UK allow for some 20 standing passengers). The main reason why this is an advantage for bus operation as well as for the passengers is that the boarding/alighting rates are so much faster that passenger service times at bus stops would be much shorter, thus increasing the commercial speed. As mentioned in Chapter 2, commercial speed is crucial to decisions such as the fleet size needed to offer a given service frequency as well as being important in enabling passengers to reach their destinations more quickly. So making the passenger density inside the vehicle is not only important for the courteous city, but also essential for the active and inclusive city.

The aesthetics of the bus are important in terms of enabling people to travel more comfortably and in a better state of mind. Colour schemes, the comfort of seats, the provision of good and timely information – and the sensible management of the number of people on the vehicle as just discussed – all contribute to this sense of being in a good place and thus help people to arrive at the end of their journey in a good state for engaging in their subsequent activity.

The New Routemaster for London went for a 'retro feel' in the sense that it looked back to the original Routemaster buses, which were characterised by small windows, relatively dark (maroon and cream) interior and (in the main) dark red seats. The New Routemaster for London has dark maroon colouring for the lower part of the interior walls and a light cream for the upper part, with a lighter tone of dark red fabric than its predecessor for the seats, which are backed in grey, and bronze poles. This gives a sort of warm womb-like feel, although it does come across as being rather dark, a characteristic emphasised by the small windows and the 'spotlight' effect of the LED lights above the seats. The upper deck of a New Routemaster for London has small windows which help to illuminate the lower part of the cabin (during daylight hours at least), but leaving the light-coloured upper part feeling quite dark, emphasised by the maroon trimming in the ceiling, which highlights the low height over the seats – in fact it is quite hard for even not very tall people to stand up on the upper deck. The positioning of the poles assumes that a passenger would be able to grab poles alternately on each side, which is difficult to accomplish if carrying bags in one hand, although the long horizontal hand rail on the upper deck near the stairs is really good. It is, however, generally difficult for two people to pass each other.

The previous London buses have much larger windows, were more 'boxlike', did not have the ceiling lowered to accommodate air conditioning ducts (they have a chiller unit placed over the stairs with minimal ducting on one side only), so feel higher inside. Their internal colouring varies according to the operators' different specifications. The latest generation of London-Specification buses before the introduction of the New Route-master for London have larger windows, lighter colour tones – for example, in our own bus there is light blue rather than dark maroon, and lighter grey and the seat fabric is similar in tone (rather more yellow in tone perhaps) to that in the New Routemaster.

There is a tendency for bus seating to be arranged in forward-facing mode, but as noted earlier in the section this does carry implications for standing capacity in the peak and if the spacing between the seats is too tight, it can be hard to enter and leave the seat while carrying shopping or other bags. Many people use an adjacent seat for their baggage, especially where this is too bulky to accommodate on their lap. Given that there is little space on the floor near to a passenger seat, this means that, in practice at least, the number of seats we should account for in the bus at off-peak times is perhaps as low as half the number of seats actually fitted to the vehicle. This is important when calculating the provision of capacity, particularly in services serving types of activity that can be expected to encourage the use of bags: street markets and supermarkets, shopping centres, sports venues, transport interchanges such as airports and so on. Taking the approach that seats could be legitimately used for this purpose reduces the need for designing special vehicles and thus saves on costs and complexity in the operational schedule. It is a good question to consider whether there would be implications for the design of seats in this case to support their use in this way without causing or damage to either the seats or the bags. For example, the priority seats in some buses are fitted with fold-down armrests. With some thought to the design of these armrests, they could serve to help retain bags within the confines of the seat and thus make the process safer. Actively making the use of seats in this way – for example, by promoting this type of use – would make the bus feel more suited to supporting access to activities. It would also ensure that the circulation space in the vehicle is kept clear, thus making the vehicle more accessible and free-flowing for passengers.

It is important to think of all the activities in the city and design the bus vehicles to supply the services that satisfy the passengers who want to avail themselves of the activities, rather than just one – important but rather limiting – type of employment pattern.

In terms of control, it is important to ensure that schedules and frequencies are appropriate to the needs of the people trying to reach their chosen activities. Increases in part-time and flexible working mean that people are travelling around much more during the day and through the night than when most work was full-time and largely at the same time each day. Activities need to be reachable when people want them, not just when the bus system decides to provide a bus, so there needs to be a strong relationship between the bus system planners and the activity providers in order to determine what should be provided when. This then needs to be communicated to the population so that people do not have to guess when the bus might come or where it might go.

6.2.3   The city as a public space

In some ways the bus is a symbol of the city as a public space – every city has some form of bus system (unlike, for example, a metro), it generally works on the surface, so is visible and the bus is both the means of reaching the public space and a part of it. The bus therefore has to be accessible in terms of its physical and sensorial properties, but also in terms of its affordability and ability to be understood.

In terms of affordability, it might be tempting to make the bus free at the point of use. In principle, this has advantages of simplicity and availability, but in reality this appearance is illusory. If the bus passengers do not pay a fare, the bus system becomes a sensitive political issue – it will consume a large part of the city's budget – and the system will inevitably be reduced to the absolute minimum in order to reduce the impact on the budget unless the system is very carefully designed (see for example, the case study of Asheville in Chapter 8 – but even this is being discontinued). This will reduce the service network and the services themselves, almost certainly the quality of the vehicles, their operation and the maintenance of both the vehicles and the associated infrastructure assets such as bus stops and the road network.

To try to reduce the political influence on the bus system, some cities have opted to allow the commercial sector to determine the bus service network. This is true of all cities in the UK apart from London. In these cases, where the city is prohibited by law from controlling the bus network. The result is a very uneven service within the city, with areas that are perceived to be able to support a privately-funded service being over-supplied and the more difficult areas under-serviced. A couple of years ago I met an ex-student of mine who worked for the public transport section of a provincial city in southern England and was in the process of having to decide whether to support bus services in the evenings (after 6 pm) or services at the weekends. Neither was deemed by the commercial sector to be economically viable and the city could not afford to support both. In another city in the north of England, the commercial operator decided to remove all its bus services as they considered them all to be uncommercial. Imposing a fare therefore places some level of control in the hands of the passengers – even if only in the sense of being customers – rather than expecting the entire system to be seen as something provided by the city. 'Public' does not therefore necessarily mean that it is free: even free assets have to be paid for by somebody and in this case that would be the city's taxpayers.

It would be much better if politicians, business people, planers, the public in general and members of other professions could actually understand how bus systems work, how they provide benefits for the city – and what they need in order to be a massive contribution to the wellbeing of the population as individuals and the city as a whole.

The issue raised by the concept of the city as a public space is to think in terms of not what the city provides but the sense of ownership felt by the people within the city (and also the responsibility this places on them to act in the best interests of the city as a whole, rather than to maximise personal benefits). This means that there is some sort of social contract in which the city and its citizens agree that the public space is provided and looked after by everyone, not only through the use of taxes, but also through the way it is used by people.

Chapters 4 and 5 have considered the issue of the pedestrian network and bus stops, where the sense of public ownership of the environment is very strongly recommended. For the bus as a vehicle this means that people need to have a sense of ownership – that the bus is 'theirs' – so that they help to look after it. This applies even if the buses are actually owned by the private sector. The public transport system is just that – public – and this means that the private operator is putting their private assets at the disposal of the public. This means that they also have to accept that the public has some sense of ownership and responsibility for them.

Having a bus system that works well for the people is one way of ensuring that people do not try to destroy it and this means making sure that the bus system – including the vehicles – is fit for the people's collective and individual purpose. It is in the city's interests to make sure that the buses are usable, are crime-free and do not pollute the environment because this means that activities are available to everyone, fewer people will wish to use alternative and more harmful means of reaching their chosen activities, such as the car, and more people will use the bus as part of a healthier lifestyle involving walking and cycling. Having a bus that people can feel proud of and that is easy to use is therefore an important element of ensuring that people see them as part of the public space and, as such, 'owned' by the people of the city.

This is not only a problem in the UK of course. Bogotá in Colombia has a superb bus rapid transit network (the Transmilenio – named to provide the sense of a new future in the new millennium (the system was introduced in 1999)), but this is at permanent risk because the commercial operators are challenged to be able to maintain the vehicles to the best standard and the city is unable to meet the costs of the intense infrastructure maintenance required to support the level of use. Carrying 45 000 passengers per hour per direction along a corridor, with buses passing every 8 or so seconds, imposes a massive physical and financial burden on both the infrastructure and the vehicles. The crowded nature of the buses on the Transmilenio has led to it being dubbed 'Trans-milleno' (*lleno* is Spanish for 'full') – and one would prefer that the public sense of ownership could be expressed in a more positive way.

It means of course that the system has to be designed to be adequate for the public to use – the Transmilenio enables Bogotá to function as the thriving commercial and social hub that it is, by enabling people to travel easily around the city – but the design cannot be frozen. The city has grown a lot since the system was first implemented and it is necessary to keep the buses able to meet the needs of the people – this means serious thought all the time about services, routes, vehicles, fares, information and so on. Bogotá has developed a new bus system in recent years – the Sistema Integrado de Transporte Público (SITP), which is designed to link neighbourhoods to the Transmilenio. This is an excellent system – yet it is not yet clear how the ticketing works, including where to buy tickets, so at the moment the buses seem rather empty. One of the best expressions of ownership of public space is to use it and this has yet to develop fully in the case of the SITP. It is a good system and it will work – but it is really important that it does so very soon.

One way of enabling people to see the bus as part of the public space is to use the vehicle as an information point, not only about the transport system, but about the city and public life in the city. At its most basic level this could be through on-board advertising of local events, but linking bus tickets to these events (e.g. offering a discount to people who arrive by bus), by enabling the bus wi-fi system to provide a simple portal for enquiring about or ordering tickets for events (for example, triggered by passengers seeing an event they wish to attend while riding past it on the bus), could be an interesting way to complement similar facilities at bus stops.

However, to be really innovative in making the bus feel like public space it is necessary to move on from thinking about its transport characteristics and start thinking about the role the city wants it to play in society. Making the city better for its population *through* public transport rather than making conversation *about* public transport is a very good first step. A journalist from the *El Tiempo* (the national newspaper in Colombia) commented to me that one of his great achievements in reporting about transport in Bogotá was to shift the transport news items from the 'shock and horror' of the front page stories to the more serious comment items in the middle pages of the newspaper. This is an example of changing the subject of the public conversation in relation to public transport – page 1 stories talk about the terrible things that happened (accidents, fare rises, etc.), whereas the commentary-based middle pages talk about what is trying to be achieved. Shifting the public perception of the bus system from page 1 to the centre pages is a major element in measuring the extent to which the public has accepted the bus a part of the public space.

The omnipresence of the bus in a city is a good expression of the city's intentions about the mobility of its population, and the vehicle's exterior design can become part of the city's image. London buses such as the old (and new) Routemaster are emblematic of the city, although their arrival at such a point was very different. The New Routemaster was designed to be an icon; the old Routemaster was designed to be a good engineering solution to the challenge of providing a large number of vehicles with a simple engineering maintenance profile – easy to maintain with parts-in-common – even with a number of variants of the core design. This bus subsequently became iconic – but mostly as it became apparent that they had to disappear from the streets.

Ensuring that the ubiquitous vehicle is attractive means that people will start to feel this is a vehicle they can be seen in – just as a public square or park should make people feel that they are good places to be; available, safe and accessible. To achieve this it must deliver whatever is perceived to be 'public space' – that it is a great place to be; available, safe and accessible. It needs to be attractive to all the senses – eyes, ears, touch, smell, balance, equity, emotion, to name just a few – but it also has to work well as a public space, accommodating the passengers' needs as a norm.

6.2.4 The healthy city

The bus contributes to the healthy city in a number of ways. The reduction of stress mentioned in Section 6.2.1 is one such health impact, as is the way in which the bus can enable people to exercise and gain the benefits of being outside their home. By being accessible it can make sure that people can travel to parts of the city that they otherwise would find very difficult to reach. In our Elixir project, we had a case of a person who had a stroke. He had been supplied with a taxi, which could not accommodate his wheelchair – even without him occupying it – and so he had to be lifted into the taxi at his home and out of it at the day centre he attended. On arrival at the day centre, the taxi driver had to look for another wheelchair for the passenger to use during the day until the process was reversed for the journey home. The Plusbus was wheelchair accessible and this meant that he could simply travel to the day centre in the bus without having to transfer out of his wheelchair which was an altogether more pleasant experience for him. In addition, he was in a bus and was able to chat with other passengers as he travelled to the day centre, so the journey was now a social pleasure for him. Altogether, this was a much healthier experience for him (and actually much cheaper than the taxi). Brown and Tyler (2004) explained this and the impossibility of recognising the cross-sector benefits in reality due to the funding regime in the UK – this problem is not unique in any way to the UK though.

However, the bus can also have adverse health effects. One of the fastest ways for infection to spread is by means of a bug boarding a bus on one side of a city and alighting at the other. People in close proximity can pass infection to each other and buses do not have the sort of ventilation systems we find in aircraft where these serve (coincidentally) to minimise the transmission of airborne bacteria. It is quite possible to become obsessed by these risks, but we should design the vehicle in such a way that the risk of transmission is reduced. This includes the choice of surface materials for seats, grab poles and handrails, an adequate circulation of air, maintenance of a reasonable temperature inside the vehicle and keeping the passenger density suitably low.

Outside the vehicle the bus can make a huge contribution to health, directly by the reduction of emissions from the vehicle and indirectly by being such an attractive means of transport in the city that other more polluting vehicles are used less. This means incorporating the best emissions and energy reducing technologies in the design of the vehicle but in addition designing the operation in such a way that, for example, driving techniques are successful in producing such reductions on a consistent basis. Buses are inevitably consumers of energy, but if drivers are careful about acceleration, and brake and drive in a manner that is both energy- and emissions-reducing, everyone benefits – passengers have a more comfortable ride, there are fewer accidents to passengers, less stress is caused to the driver and emissions are reduced. Some buses are already fitted with devices to encourage the driver to accelerate and brake gently in order to reduce fuel consumption, but as mentioned in Section 6.2.1 these could be adjusted to encourage the driver to limit acceleration rates to those that are less likely to cause passengers distress – or, worse, actually to fall. It is to determine these rates that Xenia Karekla's work on bus accelerations was conceived. This means thinking about the schedule so that time is available – and perceived to be such – for such driving techniques to be conceivable.

The reality is that maintaining comfortable acceleration rates will be unlikely to have a large impact on journey times. Most of the impact on passengers arises, not from the acceleration itself, but from jerk (the rate of change of acceleration), especially when the vehicle starts to move from rest. So the best benefit can be obtained by controlling the jerk over the first few milliseconds of a period of change of motion, when the bus initially changes from being stationary to starting to move or starts to decelerate – a period of time that is quite short in terms of the schedule but which can dramatically change the comfort and safety of passengers for the better. With the introduction of electric vehicles, three effects arise. First, electric motors have much better torque than their internal combustion counterparts, so are at risk from high levels of torque at low speeds. Second, they need no gearbox so there are fewer jerks during acceleration as there is no need to change gears. Third, it is much easier to ensure the level of control required to achieve this, when compared to what is possible in a vehicle that is powered by a conventional internal combustion engine. Personally, I think it is better to manifest this control by helping the driver to manage the vehicle better than simply to insert a jerk control system in the vehicle control system, as it would be a part of enabling the driver to exercise skill in making the bus journey better rather than deskilling their task. Such techniques are taught routinely to chauffeurs of high-end cars in order to train them to deliver a smooth and comfortable ride.

Enabling the driver to make the bus journey better for passengers could mean rethinking entirely the vehicle control system and its interface with the driver. For example, technology could now allow the steering system to be mechanically separated from the driver – 'drive-by-wire' – so that a much more sensitive performance could be obtained than is possible with a steering wheel, by using, for example a joystick (as with modern aircraft such as the Airbus A380). Similarly, hand and finger control of acceleration could be attained through the same sort of interface rather than with the feet. Heads-up displays rather than conventional instruments could also help relay information to the driver in a less distracting way – in fact much could be done with the driver-vehicle interface that could make a substantial difference to the quality of the passengers' journeys, to make them more pleasant and less stressful. Making the bus journey less frightening by making the journey feel less uncontrolled means that people would be more inclined to use the bus rather than not go out at all and the fear of falling in a bus would be significantly reduced. This would be a significant health improvement, especially for older and disabled people.

6.2.5   The evolving city
The bus is an agent of change and the evolving city is about how the city adapts itself over time to the changing needs of the people and the changing circumstances in which

they live. As an agent of change, the bus is very influential – over half the population in London uses the bus every day and all of the population encounters buses in some way or another – for example, seeing, hearing, touching, smelling them – on a daily basis. So how we see and design the bus is a crucial influence on the city's evolution.

One element of the evolution is around flexibility – the freedom to adapt and change the bus system to meet changing needs. This can happen within the lifetime of a single vehicle or in the evolution from one vehicle to the subsequent generation. The DNA of the bus – its functionality, availability, accessibility, mobility and so on – can adapt both in and through generational change. Changing the seats, seating arrangements and internal décor are of course relatively simple to do at any time, but some adaptations could be more complex and require a completely new vehicle to enable the change to happen. Others are a bit more of a mix between changing existing vehicles and requiring new ones. For example, changing the engine could be done on existing vehicles to improve fuel consumption, emissions and noise reduction, as could the development of better operational control. Some changes would need a new generation of vehicle – maybe changing the entire energy source for the vehicle could be tried out in existing vehicles but for mass take-up it would be best to design a new vehicle on the basis of what has been learnt from such pilot experiments. A change to the structural design (such as the introduction of low-floor buses) would require a new vehicle.

The way buses are procured could alter one's view of how they evolve. Some lessons could be drawn from the aircraft industry, where aircraft engines are neither bought nor leased – what is procured is the number of hours service they will deliver. It then becomes a joint matter between the operator and the manufacturer to manage the life of the engine. It is in both their interests to ensure that the engine is kept in perfect condition. Engine manufacturers monitor the performance of their engines at all times they are in use and advise the operator if they detect something which indicates that there might be a potential problem before it becomes serious. The operators can do likewise. Some buses have this capacity already, but the governance is not yet routinely in place. This would allow easier changes and updates, with risk being shared instead of being borne solely by the operator. This has served the aircraft industry as a whole very well in terms of maintenance, reliability and safety of course, but also in terms of attitudes towards innovation, which are far more active in the aircraft industry than in the bus industry. In particular, this could benefit in terms of control systems, propulsion systems, energy management systems, fuels, materials, communications and many more.

The procurement of the New Routemaster in London is an example of a bold attempt to change the bus. A competition challenge set by the Mayor and then achieved by close cooperation between TfL and the manufacturer has produced a bus which is a step more advanced than its rivals. However, the process has also yielded some problems. It has proved difficult to open the supplier base to more than the original manufacturer, thus slowing down evolution and potentially increasing the price.

What drives evolution in the natural world is the combination of stability across generations, diversity brought about by mixing the gene pools and random mutations generating new characteristics, which then turn out to be successful over many generations. The combination of these three processes keeps a species thriving, adapting to new circumstances and discarding unhelpful characteristics, either because they simply do not work or because the world has changed and, although once successful, they are, in the new circumstances, not required or insufficient. In the natural world, this just happens through the breeding process, but in the constructed world we need to instigate such change as a deliberate act. Or do we? Perhaps just being much more sensitive to what is happening would prepare us better for the potential for flexibility and adaptation.

The experiment to use articulated buses in London taught me three things: that increasing the number of doors had a huge impact on reducing the time spent at bus stops, that the availability of so many seats to people with reduced mobility opened up many more travel opportunities for them and that the length of the vehicle was not comfortable in the narrow streets and multiple junctions of London. Increasing the number of doors on all buses requires a new generation of vehicles – and this is happening with the New Routemaster. However, just increasing the number of doors does not help much unless the design of the doors and the space inside the vehicle are thought through in terms of the dynamics of passengers moving around, as well as into and out of, the vehicle. The thinking about this could be done for existing and new vehicles. Improving the availability of seats for people with reduced mobility needs a much better understanding of their needs, but could be applied to both existing and new vehicles.

The thorny question of having a second wheelchair space in the bus – something that is desired by many wheelchair users – is going to become much more of a requirement in the circumstances of an ageing population and we really cannot dodge this issue any more. There is a natural conflict here: the wheelchair space needs to be open without obstacles such as grab poles with good open access between the designated space and the door(s). Even just the wheelchair space itself means the removal of a number of seats. Ambulant people who, like many older people, have poor balance and agility need means of support to enable them to move around the vehicle and into and out of seats – especially when the bus is in motion. However, this is in direct opposition to the provision of more wheelchair spaces. The extra wheelchair space could easily make the situation worse for this population while improving the situation for the wheelchair users unless the design is particularly well thought-through.

As mentioned in the discussion about bus stops in Chapters 4 and 5, the question of bringing the bus close to the kerb at bus stops is a major challenge. In part, as described in Chapter 4, this is a question of designing the bus stop with a recognition that it needs to interface with the vehicle while the vehicle is approaching the bus stop. Just as with an aircraft approaching an airport, how the bus parks at the bus stop is a one-shot manoeuvre and how this ends up depends crucially on the precise approach path. Unlike aircraft though, buses do not have an air traffic control system to guide them in the context of the surrounding traffic and physical environment, so this is at present in the hands of the driver. At present, the driver is not provided with any assistance to perform this task, but that could change rapidly in light of new technology. If we want good performance at bus stops, we need to remember that there could be as many as 50 or

60 along the course of a bus route, and each one is a part of the service provided by many buses every hour. Each one is different – but all require the same precise performance to achieve a properly accessible bus service. This is, however, quite possible.

For example, the bus could be equipped with guidance technology that could suggest an appropriate path towards the perfect stopping position, based on the actual design of the bus stop infrastructure. Such technology already exists – high-end cars have systems linked to the steering system and a rear-view camera to guide reversing; laser guidance systems exist that could locate the bus in relation to the bus stop; the steering system does not have to be a mechanical affair and could be controlled electronically (electric propulsion is much easier to control as a system without relying on the drivers' podiatric sensitivities); heads-up display technology could reveal essential information to drivers as they manoeuvre towards a bus stop. These technologies already exist: the innovative evolution is to apply them to the particular problem of docking properly at a bus stop. This could mean transferring control of the vehicle from the feet to the hands, allowing the driver to adjust the path, speed and orientation rather than divert it completely. Possibly this would mean replacing the steering wheel with something more like a joystick, allowing for the higher sensitivity of hands and fingers to manage the subtleties of the approach, rather than feet and arms.

A 'radar' system to advise of surrounding traffic could help to reduce the driver's workload even if the detection of pedestrians and cyclists is a more difficult challenge. Being able to obtain and process the data is certainly feasible – the delivery of the resulting information to the driver in a way that is helpful is more difficult. Even the position of the driver in the vehicle – at the front off-side of the vehicle, which is far away from the point of difficulty (which is really the front near-side of the vehicle) – could be thought through to make the task easier. This requires research, with much involvement of drivers, before a vehicle could be developed with these capabilities for use on-street – but I would argue that this is entirely necessary to enable the bus system to evolve with the needs of future generations. Right now, they are nervous of the idea, but none has seen anything of such a system and so is not really in a good position to judge. Wilson (2015) raised this issue in some depth with drivers and found that they would welcome this sort of discussion.

On a more mundane level, the suspension system could be improved to allow a greater difference between the ride height and the level of the floor at the bus stop, so that level boarding could be achieved. The intriguing thing about all these ideas is that they would not only provide a staggering improvement in the accessibility of the bus, but they would also improve the performance of the system as a whole. We know from the train experiments in Pamela that the difference in boarding flow rates with level access is significantly better than when any size of vertical gap is involved. This could amount to a few seconds per bus stop. Karekla and Tyler, 2012 and Karekla et al., 2011, in a study of the London Underground Victoria line, observed that reducing the passenger service time of a train by 1–3 s at each station, could, over the course of a day, result in saving the need for one train in providing the same level of service to passengers. This result could transfer across to the bus system, although the relationship would be a little different – buses do not have rigid signalling systems and can perform at much higher vehicle frequencies than trains – but the principle would apply nevertheless: buses have many more bus stops than trains have stations and the proportion of dwell time to running time along the whole journey is much greater (maybe more than 50% in some cases), so small reductions to dwell time could result in disproportionately large outcomes in terms of operational and economic performance. Another example is the technology that could help fix the vertical gap problem raised earlier in this chapter and in Chapter 4. The latter alone could give a business case for undertaking this sort of investigation and the investment in equipment that could follow.

If the bus is to evolve in line with – or even in advance of – the evolving city and its people, we really need to think about these technologies now.

6.3. The bus as a vehicle

In the first edition of this book, I described the approach we took to the specification and design of a bus for a rural environment as required by our Aptra and Elixir projects. The issue of interest here is not so much the detail of what was specified or attained, but the thought behind the specifications: how to make a bus as accessible as possible, given constraints of budget and environment. Many of the features included specifically in that case were innovative at the time, but are now included routinely in bus specifications. A bus that complies with the EU Bus and Coach Directive will, by and large, be accessible. I will now consider the extent to which this situation could be improved to meet the needs of passengers in a better way.

We recently bought a new London-specification double-deck bus in order to study more about how 'normal' public transport services might be logged and improved for the benefit of passengers and the city as a whole. As mentioned earlier in this chapter, we use the bus in three basic lines of research: accessibility issues, energy use and operational capacity. One of the interesting things that arise though is where the three lines come together – where accessibility improvements are facilitated by different approaches to energy use and in turn help to improve capacity and vice versa. It turns out that the three areas are intimately connected.

The increasing adoption of electricity as the energy to support vehicle motion comes, of course, with benefits in terms of reduced vehicle emissions. However, it also provides the opportunity to change the means by which motion is controlled. A series hybrid bus provides an opportunity to control aspects of the motion – in particular acceleration rates and jerk – through control of the electronics. A vehicle driven by a normal internal combustion engine is only able to provide such control through mechanical valves (altering the amount of fuel being injected into the combustion chambers) and/or a mechanical gearbox, which controls the speed of the wheels compared with the speed of the motor. Because the electric motor can be controlled through software, this allows for much greater sensitivity and control. In addition, the physical separation of the driver from the mechanical action of the wheels means that not only the speed of the motor (and thus the wheels) is controlled through software, but also other key aspects of motion, such as the steering.

The drive-by-wire vehicle is with us already and it provides an excellent way to ensure that the vehicle motion is suitable to meet the accessibility requirements of all passengers by imposing controls over the acceleration and speed profile of the vehicle. The parameters for such controls can come from research such as that being undertaken by Xenia Karekla in finding out what the reasonable tolerances might be for jerk and acceleration in buses. This is becoming increasingly important in the case of electric buses (including hybrids). This is because the sensorial systems people have, as referred to in Chapter 5, are part of the way they handle issues such as changes in acceleration. This is another case of the preconscious processing of sensory stimuli that enables people to function.

With a conventional internal combustion engine (ICE) bus, the start of motion from a standing position is preceded for a few milliseconds by a change in engine noise, accompanied by an increase in vibration within the bus structure. Together these provide an acousto-haptic stimulus. Experience suggests that this stimulus means that the vehicle will start to move and the sort of preparations for this change of state begin – bracing the knees against the shift, grabbing a handrail and so on – so that to a certain extent the body is prepared for the event before it actually starts. In the case of an electric bus, there is no such stimulus because there is no change in sound and the vibrations from the motor are much less than those from a normal internal combustion engine. Also, there is less of a time lag between the energy being applied to the motor and the movement starting. As a result, there is a sense that electric buses are more problematic, with the sense that they are accelerating at a higher rate than the ICE buses. The key point, though, is that the problem is the initial jerk, rather than the acceleration rate, and because it comes without those acousto-haptic stimuli, people are less prepared for it. The more continuous (no hiatuses during gear changes) – and possibly higher rate of – acceleration does play an important part in the problem though: it gives less chance for recovery before this becomes impossible and a fall occurs.

Improved monitoring of the passenger space in the bus provides the opportunity to use CCTV images to determine operational decisions, such as if it is desirable to turn the bus short of its destination, to decide when additional buses might be beneficial to maintain the operational service level and if there are problems for older or disabled people in moving around the vehicle or finding a seat. The results of analysis of CCTV data could also feed into the operational parameters to control acceleration and braking, as knowledge of the loading and distribution of passengers around the vehicle could be important when making such decisions in order to maximise comfort and minimise injury, while ensuring that the vehicle is operating within the limits posed by the schedule.

Accessibility also enhances capacity. In one way, making sure there is enough space for easier movement of people in wheelchairs, who require larger space of moving and turning, will mean that higher or faster flows of people could be accommodated without further adjustments to the vehicle. However, simply creating additional space is not in any way sufficient. For some people the larger space afforded by the accommodation of physical restrictions to movement are in fact the cause of additional difficulty – the obvious example being the conflict between the open space required for wheelchair manoeuvrability compared with the need for handrails and physical support for people who are ambulant but frail. The provision of accessible information is crucial to the greater accessibility of any system, but to ensure that information is both intelligible and readable – or at least visible – would be a major improvement in many transport systems around the world. Buses suffer even more than metro systems in this regard as their networks and schedules are often much more complex. Yet somehow it seems to be impossible to encourage the operators or planners to consider those people for whom the network and services are a mystery when they are planning their information systems.

Martha Caiafa (2010) investigated how older people deal with information during the course of a whole journey, including the pre-journey planning process. Participants were asked to plan a journey and were given the opportunity to choose from a wide variety of information to help them. The following day they were asked to undertake the journey they had planned. It became immediately apparent that the journey planning had not been particularly helpful for the real journey. Some of them had barely planned at all, basing their approach on the idea that they would find a map or information near to the destination or that they could ask someone the way once they were fairly near. What the real journey showed was the clear lack, or, at best, insufficiency, of in-journey information. This situation has improved markedly in recent years, with the introduction of in-bus announcements of the next bus stop, the Legible London signage on the footways and at bus stops, to mention two initiatives provided by TfL, and the increasing number of smartphone apps that make use of real-time bus data to inform journey planning before and during the journey.

One gap that persists is the lack of information inside the bus about the service it is providing. London buses do not have even a static copy of the route the bus is following, and more useful information about what is going on outside the bus along the route – places of interest, landmarks, connections with other services – is at best limited to the announcement of the next stop. Chris Cook, in his 'Going Places' research with young people with learning difficulties, showed how important this contextual information is in helping a passenger understand where they were as the bus carried them towards their destination to give them reassurance that they were in the right bus, travelling in the right direction so that they could prepare better for the time they would have to leave the vehicle. Having this knowledge available makes the journey much less stressful.

Figure 6.6 shows a simple information sign in the metro in Buenos Aires, Argentina. This shows, for each station on the metro line, all the bus services that call there, and whether or not there is a public bicycle station, taxi rank or other transport interchanges. Figure 6.7 shows how stations are highlighted – red for stations already passed, green for stations to come – as the train progresses along its route. Figure 6.8 shows some of the road names and other places of interest near to each station. This sign also shows (although it is not completely clear to the first-time user) that some stations only operate for trains in one direction (these appear as a semicircle, rather than a circle, with the highlighted part indicating which direction is served).

Arguably, the most innovative new bus to appear in the UK at least is the New Routemaster, commissioned by TfL, designed by Thomas Heatherwick and built by WrightBus.

Figure 6.6 Multimodal information in Buenos Aires, Argentina

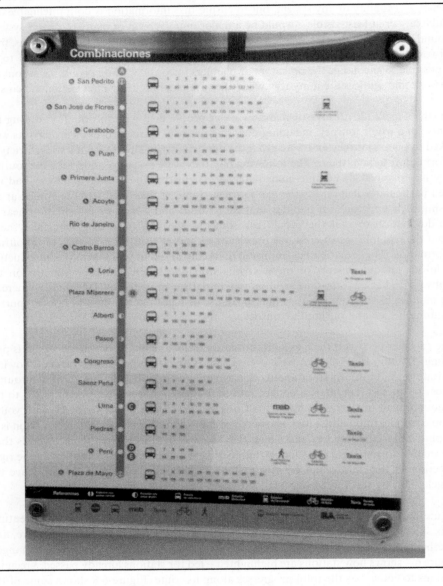

The bus carries many – but not all – of the innovations mentioned above and is intentionally designed to appear to be an evolution of the old Routemaster bus used in London from the 1960s. The Mayor wanted a bus that replicated the 'hop on–hop off' open platform at the rear of the vehicle, but which retained the other doors to which passengers had become accustomed for boarding and alighting, and the rounded contour of the body, particularly at the back on the upper deck. The interior is coloured in a retro-style, reminiscent of the original, but with a modern twist. It is a series hybrid

Figure 6.7 Progression along Línea A, Buenos Aires, Argentina

vehicle and is intended to deliver very low fuel consumption and, importantly, low emissions. A lot of attention was paid to the appearance of the vehicle – an unashamed attempt to produce an 'iconic vehicle for London' – and its interior, and to produce a vehicle which would help to reduce London's air pollution problems. In much of this

Figure 6.8 Line map from Linea A, Buenos Aires, Argentina, showing intermediate streets, interchanges and station availability

it has succeeded. Indeed, London now has a unique bus, distinctive and instantly recognisable as 'London'.

It is worth examining this vehicle in a little more detail when it comes to its operation. First in terms of its technology, it has a series hybrid stop–start drive, with a relatively small diesel motor. This seems to deliver fuel savings and emissions reductions, but the small motor seems to have to work rather hard to maintain the energy required by the vehicle's electric drive, suggesting that there might be room for improvement in the energy management in the vehicle. The motor is running for much of the time at relatively high speed and is much noisier than the conventional buses it is replacing. This is strange, as the small speed range of the motor in this mode of operation means that its noise spectrum is highly predictable and stable and so it is relatively easy to design a suitable noise reduction/baffle system, which should be able to eradicate almost all the noise. It is not clear how much of the energy captured by regenerative braking is actually retained for use – this is a notoriously difficult problem as batteries are not good at receiving the peak energy flows obtained from this source. Nevertheless, the energy performance is deemed to be excellent. Second, and with rather more concern, is the vehicle's performance in relation to passengers.

The open platform provides the opportunity for passengers to board and alight anywhere along the route, but the safety requirements for this mean that a member of staff is required to oversee these manoeuvres. This, of course, nearly doubles the cost of the crew and so is only available at certain times of day – for some of the morning and afternoon peak periods. The rest of the time the rear door remains closed whilst the vehicle is in motion and as noted in Section 6.2.1, only opens partially at bus stops.

On arrival at a bus stop, the use of three doors should reduce the dwell time by allowing three points of access/egress instead of the more conventional (in London) two. However, the passenger flows between the doorway and the inside of the vehicle soon become blocked, reducing the flows to become unidirectional and often stopping altogether while internal conflicts become resolved, for example, between the flow entering by the front door aiming to go up the stairs or into the main seating area behind the central door, and the flow entering by the central door intending to go up the stairs or moving towards the seats forward of the central door. These streams of passengers only need to contain a couple of passengers each for the process to become blocked. The front and centre door, although wider than the rear door are relatively narrow, meaning that passenger flows are slightly better than at a narrow door, but do not allow a double stream of passengers. This precludes simultaneous movement in both directions and results in only a slight increase in flow in one direction.

The narrowness of the entrance into the lower saloon from the rear door means that the flow into the saloon is quite slow and the stairs are not the fastest onward movement for a boarding passenger. The net result is that a cluster of passengers congregates in the bus stop area around the rear door waiting for passengers to alight and then for passengers to board – often some give up and move to the centre door. The potential benefits of the three doors are not realised in this vehicle – although it is better to have three doors than two.

Inside the vehicle, the provision for wheelchair users is within the PSVAR (PSVA, 2000a, 2000b) requirements but it is a tight manoeuvre to enter or leave the space. Handrails are a subtle gold colour and this, combined with the mellow dark red of the walls and furnishing make for difficulties for people with low contrast sensitivity, although, as mentioned in Section 6.2.1, the haptic quality of the rails is good. Some of the equipment in the bus is positioned rather unfortunately. I mentioned in Section 6.2.1 the placement of the Oyster Card readers in the middle of the vehicle: these are positioned on handrails just where passengers want to hold the handrail, thus necessitating holding the rail either higher or lower than desired and this is important because it applies mostly when a person needs to grab the pole quickly as a result of some unpredictable movement by the vehicle. Passengers descending from the front stairs find that they cannot hold the handrail positioned at the bottom of the stairs to support the turn in the stairs because the iBus information display is attached to it at exactly the point that a passenger would want to hold it as they come down the stairs. This is crucial, because these are not only used when the bus is stationary, but when it is in motion, when instinctive grabbing of the pole or handrail may be required at very short notice because of the unpredictable movement of the bus.

The source of much comment has been the air quality of the vehicle. In order to preserve the smooth lines of the vehicle it was decided to forgo opening windows so the air circulation relies on the mechanical air circulation system and the periodic opening of the doors. The circulation system is basically inadequate for the purpose – it is positioned centrally in the upper deck and there is no provision on the lower deck. The interior temperature of the vehicle in summer has been recorded to reach 38° and the lack of circulation, despite the system obviously working very hard and noisily, means that the air feels hot, humid and still. The physical and psychological need to be able to open the windows, at least to allow some air movement, would be a real benefit, but this is not possible.

The seats are not a great design – rather low in the back and short in the swab in the main, apart from the 'tall' ones rear of the centre door where they do not allow for the natural curvature of the spine as people sit, and thus feel rather uncomfortable.

The points raised here are critical for the passengers. The lesson to learn here is that the desire to produce an iconic bus, on which the specifications (TfL, 2013) are absolutely clear and which has been met, has somehow managed to forget that the passengers who will use the bus need to be accommodated properly within a vehicle that is in motion – and a motion that is likely to be unpredictable – for a reasonable period of time during a journey. It is a matter of setting the priorities, and future commissioners of buses should learn from this example.

So what should a city vehicle be like?

The first thing to say is that there is a set of compromises involved in any public vehicle, such as a bus, in which suboptimal solutions will be required. Which, and by how much, suboptimality should be permitted is a matter of rigorous consideration of the achievement of the bus system's objectives and which factors lead to successful attainment and which lead to failure. Let's start with looking at the optima.

First, the doors should be wide enough to accommodate two flows of people to use them at the same time. This means an opening width of around 1.7–1.8 m. If plug doors are used, the overlap of the door over the gap in the bodywork means that the actual gap – and thus the width of the doors themselves – needs to be about another 200 mm overall. This is wider than most bus doors (although in Italy there are buses with a central door rather wider than this, at 2.4 m). The advantage is that the overlap allows an internal handrail to be inserted which does not intrude into the boarding and alighting space. Doors of this width come with disbenefits as well. They must be bigger – and heavier – doors, which then require more powerful motors, which are heavier and require more energy to shift the doors in a reasonable time and would possibly create structural problems, particularly for double-deck vehicles. Doors may require handrails so that passengers can hold on to something in order to maintain their stability as they enter or leave the vehicle. This applies especially to alighting passengers. Those handrails could easily reduce the available width and thus the flow of passengers. All of this is much easier if the interface between the bus floor and the bus stop platform is level. The hop-on–hop-off arrangement is something of the past but seems to come with a lot of difficulties.

Second, the area inside the doorways needs to be open and free of obstacles so that the flow out of and into the vehicle is unconstrained: the ideal is that boarding and alighting should be completed without any hindrance from objects or people slowing down the process. A good move is to keep the ticket validation away from the doorways – even if this is a matter of just passing a smart card over a reader, this will cause a delay (we found a reduction in flow rate of some 15% just from adding such a reader to the boarding process). Some people will inevitably enter the bus before they have located their smart card, or there could be a communication delay between the card and the reader, and this will hold up the boarding process even more. The space has also to be large enough for alighting passengers to pause on their way out as they work out where the bus stop platform is. This effect can be reduced by reducing the vertical and horizontal gap between the bus and the platform, but it will always occur to some extent. This means that the internal storage for passengers needs to be slightly larger than the actual flow observed at the doors might suggest.

Third, handrails and grab poles need to be completely accessible and not used for equipment which precludes their use as support mechanisms, especially at heights where it might be necessary to grab them in order to overcome shifts in balance as a result of unpredicted movements of the bus.

The bus requires circulation space – so it is important to ensure that the bus is not expected to operate with all the non-seating space occupied by standing passengers. The routes by which passengers circulate need to take into account that the bus is in motion when a lot of these movements need to occur. Current computer pedestrian flow models do not allow for this, neither do they account for the ways in which people contort themselves to account for the strange shapes of available space that are left when in a crowded vehicle.

Seats need to be fit for purpose – maybe a more robust tip-up seat could be designed so that the higher flows at peak times could be accommodated while leaving more seats available for off-peak passengers, but we should note that the voluntary non-use of tip-up seats has not been observed anywhere where such options have been available.

It should not really need saying, but basic accessibility requirements are just that – they are fundamental to the availability of the public transport system to the public – that is, everyone. These should be the starting point for design, not an add-on.

Finally the ambience, colour, feel, temperature and air quality need to be appropriate to the local climate and the perceived comfort of the population. There is no reason why this should be an add-on. As mentioned earlier, I recall going to school on buses where I had to scrape the ice off the inside of the windows in order to see where we were and I recall the arrival of what was optimistically called a 'heater' (actually just a vent at the front of the lower deck blowing warm air from the engine into the freezing passenger compartment) and thinking this quite a luxury! Today's passengers deserve more and better – proper acclimatisation, humidity and circulation of air – we can do this on an aircraft at high altitude: why is it such a luxury on a bus at street level? Air circulation is an example of another issue, which applies also to the urban realm, and that is that we should concentrate more on designing the spaces between the structures, including the reality that the spaces (or at least part of them) are going to be occupied by people, thus changing the shape, feel and thermoacoustic properties of the space as time unfolds. We need to design to accommodate that change. How will the air circulate with the people in the bus – who are breathing in and out, exhaling warm, wet carbon-dioxide-laced air and needing to inhale clean oxygenated air? This has ramifications for heat, humidity, filtering and so on. Think of the health implications if we were to pay the same attention to the air quality inside the bus as we do to the emissions it produces from its motor. Buses are potential transmitters of airborne infection – a bug boarding a bus at one end of the route will take its infection to the other end far faster than any biological transmission pathway – but only because we allow the air quality to be poor. Why shouldn't a bus be a source of clean air, both within it and also in terms of the air it leaves in its wake? This is easy to resolve and should be done as a matter of course. If a bus is not a healthy pleasure to use, why should we demand that people use it?

The city of Porto in Portugal is proudly adding wi-fi to their bus network – yet the bus network itself is very difficult to know about and understanding how it works is a challenge in itself. The addition of wi-fi might make this better, but the first thing to achieve is to understand where the buses are, where and how to buy a ticket and when the buses are likely to appear – without successful negotiation of these issues, the on-bus wi-fi is unavailable to anyone. To be fair to the bus system, the ticketing system in the city's metro is just as impenetrable! What is desperately needed in this city is that the authorities engage someone who realises what is needed from the perspective of the passenger who knows nothing. Perhaps this is the most extreme version of allocentric thinking – but this is the starting point for any information system for any city anywhere in the world. The best transport system in the world will fail its potential users if they cannot understand how to find it in the first place.

Simpler ticketing systems also mean faster engagement with the vehicle. In the case of buses this is extremely important because for the majority of bus systems this interaction happens during or soon after the boarding process. The vehicle needs to be designed to facilitate this. The cost of reducing the flow rate by 15% as a result of introducing a card reader to the boarding process is enormous in terms of the need for extra vehicles and drivers to attain a given capacity, so this is a serious issue for the planners and designers of bus systems – and at least one element of this lies within the design of the vehicle. It is generally sensible to separate the ticket validation process from the boarding and alighting processes. If there are concerns about non-payment, these should be addressed separately. Porto has already lost out because it was so difficult to transact the ticketing process legitimately that in the end I could not buy a ticket for some journeys, meaning that I had to make the journey in another way. The complexity of the transaction process was made worse by the fact that the instructions were printed in such small text (about the size one would expect in a book) that it necessitated using reading glasses – why should a public transport system, which operates out of doors and not in a hotel, office or home – need people with 'normal', but not particularly good, vision to have to produce the sort of assistive technology needed for reading a book simply in order to find out how to use the system? The transport operators have already lost out because of the complexity and poor information about their systems so investing in clarifying them would yield immediate benefits.

Similarly, service maps are vital, yet many bus systems fail to carry these on their buses. Even with audio-visual real-time information available on the vehicle, there is still a need for people to be able to see the whole service at a glance, including estimated journey times and indications of interchanges with other services and modes of public transport. In London, there are several smartphone apps that can provide this function – it should be possible to tap into one of these to provide this sort of information. It would also be beneficial to have some form of service enquiry portal – a journey planner would be a good example that would benefit those with no access to smartphone technology but with a need to find information about the service they are currently using or may wish to catch. If this conveyed accessibility information it would be really helpful. If suitable internet connectivity could be obtained, this could form a two-way communication system, but there is a need to ensure that individuals do not monopolise the system and thus deny others the opportunity of making use of it. Provision of several terminals around the bus (including at-seat access) could be an answer to that problem. The key message here is that the easier it is to use the system, the more likely that people will choose to want to use the bus system – and be able to do so when they actually make that choice.

Remember that I am familiar with transport systems, so at least I understand what they might be trying to do, even if I am unfamiliar with the details of a particular system –

what must it be like for someone who is less familiar than me? Designing systems for people who are unfamiliar with them is a key component of making public transport systems 'public'. The investment in ticket validators all over the bus, and accessible from every seat, would be a good way forward – the excuse of not being able to validate would be virtually nullified. Drivers being able to converse with the passengers would also be useful – to indicate potential alternative interchanges, routes and opportunities would also improve the experience for bus passengers. For passengers with particular difficulties, such systems could provide useful advice about their journey, including better places for alighting.

Other indicators to passengers that are being tested at the moment include the display of empty seats inside the vehicle – particularly on the upper deck. The idea behind this is to try to help passengers decide to move upstairs when there is space available rather than wait downstairs and occupy crowded circulation space, which then clogs up the boarding and alighting process. Various technologies are being tried for this purpose – analysis of the CCTV recordings or pressure pads on the seats (the former probably being more feasible than the latter).

A major issue in urban buses is the use of space within them. The complication arises because of the need to have free circulation space so that people can move around the vehicle in order to find a place where it is convenient to remain whilst travelling. One example of such a place is the seat, but others are standing places. Unfortunately, this means occupying space that might otherwise be used for circulation, as there is very little space within a vehicle to accommodate standing passengers other than in the circulation space unless a number of seats are removed, which would reduce the number of spaces for seated passengers. Typically, buses in the UK tend to have more seats than their counterparts in other countries, thus the competition between standing and circulation space is greater.

In order to walk through a bus and be unconstrained by the fittings within the vehicle, the gangway width needs to be a minimum of 650 mm wide – but even this does not allow for a passenger to be carrying shopping or other bags, which would need to be arranged in front or behind the passenger while they are walking. Defining such a virtual corridor in a way that would close off space to standing passengers would, in current layouts, leave for standing passengers only the space near the doors and the wheelchair space, neither of which is desirable. Removing seats, especially from the lower deck of a double-deck bus, where they are relatively few in number anyway, would have a negative impact on the accessibility of the vehicle to those people who need seats.

Really, the answer to the problem of hyper-congested buses is an increase in the service frequency. This could require bus stops to be designed to handle more buses at a time (see Chapter 5), and almost certainly some form of traffic restraint in busy city centres, but would reduce dwell times and make journeys more comfortable and attractive.

People do not tend to move far into the vehicle, not least because they are concerned about being able to find their exit path.

The aim is to make travelling on the bus easier and more pleasant so that people feel happier about using the bus system. This in turn reduces the traffic flow and its associated pollution and general congestion – which in turn enables the buses to run more smoothly.

6.4. Conclusion

The bus comes in many shapes and sizes. Which particular variety depends on a range of factors, but primary requirements dictate that it should be satisfactory for and to the passengers. This means that the vehicle needs to be accessible, not only in terms of being able to enter or leave the vehicle in a civilised manner, but also being able to move around inside the vehicle, find and access a seat, understand where the bus is along its route and details of the service(s) available in and from the vehicle and an acceptable internal environment in terms of climate and crowding. The bus should be a source of health – clean air and surfaces, appropriate climate inside and outside the vehicle. The vehicle should also be sparing in its use of energy and should not add to the air pollution within the city. Without these primary functionalities, the bus fails. People charged with specifying vehicles need to keep these aspects of the vehicle at the forefront of their thinking and all other considerations, including price, come as secondary considerations.

REFERENCES

Brown IEW and Tyler N (2004) Community-run rural bus services: can theoretical cross sector benefits be realised in practice. *Proceedings of the Tenth International Conference on Mobility and Transport for Elderly and Disabled People, Hamamatsu, Japan, 23–26 May.*

Caiafa M (2010) Cognitive approach to accessible information systems. PhD thesis, University College London.

Karekla X and Tyler N (2012) Reduced dwell times resulting from train-platform improvements: The costs and benefits of improving passenger accessibility to metro trains. *Transportation Planning and Technology.* doi: 10.1080/03081060.2012.693267.

Karekla X and Tyler N (2015) Gait and balance of moving bus passengers. *14th International Conference on Mobility and Transport for Elderly and Disabled People.* Lisbon, Portugal.

Karekla X, Fujiyama T and Tyler N (2011) Evaluating accessibility requirements to public transport including indirect as well as direct benefits. *Research in Transportation Business and Management* 12: 92–100. doi: 10.106/jrbtm.2011.06.010.

PSVA (Public Service Vehicles Accessibility) (2000a) Public Service Vehicles Accessibility Regulations 2000. http://www.legislation.gov.uk/uksi/2000/1970/contents/made (accessed 15/10/2015).

PSVA (2000b) Public Service Vehicles Accessibility (Amendment) Regulations 2000. http://www.legislation.gov.uk/uksi/2000/3318/made (accessed 15/10/2015).

TfL (Transport for London) (2013) *Amended and Restated Design and Supply and Maintenance of Double Decker Bus Vehicles Contract.* TfL, London, UK.

Wilson S (2015) *How Technology Can Help to Reduce the Horizontal Gap at Bus Stops.* MSc thesis, University College London, London, UK.

publishing

Chapter 7
Public participation in bus system design

7.1. Introduction
7.1.1 General issues

Throughout this book the involvement of the public in the process of making bus transport accessible has been advocated. Public participation in this process is much easier to talk about than to do, and I would like to explore the ways in which such participation can be achieved.

The different perspectives of different participants in the design process, including the general public, the bus industry and local government, have been described. These are summarised in two diagrams (Figure 7.1, which shows the common communication paths between these agents, and Figure 7.2, which shows a more participative approach). This book emphasises the need to encourage the inclusion of users (including current non-users) in the design, development and operation of bus systems. In the main, adopting this approach to bring the implementation of the bus system closer to the people – in terms of service, network, infrastructure, vehicle and information design – makes it easier for everyone to use. This has meant placing the users and potential users at the heart of the development process rather than leaving them as an afterthought where they are left to put up with whatever has been designed on their behalf.

The idea that a 'successful' bus service is one with few empty seats is easy to understand – even if it is wrong. However, I am seeking to measure the success of a bus system using measures that reflect the needs of the community. These include the extent of social inclusion, the social and economic contribution that the service facilitates within the local community, and the degree of independence that it generates. These characteristics may result in increased numbers of people using the service, but even so it is quite likely that society will have to accept some share in the financial support for such an outcome. This view of financial support is not, of course, just for the bus service as a transport resource. The bus service is merely the vehicle that brings about the level of social inclusion, cohesion and independence we seek. Society's support is, therefore, for the development and attainment of these objectives, which are only achievable if the service is truly and broadly accessible. Given the difficulty of achieving any of these without an accessible public transport system, the success of accessible bus services (as part of the public transport mix advocated in Chapter 2) in working towards these goals is good value for money. Brown and Tyler (2004) describe a project to realise some of these cross-sector effects so that we could learn how investment nominally directed towards public transport might obtain benefits in other sectors, including health and social

Figure 7.1 Current participation in the bus system design process

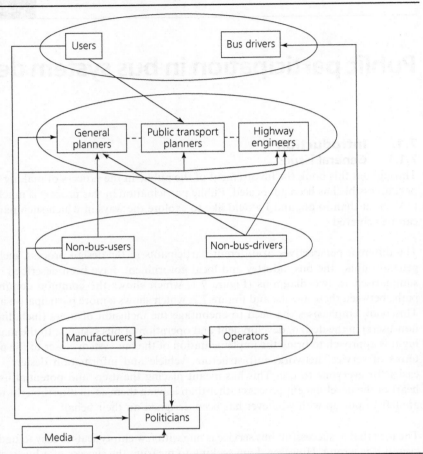

services. However, seeing a bus service in this way requires a steep change in thinking about public transport, not only on the part of bus system planners and operators, but also by the people who will be an intrinsic part of the system – the public.

It is fairly easy to see how planners, designers and operators of bus systems can set out and measure their achievements in conventional terms. They have data on residential areas, passenger numbers, fares taken and costs incurred to help them evaluate a bus service in these terms. As the public is indeed an intrinsic part of the system, it should become involved in the processes of planning, development, design and the provision of bus services.

7.1.2   Legal issues
Since the publication of the first edition of this book, public participation has become more important in the implementation of projects, especially where these relate to transport schemes. However, there is some concern about the extent to which a public

Figure 7.2 Participative approach to the bus system design process

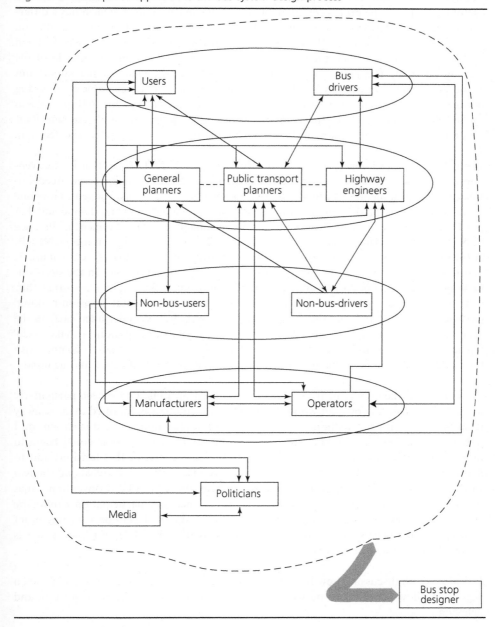

participation scheme is genuine and whether or not it is just a box-ticking exercise that is carried out rather perfunctorily for the purposes of saying that it has been done. It is therefore worth considering exactly what we mean by public participation and then thinking about how this could be achieved in practice.

There is a distinction between public consultation and public participation. Each is a useful technique in the process of involving the public in decisions, but each has a different emphasis in relation to the way in which the public are involved. Public consultation is the process whereby the public is approached for its views, which are then considered by the decision-maker, who then takes overall responsibility for and ownership of the ensuing decision. The public participation process seeks the views of the public, but encourages them to be actively involved in making the decision, for example by choosing options to be assessed for their technical merit and then choosing the one to be progressed to completion. In the public participation process, the public not only provide their views, but also take some share of the ownership of, and responsibility for, the decision.

The United Nations Economic Commission for Europe (UNECE) states that its 'Convention on Access to Information, Public Participation in Decision-making and Access to Justice in Environmental Matters', otherwise known as the Aarhus Convention, is one of only two legally binding international instruments on environmental democracy that put Principle 10 of the Rio Declaration on Environment and Development in Practice (UNECE, 2014a). This came into force in 2001. The UNECE Convention (UNECE, 2014b) is clear that the public participation is in decision-making (Article 3 Clause 3) and that information must be made available to the public at a point in the decision-making process which allows 'sufficient time for informing the public ... [so that they can] prepare and participate effectively during the environmental decision-making' (Article 6 Clause 3) and that the public participation should be undertaken early in the process, '... when all options are open and effective public participation can take place' (Article 6 Clause 4). So it is clear that consultation is not nearly enough to comply with the law and that public participation needs to be implemented, effective and genuine.

I have brought the involvement of users into all of our projects. I have been particularly interested to include people for whom transport is difficult to use. I wanted to move away from the idea that participation would be covered if a questionnaire had been sent or a public meeting held. I have been looking for a means by which people could begin to understand the underlying issues, including technical matters, of the decisions and to agree the extent and detail of the inevitable compromises between the ideal and the real world. This approach is important if the requirement of the UNECE Convention – that public participation should be effective – is to be met: the participation cannot be effective if the public does not understand the issues and there has to be a starting point at which all the necessary information is made available in a style and format that is genuinely accessible to everyone.

It is also worth discussing how the decision-making process can be structured in such a way as to allow for effective public participation to take place without distorting and delaying the process.

7.1.3   The decision-making process

First of all, who is the decision-maker? Table 5.1 shows how a decision can be broken down and responsibilities identified for each component. In the case of bus systems, the decision-making process is often concerned with local issues in which the decision-maker is the local authority. However, in arriving at that point, it is important to realise that most decisions are actually made up from a set of other decisions and not all of these have to be made by the local authority which is responsible for the overall decision. To take a simple example as an illustration, the location of a bus stop can be considered to have three broad issues that need to be addressed: the safety issues which are the responsibility of the relevant legal authority (in the UK, the appropriate Highway Authority (HA)), the technical issues for which the local authority might be the possessor of the requisite knowledge or is in a position to acquire it and the other issues which, subject to satisfactory resolution of the safety and technical issues, have little concern for the local authority – but might be of major concern to local people for example.

In our Puppit (Public Participation Processes in Transport) project, which was located in the City of Brighton and Hove in the south of the UK, the local authority wished to redesign their bus stops to make them more accessible. This could require relocation in some cases, but in all cases it required a significant change to the design of the infrastructure. The first action in the project was to identify the three classes of issue as described above. What did the local authority actually have to decide? There were certainly road safety issues – sightlines, location of pedestrian crossings, traffic issues and pedestrian capacity and so on – and these were clearly the legal responsibility of the local authority. There were also technical issues. In this case the local authority was indeed in possession of some technical knowledge but as they were considering how to make the bus stops accessible they required other technical knowledge, which is why they contacted us. We could then explain the technical issues to their engineers and planners and they could then apply their technical expertise to drawing up suitable designs that would satisfy the technical requirements. However, satisfaction of these two issues resulted, in most cases, in there being a number of solutions that would satisfy the legal and technical criteria. This is where the public were brought into the process. If a bus stop was legal and technically competent, the detail of exactly where it would be located and which choices of competent options should be made, other aspects of its design were really matters for the people who would be using and/or living or working near the bus stop. So the authority held public meetings to explain the legal and technical issues and to discuss with the public where they would like the bus stops to be located. This process managed to accomplish two important outcomes.

First, issues were discussed at the meeting of which the authority was unaware, and resolution of these issues was obtained at the meeting. This prevented the problem of having to alter a critical feature (such as the location) of a bus stop half way through construction, which is highly expensive and disruptive and potentially could damage the reputation of the authority. Second, it meant that when these bus stops were installed there were no public objections, which had caused considerable delays to implementation of previous installations in the authority's project. This saved money and time which had been lost due to the delay process and left the local people feeling that they had some sort of ownership of the outcome. The authority was unable to provide a cost for the work required to answer the objections – the investigations, searches through archives, developing reports, consulting local politicians, writing letters to the petitioners and so on, all of which caused further delay to the scheme of concern as well as others.

So participation means taking part in making the decision – and taking ownership and responsibility for it – and Brighton and Hove is a clear example of that taking place and working. However, this example took place before the UNECE Convention had actually come into force and there has been time since then to consider further how public participation should become part of the whole design and implementation process.

In Chapter 2 I discussed the structure of a decision model and how the public needs to be participating in the development of the strategy (see Figure 2.6) so that the decisions to be taken are in fact defined during the participation process. Then the participation arises in the actual decisions (see Figures 2.3, 2.4 and 2.5) within the process of defining the success factors and limitations, the definition of the actions and their evaluation. This raises the question of who is the 'public'.

The public has an important role in the process of making the decisions – even actually making some of the decisions within the process – so it is important to be clear about who the public is and who might represent them. There is a common use of the term 'stakeholder' in decision-making parlance. This is to acknowledge that there are many people and parties who have a 'stake' in the decision. One of these is often the 'public' but the public could have many different elements with different views about the decision, some of them conflicting. It is essential that all parts of the public are able to have their say. This means thinking beyond just the stakeholders as these are, by definition, parties who actually have a set of vested interests – they are not neutral and should not be treated as such. The actual public also may have views and these should be heard. Indeed the decision-maker is in the position of having to make a decision given all these inputs and of course including their legal and technical obligations. In some cases it might be helpful to have an independent person who has no association with the decision and its stakeholders to act as a knowledgeable referee to advise the decision-maker who, for all the public and stakeholder participation in the process, actually has the responsibility for making the decision in the end.

I have had the role of a neutral adviser in a number of decision-making processes outside the UK. In these cases one of the principal activities has been to identify who exactly should be making which decisions, sometimes bringing people into the room who had never previously managed to sit at the same table as each other. Another feature of this role has been to structure the decision – this is where and how a lot of the decision-making models and structures described in Chapter 2 were developed. Enabling all stakeholders – including members of the public and the decision-makers – to identify the correct questions to ask is a major element of improving the decision-making process.

There are four crucial points to remember when setting up a public participation process to enable a decision to be made:

1   Everyone has some knowledge and experience, but nobody knows everything.
2   It is essential to decide who has to decide on:
     (a) The technical constraints that are unchangeable: 'the laws of physics' as we called them

(b) The legal duties and responsibilities that pertain to the decision
(c) Everything else.
3 Enabling people to present their concerns, desires and needs does not mean having to accede to them.
4 The decision is larger and more important than any participant in the process.

Within this process, and especially if there are conflicting views, the question of evidence will arise. In the main, the public will have less access to evidence than the other stake-holders – this is the reason for the UNECE Convention: to make such evidence as freely available to the public as possible. However, it is important to realise that the evidence itself does not contribute to the decision. It is the meaning derived from the evidence that informs the decision.

7.1.4 Evidence and meaning

Different people in the process will draw different meanings from the same evidence, sometimes based on their technical knowledge but usually on the basis of a different perception of the question. I learnt this from a clinician in an Accident and Emergency department and the story is worth repeating. One evening, the parents of a very young (about 2 weeks old) child brought their child into the hospital because he had fallen on his head at home. They were of course extremely worried. The clinician examined the child and was satisfied that there was no serious problem. He was unable to undertake seemingly obvious tests because of the resulting radiation impacts on such a young child. He assured the parents that the child would be fine. The parents pointed out that he had done no tests on the child apart from a superficial examination. The clinician explained that he could not do other tests because of the radiation risk, but that in his view the child would be fine. The parents then asked why he could not do the additional tests and after explaining again he said that they, as the legal guardians of the child, would have to require him to do the tests. They then said that they did not have the knowledge to enable them to do this – the provision of technical evidence was his job.

Then he realised that he was passing on the wrong information. The details of the tests and why they could not be done might be factual evidence, but this could not support his statement that the child would be fine. The parents needed more than his pronounce-ment, however well-based it was on knowledge, experience and evidence. What did his 'evidence' actually mean? It meant that there was nothing that could be done for the child in the hospital at that point and there was no detectable immediate danger. That the child and parents would be more comfortable at home, but that what they needed was information about how to identify a situation that meant that they should return to the hospital and a reassurance that the child would be looked after at that point. Detection of the useful symptoms did not require clinical expertise, so he explained to them that if certain easily seen symptoms were to appear they should bring the child back to the hospital immediately and that he would see the child straight away. Satisfied, they took the child home. A few days later they reappeared at the hospital with the child. They wanted to thank the clinician as the child was apparently quite normal and had fully recovered. What are the lessons to be drawn from this story?

1 Evidence, based on high quality knowledge and experience and the best data possible in the circumstances, is essential to the decision-making process.

2 However, evidence on its own is likely to be confusing. It needs to be presented in a way that is meaningful for the recipient. The 'expert' understanding what the evidence means is not enough: the person who actually needs to understand the evidence must be able to understand what it means without having to be an expert.

3 Translating the evidence into meaning means understanding what the recipient's problem actually is and that this is necessary before it can ease the decision process.

4 In this case, the parents became part of the decision-making process – they decided to take the child home and, crucially, to know what to look for and what to do if important symptoms were to appear – and had been given enough information to reassure them and to enable them to act if something untoward were to happen.

5 The technical competence was not enough. It needed to be combined with 'emotional competence' to understand what the parents felt, and how they were concerned, and it was addressing this emotional issue that led to the resolution.

The same applies to public participation in decisions about urban planning and the bus system.

7.2 Participating with the public

The plain fact is that, whatever the law says, public participation will happen. The reason for saying this is quite simple: the availability of sensors and applications on mobile phones is becoming ubiquitous. The expected number of smartphones to be shipped to Africa in 2015 is 155 million, with almost half of these selling for less than US$100 and 75% under US$200 (IDC, 2015). The significance of this is that these smartphones – even the cheap ones – have capabilities to record information and make it available to the user – and to others via the Internet – in a way that has hitherto not been seen. The effect is that the general population has become data enabled, even in the poorest countries. This is transforming the way that local economies run but also how people might respond to what they perceive to be threats or risks to their perceived quality of life.

It is important to distinguish between data and information. I said that the population has become data enabled, not information enabled. There is a research field based on the data-enabled phenomenon, called citizen science, which enables people to collect their own data so that scientists can help them analyse it to provide information. Citizen science projects have been run for many disciplines but, as Haklay (2013) says, this is especially pertinent to the use of mobile phones with their range of inbuilt sensors and ability to locate the data point within a geographical and temporal range. This means that people within a city have already become able to collect their own data and this will happen increasingly in the coming years.

Enabling people to interpret their own data empowers the population (especially in areas where the authorities do not particularly wish to travel). Pollution, noise and accessibility are just three possibilities for data collection, and current smartphones are quite capable of delivering data, geocoded and time stamped, that is suitable for analysis. The citizen science discipline brings scientists and a population together so that this data can be analysed properly and robustly so that the public can deliver their own analyses of existing problems, their own responses to proposals or their own proposals for potential projects. City governments are no longer the unique owners of information and expertise and therefore they will have to deal more directly with the public, whether they want to or not.

The better way to tackle this issue is to see it as a positive rather than a negative phenomenon. The principle that underpins both the five-cities model (Chapter 1 – see Figure 1.7) and the outcomes-based decision model described in Chapter 2 (see Figure 2.3) emphasises the need for people to be at the centre of the process and for the evidence to assess and support decisions to be meaning based. There is no better way to achieve this than the mechanism of empowerment through the sort of personal data collection technology that is now available, especially when coupled with the enabling and supporting approach of citizen science. I would argue that this is a far greater paradigm shift in terms of information systems than the mere existence of 'big data' filtered into and used by corporate or government organisations.

So public participation is not just 'nice-to-have' any more, as it was when the first edition of this book was written. It is now a fact that makes the path to a better quality of life easier to achieve. The question is how to set about making the most of these opportunities. I think the way to look at this is two dimensional.

1   'Who' is involved in the process and how to organise the relationships between the various sectors of the population (we loosely talk about 'the people', 'the population' or 'the public', but in reality these groups contain a large number of different subgroups that are often in direct conflict with each other).
2   'How' the process proceeds and what is involved in the participation at different levels and stages of the decision process. Participation is required throughout but there is a difference in what would be required and how this would be achieved when considering, for example, an overarching vision, or the actions to be taken at a specific point in the network.

Playing across these dimensions is the concept of 'meaning' – the need for evidence to be understood, to have meaning, was explained in Section 7.1.4 – and there is a really important issue of how the data being collected by people is understood – by the people collecting it and by others who have to interface with it. Take the example of aircraft noise. There are established formal techniques for collecting aircraft noise near airports, and data being presented as evidence to a planning inquiry would need to follow these procedures to avoid the 'other side' calling the data into question. Often the assumptions about the data and collection processes are based around scientific methods, established for scientific methods, established for scientists to put in place and require scientists to explain what they mean. However, the issue of noise around airports is not a matter of a few readings taken from highly expensive technical equipment but one of comfort, annoyance, sleep deprivation, reduced social communication and increased severance. The data is just a series of numbers, which can be modelled; the meaning of obtrusive noise is a mix of social, pervasive, perceptual and even cultural factors. So which data carries more value – the scientific acoustic data from the meters or the meaning felt by the people? The former will have highly precise, but possibly meaningless content, the latter might have less precision but much more meaning – which is more useful for society to include in its decision process about the airport? The significant change here in very recent times is that the ubiquitous nature of the proliferation of smartphones with sound level meters, accelerometers and geocode/time data stamps means that the basis for that meaning is far more widely spread, based on quantifiable, repeatable data than was imaginable at the time of writing the first edition of this book.

Aircraft noise has a set of regulations built around it, and this applies, although to a much lesser extent, to buses. Mostly these refer to the noise level of a bus passing by a given point – which could be chosen to be less problematic (e.g. at a point when the bus is not accelerating). Some of the (older) buses in London are very loud – their cooling fans can be heard from a few hundred metres away, especially when they are accelerating away from a bus stop or traffic signals. Ensuring that the bus noise actually proves to be satisfactory for the public in their ordinary lives (e.g. chatting on the street or hearing other traffic) is a matter, not of complying with some standard but with providing a socially acceptable outcome. Public participation is the means by which these outcomes can be determined and policed and the ability of the public to undertake this task has never been as great as it is now. We can only expect this to increase in the future. This changes for ever the whole concept of data, who owns it, who interprets it and who legislates for it in terms of how public decisions are made. The legislative processes have yet to catch up with this fast-moving reality, but it is best that everyone – the public, the legislature, the officials, the technicians, politicians, operators and manufacturers – become familiar with the implications.

I mentioned the difference between consultation and participation in Section 7.1. I will now describe some examples of participatory processes in which I have been involved to try to show what might be possible to gain from such exercises in terms of generating a better future world. I shall do this considering the two categories – the 'who' and the 'what' – that were just mentioned.

7.3   Public participation – the people

A good first question is 'who should be included in the participation process?'. The simple answer of course is 'everyone', but this is not always possible. However, the ubiquitous nature of data collection referred to in Section 7.2 means that a very sizeable proportion of the local community can be involved – the days of a few people turning up to a public meeting at an awkward time in an awkward place really are numbered. The key I use in these exercises is not so much public participation as much as education. The exercise is not to inform people about issues and then ask them to become instant decision-makers. This is unlikely to yield good decisions and leaves the process open to what I call the 'tyranny of democracy in small places' – where a small vocal group can dominate the discussion, and divert the decision to their own self-interests rather than the common good, all in the name of so-called democracy. This is just a distortion of democracy and is not public participation at all.

So I start from the premise that the issue is education. For the public to be able to participate genuinely in a decision process then they must know what the issues are, how the decision process works, and what the implications of different decisions might be – all from an objective, allocentric, data-rich but meaning-driven viewpoint. This process will be discussed in Section 7.4. Here I will discuss how to garner the inclusion of the public – and who we mean by the public in the first place.

For me, 'the public' is everyone concerned in the decision. The decisions we are talking about are public decisions, which are made in order to achieve some public purpose. So the first barrier to break down is to remove the distinction between the people who make the decisions (usually perceived to be people like 'the council', 'the developer' or 'the government') and everyone else. A public decision has to be genuinely public, so there are no sides to the argument, just people involved and interested in obtaining the best outcome for society. So it is important to reach out to all sectors of the community – the older people, younger people, people in different socioeconomic groups, with different education achievements, different interests in the community, different prospects for putting into the decision, and different possibilities for gaining or losing from the decision. The completeness of the involvement is crucial.

When I was Head of the Department of Civil, Environmental and Geomatic Engineering at University College London, we decided to update our civil and environmental degree programmes. This involved all the staff in the department. One of the most important processes was to decide what needs to be taught in the programmes. The usual way of doing this is to ask the people responsible for teaching the various specialisms to come up with a list of subjects that would have to be included in the curriculum. The trouble with this is that everyone thinks of all the inputs they need to teach their specialism to its utmost and includes these in their list. So you end up with a set of enormous lists of topics – and an unteachable degree programme. So instead of doing this I set up groups in which disciplines were clustered. In these cases, each cluster was given an outcome and the group was required to determine what would need to be learnt in order to achieve that outcome. The outcomes were that the cluster should deliver

1   the context in which the engineering skills had to be considered
2   the ways in which that context could be changed for the better
3   the mechanisms needed to effect those changes
4   the tools needed to support the first three points.

So all disciplines represented in the department had to be represented in each of the clusters. This meant that people's starting point was no longer what they needed to include in order to teach their discipline, but how their discipline blended with all of the others to deliver that outcome – and thus what the learning opportunity would be. The actual definition (and delivery) of the engineering programmes was a level above this – the clusters delivered between them the whole programme, which was not to teach civil engineering, but to create people who could use civil engineering thought and practice to make the world a better place.

In terms of the vision, strategy and actions (as discussed in Chapters 1 and 2) the approach was to

1   define the vision (to make the world a better place)
2   determine a strategy for achieving this (to create people who could use civil engineering thought and practice to make the world a better place)
3   work out the tactics for doing this (define what needs to be learnt in order to create people who could use civil engineering thought and practice to make the world a better place)
4   put in place the actions (create the learning opportunities to deliver what needs to be learnt in order to create people who could use civil engineering thought and practice to make the world a better place).

The point from this story is the involvement of all of the people (including technical and administrative staff) to understand all of the problem and not just their part of it. They could contribute their part into the whole process of a group determination of what decisions needed to be made and how they would be implemented. This contribution required them to have that overall understanding. The same goes for public decisions.

So the first part of public participation is to educate people about the decisions to be made and what the underlying issues are that will drive the process. To a certain extent, this can be done through schools and the basic education being delivered within the community. However, it is likely that the specifics of any particular decision will still require some element of education for that decision. Added to this of course is the need for the process to be participatory, so the education needs to take the people's views as the starting point, add some new ways of looking at these in the light of the decision to be taken and then to come out with a perspective that they can deliver into the process. Importantly, the process is participatory for everyone and – like the clusters in the engineering department – cross-cutting. Nobody has primacy simply because they belong to a particular group – everyone is on an equal footing. Just because someone is a transport expert, architect or designer does not give them automatic rights to be heard; their right to be heard is because they are a person from the community and they have a contribution to make on the basis of their experience and skill, just like anybody else in the room. Of course their expertise needs to be listened to, but in other areas they may be as unknowledgeable as everyone else. Learning how to adapt from soloist to accompanist is something musicians learn from a very early stage in their education and when they come together in an orchestra these skills are in some ways the most important. A public participation exercise is rather like an orchestra – everyone contributes according to their skills and experience and the overall outcomes is dependent on the quality of those interactions, the mutual respect and that sense of completeness from the whole rather than the sum of the parts. The secret is to have everyone in the process and a lot of care needs to be put into the process to ensure that this is achieved.

7.4 Public participation – the how (and what)

There are several ways to conduct a public participation exercise. In this section I will discuss the core issues and illustrate these with examples from different exercises I have conducted. If you have your core principles clear then the method can then be devised to deliver them. On the other hand, if your core principles are not clear, simply choosing one method over another will not help achieve the target.

The first and most important core principle is the axiom from Confucius 'I hear and I forget, I see and I learn, I do and I understand'. The principle behind public participation is participation – the public must actually do something in order that their understanding is increased. Public participation is not about telling the public what you want to do and neither is it listening to the public telling you what to do. It is a process of mutual learning about what is on the agenda, the overall intentions, the desires and needs, the possibilities, the impossibilities, the easy things and the hard things, so that the understanding is mutual and the eventual worked-out approaches are agreed, accepted and understood by everyone. So it is important that everyone – including the proposers of the project – enters the process with a mindset of learning in an open environment.

Different content will be required for different stages in the process and this will need to involve different approaches, according to the point in the process being considered at any particular time. For example, when asking the public to participate in constructing a vision, this will involve very different questions and inputs from those needed in the process of working out how to implement a particular intervention. I will discuss this by taking you through a particular example of such a process as we conducted it in a project in Latin America, where we had been invited to work with some local cities to work out how to implement policies designed to reduce their greenhouse gas emissions. Although this is a very specific example, the lessons that can be drawn from it are many and generic.

7.4.1 The general format

The basic format was to hold a set of workshops over three half-days – usually Tuesday, Wednesday or Thursday mornings. This was because the technical and professional people could not guarantee to be able to attend for whole days and it was important that they attend throughout the programme. This also allowed the participants to have a break from the workshop – to think about what they had been doing, or just take a break, as well as enable them to carry out any pressing duties from their day jobs.

The programme on any one day was one structured around participatory activity, usually (but not always) with the participants working in groups. The groups were organised very carefully so that each group included someone from technical, political, professional, and a variety of social groups (including age, gender and socioeconomic group), while keeping the groups to a manageable size. We find that a group much larger than six people becomes fragmented, and one much smaller is too limited, so it is best to keep the group size around that number.

The group activities are then punctuated by short informative contributions from the team – the subject matter for these depends on the particular moment, but in this case these explained the five-cities model, the decision process and the importance of scale. These contributions were very short – a maximum of 15 minutes – because we wanted the primary activity to be the group work and these contributions were to inject new ideas into that process, change the pace a little, and the details could always be discussed later.

So, in the first set of workshops, on day 1 we considered the construction of a vision, day 2 the strategy and day 3 the interventions that might be used to apply the strategy to achieve the vision. In the second set of workshops we did a quick overview/reminder of the first workshop outcomes, and then discussed scale – thinking about the city from the city-wide scale, through from meso-scale (neighbourhood) to micro-scale (local street) interventions.

7.4.2 More specific issues

It is important that the exercise enables the public to contribute their views rather than being one in which the public hear the views being promoted by the decision-maker. So, we started by asking the participants for their view of what is the city's vision. We received a number of answers to this but in the main what they revealed was that the concept of a vision was nearer to one of a politician's strapline – 'more parking', 'more housing' or 'better health', rather than something more overarching. So we had to enable them to set aside their current views of problems and visions, not because these were necessarily bad but because we wanted to open their minds to different perspectives. We achieved this using a technique called the 'doombox'. This involved asking the groups to identify and write down on sticky notes all the problems the city faced that would prevent them from reducing greenhouse gas emissions. That was quite easy for them as they were living with these issues all the time. After asking them to present their lists, they then put all the sticky notes into a black box – the doombox – so that they could be removed from further discussion. This proved to be an extremely useful device as it prevented people rehearsing the 'usual' issues – the participants would chide each other if someone mentioned one of them later in the workshop, saying 'that is in the doombox and we do not talk about it here!'. To move from this level of statement to something more visionary, we encouraged them to think more openly about what they considered to be the best outcome for the city and to work within their groups to produce their own vision statement, which incorporated the views of the whole group rather than just one part of it. These turned out to be very long, so the final exercise of the session was to select a set of single words that would encapsulate the ideas. We then opened up the session to the whole group and, using a word-counting software, we asked them to vote for their word(s). The software displayed the size of the words according to their popularity so it soon became clear that for the group as a whole that there was a sense of certain words being important and it was these words that were then taken forward as 'the vision'.

To create a strategy from the vision requires a sense of what is needed to meet the requirements of the vision. So, if your vision word was, for example, 'an accessible city', then the action is to work out what would need to be in place in order that the city could be described as accessible. This gives a set of conditions that various elements of the city would have to meet – for example, wheelchair-accessible buses, good-quality footways or adequate information in a variety of formats – and the strategy is about the processes that need to be put in place in order to achieve those conditions. The processes range from collecting the data that is necessary for the design through to the appropriate procurement processes to ensure that the requirements would be delivered for a suitable price. This could be viewed at different scales – the policy across the city, the desires for implementation of that policy in different localities and then the detailed way of implementing the policy at a particular point in the street network.

The actions are then defined (e.g. what exactly do we mean by an accessible bus stop?) so that for each particular location a suitable specification can be defined and procured. To do this, we took the participants out on to the street so that they could work in groups to determine what would be necessary to fulfil the vision. This meant visiting the micro-scale situation of a small piece of the city – perhaps part of a square or a street – and deciding how to redesign it to make it fit the vision. What is interesting is that sometimes it becomes clear that, to achieve the vision, a great deal of work and expense is required, but that sometimes it is quite possible to achieve a lot with very little work, or even, expense. One example in Panama City was to turn around the bench seats placed around a large square so that they faced the gardens of the square rather than the traffic so that people sitting in the seats had a more pleasant view. By enabling the participants to make such interventions, they learnt that it is possible to achieve a lot with small actions – if they were aligned with the overarching vision. This provided the finishing point for the second day – a set of things to do on the third day.

So on the third day, the outcomes from the second day were fed into a design process where this thinking could be exercised in the form of some 3D models made at a scale of 1 : 100 to show how their thinking could be incorporated into the area. One of the really interesting points in this exercise was that we introduced scale models of people, and required the participants to scale everything they did around these models so that the whole design had a sense of providing outcomes at the human scale. During this exercise the participants were all able to create the model – using the skills of everyone – so that they could explain to the rest of the groups what they had achieved and why.

In another case, we wanted to find out what people thought about bus stops. One of the exercises to do this was incorporated into the TfL Year of the Bus event in Regent Street, London, and was described in Chapter 5. Here we redesigned two bus stops (See Figures 7.3 and 7.4) in order to break people's perceptions of a bus stop. This was so that we could start to build new possibilities of what might be incorporated in to their design in order to work on achieving wider objectives towards the overall vision. Changing the design of the bus stops and making the opportunity for people to respond was a really important part of seeing what might be possible when it comes to redesigning real, working, bus stops for the urban realm. This is discussed a little more in Chapter 9. Again, the principle was that all the public should be able to join in, that it was educational and enjoyable as well as challenging preconceptions of what people thought about the issue beforehand. Our job – in the workshops or at the bus stops – is simply to listen so that we can then consider the implications of what might be possible later on.

Figure 7.3 A bus stop asking the question 'what would you like a bus stop to look like?' Part of the Year of the Bus event on Regent Street, London, June 2014

Figure 7.4 A musical busk stop that asks the question 'what would you like to bus stop to sound like?'. Part of the Year of Bus event on Regent Street, London, June 2014

The key in all of this is the sense that the exercise is about learning, not teaching, promoting, advocating or proposing. Everyone needs to realise that they might leave the process at the end having changed their minds about many things. It is this mind-changing process that characterises good public participation processes – however they are actually done. In my experience, they work best when everyone is a participant and all the participants engage in 'doing' rather than watching or listening. So the question is 'what is the best way of encouraging and supporting people in 'doing' things so that they learn?'.

In Colombia and Panamá we had the groups go on to the street to create interventions – one group drew a zebra crossing on a street, another put post-it notes on badly parked vehicles proposing a fine. In another case they added a warning to one sign to vehicles entering and leaving a car park, pointing out that vehicle drivers should take care of the pedestrians (see Figure 7.5. Of course these interventions are temporary (although one was still in place in a later visit some 6 months after the workshop) and informal, but they showed the participants that they could actually do something, that often small things are important; that if you have your clear and agreed vision then small interventions can help you to move in the right direction, and it is not the case that the only answer is a huge project, for which money is not available, and therefore nothing can be done.

Figure 7.5 An intervention from one of our public participation workshops in Colombia – 'Caution! Vehicle entry and exit' was turned into 'Caution! Pedestrian right of way!'

7.5   The roadmap in Lima

Another case where we involved the public in a decision-making process was in the generation of principles relating to how a reduction in greenhouse gases could be achieved in the city of Lima. As part of a project funded by the UK Foreign and Commonwealth Office in Peru, we were asked to help the Peruvian Government to draft a document which describes the actions that the government would take in order to reduce greenhouse gas emissions in the transport sector. The document is one prescribed by the United Nations called 'Nationally Appropriate Mitigation Actions' (Nama); we were asked to work with various national ministries and local government to generate a draft Nama. The draft Nama document therefore set out the broad identification of the problem to be solved.

Reductions in greenhouse gas emissions will require some form of change in behaviour by the population and, although there are opportunities through technological shifts, much of the responsibility lies in the government to facilitate such a change. This requires cooperation on the part of the population, so it was necessary to engage with the local population in order to secure their engagement in the process. As per Table 5.1, we therefore needed to engage the population in the conceptualisation of the problem (Stage 2). Arguably, the Legal (Stage 2.1) and Technical (Stage 2.2) issues were covered in the process of drafting the Nama document. Although there was also activity with the civil society during the drafting of the Nama document, the civil society inputs really came into their own when we asked them to draft a roadmap to describe their own views about how the Nama should be implemented (Stage 2.3). To achieve this we facilitated the formation of, and engagement with, a consortium of non-governmental organisations, local universities and charity bodies with interests in the transport system. These organisations ranged from those interested in transport in general, such as Fundación Transitemos and Luz Ambar, to ones with specific interests, such as road safety (Cruzada Vial), or environmental change (Lima Cómo Vamos). We also worked with some local consultancies with particular experience of the local situation (Libélula and Swisscontact). The consortium also met with the city authorities in Lima and national government officials. The idea for this group was to generate a roadmap which would show how the draft Nama could be implemented in the coming years, which would be Stages 3–8 in Table 5.1.

The key component in this case was that the local people led the project from the outset – our role was to provide them with technical advice and to provide capacity-building courses, workshops and seminars and facilitate contacts with external bodies (e.g. Embarq, Transport for London). In other words we were the 'External Experts' of Table 5.1. It is crucial that the local people owned the output. They had to lead the process and our role was to help them with the technical issues – the local knowledge, sense of the problems that needed to be tackled and sentiments were clearly their domain.

With our assistance, the civil society group produced a Roadmap (*Hoja de Ruta*) (Transitemos, 2014), which was then presented to the Lima government. It expresses the sentiments and preferences of the people represented by the consortium members. It also formed the basis for the design of some pilot projects, for which funding has just been announced as this book goes to press.

7.6. Discussion

So how does the public participate in a project? I would like to consider these issues in three groups

Subject matter:

1 the information being provided
2 the method of presenting the information
3 the timing of the process.

Involvement process:

- input by members of the public
- the empowering, encouragement and facilitation of people to make informed judgements
- the understanding and acceptance of appropriate compromise
- the shared ownership in the resulting decision
- the appropriate distribution of power and responsibility to include both the controlling authority and the local people
- the use of votes to ensure equal and appropriate representation of all parties
- evaluation of the effectiveness of the detailed project and the involvement process itself.

Administration:

- formal involvement, including reference back to the community when amendments are being considered
- the users placed at the centre of the process
- separation of control from the spending body to the users' body.

7.6.1 Subject matter

We have seen that the subject matter can vary – for example, from the generation of strategy to the design of bus stops. Appropriate information must be made available and must be designed and presented to aid understanding. Under these circumstances, any subject involving people should be able to include the users' views as a central part of the process. Involvement should start at the very beginning of the project. The subject should be continually revisited and revised so that conditions continue to improve into the future.

7.6.2 Involvement process

Involvement includes the active participation of the public in a decision, using many different processes, but I contend that they must be characterised by the factors listed above. All potential users should be involved in decisions that are likely to affect them, and the process should also ensure that the whole range of users is given the opportunity to provide inputs to the decisions if they wish. This means that a concerted effort has to be made to contact people from all potential groups as the project proposals are being developed. Talking to representative groups is necessary, but not sufficient. The process should ensure that everyone, no matter whether they are confident or diffident, can have their say and be taken seriously in the expression of their concerns in the matter. This could mean setting up ancillary groups to enable some people to discuss the issue and come to a collective view before discussion of the issues in public and setting up, for example, workshops so that people can learn how to take on technical tasks and relate more equally to those in power. This would be appropriate where specific interest groups are involved, but where they might have conflicting interests. Disabled people have many different, and sometimes conflicting, interests and it is important that they can come to a collective view about the issue at hand so that they can present a unified approach to the wider discussion. Otherwise it is too easy for other more single-minded groups to argue against them.

People should be encouraged to make judgements and to have them taken seriously, even if the majority disagree. With more involvement, personal judgements will become more informed and, in combination with better understanding of the issues, more directed to the problem at hand.

Understanding and acceptance of appropriate compromise means that principles and policies, technical matters and design issues must all be explained in plain accessible language so that everyone can understand well enough to make a sensible decision about the proposal. Again, continual reference to the public will make this much easier, but it is time that we all (including university researchers) made our knowledge plain to the public we are attempting to serve. Hiding behind jargon is not an option any more.

A key element of public involvement has to be the ownership of the resulting decision. Decisions should not be made by one group and imposed on another: they should be made by all parties and understood by everyone (whether or not they are agreed by everyone). With the shared ownership of the decision comes a shared responsibility, both over the decision itself and of its implementation. In the scenario of public involvement, decisions are not isolated events that can be forgotten, but are ongoing processes that need to be monitored and evaluated so that improvements can be made and mistakes rectified in good time. The sharing of ownership of and responsibility for decisions puts power in the hands of the community in which they are applied.

Voting regimes need to be established so that people feel that their views are taken into account in the decision process. In short, the involvement process needs to feel real as well as inclusive.

All decision processes should have an independent evaluation element to check that the decision outcome is working and that the effects are as desired. Involvement processes are no different in this respect, except that the outcomes of such evaluation should be more explicit and more widely available to the public than is currently often the case.

The involvement process should continue beyond the end of the project so that benefits are not lost simply because the particular project that brought them changed its funding

338

regime or stopped altogether. Apart from changes in funding, the world changes and public participation is a good way of making sure that a project keeps up to date with progress (e.g. more general availability of accessible buses may alter the way in which other resources could be used).

It is important to have a schedule of meetings so that everyone knows when there will be an opportunity to re-evaluate problems and their solutions. The existence of a schedule provides the necessary power for the user to keep the pressure on the technical and political partners in the decision process. This prevents the meetings from becoming a superficial talking shop from which no practical solution ever emerges.

Decision-makers also need to resolve the difference between wishing to include the public, including disabled people, young and elderly people and other typically excluded groups, and the practicality of doing so. Inevitably, involvement means setting up procedures so that these groups, who are typically very difficult to reach, are included in a way that makes their involvement real. This suggests the organisation of discussion groups, focus groups, public meetings and other diverse techniques to ensure that the involvement happens and is genuine. It is a very different world from the usual decision-making domain, where control is wholly in the hands of providers rather than the users of services.

7.6.3   Administrative process

The process needs to be formal in order to make sure that it happens and that people are aware that any subsequent decisions take the outcomes of the participation process into account. However, it must also feel 'human' and relevant to everyone in the community. As a result, there is no 'one-size-fits-all' solution and the likelihood is that a variety of methods will need to be brought into play. Involvement needs to be incorporated formally into every process so that users are included as a norm at the centre of the process and not just in a series of meetings at the periphery. Participation is not a favour that can be dispensed with or withdrawn at will by anyone, whether they are a member of a community or a local authority. A central issue is the placing of control over spending. This is often retained by the spending authority on the basis of its legal responsibility for the proper use of public money. Users' involvement means that some of this control must pass to the users. This issue has already been addressed in the management of some social housing estates.

As long as the administration process is correct and the users are involved as stakeholders in the process, there is no reason to suppose that the involvement of users is any less 'proper' than an approach which does not involve them. In fact, I would argue that a process that does not include users at such a level is not a proper process at all: proper use of public money is surely to ensure that it is being spent wisely and to the greatest benefit of the potential user groups. Sharing responsibility for spending of public money in the social services area has already been started: the direct payments approach to funding a user's social-services needs delegates to the user the decisions about how the money is spent, even though the local authority has the legal responsibility for the resources. Involving users in the decision process as suggested here would work on a similar basis. Proper spending decisions have to involve the users, and the inclusion of users in the decision process is a necessary condition to enable such decisions to be made.

The workshops in Colombia and Panama and the roadmap in Peru show that it is quite possible for civil society to take an active part in conceiving, designing and implementing their own decisions. Changing the relationship between civil society and the local/central administration to one of equals is both important and possible.

7.7. Conclusions

Different methods are useful in different contexts and it is important to have a full range of options available so that the best ones can be used in each case. It is important to review the process so that improvements can be made in the future.

Involving the public is an ongoing task, which means that procedures have to be set up to enable it to happen on a permanent basis. It is all too easy to forget the public once the service has been put into operation or the bus stops built. Once people believe they will be taken seriously they will become involved, and this involvement provides a project with a great benefit. Apart from the advantage of making sure that the project is appropriate for the local community, the public participation process lends the project's promoters a level of authority that is difficult to dispel. I use the word 'lend' in this context because the support of the public needs to be earned on a continuing basis.

Public participation carries with it some costs – costs of implementation (e.g. the cost of meetings) and of time (it requires enough time for the public's views to be heard and acted on). It would not be appropriate to use the display approach instead of the first meeting as it is this meeting which enables the public to discuss the project in the light of its overall principles rather than in the fine detail of particular solutions. This aspect of the Puppit project was a success (I mentioned above the change in attitude of the public in the course of the first meeting) and shows that a more mature approach to such detailed issues is possible.

Involving the public is an essential element of a modern decision process. It is important that the public is able to participate fully throughout the process. Presence at meetings and completion of other consultation exercises, such as questionnaires or interviews, are basic forms of involvement. However, participation means that people must be informed about and understand the knowledge they need in order to be able to make a contribution. Many of the issues that cause members of the public to feel left out of the decision process arise because the reasons for the decision are not given or are not understood. For example, the solution that would be optimal from the public's point of view might be illegal, or technically impossible. In some cases, although the details of the design of infrastructure are constrained for technical or practical reasons, they could be adjusted to suit local preferences (e.g. moving a cycle rack from one side of a bus stop to the other). Explanations and discussions about what is possible mean that the public feel better about the outcome, even if their own preference has not been chosen, because the decision was made with, and at least to some extent by, the public rather than by somebody acting in apparent isolation at the town hall. Every decision is the selection of one compromise from a set of different suboptimal options. It is important that the rationale for this choice is understood by everyone. It is this sort of issue that was so well dealt with through the workshop mechanism. The groups – mixtures of professionals and civil society – learnt from each other and discovered how to tackle such problems.

It is important to ensure that the 'right' public is involved in a decision. Local decisions are clearly important to local people, but others may also have reason to have an input. Bus users, for example, might use a bus stop even though they do not live or work anywhere near it. A particular issue is the involvement of disabled people. I have mentioned the need to ensure that they have a voice in all decisions, sometimes with the opportunity to discuss the issues between themselves beforehand. Disabled people fill two roles in the public participation process: they provide their knowledge of their local area and they provide knowledge about at least some issues of importance to disabled people in general. It is essential that disabled people are included in every decision, even where it does not involve their immediate locality, so that the needs of disabled people can be included in every decision. This suggests that the initial publicity and associated information about the participation process must be made widely available before the process starts – if people do not know about the forthcoming issue, they cannot be expected to participate in helping to resolve it.

The inclusion in the decision, design, implementation, operation and management processes of groups such as disabled, young or elderly people is of course essential in order to ensure their inclusion in the eventual design and operation of the resulting system. However it is also important for another reason. There is a tendency to design for 'norms' or 'standards' – a lot of conventional ergonomics is based around designing for e.g. the '95th percentile' size of body part (e.g. arm length, foot size, grip strength, visual capability, etc.). However, this not only excludes the other 5%, but it also ignores a central tenet of design, namely that it should be considered on the basis of whether it achieves the required functionality. This functionality has to apply to the whole population and the use of percentiles in this way leaves the designer in a position where they do not know who they are excluding. In other words the person is excluded from the process. Because groups of people – and disabled people are only one such group – have different needs but all have to have a place in the overall vision, the particular needs of these groups are crucially important if we want to have a fully inclusive society. So their direct inclusion in the design process is not only a 'nice-to-have' but is a prime necessity in order for everyone to understand where the real limits lie in terms of functional design.

Formalising public participation by setting up a community company is an exciting and empowering way to enable people to take control of some aspects of their community life. The example of a community's control over its local bus service shows that this approach can work even where the operation concerned is complex. Such involvement requires a lot of time and effort. Comparison between the Cumbria and Hackney examples shows that implementation of full public involvement needs time and patience to establish a climate in which new initiatives can be easily established. This, coupled with the number of people living in the local area in each case, affects the range and depth of the available human resource and thus the rate at which public involvement processes can be introduced in different places. When public participation schemes are being devised, due account has to be taken of the available skills and the number of people able and willing to contribute to their local community in this way. When a full and inclusive public involvement programme is achieved, it can provide the most democratic way of making public decisions in the community's interest.

A final point is that the link from the high-level vision to the low-level action is crucial – it dictates what can be done to help achieve the vision even if the action is quite small. It is not necessary to wait for an expensive mega project to happen in order to achieve an improvement.

REFERENCES

Brown IEW and Tyler N (2004) Community-run rural bus services: can theoretical cross sector benefits be realised in practice. *Proceedings of the Tenth International Conference on Mobility and Transport for Elderly and Disabled People, Hamamatsu, Japan, 23–26 May.*

Haklay M (2013) Citizen science and volunteered geographic information – overview and typology of participation. In *Crowdsourcing Geographic Knowledge: Volunteered Geographic Information (VGI) in Theory and Practice* (Sui DZ, Elwood S and Goodchild MF(eds). Springer, Berlin, Germany, pp 105–122, http://dx.doi.org/10.1007/978-94-007-4587-2_7.

IDC (International Data Corporation) (2015) Middle East and Africa Smartphone Market to Top 155 Million Units in 2015 as Sub-\$200 Segment Surges. *International Data Corporation*, 12 July. See https://www.idc.com/getdoc.jsp?containerId = prAE25737515 (accessed 12 October 2015).

Transitemos (2014) *Hacía una ciudad para las personas: Hoja de Ruta para una política de transporte y movilidad sostenible para Lima y Callao* (in Spanish). Fundación Transitemos, Lima, Peru.

UNECE (United Nations Economic Commission for Europe) (2014a) Rio Declaration on Environment and Development in Practice. See http://www.unece.org/env/pp/welcome.html (accessed 27 April 2014).

UNECE (2014b) UNECE Convention. See http://www.unece.org/fileadmin/DAM/env/pp/documents/cep43e.pdf (accessed 27 April 2014).

Part 3

Examples – Where?

ICE Publishing: All rights reserved
http://dx.doi.org/10.1680/aabs2ed.59801.345

Chapter 8
Examples

Many of the ideas and concepts raised and discussed in this book are too new to have been implemented. They have, however, emerged from some years of observing bus systems in practice in a variety of cities around the world. Rather than just being a collection of best practice from these cities, however, I have tried to treat them more as influences on a developing idea of what a city should be trying to do to help the members of its society strive to achieve their aims and improve their quality of life and wellbeing – and how the bus system can help that come to fruition. It might be better to think of this as the influences that combine to influence a live performance: always there, always changing and always new – permanent yet ephemeral, repeating but never repeated. There is, as yet, no extant example of the ideas in action, but there are examples of parts of them in different cases. The ideas continue to develop, of course, and in order to help others come to think about the bus system in different ways, I am now going to describe a number of examples that either have proved influential, or seem to be interesting examples of how people in city authorities, with all their constraints, have sought to enable their bus system to help people achieve their goals.

8.1.　Medellín

However one chooses to look at it, in the 1990s, Medellín was in a dark place. It was the centre of an intense narcotrafficking industry with all the associated gang wars and violence. Over 500 policemen were murdered during 1990 in the city and the murder rate peaked at 381 per 100 000 people in 1991 (for comparison, in that year the murder rate in New York, NY, USA, was 14 per 100 000 of the population (DC, 2015)). Something had to be done.

One of the local drug gang leaders was arrested and the mayor took advantage of this change in dynamics to address the challenge of how to make the city one in which people would want to live. This meant not just building infrastructure or other major projects, but changing the culture of a city in which people were scared to walk in the streets and participate in local democratic processes, in addition to encouraging people to acknowledge civilised behaviour (such as car drivers waiting for pedestrians to cross the road in front of their vehicle) and to feel able to indicate when behaviour was not so civilised. He employed mime artists and actors to help with this.

One of the innovations was the introduction of a system of 'Proyectos Urbanos Integrales' (Integral Urban Projects) (PUIs). It is essential to realise that these were projects and not plans – Alejandro Echeverri, who developed the concept, insisted that they had to be projects because plans never translated into reality. This translated into implementing the simpler things immediately while planning around the more complex elements of the project. The PUIs were implemented, starting in the poorest neighbourhoods. They were highly participatory – the projects were defined and specified by the local community – and involved both attention to improving footways and making places deemed by the local population to be important accessible to the population as a whole, as well as constructing larger projects such as housing schemes, libraries, centres for small businesses, and schools. By doing the participatory process right at the start and while determining the local desires for improving present conditions, they could proceed with constructing the other elements. Thus PUIs tended to deliver – 80% of the PUI intentions were delivered within 4 years. PUIs were a demonstration that the city believed in its communities – there is the sense that the previous drug-related problems were in part a result of the city absenting itself from some of the more remote and poorer communities, thus leaving the turf clear for criminal elements to enter. By showing that the city does care – introducing community policing, employment, training schemes, education and using high quality materials, techniques and design in the construction of the projects, the city showed its belief and trust in the local population.

One of the other aspects of this story – and the one of most interest for this book – is the recognition that Echeverri realised that how people exercised their need to move around the city was crucial to how the city would develop. This was not just about economic development but also about a social change that meant people felt they really could move around the city, without fear, and with a sense that this would bring social as well as economic benefits. Echeverri used the metro line, which had been constructed earlier along the main conduit of the city as a device to encourage a better sense of community. Now, the important thing here is that this metro line, which appears normal in many respects, was not really a transport system. Of course, it carried passengers to and from work and other activities, but an example of its real intent can be seen from one of its more unusual characteristics. This is that the drivers of the trains are university students.

Why?

The answer is that the metro line is an instrument of social cohesion. The students will one day become the future engineers, lawyers, medical doctors, sociologists, teachers and so on of the city; their job during their university career shows them that every time they drive their train into a station, they see society standing on the platform and their role is to bring that society together. Yes, people are travelling from A to B, but they are doing this together, in a city where this would have been a real risk only a few years before. So, Lesson 1 from this example is that having a high-order vision for the nature of society can be translated into a day-to-day practical reality by the way you choose to operate the public transport system. For me, this is such an important point that I coined a word for it! The actual meaning of 'infrastructure' is 'that which supports a structure' (OED, 1989). We normally think of this (at least in civil engineering) as that which supports our road or rail systems – the bridges, railway tracks, stations etc. However, the 'structure' in the definition does not have to be made of concrete! The structure of society needs to be supported as well. So infrastructure as a word could refer to the systems that collectively support the workings of society. However, before we can have a society, we need a culture. This is what the Mayor of Medellín recognised and enacted through his campaign to recognise good and bad behaviour – and then through the metro system and the way it operated and the PUIs and the way they were implemented. The Medellín metro supports this culture, so the word I coined is 'infraculture' – that which supports a culture – and in this case the culture then supports society. This is a truly 'public' transport system.

The city government believes that another cultural quality is obtained from reading; words formed into poetry or prose. So their 'infracultural' metro system has book dispensers at each station, to allow people to borrow books – specially produced to be a size that is easy to handle on the train – and then to return them at another station. There is also a whole educational programme for schools in which the concept of social behaviour and how this pertains to travel on the metro, and social behaviour in general, is taught. *The Economist* quotes Ramiro Márquez: 'People are the raw material. You need to educate them' (*The Economist*, 2014).

However, like most metro systems, the Medellín metro is only able to satisfy demand along its line of route. The poorer communities in the city lived some way away from this – actually vertically quite a long way above it. This height difference means that it would be impossible to reach them by metro and the existing bus systems had to climb up over 500 m to reach these communities (the centre of Medellín is located 1500 m above sea level and the poor areas tend to be located above and away from the centre), meaning a journey of some hours in uncomfortable conditions. The answer was to construct a cable car system and link it to the metro. This reduced the journey time from the periphery to the centre of Medellín to 25 minutes, thus enabling people from these communities to work or trade – carry out activities in the city centre – more easily. In all, three 'Metrocable' lines were built to provide a well-connected metro network.

In a fourth area, however, the disadvantage of the cable car (and actually of the metro itself in a way) was highlighted. This is that the main benefits of these systems accrue to the people who live near to the stations – those in between the stations still had a difficult journey to make to reach the system (even though this was much easier than what was previously on offer). So in the fourth area a public escalator was installed. This stretches for about 450 m up the mountainside. Here again the higher-level vision came to the fore. The escalator had to be built in seven sections. By encouraging and training teams of school students to look after each section and to supervise its use, not only was the escalator constructed, but the sense of community ownership was built. There is a real sense of pride, public (rather than city) ownership and belief in the city that was hard to imagine 30 years before.

The approach extends to the implementation of a bus rapid transit system, tram, public bicycles, pedestrianisation in the city centre and so on. Inevitably there is more to be done, but the message from this example is about that higher-order visionary approach which then leads to how the city, and especially its public transport systems, can be designed to provide a greater sense of city development for the people. Public involvement in the operation of the public systems is crucial – the ownership and sense of responsibility conferred upon the people in the city is an illustration of the trust placed in them by the city leaders. It also shows that the transparency which arises from such a participatory process reduces the incidence of corruption and thus increases trust in the city leadership as well.

Crucially important to the changes in Medellín, though, is the way it has financed these social changes. The Empresas Públicas de Medellín (EPM), established in 1955, is a group of companies which, between them, provide electricity, gas, water, sanitation and telecommunications. Initially the company served only Medellín but now it has operations elsewhere in Colombia and beyond. It also leads a fund for university education which benefits many students in Medellín. In 2013 EPM generated nearly $870 million in profits, but because the Board decided to contribute to the city from its profits, it allocates 35% of its profit to the city. In 2013, of which $640 million was contributed to the city's accounts. In the decade from 2003, this resource has generated over $3 billion for the city, which accounts for about 25% of the city budget (The Economist, 2014). EPM is an industrial and commercial enterprise owned by the municipality of Medellín and is subject to great interest from the city's population – *The Economist* asserts that 'politicians mess with EPM at their peril' and quotes the chief executive as saying 'There is a massive social control of what we do'.

EPM's mission is corporate social responsibility. This is not an add-on to the company's main business, but its core purpose. It sets out to achieve this by seeking to improve the social wellbeing of the city through supplying water, electricity, gas, telecommunications, social housing, education projects and more. It has a programme of 'Units of joined-up living' (*Unidades de Vida Articulada* (UVA)). UVAs are projects where the company's water business opens up the areas around its main assets (large water tanks) to the local community, providing resources for play and education, access to internet, art and other opportunities as a way of helping people lead more complete lives. This company is part of the ethos of the city – and that delivery of budget to the city for use on socially beneficial projects is a major support to the city in its endeavours to change its world.

It illustrates the potential of thinking about how cities are financed if they are directing themselves to improve the quality of life and wellbeing of the people living there.

Medellín is one of the main inspirations for the five cities model I described in Chapter 1. It demonstrates the importance of setting a higher-level vision and ensuring that projects are implemented to attain it. This is crucial to the development of a better societal outcome. In addition, it shows the importance – and opportunity – of thinking laterally about the way a city is financed and supported in its societal mission.

8.2. London
London – and in particular, Transport for London (TfL) – won deserved praise for its hosting of the Olympic and Paralympic Games in 2012. This was a games in which accessibility was a major aspect of the planning and implementation. In terms of the

transport system, it managed to handle half a million additional people heading to and from venues across the city while maintaining the commercial and residential activities that make the city the global powerhouse that it is. All of this with a transport system that operates within a hair's breadth of its physical capacity on a normal day, let alone with the additional pressures of such an event. The public transport system worked.

With all the success of the games, it is easy to forget just how nervous everyone was beforehand. Encouraging people to change their travel time, to walk a little more, the stentorian warnings from the mayor ringing across public address systems in railway stations, the rigid application of loading/unloading and delivery times, all reflected a deep concern that the games could be a disaster for London's transport system. So it is interesting to reflect on what worked well and what this might mean for a transport system – especially a bus system – under more normal operating conditions.

It is also easy to forget that in the early 1930s London's transport system was on the verge of collapse and the bus system was no exception. A plethora of operators, no investment and poor maintenance meant that the system was rapidly becoming dysfunctional. In 1933 the London Passenger Transport Board (LPTB) was created by the London Passenger Transport Act 1933 to bring some order to the situation. The LPTB brought together some 92 companies including all the bus companies, the Underground Electric Railways, the Metropolitan Railway and all the tramways and covered an area (the London Passenger Transport Area (LPTA)) from High Wycombe in the west to Tilbury in the east and Baldock in the north to Horsham in the south. With this unified organisation a massive capital investment programme was initiated, mostly in the form of extensions to the underground railway network, new trains, the tramway network replacement by what would become one of the world's largest trolley bus systems, and the development of a new standard bus.

LPTB commissioned a number of iconic design standards that provided a corporate identity, bringing in designers and architects such as Charles Holden (underground stations) and Wallis, Gilbert and Partners (bus garages and depots) and a more standard approach to bus stops and shelters. In addition there was an imaginative poster advertising activity to promote the network.

The LPTB was replaced by the London Transport Executive in 1948 as part of the more general nationalisation of transport implemented at that time. London Transport (LT) continued in a similar vein to LPTB, but as, in effect, a nationalised entity. In the post-war austerity period, investment inevitably reduced and some pre-war schemes were never restarted following their suspension during the war period.

In the mid-1980s, the Thatcher government deregulated bus systems in the UK outside London. LT started a process of tendering its bus services to private companies while retaining ownership and responsibility for the route and service network. However, the management system in London was still highly fragmented. The abolishing of the Greater London Council in 1986 left no single control of the city, so political decisions were taken, in effect, independently, by each of the 33 boroughs. This meant that LT had no political direction other than from the Secretary of State for Transport. It was thus simply the body that provided transport in the city. There was no sense of its involvement with the city as a social space. In order to improve this situation, Transport for London was formed in 2000 and was placed under the direct responsibility of the new mayor (a role that was created in May 2000).

TfL is responsible for all the transport in the Greater London Authority area (rather smaller than the LPTA). In its most recent reorganisation (2014), it now has three divisions (Surface Transport, Subsurface Transport (effectively the underground and overground railways) and a special division with responsibility for the massive CrossRail development.)

Surface Transport has responsibility for all the transport on the surface, including buses, tram, taxis, boats, public bicycles, cable car, streets and traffic management on the strategic road network (other roads are managed by the 33 boroughs). This brings much closer the prospect of service integration across all modes and the simpler relationship between Surface Transport and the various railways in the city means that integration between rail and road public transport is much easier to obtain. The responsibility to the mayor meant that transport became one of the levers open to the mayor for social change. This was exercised in the introduction of the congestion charge, investment in bus system under the first mayor and the incentives to cycling by the second.

This was tested before and during the 2012 Olympic and Paralympic Games, when it was necessary to insert an additional million users into the transport system over a period of a few weeks in the summer. On a normal weekday, London's 8.5 million population is supplemented by 2.5 million commuters, most of whom head for central London, and the transport system just manages to cope. So the additional users could all too easily have pushed the system beyond its capacity. The ability to use the overall management structure to predict and act on possible congestion problems in real time was only possible because of the integrated management and operational structure. A single control room was set up which housed the operational controllers for all the transport systems, including National Rail. Thus, for example, the National Rail controller, knowing that a very full train had left Newcastle 300 miles to the north of the capital with most of its passengers bound for London, could inform London Underground controllers to expect an influx at King's Cross 2.5 hours later, which could then be managed both within the station itself and on the associated underground lines. The bus controllers could advise buses of appropriate action to relieve the problems that could arise if the Underground system could not cope – by permitting Underground tickets to be used on the buses, for example, or by ensuring that sufficient buses were available traffic, or by managing to enable the buses to move easily to resolve the problems raised by congestion by arranging the influx of passengers at an appropriate time. The lessons learnt from this informed the recent reorganisation to maintain that structural cohesion for the more normal operation that is needed every day.

The bus system is operated on a tendered contract basis. TfL retains the risk in relation to demand and revenue – the operators compete on the basis of reliability, quality of service, and cost, but are not required to estimate the present or future demand or revenue. Contracts are therefore full cost (including profit) for operating the service as required by Transport for London. Contracts run for 5 years with a possible extension to 7 years if performance has been satisfactory. Operators are continuously monitored for performance and key performance indicators are published monthly. Poor performance may be penalised and exceptional performance may be rewarded, in both cases the change being financial. Vehicles are purchased according to a TfL specification, but the risk is taken by the operators – loss of a contract could leave them with vehicles (and staff) that are no longer needed. This has not been a major problem in practice – most of the operators have operations elsewhere in the UK and can displace the London vehicles elsewhere if necessary, or might be able to sell them to the subsequent operator on the same service. Similarly, the drivers may be transferred to another operator. The result is a system of systems, which is basically stable, well-managed and innovative.

The keyword here is integration. London's transport is a whole system with a number of different parts which are all integrated, nearly completely through the ticketing system and operationally through the overall management offered by TfL. Another interesting lesson is the mix of public and private sector involvement in the delivery of transport in the capital. The public section takes the social risk of ensuring that the city population will improve their quality of life through equitable access to connectivity and movement between their chosen activities. This social risk takes on a financial aspect when this is translated to estimations of demand. This provides a stability for the people and ensures that the supply of transport will be predictable. The private sector provides the delivery and takes the operational risk of doing so, but does not base financial risks on their own estimates of demand. Therefore it is possible to have an integrated equitable and reliable transport system with a societal mission to contribute to improvement in people's lives.

8.3.   Asheville, North Carolina

Asheville is a small city in the USA (the population is about 85 000), so is very different from the example of Medellín (1.5 million) or London (8.5 million). However, the USA is not well known for its sympathy for public transport, at least outside the major cities such as New York, or special cases, such as Portland, Oregon. So the efforts being made by Asheville are really exciting.

Prior to 2009, the city operated 24 bus routes, mostly at an hourly frequency with some operating an additional service at peak periods, a night service was operated and there had been a 90-day trial of a free-fare in the central area and these are thought to be the main reasons for an increase in ridership since 2003, giving a daily ridership of over 5000 trips. However, there were several concerns. These included complaints about poor on-time performance, slow running, old vehicles and uncoordinated services.

In 2009 the city developed a Masterplan (the Asheville Downtown Masterplan) so it is worth having a brief look at this. I will not go into the full details of the plan – these can be found at (Asheville Downtown Masterplan, 2009) but I will discuss some of the main issues here. The Masterplan was built on a long history of community involvement, which had started some 20 years before, when the community came together to create an urban design and enterprise model for the city. This was that the city had to be vibrant and 'a place' with its own character: for example, national trading chains wanting to set up in Asheville had to adapt to local needs. This led to a strategy of supporting local businesses through targeted investment and encouragement to make Asheville their home as well as their base. The community is proud of the city and encourages tourism.

First of all, the plan was developed to address four issues that were arising in the city at the time (i.e. up to 2008):

1   There had been a strong upsurge in development interest in the downtown area in the previous 5 years, mainly in the form of housing, hotels and retail, and this could be expected to continue.
2   The development interest was in danger of threatening some of the city's most celebrated assets, including historic buildings, affordable places for local entrepreneurs and artists, locally owned retail, the breadth of housing options available to residents, entertainment services, restaurants and views of the surrounding mountains.
3   There were increasing difficulties in managing the planning process in the face of the development interest, so that the main characteristics of the city as outlined in the previous City Development Plan (2003) were being increasingly threatened and a better way to plan the future development of the city was badly needed.
4   Economic uncertainty made it difficult to plan – whether the economy were to grow or diminish would affect the planning needs.

Asheville has several nationally recognised historic buildings which had been looked after by local people. There was a concern that the new developments had – or were threatening to – disturb the balance of new and old and issues such as the skyline were clearly apparent, including how this affected views of the surrounding mountains (a similar issue arose in Vancouver, Canada). A characteristic of which the population were very proud was the high number of locally-owned retail, entertainment and artist venues with pedestrian-friendly frontages. Although difficult in some places because of the topography and elsewhere being under threat, the city was felt to be essentially walkable and this was something appreciated by the local community. The downtown area was characterised by plenty of person-friendly public space.

It seemed that the main priorities for this Masterplan would be to retain characteristics of the city that were related to people, pedestrians, maintaining a human-scale for the city environment.

In response to this need the Masterplanners went to the local community and engaged in a strong exercise of public participation. This resulted in a whole series of events, including large interactive public meetings, workshops looking at visions, strategy and so on, one-to-one interviews, affinity group sessions, facilitated summits and other gatherings with targeted community organisations, residents and members of the city

Figure 8.1 Visions and strategies for Asheville (Asheville Downtown Masterplan 2009, p. 44)

business communities, and these took place over a period of about a year. The range of different activities is important in public participation – different issues need different fora and different methods of engagement in order to be dealt with properly. People were asked to 'dream, think, co-operate and fine-tune their aspirations' (Asheville Downtown Masterplan, 2009) for the city. The outcome was that the eventual plan had been effectively drawn up by the community and achieved the broad support of the community as a whole.

The outcome of this process was the generation of a Masterplan in which seven visions were set out, and a set of seven strategies were devised to put them into practice. These can be seen in Figure 8.1. It is interesting to see the importance of the strategies in cultivating the creative, cultural and historic character of the city, the intention to expand the access and mobility in the area, the sense of place and community, the need to be transparent and how these overlap a number of visions. The Masterplan relates the transport-related strategy (Strategy 2) to Visions (1) 'sustaining the dynamic culture, (2) enhancing the centre of community', (5) 'good, interconnected transportation choices for access and better health' and (6) 'making the area a national model of sustainable development'. I think that if more creative approaches to bus stop design and their connectedness to the pedestrian network were incorporated, the strategy would also apply to Vision (3): 'strengthen the area's identity as a series of residential neighbourhoods' and (4) 'preserve and enhance diverse architecture, historic resources, public realm and view corridors that create Downtown's unique legacy'.

The Masterplan provided a high-level vision for Asheville, with support from creative ideas. It was in light of this Masterplan and its development processes that the Transit Plan was constructed as part of the implementation. In 2009, the Transit Masterplan adopted a new approach, which was badged as 'Asheville Redefines Transit' (Art). This approach was to make the system much more responsive to the needs of the population. The issue was that the public transport system was growing organically but without any particular direction – community requests were met, but there was no overall sense of where the city wanted – or needed – to go in terms of its transport systems. The idea was to put transport in a different place, and to have a sense of a transport system. The existing system was responsive but difficult to market because it made no overall sense and had no overall 'image' for the people as a whole. There was also a problem because the economic situation meant implementing the Masterplan without direct resources.

Crucially, the Transit Masterplan was not only about transport – it had to embrace economic development as well as a multimodal approach including pedestrians and cyclists. This meant thinking through how infrastructure such as footways and cycleways could be provided. The transport system also had to support local businesses. The Downtown area is expensive to live in but that dependence of tourism as a business means that wages are generally low – the City Council is trying to bring more affordable housing into the Downtown area, but the wages problem means that fares are important. As a result, the city fare was set at $1. However, another characteristic of tourism is that it is a 7-day-a-week business and no buses on Sundays meant that many workers were having to pay maybe $20 for a taxi to take them to work. As a result, there was a strong desire from the community for a Sunday service and this features in the Transit Masterplan.

Proposals for the first year were to increase the frequency on the heaviest corridors, add new transfer locations out of the main central area, improve the on-time performance, reduce the number of route deviations, either to eliminate the dial-a-ride service or convert it to a fixed-route service, speed up the longer routes and keep the whole system simple for new users. In terms of schedules, the proposal was to offer all routes from 6 am to 6 pm at least, to be able to add additional capacity based on demand, every route should have at least an hourly service, evening routes to be combined with the equivalent daytime route, add a Sunday service to the most productive routes and eliminate the Saturday service on the least productive routes.

The proposals required a considerable investment – an increase of 70% in the city funding level. How was it that a transportation plan had such a community-driven approach? The strong community involvement in the city made sure that the Sunday service issue was at the top of the agenda, but it could not provide the resources to pay for its implementation. The crucial point here is that the long-term public participation over more than 20 years meant that a sense of trust had developed between the people and the city authorities. This meant that even though people understood that the city did not have the resources to support such a service, the message was understood that the city would do whatever it could to help. The community believed that the scheme would eventually happen even though it might not be able to happen right now. In fact the link with jobs meant that the Sunday services could be supported at 50% by a Federal 'Job Access and Reverse' fund and the service was implemented at the beginning of 2015.

If I were to compare this with the five cities model, I think the Asheville plan fits quite well with that approach. The creation of the city visions can be fairly easily mapped onto the five cities. Visions (2) and (3) are clear drivers for the courteous city. It is also interesting to see the predominance of pedestrian activity in the thinking and the strength of feeling in keeping that characteristic as a feature of the city – unusual in a North American context. The active city is represented by the clear concern that the activities should be available to everyone and that they should encourage local businesses rather than national chains, to retain the community feel that has developed in the city over many decades. Similarly the city as a public space is evident: the importance of ensuring that the public space is truly public, safe and secure is retained in Visions (1), (2), (3) and (4). The sense of ownership is palpable: the City Transit Planning Development Manager says 'we want the community to feel proud of the system they are riding on'. This means transforming the buses (most were old) and bus stops – 'we did not have bus stops: we had dirt!'. New buses were brought into the fleet, the older ones scrapped and a programme of enabling community groups to design their own bus stops brought a clear sense of ownership and pride. Not much is said about the health aspect of the city, although the Masterplan does state that Asheville has been accorded the distinction of being in the top 10 places to live for healthcare (p. 8), otherwise the vision that transport can help to secure better health is the only directed ambition in this area. The evolving city is well-represented – much of the point of the Masterplan was to secure the sort of future for future generations that would enable them to have options rather than have them foreclosed by the nature of short term development.

Asheville transformed their transit system and in doing so helped to transform the city for future generations. A key message from this example is that if you have a clear vision, which outlasts the political cycle and is accepted by the community as a whole – largely because they developed it – it is always possible to make a positive difference. It is not necessary to wait for the funds to start a massive project – lots can be achieved by doing the small things you can now. The vision is necessary because it prevents this approach from just doing anything in an uncoordinated way (the 'undirected' approach that happened before 2009 was a good example of that) and thus the short term actions are actually part of the long term vision. This also works well for community engagement in the process – the ownership of the bus stops will stand them in good stead for generations to come. Yes, 'it's the little things that count'!

8.4. Lima

Lima is a city of around 8.5 million. Its governmental structure is complicated for historical reasons, with the result that there are in fact two governments involved in the operation of the city (and in particular its transport system): Lima (responsible for the other 7.5 million of the population) and Callao (responsible for about 1 million). Consequently, trying to develop a single approach to the transport system has been a very difficult process. In 2010 I was asked to help with a programme of capacity-building in order to develop a concerted approach towards the development of a programme of

Actions as the submission by the Peruvian government to the United Nations on reductions in transport-related greenhouse gas emissions. These documents are called 'Nationally Appropriate Mitigation Actions' (Namas). The Lima conurbation has about a third of the Peruvian population, is responsible for about 50% of the Peruvian economy and 80% of its emissions, so the city had to play an important part in the national policy.

The bus system at that time had been chaotic for many years – made worse by the liberalisation of imports of second-hand vehicles in the early 1990s – and consisted of about 30 000 assorted mostly small buses in pretty terrible condition operated by almost as many operators (typically a driver owned (or rented) the bus he was driving). There was a sort of aggregation of these individual operators into 'Committees' which loosely formed a route and controlled the drivers (mostly to ensure that revenue was evenly divided between them, so it mainly tried to prevent late- or early-running 'stealing' passengers from another driver). On-street competition was rife, the quality of service was appalling and the resulting congestion and pollution, particularly in the centre of the city, was dreadful. This was complemented by a more-or-less unknown number of taxis (estimates vary from around 100 000 to 200 000), which were mostly illegal. Efforts to regulate them were made but this fell foul of the dual-authority mentioned above. Taxis could be registered in either Lima or Callao. To operate in Callao, a taxi had to be registered in Callao, but to operate in Lima it could be registered in either Lima or Callao. This was important because the port and international airport were both located in Callao. The excessive number of taxis in Lima caused the Lima government to cease registrations, but Callao continued to register them. As a result, the number continued to rise. There was no quality control, although gradually regulations appeared to limit taxis in terms of entering the city centre. However, the huge number of illegal, informal taxis meant that regulation was always undermined.

If Peru – and thus Lima – was going to act on transport-related emissions, it was inevitable that they would have to do something about both buses and taxis – yet the odd governance of the city of Lima made this very difficult. Accordingly, this story is about how to try to improve the situation on the street (or, in reality, in the air) with such a difficult government structure. The resulting draft Nama (Tyler and Ramírez, 2012) contains the details and I will not go into these here.

The first issue to contend with was that the governance structure was a matter for the Constitution of Peru. This was not going to be changed very easily (or quickly). So solutions had to be adopted that would somehow avoid this problem until it could be resolved. Lima elected a mayor who was very keen to resolve the transport problem (it was a major issue in the election). Construction of a BRT system (the Metropolitano) was started in 2006. The mayor set up an organisation to manage the bus system, Protransporte, and set them to designing and implementing a BRT system in the city. The first line of the Metropolitano was opened in 2010. Lima also has one metro line, which started construction in the mid-1980s but was only opened in 2013. This is operated by the central government (Ministerio de Transporte y Comunicaciones) because it had originally been a Presidential project and also because they did not consider that the Lima government had the capacity to run the system. This added a complexity to the Lima government's transport planning processes as they had no control over where this – or any subsequent – line would actually run, or what frequency of service would be offered. Clearly, this makes it difficult to plan infrastructure or services such as a BRT system.

The BRT operates extremely well and is very popular, but one express bus corridor is of course only a very small element of the transport systems of a huge city like Lima. It is necessary to integrate it with the rest of the bus network – but how to do this with such an informal system in the rest of the city? Clearly order had to be brought to the bus system as a whole. The process of doing this was fraught with difficulty – the mayor had to fight off an attempt at impeachment because the existing bus operators complained – but eventually, in 2014, another corridor was opened, this time not with a BRT system, but with organised buses operated by Protransporte and the informal buses banned from entering the corridor.

The new corridor is the first of a series of 'Complementary Corridors', which are intended to complement the BRT system but which do not have the full segregated infrastructure of a BRT. These formed part of a proposed full bus network which consisted of a number of BRT lines, several complementary corridors and a set of feeder routes which would reach into the local communities. Constructing the BRT system would be expensive and take a long time (Line 1 had taken about 3 years, just in the construction phase – the planning took some years before that) and respite was urgently needed. So the complementary corridors were seen as a mid-way stage in the improvement of the bus system, basically bringing some order to a system which has been characterised by its chaotic informal approach for several decades.

The main point was to consolidate a high-vehicle-flow situation into a lower bus flow but with greater capacity for passengers. This meant that Protransporte had to deal with issues such as the unemployment of drivers and fare collectors (they resolved this by offering training schemes for other employment). The operation of the new bus system in the corridor had to be taught to the public, who had been used to the fraught *modus operandi* that had been the case for several decades. It also had to be taught to the drivers, who had to learn new skills – controlled driving, where chasing after the next passenger and competing with other buses for the passengers was no longer acceptable – and so the system ran for the first month without fares. It is now operating very successfully. However, with a change of mayor in early 2015, the main protagonists in Protransporte have all been replaced and the future of the approach is now in doubt.

Central to this process, and enshrined in the Nama, was the direct involvement of civil society. Peru is fortunate to have a number of civil society groups with specific interests in various aspects of transport, notably Lima cómo Vamos, Luz Ambar, Cruzada Vial, Transitemos. We helped these groups to work together through a series of workshops to produce a White Paper, in which they set out a pathway (*Hacia una Ciudad para Personas* ('Towards a city for people'), Transitemos *et al.*, 2014) for transport policy in the future, which was presented to the Lima and national governments. The Pathway set out seven key milestones:

2014–2016

1 Pilot project to reform the accessibility integrating two complementary corridors and the environment, including a System of Public Bicycles.

2 Pilot Project for accessibility to mass transit system including metro and metro interconnection. The two major forms of mass rapid city transit to be planned in a complementary way and not competing with each other, and access to this system to be by means of public transport and non-motorised access.

2015

3 Unified Technical Authority created based on a metropolis-wide consultation. We are aware that this is a difficult decision that can only be achieved progressively, starting immediately with a pact for mobility.

2013–2020

4 Formation of a team of professionals and world-class technicians to lead the substantial change in mobility management, road safety, transport and logistics in the city. Immediate allocation of budget for this purpose.

2016

5 Final design and implementation of the integrated mobility and sustainable transportation system for Lima and Callao.

2014–2020

6 First South American Pacific Green Urban Area, where all urban services are neutral or low carbon (transport, energy, water, solid waste management, etc.).

2015–2020

7 Freight integrated by the development of dry ports, logistics corridors, coastal shipping and rail planning.

The lesson here is that although the need to define what the city was trying to achieve was particularly difficult as, in effect, there are two cities, it was possible to create a new transport system within a difficult political and operational scenario and make it work. This relied on having a determined management that was prepared to learn from other experiences around the world and to face up to the political and practical challenges. Having a clear vision, which rose above the level of the transport system itself, was crucial to this endeavour. Creating the technical capacity to design and implement such a project was also hugely significant. Lima is not out of the woods yet, but at the time of the publication of the Roadmap, it was certainly a lot nearer to this ideal than it was just a few years before. It also shows the risks that arise if the technical contribution to the city is too dependent on political appointments: the removal of the technical leadership of Protransporte after the new Mayor was elected has meant a loss of continuity at best and a period of dismantling hard-won achievements at worst.

The Hoja de Ruta is built around the five cities model and shows how such an approach to developing the vision of a city can be understood and adopted by the civil society as a way to drive the sort of transport solutions that they believe would help to achieve a city that is better for the populations and its descendants.

However, following the change of mayor after the mayoral elections in late 2014, the entire programme has been halted. All the city technical officers working in the transport system were removed from their positions. It is still too early to tell exactly what will happen in the city as a result, but it is clear that there is a real danger that the tentative steps forward, made over the last few years, are in clear danger of being reversed. Herein lie the perils of a lack of continuity and weakness in the technical competence in the city to withstand the changes arising in the political cycle.

8.5. Conclusions

What lessons can we learn from these examples?

First they are all examples where the vision of the city has been set at a high level and then the transport system has been engaged as a part of the delivery of that vision. In none of these cases has the transport system been developed separately from the city vision: the transport planners have been presented with a challenge to join in and contribute to the city vision.

Second, the active participation of the population has been central to the development. In some cases they are included more actively than others. Medellín, for example, through the PUIs, actively involved the population in crucial decisions about what they wanted and where it should be located, what it should look like. In Asheville the strong, varied and open approach shows that the population was engaged in fundamental aspects of the generation of the vision and its proposed implementation. London has a 20-year strategy for the city, with associated strategies in different sectors, including transport, which have to feed into the higher-level strategy. Both levels are generated after a period of active consultation, which allows for continual adaptation over time, independently of the political situation. Lima is in the early stages of this sort of engagement with the public, but the active involvement and acceptance of the civil society in the form of a group of non-governmental organisations (NGOs) is at least a sign that this is the path that could be followed in the future.

Third, the examples show that the size of a city is no restriction on the extent to which the vision can be applied. London and Lima each has a population of around 8.5 million, Asheville about 85 000. Whatever the scale of the city, the message is that the population interacts with the city as a set of individuals. Whatever the scale of the enterprise or project the one common feature that determines everything is the person. Starting from the point at which the individual person interacts with the city – physically, cognitively or sensorially – means that the constraints in other areas – the 'laws of physics', the 'laws of the land' – are secondary to the people. Lima had to find ways around its complicated legal situation in order to have a transport system that would work for its people. The London story is about how the organisation of its transport had to be adapted – in this case over several decades – to meet the needs of people to move around the city under the severe constraints of a historic infrastructure and how the realisation came about that the governance had to be right in order to achieve the true integration between the modes of transport so that journeys could be as seamless as possible. Asheville learnt that its people-scaled environment was under threat from more money-focused development, and had to change its planning laws to meet the people's desire for a more human-scaled city centre. Laws of the land can be changed (although it might take some time to achieve this), but the laws of physics are only rarely able to be broken – except in certain circumstances, for example the availability of a new technology. These need to be mitigated in order to meet the needs of people. For example, the size of infrastructure or vehicles should be dictated by the people's needs rather than the convenience of the materials: the size and shape of a bus shelter needs to be determined by the needs of people, not by the convenient modular size of the panes of glass or the steel structure, both of which can be adapted to suit.

Fourth, Medellín shows the advantage of having a resource available to the city which is not derived only through taxes. Although the EPM is highly singular, the questioning of how the private and public sectors come together to the advantage of the city is a matter that has enabled Medellín to develop a highly societally-driven transport system and London to maintain a high quality transport system. This shows the importance of thinking hard and openly about how resources are obtained, secured and used to the benefit of the people of the city.

Lastly, the five cities model can be applied to each of these cities, either retrospectively or in a forward-looking way that can affect future policy. The idea of this model of a higher-level vision, which requires the different sectors to see how they can meet the requirements, works well in these examples. The key role of the transport system as one of the major means of social integration makes it crucially important that it is not constrained by ideologies about how it is delivered – whether a solution is a bus or a metro system should be decided according to honest assessment of the fit between each system's capabilities and the need, not because one is more politically attractive or 'modern' than the other. The five cities model imposes on the transport system the need to deliver accessible support to the attainment of the five principles. However, the case of Lima shows the danger of not having such a high-level vision and how that can all too easily result in stunted progress.

REFERENCES

Asheville Downtown Masterplan (2009) See http://www.ashevillenc.gov/Portals/0/city-documents/economicdevelopment/D34831%20COA-PNDV%20Ins.pdf (accessed 25 May 2015).

DC (Disaster Center) (2015) *New York Crime Rates 1960–2014*. Disaster Centre, Washington, DC, USA. See http://www.disastercenter.com/crime//nycrime.htm (accessed 13/10/2015).

OED (1989) *Oxford English Dictionary*. Oxford University Press, Oxford, UK.

The Economist (2014) The trouble with miracles. *The Economist*, 7 June.

Transitemos (2014) *Hacía una ciudad para las personas: Hoja de Ruta para una política de transporte y movilidad sostenible para Lima y Callao*. Fundación Transitemos, Lima, Peru.

Tyler N and Ramírez C (2012) *Developing Low-carbon Transport Policies for Peru with Capacity-Building for their Implementation: Draft Transport NAMA*, Report to the Foreign and Commonwealth Office, Accessibility Research Group, UCL.

Ingenuity – How?

Accessibility and the Bus System: Transforming the World
ISBN 978-0-7277-5980-1

ICE Publishing: All rights reserved
http://dx.doi.org/10.1680/aabs2ed.59801.365

publishing

Chapter 9
Opportunities

How can all the issues discuss in the book be drawn together to make a coherent and transformative bus system?

9.1. Can the bus system work for us?

The first realisation is to believe that the bus system can have a transformative effect on the city and its population. Too often, the bus system is seen as a necessary evil that has to be tolerated, rather than a positive asset that can make it easier for people to achieve their aspirations. Without this belief, the opportunities that the bus system can release will not be made available to the people. It also changes the frame of the questions that can be asked about how the system should look, feel and operate. What is the evidence to support such a belief?

Bus systems can operate at much higher capacity levels than is often thought. Of course, there are the 'big infrastructure' systems such as the BRTs in places like Curitiba and Bogotá, which can deliver very high capacity indeed – but require large infrastructure to do so. Not every city has the space for such a system or the environment where the infrastructure would be appropriate. But much can be done at a much smaller scale, which can deliver major improvements that can be part of a transformative system. The first realisation for this is that the bottleneck for bus system capacity lies at the bus stop – the modal interchange between pedestrians and passengers. A lot of conventional thought about bus systems emphasises the capacity delivered by carrying passengers and so reduces the importance of the capacity afforded to the process of boarding and alighting at bus stops. Bus stops are rather like the taps in a water system – they are the points at which the water/passengers emerge into the environment or enter the network, they can allow the flow to happen freely or they can restrict it – and making sure that the taps can be opened sufficiently wide is crucially important to enabling as free a flow as possible.

In essence, the bus stop capacity challenge is driven by ensuring that the dwell time is as short as possible. This means that the transfer to and from the bus is as smooth as possible. This in turn requires sufficient space to be available in the bus and at the bus stop for passengers and the smoothest possible transition from one to the other – level access and no horizontal gap between the vehicle and the platform. The latter means being honest about the space required for the vehicles to achieve this performance consistently. These issues have been discussed in Chapters 5 and 6. It is absolutely possible to ensure that bus stops work properly – if the issues are properly understood; the key is to understand that the bus stop must be properly accorded the importance it has within the context of the bus system.

9.2. The role of the vision

Once the belief is in place that the bus system is a tool that can be used to transform society, the next issue to consider is the sort of society the city desires. The approach adopted in this book is that it is necessary to spend time deciding this issue and that it is essential to do this in the context of close discussion with the people who live, work and play in the city and enjoy the kind of life they can lead in that environment. In Chapter 1, I mentioned the five cities model as a way of framing the development of such a vision. The importance of the five cities model is that it lifts the questions that need to be asked out of their sectoral comfort zones. To respond to the questions posed by the five cities it is necessary to think about the city as a whole first, and only once that is resolved to challenge each of the sectors, individually and jointly, to consider how it can contribute to that vision.

The five cities model asks about how the city wants to feel about things such as the interpersonal interactions between people in the city, what sort of activities the city wants to have and where these are, the view about public space and its accessibility, the sense that the city is a positive influence on health and how the city should be able to adapt to changing needs in the future. The bus system plays into each of these and by determining what the city's vision is it is possible to determine the characteristics of the bus system that will best deliver a satisfactory contribution to that overall vision. This can only be done if the vision is set out clearly in the first place. As discussed in Chapter 8, Medellín, London and Asheville all show this process working well, although I think that Asheville wins the prize for the most active public engagement in the process of defining the vision, and Medellín is the most adventurous in resourcing more people-centred approaches as a means of driving societal change and improvements in wellbeing and quality of life. In Lima I think the situation is a little more complicated, but the response of the civil society through its Hoja de Ruta – and the acceptance by the city of the legitimacy of this response – is good evidence that there is a thriving civil society in the city and that this can be brought explicitly and successfully into the decision process. Lima also demonstrates the fragility of that process and its dependence on the desire of the politicians to create, not only ideas and projects, but also the continuity that the city and its populace deserves.

Of course, the public engagement needs to be a continual process so that the vision can mature well and the ownership of the vision rests clearly with the people and not with one political group – which can easily change after an election and thus does not offer a sense of continuity to the city. It is important to remember that politicians and their technical teams are just stewards of the city, looking after it for a short time. The city – which is essentially its people – is far more long-lived and continuous: in London a mayoral term is 4 years, whereas there is evidence of early infrastructure in the city, showing that it is more than 3500 years old!

9.3. Structuring the decisions

Chapter 2 sees the discussion about decision-making. It is important to realise that the process of making a decision is much more than just the final act. Decisions need to be constructed just as thoughtfully as any building. Indeed, the decision-making process is a part of the city infrastructure just as surely as the roads, water and communications systems. The outcomes-based decision model is a simple way of structuring the decision-making process so that it links directly to the vision. By declaring the desired outcome before considering any other aspect of the decision, the vision is contained in the process as the director of priorities and requirements. By being clear about what would lead to success in achieving that vision and how that could be measured it sets out one-half of the pathway to success. The other half is an explicit recognition that there are limiting factors that can reduce or possibly prevent success in achieving the vision. By opening these up to scrutiny, it is then possible to see what the actions need to be so that these are eliminated, and if that is not possible, what needs to be done to obtain a level of mitigation which is sufficient to enable success to be achieved.

The importance of linking every decision clearly to the vision – including the overarching high-level vision – is twofold. With very high-level visions, no single decision is going to deliver achievement, so it is all too easy to become lost in the immediate challenges of much lower-level decisions without realising that a decision taken at a small scale might have an unintended negative consequence for the high-level vision. A clear linkage in the decision model means that this is much less likely and if such an issue does arise it can be caught early.

It is crucially important that all decisions, including determining the vision, are the result of a distinct, coherent and honest programme of public participation.

The second issue is also important. The scale of the 'project' to achieve a high-level vision is, by definition, huge. Therefore, it is complex and requires huge investment. This is a very good reason not to start working on the project – too difficult, too expensive. However, with clear linkages between the vision and the associated decisions throughout the hierarchy, it is possible to start working at a much lower and more achievable level safe in the knowledge that these decisions will work towards achievement of the higher-level vision. Choosing to locate a bench at one point rather than another in the pedestrian environment might actually cost very little indeed, but its position in the environment might easily permit or prevent achievement of the higher-level vision. Having the linkage made very explicit at all points in the decision hierarchy means that much can be achieved by small interventions – it really is the case that 'it's the little things that count'. This approach means that the project can be started and worked on even though the whole thing is huge.

The bus system is an interesting case in point. The bus system may well be a huge element of the city transport infrastructure, but the interaction between the population and the bus system occurs at the level of the individual person – how he or she sees, feels and thinks about the bus will drive his or her whole way of using it – and thus how the city will be able to function. In some ways the bus is one of the closest interactions the city has with its people. This is why the detail of the bus stop, its aesthetics, its relationship with the pedestrian realm, the activities, the delivery of clean, breathable air and so on are all so important to the achievement of the city vision. Investing in making these interactions right is not at all just about making the bus system go faster, it is about how people may live and thrive in the city as a whole and how they feel about the future. This is why the bus system is so crucial when we want to transform society – the way people feel about using the bus stop will affect how they feel about living in the city, so making sure this interaction is the best possible quality is crucially important. Chapters 4 and 5 consider this issue in the way we look at how to design a bus stop. Not only is this for the benefit of the bus system but it is also for the benefit of the people and the city as a whole.

9.4. Systems and value

Throughout this book I have referred to the 'bus system'. Indeed, the concept of a system as a whole consisting of a set of elements (which are systems in themselves) is illustrated very clearly by the bus system. The complexity of such systems of systems is huge and it is important to make sure that we embrace this complexity rather than try to simplify it away. Yes, it is important to understand how each of the elements works, but it is only in the way they come together that they are able to produce the desired outcome. A system that works perfectly within itself but fails to interact positively with the other systems is not going to be workable for very long. This is another reason for the strength of the five cities model: because the five cities are requirements which extend beyond the realm of any one of the constituent city systems, it forces thinking about what, how much, when and how each component system might contribute to the whole – on its own behalf and in combination with the other systems – to maximise their contribution as well.

In Chapter 1 the topic was raised of value engineering. As I mentioned there, the concept has been abused recently to become a term used to describe fiddling around with the numbers to demonstrate that 'value' has been achieved by maximising return and minimising cost. This is a shame and it is quite wrong. As described in Chapter 1, value is not just about cost at all, but about functionality. I showed that we can look at functionality by considering how well the functions of an object, system, activity and so on combine to achieve the aspirations pertaining to its functionality. However, I include as a function the function of appealing to the senses – delivering aesthetics – to everyone as individuals and society at large. Function is not just 'working' in the mechanical sense, but also working in a multisensorial way to deliver a better quality of life and wellbeing.

That sense of how much it is possible to achieve – satisfaction – in the multifactorial sense of functionality compared to the aspiration is a tough standard to meet. Satisfaction is not only a question of asking people if they are satisfied with something. It is necessary first to establish their aspirations and then to see how their aspirations have been met. This is a challenging idea – one of the respondents to our musical bus stop exercise in Regent Street (see Section 7.2.10) responded 'I never had any expectations whatsoever for a bus stop. This has opened a whole new world up for me!' – so how do you evaluate achievement over an aspiration that did not previously exist? The answer is that there needs to be an engagement, rather than 'just' a participation or consultation, between the composer of the system and the public. It is necessary to stimulate responses from the public by showing them ideas for real and letting them respond. Sometimes, this can be a one-off case – like the Regent Street bus stops – but sometimes this might need to be a lengthy trial. The Cumbria Plusbus took about a year of operation before people become confident enough to change their lifestyle and began to use the service; sometimes the pilot trial could need to be quite lengthy in order to enable people to have a feel for what is really being offered.

Sometimes of course it is too difficult to run a full-scale pilot trial, so it is necessary to consider how best to represent the essence of what might be offered. The concept of Value Engineering as advocated here can help with deciding what to test. Being clear and explicit about the aspirations that are under consideration and what signifies achievement should suggest what elements of the proposed system would provide enough information for people to be able to determine the extent to which satisfaction is obtained, even at a small or partial scale. Therefore ensuring that these are present and detectable – and that the outcomes can be measured and evaluated – becomes the driver for deciding what is included in a pilot trial. Expecting people to imagine a new concept is ambitious – it is very hard for people to imagine something they have never seen or experienced before.

9.5.   Buses and the city

A core issue running through the entire book is that buses and their associated infrastructure constitute a transformational agent of change in helping society to become more sustainable, equitable and congenial – civilised – in the future. However, that does not just 'happen' – it requires, as with all art – a great deal of objective preparation, determination and skill to achieve this end. The first principle is to have a clear idea of the concept of the ensemble of the city, in which the bus system is one element. To produce a coherent performance, it is necessary that each element has a clear perception, understanding and respect of each of the others, individually and in combination, in space and time. The responsibility of each performer is to bring the requisite skills to the event so that the collective whole is the best possible and most satisfying performance in the minds of the audience. The end objective is that of satisfactory performance, not the demonstration of particular individual skills.

I have emphasised that the attainment of a civilised city depends on the ability of the bus system to complement the other city systems – immediate examples are its relationship with the pedestrian environment and the people who populate the city. This is why it is important to understand the necessity of making the aesthetics of those parts of the urban realm that are also parts of the bus system so important. This is not an added extra – what the system looks, feels and sounds like is as important to the shape, life and civilisation of the city as works of public art or the architecture of grand buildings. The key issue to consider is how the bus system contributes to people having a better quality of life. Enabling people to travel around the city to reach the activities they want or need to do is one part of this function. Another is the extent that it contributes to people feeling better about the space and community with which they live. Enabling – and encouraging – people to linger in, rather than just pass through, a space is important for civilisation and the bus system can contribute amply to these social activities, as long as it is designed to achieve this while also performing its function of carrying people from one place to another.

Chapter 3 considers how the view of the bus system in the city as a social integrator translates into an expression of needs. An important step is to change the idea that somehow passengers are different from other people. Thus breaking down the way we look at people in relation to the bus system shows us that, in addition to being passengers, they are also pedestrians and the transmutation between these two states, the 'pedenger'. The concept of a pedenger is useful because it emphasises that one area of difficulty in interacting with the bus system is the set of changes that are necessary in order to be able to use it. By acknowledging and accommodating these within the design of the system, it is possible to design the system as a whole to make it easier to use. Incorporating the state of a pedenger in the design process is one way to ensure that this issue is taken into account throughout the process of planning, design and operation, but it is important to remember that throughout, pedestrians, pedengers and passengers are all people and this is all about making people's lives better. It is thus essential that these functions are well understood and incorporated in the value engineering model for the bus system. Shifting the sense of performance on from 'just' how the buses work to the sense of how well they contribute to the wholeness of a civilised society lifts the quality requirements of design from the simply efficient to the transformational.

'How the system works' is often measured by something called efficiency, but actually this is quite wrong. Efficiency is just a ratio between one set of inputs and another set of outputs. Superficially this tells us how the system is working – but this superficiality is a chimera: it looks attractive but is in fact impossible – it conceals a really dangerous inner monster.

To take one example, 'cost-efficiency' is often expressed in the form 'some measure of output compared with the cost of achieving it'. So it is possible to have a very cost-efficient train: lifetime capital and operating costs could be very low and the number of people carried during that period could be extremely high, to give millions of passengers per £ of investment. However, this gives no indication of the quality of the journey, or even the time it takes. Trains (or buses) that are full are appallingly bad at operating at stations (or bus stops) because of the difficulty of boarding and alighting in these conditions. Therefore, the system could be cheap in one sense but very expensive (figuratively and in reality) in others. The additional time taken in the stations could easily worsen the operational cost and the quality of the journey could be so bad that people move to another option as quickly as possible, thus reducing demand. The fact that each of these outcomes can be converted into a financial term is no excuse for regarding cost-'efficiency' as anything other than a simplistic measure of not very much – even though it is attractive to those who do not think further than the surface. Because of this illusion, it is important to evaluate the quality and time of the journey explicitly in their own right and incorporate these into the evaluation rather than lose them in the single mush of 'money'. This is the underlying necessity for viewing value engineering through a lens of multicriteria analysis, which looks at what the system actually delivers, rather than some inappropriate proxy for performance.

Another issue that is highly pertinent in terms of the bus and the city is the scale of a project. One of the reasons for including the vision and decision-making processes in this book and emphasising their usefulness is that having clarity about what is being desired as an overall outcome makes it a lot easier to design suitable projects. There is often a tendency to think that a project must be a substantial size to achieve a useful outcome for the city. However, it is often the case that great impacts can be obtained through small-scale interventions. For example, changing the design of a bus stop to make it both more attractive and easier to use could encourage more people to use the bus system and create a different atmosphere within the city. However, this can only be successful if there is a clear link between the overarching vision and the change to the bus stop. If this alteration is clearly directed to achieving the vision it can often be the case that just a small adaptation can yield great outcomes. If there is no clear link to the vision, this would result in a real problem – there would be a set of disconnected interventions which make no consistent sense and would increase the disconnect between the people and their bus system.

The infrastructure is one thing, of course, but the vehicles are often how people see the bus system. In cities such as Lima, the provision of quality buses is a difficult political issue in the face of the existing operators and their own vehicles. The vehicles themselves – and their owners – are examples of an acceptance that buses have to be poor quality and poorly maintained because otherwise they would be too expensive to afford. This is a case where, if your expectations are low, you will at best achieve only a low quality outcome. It will still be expensive to operate – the distinction is that the difference is made up of the passengers' additional travel time and discomfort, which carry no quantifiable evaluation even if they did interest planners enough to change the system. In addition, the bus operators form a formidable constituency – it was not so difficult for them to carry enough support to be able to start impeachment proceedings against a mayor who did not accede to their wishes (as in Bogotá and Lima). The reality is therefore that planners and designers would like to change the system but the political inertia is too strong in the face of severe opposition. It is only if the political side is prepared to take on the opponents – Bogotá is a good example where this occurred and in fact Lima is another, although that process is still in its very early stages and very fragile – that there is a glimmer of hope for real and substantive improvement to the bus system. At that point, the technical skills need to be ready – and this is the point of this book.

9.6.   Implementing a transformation

Transforming the world, from one where life is mundane, controlled by daily patterns that are in turn controlled by others, to a world in which people live for the future, enjoy living in their environment and can improve the quality of their life and wellbeing is a shift that helps to give life to a city. Transformation means making it easier to do things that are good for society – survival depends on societal cooperation and this is obtained by making it better for people to seek societal objectives as a first-order aim and their own objectives afterwards.

Transformation should therefore make it easier to be a citizen, giving opportunities to give time and space to the city. So, a first action could be to make it easier to linger and enjoy the city instead of just rushing through it. Lingering is a lost art, but where opportunity is given that encourages lingering, it creates a sense of calm activity. Providing

Figure 9.1 Seats arranged with angles to make it easier to chat while passing the time. Osaka, Japan

benches so that people can sit and chat causes them to want to stay a little longer and this creates a backdrop in which society can flourish – people begin to care about what is happening around them, rather than try to stop it or ignore it. To achieve this, benches need to be set so that it is easy for people to talk to someone, or not, as they choose (see Figure 9.1). A simple straight bench is reasonable, but one with angles and corners that make it easier for people to sit in a more conversational way is a lot more effective. An attempt to achieve this more flexibly is shown in Figure 9.2, where quadrants are provided for seating in a pedestrianised street in Kumamoto, Japan. These are on wheels and people can move them to create seating units of different shapes as preferred. In Figure 9.2, the seating is arranged as an 'S' bend, but it could have been made into a half circle if people had preferred. If the idea could be stretched to make the seating itself more comfortable that would be even better: for example, there is no back support, which makes it unattractive for older people. The size of the space in which these conversations happens also needs to be right. Plaza Bolívar in Cartagena (see Figure 4.9) is an example of a relatively small square, which has a good number of people in it most of the time, chatting, sleeping, eating, watching, able to see enough to be interested and to feel safe, yet small enough to feel intimate. Other examples abound and yet it is quite possible to fail miserably in creating a space in which people want to be and which thus creates a social space in the sense that this is where society is actually coming together. A counter-example could be Paddington Basin in London (see Figure 9.3). This is a space where people are definitely unwelcome – the only 'person' there is in fact a statue! There are no seats, the light is poor and the general feeling is one of being drab and dull.

Figure 9.2 Flexible seating in Kumamoto, Japan

Making the urban realm attractive for people to use and enjoy makes for a more civilised city. Figure 9.4 shows a starting point for creating a new approach to public space in Santa Marta, Colombia. The photograph shows part of a model produced as part of a workshop we ran as part of our Foreign and Commonwealth Prosperity Fund programme on implementing a city vision. The participants were encouraged to think of the

Figure 9.3 A barren pedestrian space – Paddington Basin, London

Figure 9.4 An approach to public seating in Santa Marta, Colombia (part of an output from one of our capacity-building workshops on the implementation of a city vision

person as the centre of the process – and this was emphasised by asking them to create a part of the city at 1 : 100 scale based on people as the units of measurement. Figure 9.5 shows the use of trees to provide shade, coloured seats in a curved modular form that people could move to make conversations easier in a similar way to those shown in Figure 9.2. The workshop also showed how techniques like this could be used by the city authorities in public engagement activities.

Creating social space that people want to use does not necessarily mean making things complicated. People will create this where they can. The secret is not to create the space but to create the opportunity – people will then take up the opportunity and create their space, thus creating that sense of ownership that is so crucial to making people feel that the public space is 'theirs'. Figure 9.5 is an example where people are encouraged – by a statue – to take over a traditional building and its doorsteps as a comfortable place to while away some time. These people also provide a part of the urban realm – they soften the edges of the buildings and make the place seem more friendly. Designing spaces or accoutrements that enable people to own the environment in this way is a great way of creating social space. Figure 9.6 shows inverted bronze cannons being used as bollards to exclude motorised vehicles from the historical centre of Havana, Cuba. By midday, these have been taken over by people – it turns out that inverted cannons are a good height for leaning – who use them to support lingering and the boundary becomes human, rather than metal (see Figure 9.7).

Figure 9.5 A place where people are encouraged to make their own social space (Havana, Cuba)

Figure 9.6 Bronze cannons inverted to form the boundary of the pedestrianised historical city centre of Havana, Cuba

Figure 9.7 Creating a person-friendly boundary infrastructure: using historic cannons as bollards provides just the right height for people to lean and chat (Havana, Cuba)

The bus system can build on these spaces by joining them together, but, crucially, it can also help in another way. Bus systems need bus stops and these could be designed to be person-friendly so that they became great places to be. The edible bus stop is one such example. Providing bus stops as a contribution to an urban realm which people find interesting and positive is a great way to changing the way society interacts with its environment and thus contributes to the transformation of society as well as the environment itself.

In our event on Regent Street, Liliana Ortega asked people what they thought about bus stops, as they are now and what they would like in the future. Interestingly, many of the responses were directed towards quite different aims than just waiting for a bus, which leads to the thought that perhaps bus system designers are being rather bashful about what a bus stop could be like. The general message seems to be that they should be comfortable, attractive, stimulating – but should also show information about the local area and bus arrivals.

9.7. Grasping the opportunity

Having the opportunity to transform the world sets a challenge. In this book I have set out some of the issues that I believe are the essence of responding to that challenge. It is all very well having the opportunities but they are only meaningful if they are grasped and implemented. I visualise this as a cycle. Each element in the cycle can be transformative in its own right – the process described in Chapter 5 and illustrated in Figure 5.2 applies to each. This, what I call the 'opportunity cycles', brings them all together in an overall transformation process. I will now briefly describe each element of the cycle, starting with the city.

9.7.1   The city

The bus system is working within the city. The city is its people and their aspirations. So it needs to work out how to make these aspirations work out in practice. Crucial to this is engaging the political body in the understanding of the issues and the opportunities afforded by a properly conceived, composed and implemented integrated mobility system, in which the bus system is a vital element. One way of doing this is to formulate a set of principles for the mobility to be provided in the city and just such an approach has been adopted in Latin America.

In August 2014, 18 mayors from major cities in Latin America signed an agreement to support each other in developing integrated mobility systems for their cities (Musal, 2014). I was involved in drafting this agreement and it includes many of the features explained in this book – the five cities model, the transport hierarchy and so on. This sets out the principles under which their cities will view transport – all their subsequent transport projects will need to be tested against this agreement. The unusual feature is the international level of the agreement – why should cities agree internationally to take up such a set of principles, when each is operating under a different national and political framework? The answer is to support each other in maintaining this political stance in the face of local opposition and intransigence from international funders. We shall see how it will work in practice, but the initiative is extremely encouraging and a model which it would be interesting to see followed elsewhere.

9.7.2   Heraclitus

Heraclitus said that a man cannot jump into the same river twice: both the river and the man will be different on the 'second' occasion. The start of the transformation has to take into account that everything changes over time – and that this is the normal way of things: nothing is constant; nothing stays the same. The opportunity is to capitalise on this characteristic by providing a comfortable difference – one that is not confusing or threatening, but one that is pacifying and generally perceived to be pleasant. In our Regent Street event, we used music to stimulate responses from the public. This could be done – some London Underground stations play classical music and there are bus stops in France where different music can be selected by listeners – but this does raise the spectre of excluding people who do not like the music that is playing at the time. Other sounds might be more acceptable. An example could be to play birdsong in the bus stop shelter. Rather than just play a soundtrack, different birdsongs could be driven as a result of the positions people chose to sit, thus the actual sounds would be different all the time. There could be a form of quiz for people to try and identify which birds were represented.

9.7.3   Space/time

This brings us to the concepts of space and time. These are related by speed, of course, but I would like to draw out some issues that challenge the way we look at them. How far apart people are from their activity is a clear factor of how they are going to choose to

Figure 9.8 A timeline expressed as a helix

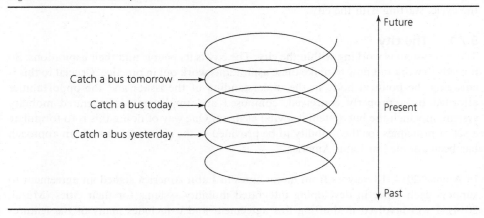

travel towards it. If we can make more of the city reachable on foot we can help to inspire the city to become more human in scale. The bus system is a way of dealing with the compromise that arises from the fact that not everything can be within easy walking distance of the entire population. There is also the question of lingering and the social benefits that accrue as a result of people staying in a space. Mobility is not all about movement – it is about how people reach their chosen activities and this should include the opportunity to stop moving and spend time in the environment.

Ask people to draw a timeline and they will usually draw a straight line. However, time is not really like this. Things repeat over time – a commuter catches the bus every day at the same time – but although the time as seen on a clock looks the same, in fact it is always different – for example, the day, the weather, the surrounding environment will have changed – so the time is always repeating but is never repeated. Time is better visualised as a helix, where the repeating/non-repetition nature is represented rather better (see Figure 9.8).

We also are very poor at visualising the duration of time. I mentioned in Chapter 3 about the way in which time in the past is compressed so that we think things have happened much more recently than in fact they did. Similar distortions arise when we try to perceive time in the future. Figure 9.9 is a representation of this misperception of time, where each line represents an event which is recurring at equal time intervals. Both past and future are compressed and the present is extended.

Figure 9.9 Perceptions of time in the past, present and future

Our ability to perceive the present time accurately is highly variable (as I also discussed in Chapter 3) so the idea that time is a constant clockwork measure is questionable when we are faced with people's perceptions. However, people always do this – so their changing misperceptions of time go with them throughout their life course. This means that the concepts of time in Figures 9.8 and 9.9 are overlaid on each other. What I would like to do is to make the time spent interacting with the bus system more pleasurable so that it yields good memories and a desire to repeat the experience. If I want to make a bus system work for people in the present, I have to deal with the fact that the time-perceptions of the passengers now will be based to a considerable extent on their perceptions of the past, present and future – all of which are likely to be wrong. If I want people to use the bus system tomorrow, I need to ensure that their memories of the misperceived past and present are positive enough to wish to repeat them in the misperceived future. It means making the bus stop and the bus great places to be – and the pedestrian environment a great way of reaching them. Providing comfort, superb stimuli, places to rest and linger, with good information about the locality and the available transport would be a good start.

9.7.4 Vision

Given our misperceptions of time, the city vision is created on the basis of an incorrect perception of the future. We need to inspire and create a vision for the city that is felt by everyone who interacts with it. This suggests a strong exercise in practical public participation, so that the vision really does have buy-in from everyone, in particular by the differing political factions, so that the city and its people can function with a sense of continuity over time. The vision can be adjusted according to changing public desires, but should always maintain a long-term horizon. The London 20-year plan, adjusted by 4-yearly revisions to the associated strategies is a reasonable way of achieving this. Keeping the vision high-level and based around non-sectoral perspectives is crucial both to attaining buy-in and to ensuring that every sectoral function in the city has targets to work to which are explicitly driven by the need to develop their own contribution to the creation of a better quality of life, wellbeing – and city. This is why the concept of the evolving city is so important – we have to allow future generations to correct for our misperceptions and to ensure that we leave options open for them so that they can adapt as required.

9.7.5 Multisensorial

As discussed in Chapter 5, the need to embrace all the senses is crucial. The more we can respond to the information gathered by our physiological, environmental and interpretational sensors, the more we can ensure that the bus system will seem more suited to our needs. Opening up to the challenge of incorporating all the senses in the design process yields a much more complete outcome, which is more attractive to more people. Creating a bus system based on a set of functionalities which include aesthetics as well as operations, which sets out to respond to the desire for fairness and which is attractive to people who are not strong in all capabilities, means having to take into account at least the broad set of senses discussed in Chapter 5.

9.7.6 Composition

Composition, of course, is the means by which multisensorial design is incorporated into the spatio-temporal world of the transformative bus system. Bringing all the elements to bear on the issue is the essence of the composition process, opening design to a much higher dimensional opportunity for creativity and outcomes which are better suited to more people for more of the time. The composition approach makes it much easier to respond to the needs arising from the variety of capabilities presented by the entire population – all ages and all capabilities are inherently included in the process. Composition brings together multiple senses, space and time to create an environment in which all people can feel welcome, a sense of ownership – and a sense of responsibility for its continuance – so that the sense of wellbeing is enhanced.

9.7.7   Instantaneous/ephemeral

This is another view of time. Not all considerations of time are long-lasting – or even repeated on a regular basis. The immediacy of an interaction, say between two people as they encounter each other at a bus stop or just passing each other on the footway, is part of the life of a city. Such interactions are the basis of both stability and progress in society. On such tiny evidence people base their judgements on whether a situation or person is safe or worrying. Yet these interactions are instantaneous, sometimes just the flick of an eye, a tone of voice or the slight brush of a sleeve. They are unlikely to be repeated, so they are quite ephemeral. Encouraging positive instances of these tiny, but significant, interactions and discouraging negative experiences is a real challenge in the bus system. Composing the system to enable such interactions to happen without disturbing people has implications for movement, lighting, and the number of people in a particular space at a particular time. A crowded bus often imposes non-instantaneous and non-ephemeral interactions: people trade in their choice about to whom they are in sometimes very close proximity in order to make their journey at a specific time. It is a good question to ask if it is reasonable to require such a trade-off on the part of the passengers. In making the bus system more civilised it is good to think about reducing or eliminating more forced and unwelcome contact between people and how to enable and encourage positive instantaneous and ephemeral interactions. Society needs such interactions: these are the basis of societal advance.

9.7.8   The city has to work!

Nevertheless, given all the constraints and challenges, the city and its bus system still have to exercise full range of functionalities. This means that there might be a lot of compromises – in both space and time – that have to be considered and accommodated. This does not mean that they have to be tolerated for all time though. We should always be looking for ways to improve the experience of using the bus system. Sometimes technology can resolve the problems and sometimes they can be reduced through changes in accepted behaviour. Opportunities all come with challenges and all need to be addressed, even if in the end some have to be tolerated as being necessary in the meantime until a better solution is found. All should be addressed and the reasons for an inability to resolve them understood so that improvements can be made once they become feasible. The important thing to remember is that it is necessary to have in mind the best possible bus system so that the one that exists has a target to aim for. The bus system is there to help make the city work on a daily, hourly basis and to help with the longer-term vision of improving wellbeing and the quality of life.

Figure 9.10 The opportunity cycle

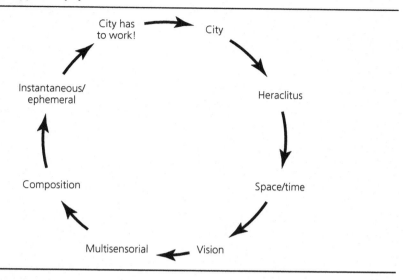

The cycle then continues back to the city for the next turn around the cycle, when new opportunities will arise for improving the system to move a step near to that vision. The 'opportunity cycle' is shown in Figure 9.10.

REFERENCE

Musal (Movilidad Urbana Sustentable de América Latina) (2014) *Lima Declaration: White Paper on Sustainable Urban Mobility in Latin America.* Movilidad Urbana Sustentable de América Latina, Lima.

ICE Publishing: All rights reserved
http://dx.doi.org/10.1680/aabs2ed.59801.383

Chapter 10
Conclusions

10.1. General points

My intention in writing this book was to update the first edition, which was published in 2002. Many things have changed since then, not least the attitudes of people in general to public transport. However, in many ways the situation is still one where new thinking can be adopted to bring such changed attitudes as there are into reality. So a second intention was to write down the ways in which my own thinking has progressed over the past decade or so. This is not to say that my current thinking is the only way to do things or even that it is correct – the way to look at this book is as a stimulus to what could be done if some of the old ways of thinking about the bus system were set aside and a fresh start were made. The real transformation here is in thinking that it might be possible to transform the world using the bus system as the agent of change. Buses are everywhere, close to us in our cities, and thus making a small change can have a huge impact.

Changing a system as endemic as a bus system is also potentially dangerous – the very ubiquity of the bus system is such that if the change were negative the impact could be equally huge – but in the wrong direction. So, a crucial message from this book is that it is necessary to have a vision that overarches the political and technical details that can change so rapidly. This is why the five cities model is so important – not that it has to be exactly five cities or those cities, but that it sets a framework for creating a vision that is above the immediate decision and policymaking processes within the city. With a clear vision for the city, what happens to the bus system will follow that vision and therefore will provide a positive impact. Without such a vision, disaster could happen.

Following on from the vision, the need to systematise decision-making is a way of making sure that the decisions do in fact set a path towards achievement of the vision. By establishing the desired outcomes as expressions of means of achieving the vision, and working through what will support them and what would inhibit them, it is possible to create a set of actions that could help rather than hinder the process. Central to this systematised decision-making is the involvement and engagement of the people – all the people – and the need for everyone to make sure that understanding rather than informing is the key to better engagement. Professionals need to understand that the public need to understand why something can or cannot be done, not just be told that it is the case. No longer can a professional just 'do their job': they need to enable the people who will be affected by their work to understand – to build that sense of trust between the professions and the people that enables good projects to proceed and poor ones to be avoided. This means a transformation in the professionals' approach to the public, which in turn means a transformation in the education of both.

A core shift that helps a great deal with transforming the world is to recognise the symbiosis between the bus system and the rest of the environment. This environment actually consists of a number of environments:

1   the natural environment in terms of its use of energy and production of emissions that are noxious both to the people and the planet
2   the societal environment, including the inclusion of all people throughout the design and implementation of the bus system, from conception to evaluation
3   the human environment, including how the bus system is sensed by, and how it feels from the perspectives of, individual people
4   the built environment, including how the bus system affects and is affected by the buildings and urban realm within which it operates, and
5   the temporal environment, in which our perception of time, in the past, present and future is different from, and more influential than, the actual passage of clock time in influencing our decision-making. In other words the key influence on the bus system is not actually the design of the bus networks, buses and associated infrastructure but their relationships with the world around them.

It is because these relationships are so real – even if often unnoticed at the moment – that doing 'the right thing' with the bus system really can transform the world.

Many of the intricacies involved in the relationship between the bus system and its sur-roundings are yet to be properly understood, but I hope that in this book, by highlight-ing some of them, I have been able to start you thinking about how such relationships could be identified, evaluated and used in a positive way to improve the system. The human body is an amazing set of multiple sensors and we should use these much more in assessing the impacts of interventions on the people. The material in Chapters 4 and 5 about how people see the environment is mainly about the vision sense, but lessons to take away from these chapters include that we need to see vision in a different way, to realise just how limited this fantastic sense actually is when dealing with something like a bus system, to understand a lot more about peripheral vision and how this feeds into our mental perception of the world around us – and to understand how the design of the system could be made to speak to these preconscious processes to make the conscious ones much easier and more effective. I have used vision as the example here because, unlike most of the other senses, it is possible to see what the vision system is doing – we can see what the eye is fixating on and can thus infer from that what choices have been made by the preconscious brain, as well as the extent to which responses are different when stimulated by different design details.

This is much harder to do with, say, hearing, because we cannot yet know exactly what the ear is actually hearing and, importantly, the equivalent of the location of the eye fixation in vision, which shows what the brain is picking out as stimuli that need further attention, does not yet exist for hearing. Research in ophthalmology and medical physics has given us this technology for vision and hopefully sometime soon we might have some sort of equivalent for hearing, touch, balance and so on. So the example is one that we can talk about as being currently possible, and this is a stimulus to those working in other sensorial fields to think about doing something similar in their case. People perceive everything through all their senses, of which there are many more than we usually consider, and composing a bus system means communicating with the person through all of their senses.

Encouraging people to feel better about their bus system is an important goal to set. This is part of the development of the sense of trust that supports and encourages positive communication between people and the authorities. This is important when it is not possible to accede to requests from the community for one reason or another, but it has to be built up over many years and needs to be maintained. Trust is an easy thing to lose and very hard to regain once it has been lost. Designing for the emotions might sound rather 'soft' for something as 'hard' as a bus system, but actually it is vital. The bus system has suffered over the years and around the world from being perceived as something that needs to be tolerated so that 'other people' can move around the city. In some cases, this shifts to the extreme, when anything that interferes with vehicular traffic flow is eliminated or minimised, but the inference is clear in most cities around the world that the bus system has to be superimposed on the city and its activities. However, such a view is entirely wrong on a number of levels.

First, if people do not feel good about the bus – or any other – system, they will treat it badly. This is particularly true if they have to use it because it is their only option and this is a very common position for bus users around the world. The converse is also true: if people do feel good about a system, they will treat it well. The Asheville example is interesting because the city set out to make people feel proud of the system they were riding on and then put in place strategies, designs, operations and programmes with that in mind. To some, this might seem like spending too much time – as well as money – on non-substantive aspects of a bus system, but the fact is that if people do not feel proud of the system they will stop using it as quickly as possible. In the meantime, they will abuse both the system as a whole and the people who they see as operating it. In the longer-term, a better realisation of the importance of making people feel good about the bus system converts into what gains political support in terms of city investment and thus what happens in the future.

Second, pride is a sense and is included in the list of what I called 'interpretational senses' in Table 5.3. Designing to appeal to all senses is hugely important if we want people in general to feel good about the bus system. Aesthetics is not a 'nice-to-have' that can be appended when everything else has been done (but not until that point). It is by making sure that the aesthetics works for the population, that the system will work better, be better accepted by everyone, and will generally help to improve the sense of wellbeing of the population as a whole. This is converted very quickly into issues such as the acceptability of schemes such as bus priorities, pedestrianisation, investment in general in the urban fabric and many more. As the bus is so ubiquitous it carries a symbol of a city's pride all over the city and is a very good indicator of how a city feels about itself. The sheer quantity of bus stops is another opportunity to express good feelings about the city and its people. Indeed, aesthetics is essential if the bus system is to transform the world.

Much of the sense of pride follows from a sense of ownership. If people feel that *they* own the system, they will begin to want to feel proud of it and the system should deliver on that desire. Therefore, whether the bus system is operated by the private or public sector, it is essential that there is a sense of its place within the city. In some cities – London and Bogotá are just two examples – the city owns the network and service definition and the private operators operate to a contract, with performance indicators setting out the ways in which performance against the city's ideal are measured. In London, this works very well, with the city pushing up standards in the operation on a continuing basis. In Bogotá, the sense of ownership is rather more political and the priorities are to assuage political aims rather than to create a world in which people have civilised transport around the city. When the Transmilenio system was introduced in Bogotá, it was something of which the population was proud and Peñalosa's description of a developed city (one where the rich ride in public transport) seemed to be coming into reality. After a while, however, the system was seen as politically expensive – partly because it was sensed to 'belong' to Peñalosa and it was something to use to oppose him politically – and thus the investment flows slowed. With that reduction in investment, the system was not maintained as well as it should have been, the expansions to the system to follow (or presage) the expansion in the city were not made and as a result, the system has become overcrowded and unpopular. In London, the decisions about investment and maintenance are just as political as in Bogotá, but the sense of ensuring that the system is properly maintained, operating properly and under constant revision are actually the responsibility of strong, competent, imaginative and technical, rather than political, people within the organisation.

The five cities model is crucial for the development of appropriate objectives for the bus system which transcend the system itself. The importance of this is that it provides overarching aims to which the system can aspire and this gives a sense of purpose and direction to the decisions about future investment and planning. The ownership I have just been discussing is actually within the 'city as a public space', where people have a sense of ownership of – and responsibility for – the system. This lifts the sense of the bus system as being something that just has to cope with each day as it comes to being something which drives positively towards achieving higher city visions. This shifts the sense of the system from the negative to the positive and this is a precursor to being able use the bus system to transform the world.

10.2. Transforming the world

I have mentioned several times in this book that buses are agents of change that can help us transform the world. I started by raising the vision of how it might be possible to define what a future world would be like and described this in the form of the five cities model in Chapter 1. It is illusory to try to transform the world without a clear vision of where the transformation should lead. I have found that in many places the concept of what a vision is and how it might be defined is woefully inadequate. Usually it is defined by a political statement, policy or manifesto commitment, but rarely contains any coherent view about what the future city (in this case) should be like. In one case where my team and I were running a workshop on this topic, the participants famously responded to my opening question 'What is the vision for your city?' with the answer 'Increased parking'. None of the participants had ever been asked to produce a vision of their own – just to put in place whichever mantra emanated from whichever of the politicians happened to be in power at the time. If buses are seen as a necessity in a city, it is important that the reason why they are necessary is also seen. The necessity is not that they can carry people around the city but that they help the city achieve its vision. This requires a coherent vision to be in place. In that workshop we helped them to learn how to create a vision – and how to summarise it in understandable and brief terms, so that by the end of the first day they were talking about visions of 'accessibility', 'sustainability', 'equity', 'reduced stress' and so on.

By the end of the second day, the workshop participants had also learnt how to system-atise making decisions so that they led to achievement of the vision. We then went on to show them how, by making sure that they always aimed for their vision, even small inter-ventions could help to transform the city to attain their vision. Interestingly, in every case where we have run this workshop, the outcome has been that the participants choose to promote pedestrian and bus transport, and usually by using methods of improving the public realm – more seating, designed to facilitate conversations; shade; better bus stops; better bus operation; better buses and so on. Much of that list could be implemented at relatively low cost and in a gradual way so that massive capital funding would not be required. Even though implementation might be gradual, the link to the vision means that the public could see the direction in which the city was going and this would then make public engagement easier and more informed as the project proceeds.

I suspect that some readers might have balked at the 'transforming the world' element of the title of this book. I hope that by the time they have arrived at this point, they will understand how the bus and its associated systems – including the pedestrian, societal and public realm – with which it interacts can indeed transform the world. It needs thinking way beyond the confines of the bus system itself – into the worlds of philosophy, psychology, art, ideas, design, composition, decision-making, public engagement and so on. None of these worlds can withstand the demands of such a challenge without changing in themselves. In this book I have questioned several ideas about a number of aspects of how to see a city and how to work out what it is necessary to do in order to achieve a coherent, cohesive, pleasant – in short, civilised – city in the future. Adjust-ing the bus system is a way in which we can achieve that change – and thus transform the world.

Accessibility and the Bus System: Transforming the World
ISBN 978-0-7277-5980-1

ICE Publishing: All rights reserved
http://dx.doi.org/10.1680/aabs2ed.59801.389

Index

Aarhus Convention, United Nations
  Economic Commission for Europe
  (UNECE), 210–211, 322
acceleration, bus, 280–284
accessibility, 29–41
  access costs, 108–110
  bus stops, 10, 89–91
  connectivity, 33–35
  dependence/independence, 38–41
  disability, 29–32
  mobility, 33–35
  movement, 33–35
  spatial accessibility, 91–93
accessibility gap
  bus stops, 36–38
  specialised transport services, 37–40
accessibility index (AI), 88
accessible journey train, 35–36
accessible networks, passenger needs,
  81–89
active city, 293–299
  see also five-cities model
advertising, bus shelter, 150–151, 255–256
aesthetics
  see also design
  bus design, 284–285
  bus stops, 216–223
  operations, 273
  sensory issues, 216–218, 379, 384–386
AI *see* accessibility index
air quality, bus, 315
alighting *see* boarding/alighting process
Asheville, North Carolina, 'Masterplan',
  351–355
aspirations, 56–58
  bus systems, 54–56

aspirations and wellbeing, 21–23, 56–57
average speed, 104–108

bags, 294–295
  boarding/alighting process, 164
  pedestrians, 156–157
  wheelchair users, 157, 295
Bloomsbury, London, bus stops, 84–85, 86
boarding/alighting process, 138–139,
  156–157, 158–165, 180–182
  see also doors; pedestrians
  bags, 164
  locating the correct door, 159, 248–250,
    285–292
  locating the correct stop, 162–164
  move away from the bus stop, 165
  moving inside the vehicle, 161–162
  orientation, 164–165
  payment/validation, 160–161, 164
  stepping off the bus, 164
  stepping on the bus, 159–160
  wheelchair users, 157
Bogotá, Colombia, public spaces, 300–301
Brighton and Hove, Puppit (Public
  Participation Processes in Transport)
  project, 323–324
BRT *see* Bus Rapid Transport
bus and platform gaps, 171–177
bus as a vehicle, 307–318
  air quality, 315
  capacity, 308–309
  doors, 312–314
  electric power, 281–283, 307–308
  information, 309, 310, 311
  older people, 309
  passenger space, 308, 317